Body Dysmorphic Disorder
A Treatment Manual

David Veale and Fugen Neziroglu

WILEY-BLACKWELL

A John Wiley & Sons, Ltd., Publication

This edition first published 2010
© 2010 John Wiley & Sons Ltd.

Wiley-Blackwell is an imprint of John Wiley & Sons, formed by the merger of Wiley's global Scientific, Technical, and Medical business with Blackwell Publishing.

Registered Office
John Wiley & Sons Ltd, The Atrium, Southern Gate, Chichester, West Sussex, PO19 8SQ, UK

Editorial Offices
The Atrium, Southern Gate, Chichester, West Sussex, PO19 8SQ, UK
9600 Garsington Road, Oxford, OX4 2DQ, UK
350 Main Street, Malden, MA 02148-5020, USA

For details of our global editorial offices, for customer services, and for information about how to apply for permission to reuse the copyright material in this book please see our website at www.wiley.com/wiley-blackwell.

Library of Congress Cataloging-in-Publication Data
Veale, David.
    Body dysmorphic disorder : a treatment manual / David Veale and Fugen Neziroglu.
        p. ; cm.
    Includes bibliographical references and index.
    ISBN 978-0-470-85120-3 (cloth) – ISBN 978-0-470-85121-0 (pbk.) 1. Body dysmorphic disorder–Treatment–Handbooks, manuals, etc. I. Neziroglu, Fugen A., 1951 II. Title.
    [DNLM: 1. Somatoform Disorders–therapy. 2. Body Image. 3. Obsessive-Compulsive Disorder–therapy. 4. Self Concept.   WM 170 V394b 2010]
    RC569.5.B64V43   2010
    616.85'2–dc22
                                                                                    2009033740

A catalogue record for this book is available from the British Library.

Set in Times 10/12 pt by Toppan Best-set Premedia Limited
Printed in Singapore by Fabulous Printers Pte Ltd

2   2012

Contents

130296

About the authors

David Veale, FRCPsych, MD, BSc, MPhil, Dip CACP is a Consultant Psychiatrist in Cognitive Behavior Therapy at the South London and Maudsley NHS Trust and The Priory Hospital, North London. He is an Honorary Senior Lecturer in the Institute of Psychiatry, King's College, London. He is an accredited cognitive behavior therapist and was President of the British Association of Behavioural and Cognitive Psychotherapies for 2006–8. His research and clinical interests are in CBT for body dysmorphic disorder (BDD), obsessive compulsive disorder (OCD) and specific phobia of vomiting. He has authored about 70 peer-reviewed articles. He is co-author of four self-help books: *Overcoming Body Image Problems (Including Body Dysmorphic Disorder)*; *Overcoming Obsessive Compulsive Disorder*; *Overcoming Health Anxiety* and *Manage your Mood* (all published by Robinson). He was a member of the National Institute for Clinical Excellence (NICE) group that wrote treatment guidelines for OCD and BDD in the UK. He was a member of the Cosmetic Surgery Inter-Speciality Committee in the UK. He was an Associate Editor of the journal, *Body Image* from 2004 to 2006. He is a former chair of OCD Action and remains a professional adviser to the charity.

Fugen Neziroglu, PhD, ABBP, ABPP, is a board certified behavioral and clinical psychologist involved in the research and treatment of anxiety disorders and obsessive compulsive spectrum disorders. She is co-founder and Clinical Director of the Bio-Behavioral Institute in Great Neck, New York, USA, Adjunct Professor of Psychology at Hofstra University in Long Island, New York and Adjunct Professor of Psychiatry at New York University. She has presented and published over 100 papers in scientific journals, including *The American Journal of Psychiatry, Behaviors Research and Therapy*, and *Journal of Anxiety Disorders*. She is the author and co-author of 14 books including *Obsessive Compulsive Disorders Spectrum: Pathogenesis, Diagnosis and Treatment* and *Overcoming Compulsive Hoarding: Why You Save and How You Can Stop*. Many of her books have been translated including into Italian, Spanish, and Korean.

She is on the Scientific Advisory Board of the Obsessive Compulsive Foundation in the USA and has assisted in the development of the *Diagnostic Statistical Manual IV-TR*.

Contributing Author

Rob Willson MSc is a cognitive behavior therapist in private practice and studying for a PhD in BDD at the Institute of Psychiatry, King's College, London. He is a tutor at Goldsmiths College, University of London. He holds an honors degree in Psychology, an MSc in Rational Emotive Behavior Therapy, and a Postgraduate Diploma in Social and Behavioral Health Studies. He is co-author of five self-help books: *Overcoming Body Image Problems*; *Overcoming Obsessive Compulsive Disorder*; *Overcoming Health Anxiety*; *Manage your Mood* (all published by Robinson); and *A Dummies' Guide to Cognitive Behaviour Therapy* (published by Wiley).

Preface

Body dysmorphic disorder (BDD) is extraordinarily under-researched compared to other mental health problems and yet can be one of the most distressing and disabling of psychiatric disorders. As a group, individuals with BDD have high rates of suicide, psychiatric hospitalization and unemployment, are often housebound or socially isolated, and have great difficulties with relationships. BDD is regarded as rare, but conservative evidence suggests a prevalence rate from community surveys of 1–1.5%. A much higher prevalence has been found in psychiatric inpatients and in cosmetic surgery and dermatology settings, where the outcome of a procedure is usually unpredictable. In mental health settings, it is a hidden disorder and many individuals do not seek help because of shame and stigma.

Being *dissatisfied* with one's appearance is normal, but BDD is different. Someone with BDD is *preoccupied* with their appearance, is excessively self-conscious, and experiences marked distress and handicap. When a person with BDD finally seeks help from a doctor or mental health professional, they are often too ashamed to reveal their main symptoms of BDD and might present with symptoms of depression, social phobia, or obsessive compulsive disorder (for which there is frequent comorbidity). The onset is usually in adolescence, but when the condition is finally diagnosed after 10 years or more, it are often treated inappropriately with anti-psychotic medication or the therapist lacks an effective treatment model. We hope this manual will go some way to address this. The evidence base for both cognitive behavior therapy and pharmacotherapy is small, but we believe it is strong enough to publish a treatment manual and evaluate in a controlled trial. Individuals with BDD are generally regarded by professionals as difficult to engage in therapy and to treat. We do not, of course, have all the answers and, like us, you will at times struggle to keep your patient engaged in therapy.

We have divided the book into two parts. Chapters 1–12 summarize the current knowledge and theoretical perspectives about BDD that will inform the therapy. Chapters 13–23 cover the practical aspects of assessment, engagement, and therapy. To avoid clumsiness in the text, we have assumed that the therapist is female and the patient is male.

David Veale
Fugen Neziroglu

Acknowledgements

We would like to acknowledge the appreciation of the help and advice of a number of individuals over the years, who have influenced our thinking or have been research associates on both sides of the Atlantic. Katherine Phillips has a special acknowledgment for her enormous contribution to the field; others are in alphabetical order: Martin Anson, Anne Boocock, Tom Cash, Alex Clark, David M. Clark, Myra Cooper, Louise De Haro, Rupa Dodhia, Windy Dryden, Nell Ellison, Michelle Ennis, Edna Foa, Mark Freeston, Randy Frost, Paul Gilbert, Kevin Gournay, Ann Hackmann, Amaryllis Holland, Peter Kinderman, Michael King, Christina Lambrou, Helen Lomas, Isaac Marks, Dean McKay, Sandra Mulkens, Victoria Oldfield, Selen Osman, Sony Khemlani-Patel, Susan Riley, James Rosen, Paul Salkovskis, David Sarwer, Marc Serfaty, Roz Shafran, Fozia Shah, Emma Smith, Gail Steketee, Steven Taylor, Jessica Walburn, Adrian Wells, Tom Werner, Sabine Wilhelm, Katja Windheim, and Joseph Wolpe.

We should also like to thank Florian Ruths for translating the description of BDD by Emil Kraeplin and to Natalie Salaun for translating the description of BDD by Pierre Janet.

Finally, we would like to thank our partners, Elizabeth Nicholson and Jose Yaryura-Tobias, who have persevered with us and provided additional help and advice.

Part A
Knowledge and Theory of Body Dysmorphic Disorder

Chapter 1

The diagnosis of body dysmorphic disorder

Summary

The diagnosis of body dysmorphic disorder (BDD) is relatively easy to make but is often overlooked because few professionals ask a simple screening question. The key criterion is a *preoccupation* with an imagined defect or minor physical anomaly. The preoccupation must be sufficient to cause significant distress or handicap. An additional diagnosis of delusional disorder is made on the strength of the conviction of the client's beliefs and reflects the severity of the disorder. There is high degree of comorbidity in BDD, especially of depression, social phobia, or obsessive compulsive disorder (OCD). The differential diagnosis of BDD is discussed in other common disorders. The most common Axis II diagnoses are avoidant, paranoid, and obsessive-compulsive personality disorder.

Sections

Body Dysmorphic Disorder: A Treatment Manual. David Veale and Fugen Neziroglu
© 2010 John Wiley & Sons, Ltd.

1.1   Presentation

The diagnosis of BDD in DSM IV is relatively easy to make but is often overlooked. Patients present in a variety of settings: medical, dermatological, or cosmetic surgery. They are typically preoccupied by perceived or slight flaws on the face, asymmetrical or disproportionate body features, thinning hair, acne, wrinkles, scars, vascular markings, pallor, or ruddiness of complexion. Sometimes the complaint is extremely vague or amounts to no more than a general perception of ugliness or other aesthetic attributes, such as being too masculine or feminine. The most common preoccupations in BDD are around the face, especially the nose, skin, hair, eyes, eyelids, mouth, lips, jaw, and chin (Neziroglu & Yaryura-Tobias 1993a; Phillips et al., 1993; Veale et al., 1996 Neziroglu et al., 1999). However, any part of the body may be involved and the preoccupation frequently focuses on several body parts (Andreasen et al., 1977). Over time, the location of the main defect may change. In one of the largest surveys of people with BDD, Phillips & Diaz (1997) report there are far more similarities than differences between men and women in the location of their BDD concerns. Both genders are most commonly concerned with their skin, followed by hair and nose. Although women are more likely to have hair concerns (e.g., asymmetry, wrong color, lacking body, excessive body hair), men are significantly more concerned with hair thinning or baldness. The gender differences occur with body size and shape. Women are more likely to be preoccupied by their breasts, hips, weight, and legs, usually believing that they are too large or fat. In contrast, men are more likely to be preoccupied with body build and believe that their body is too small, skinny, or not muscular enough. This has been described as muscle dysmorphia (Pope et al., 2005). Despite such concerns, many such men are unusually muscular and large. They spend many hours weightlifting, and pay minute attention to nutrition. Others may abuse steroids. Another significant gender difference is that men are more likely to report hair thinning and preoccupation with their genitals (usually a concern that their penis is too small). However, women may report their labia being too large and seek a cosmetic operation to reduce the size (Liao & Creighton, 2007).

Phillips & Diaz (1997) note that some of these gender differences appear to reflect those reported in the general population, suggesting that cultural norms and values may influence the content of BDD symptoms. Women are more likely to pick their skin, camouflage with make-up, and have comorbid bulimia nervosa. Men with BDD are as likely as women to *seek* non-psychiatric medical treatments, although women are significantly more likely to *receive* medical treatments, especially dental treatment. Men with BDD, however, are as likely as women to have received cosmetic surgery.

The diagnosis of BDD is, however, often overlooked if the interviewer does not ask about specific symptoms of BDD as clients are often too ashamed to reveal the true nature of their problem. This seems to occur especially in psychiatric inpatients (Grant et al., 2002). Grant et al. screened 122 consecutive inpatients and 16 (13.1%) were diagnosed as having BDD by a structured interview; none of the participants had been diagnosed as having BDD by their treating physician. All 16 subjects reported that they would not raise the issue with their physician unless specifically asked, due to feelings of shame. This study underlines the importance of clinicians asking about symptoms of BDD in routine interviews and screening, especially in an inpatient population.

1.2 Diagnosing BDD

BDD is classified as a somatoform disorder in DSM IV (American Psychiatric Association, 1994) (Table 1.1). Identifying and diagnosing BDD is relatively easy if the assessor asks the right questions or uses a structured diagnostic interview; there is then a high degree of inter-rater reliability.

Table 1.1: Diagnostic criteria for Body Dysmorphic Disorder (DSM IV)

1. Preoccupation with an imagined defect in appearance. If a slight physical anomaly is present, the person's concern is markedly excessive.
2. The preoccupation causes clinically significant distress or impairment in social, occupational, or other important areas of functioning.
3. The preoccupation is not better accounted for by another mental disorder (e.g., dissatisfaction with body shape and size in anorexia nervosa).

A simple open question that can be used in a screening interview is:

"Some people worry a lot about their appearance. Do you worry a lot about the way you look and wish you could think about it less?"

Without direct questioning, individuals may present with symptoms of depression, social phobia, or OCD. Clients are especially secretive about symptoms such as mirror-gazing, probably because they think they will be viewed as vain or narcissistic. Clinicians do not ask the right questions, probably because they regard BDD as rare or believe that concerns about their appearance are part of another disorder, such as depression.

There are also validated screening measures for BDD. The Body Dysmorphic Disorder Questionnaire (Phillips, 1996a) is a brief, simple, self-report screening measure. It has a high sensitivity and specificity for the diagnosis in both outpatient and inpatient settings (Grant et al., 2001) and in dermatology settings (Dufresne et al., 2001). Cash et al. (2004) have developed the screening questionnaire into a formal scale, although a cut-off point was not set for screening. Cash (personal communication) found in a preliminary study that a seven-item mean Body Image Disturbance Questionnaire (BIDQ) score greater than or equal to a summed score of 21 would detect 98% of individuals with BDD vs. a positive screen for only 10% of the clinical (psychiatric) controls, 26% of the treatment-seeking obese patients, and 67% of eating disordered patients. Among normal controls (college students), there would be a positive screen for only 6% with a score of 21 or more. Self-report questionnaires and diagnostic interviews are provided in Appendix 1. A brief, clinician-administered diagnostic measure, the BDD Module, has been shown to have good inter-rater reliability (Phillips, 1996a).

Each of three main criteria for diagnosis of BDD is discussed below.

1.3   Preoccupation

The cornerstone of the diagnosis of BDD is *preoccupation* with an imagined or minor defect in appearance. To fulfill the first criterion, Phillips (1996a) suggests that the preoccupation with perceived defects should be at the forefront of the mind for a minimum of an hour a day. We would concur, although this threshold may be too low for some individuals seeking cosmetic surgery who desire a cosmetic enhancement (i.e., they have no "defect") and other criteria, such as significant distress, may be difficult to apply in this setting. Most clients with BDD in a psychiatric clinic describe being excessively self-conscious of their appearance; however, there are some clients who are not preoccupied as they can avoid others viewing their feature by camouflaging it with clothing. They would, though, become severely distressed if they were not camouflaged. Such clients can generally avoid intimacy or revealing their body in changing rooms or when swimming. Another pitfall in fulfilling the criteria for preoccupation is misuse of substances such as cannabis or alcohol, which may prevent the client thinking about his appearance. Others may be less preoccupied because their avoidance is high and they are housebound, spending many hours in bed, watching television, or surfing the Internet. Rather than be preoccupied, many of these clients may be depressed about their appearance and score low on standardized scales for BDD.

We discuss the nature of the preoccupation in Chapter 4, but it appears to consist of excessive, self-focused attention on body image, ruminating and comparing features with those of others. Changing the agenda and trying to define the problem to be solved as one of excessive worrying or thinking about one's appearance are emphasized in the process of engagement. The preoccupation often covers multiple locations and may fluctuate over time and shift to another area of the body.

The term *imagined defect* in the diagnostic criteria can be problematic. It is not one we use with our clients for several reasons. First, the defect(s) is very real to the individual and telling a client that he has an "imagined defect" does not assist in engagement or building a therapeutic alliance. Second, aesthetic judgments *partly* depend on personal aesthetic standards and there is evidence that clients with BDD may be slightly more aesthetically sensitive than average and have lost a self-serving positive bias in judgements about their appearance. We discuss later the phenomenology of an "imagined defect," but it is best explained psychologically as excessively self-focused attention on a "felt impression" of appearance, which is fused with past experiences and is now viewed as current reality.

The criterion can also be met if a "*minor physical anomaly is present and the person's concern is regarded as markedly excessive.*" In practice, the criterion means that the feature(s) under consideration is/are either not significantly noticeable to others or that many other people have the same or similar feature(s). However, some people with BDD are not concerned by whether the feature is noticeable by others but usually have a deep self-disgust about certain feature(s). We discuss later a psychological understanding of the discrepancy between the aesthetic evaluation by the individual with BDD and that of clinicians and relatives.

The term *minor physical anomaly* covers the normal variation in features (e.g., freckles, small breast size, or baldness) which may be noticeable, but which are not that abnormal compared to one's peers. There is clearly a gray area between those who have a minor and those with, for example, a moderate physical anomaly and yet may fulfill other diagnostic criteria, such as being excessively preoccupied, significantly distressed, and/or handicapped. The most common example is women with A or AA cup size breasts; someone who has lost a lot of weight and has excessive skin folds; or someone who has an extremely small stature. Such individuals may be very self-conscious, be quite avoidant in intimacy, and have been teased about their appearance. Although an argument can be made that these are minor anomalies or normal variations in bodily appearance, we do not generally view such clients as having an imagined or minor defect – one of the criteria for BDD. To complicate matters further, a client may have one or two features that are regarded as moderate physical anomalies that are noticeable, and others that are "imagined" or minor anomalies.

Alternatively, a feature (e.g., a skin blemish) may be noticeable if your attention is drawn to it by your client or if you look closely enough *and* raise your aesthetic standards. In such situations an individual may even acknowledge that his blemish is not noticeable to a stranger passing in the street (especially if it is camouflaged), but might feel very self-conscious in an intimate relationship or if a stranger came too close. To overcome some of the difficulties with an imagined defect or a minor physical anomaly, it might be better if the criteria for BDD in the new DSM V are modified to: "a preoccupation with one or more features in one's appearance that is either not significantly noticeable or abnormal to others."

Most clients with BDD acknowledge that they are not *disfigured*, but believe themselves to be ugly or very unattractive. Some clients may be preoccupied not with "a defect," but with one or more features being not perfect, not "right," or not equal. They might accept that they look "normal" to others but are preoccupied by self-disgust. A variation on this is a hatred of one's own race and a desire to pass as a different race.

Occasionally, a person may be preoccupied by features that have *changed* for the worse (e.g., an actual change after cosmetic surgery). Thus he may acknowledge that his "defect" is not that noticeable or abnormal but that it has changed for the worse. Thus he may be comparing himself repeatedly with old photos and be fearful of meeting people who knew him before he changed. Occasionally, a person will be preoccupied with a feature which he cannot easily explain (e.g., after a drug experience) or psychotic experience. There are, therefore, many variations on the content of the presenting symptoms, which we discuss in Chapter 4. However, all BDD individuals share a preoccupation with one or more aspects of their appearance which is not shared by others and is excessive and very distressing or handicapping. Rarely, an individual is excessively preoccupied with the imagined defects of another individual, such as a partner or close relative. This has been termed "BDD by proxy" (Josephson & Hollander, 1997; Laugharne et al., 1998; Atiullah & Phillips, 2001).

1.4 Distress and Handicap in BDD

The second criterion for the diagnosis of BDD is that the preoccupation must cause significant distress or handicap. Trying to operationalize these criteria can be problematic, although this is an issue for most disorders in DSM IV.

This criterion usually helps to distinguish between "dissatisfaction" about appearance (especially during adolescence) and a diagnosis of BDD. Body dissatisfaction is very common (Fitts et al., 1989; Castelnuovo-Tedesco, 1992). Studies have reported rates as high as 50%, especially during adolescence. BDD is, however, at the extreme end of dissatisfaction leading to significant *distress* or *handicap*. This is not usually an issue in a clinical population. The evidence from a study on a common quality of life measure (Short Form Health Survey, SF-36) has found a degree of distress that is worse than that of depression, diabetes mellitus, or recent myocardial infarction in 62 consecutive BDD outpatients (Phillips, 2000). Of note, quality of life measures were not explained by comorbid symptoms of depression. Hrabosky et al. (2009) also found that people with BDD had a worse quality of life on the Body Image Quality of Life measure than those with eating disorders.

At the milder end of the spectrum of BDD, some clients function with great effort and distress, but are usually disadvantaged in their occupational or academic functioning. Their motivation and concentration may be impaired because of excessive self-consciousness. Time-consuming behaviors such as mirror-gazing and excessive grooming impair their performance or make them late for work. However, BDD patients are more likely to be unemployed (Phillips et al., 1997) or drop out of school (Albertini & Phillips, 1999) because of their BDD.

People with BDD may have few friends or may not take any risks in social situations. They tend to avoid situations where they believe they will be evaluated negatively, such as swimming, beaches, public changing rooms, or gymnasia. In social situations they are more likely to use alcohol or illegal substances or safety-seeking behaviors similar to those with social phobia. They are more likely to avoid dating and are often single, separated, or divorced as a result of arguments and jealousy in a relationship: Veale et al. (1996) found that 74% of a sample of 50 BDD patients were single, separate, or divorced. At the severe end of spectrum, patients may be suicidal or hospitalized, have stopped working or attending full-time education, be housebound and avoid all interaction, and be totally socially isolated because of their BDD.

The final diagnostic criteria in DSM IV state that the preoccupation must not be better accounted for by another mental disorder (e.g., dissatisfaction with body shape and size in anorexia nervosa). We discuss this in more detail under each of the comorbid diagnoses below.

1.5   Suicide Attempts and Suicide in BDD

Indications of high rates of suicide attempts were found in early surveys (Phillips, 1991; Phillips et al., 1997) and Veale et al. (1996), who found that 25–30% of BDD patients in psychiatric clinic have had a history of attempted suicide. In the largest sample described since then, Phillips et al. (2005) found that 78% of a sample of 200 individuals with BDD had lifetime suicidal ideation and 27.5% had made suicide attempts. BDD was reported as being the primary reason for suicidal ideation in 70.5% of those with a history of ideation and nearly half of the subjects with a past attempt. Both suicide ideation and suicide attempts were associated with functional impairment due to BDD, bipolar disorder, and personality disorder. Furthermore, suicidal subjects often did not reveal their symptoms of BDD to their clinicians.

Phillips and Menard (2006) in the same sample were able to conduct a prospective study of 185 subjects for up to four years (mean 2.1 ± 0.8 years). Suicidal ideation was reported by a mean of 56.7% of subjects per year and a mean of 2.8% attempted suicide per year. This is approximately 10–25 times greater than in the US population. Two subjects completed suicide (0.3% per year), which is 4–13 times higher than in the US population. The findings are preliminary but suggest that suicide in BDD is markedly high. Finally, in a study of dermatology patients who had committed suicide, Cotterill (1981) noted that most either had BDD or acne; of course, the former may have been a manifestation of the latter.

1.6   Age Restrictions

There are no age restrictions on the diagnosis of BDD. Generally, BDD is uncommon in childhood; the onset tends to develop in adolescence. The clinical features of adolescent BDD are similar to that of adults (Albertini & Phillips, 1999). Although the age of onset of BDD in adults is during late adolescence (Phillips, 1991), patients are usually diagnosed on average 15 years later (Veale et al., 1996; Phillips & Diaz, 1997).

1.7   Delusional Disorder

Beliefs about one's appearance (e.g., that "my skin is wrinkled and puffy") may be held with poor insight, when it is regarded as an overvalued idea in DSM IV; or no insight, when it is termed delusional. DSM IV allows BDD to be classified on the strength of beliefs and whether there is an *additional* diagnosis of a delusional disorder. The belief must be regarded as not bizarre and of at least one month's duration. One should also exclude schizophrenia or the direct physiological effects of a substance. The older literature is confusing as delusional disorder was previously termed "monosymptomatic hypochondriacal psychosis" (Munro & Stewart, 1991) and included delusions of body odor ("olfactory reference syndrome"), infestation, or dysmorphic delusions.

A structured diagnostic interview such as the Overvalued Ideas Scale (OVIS) (Neziroglu et al., 1999) or the Brown Assessment of Beliefs (BABS) (Eisen et al., 1998) (see Appendix 1) may be used to assess the strength of conviction and whether there is an additional diagnosis of delusional disorder. The additional diagnosis of a delusional disorder generally reflects the severity of the distress and handicap experienced.

The validity and usefulness of an additional diagnosis of delusional disorder is questionable for several reasons. Phillips et al. (1994) first found no difference in the characteristics between delusional and non-delusional BDD patients. Furthermore, delusional patients respond just as well as non-delusional patients to a selective serotonin reuptake inhibitor (SSRI) (Phillips et al., 1998; 2002). Phillips, Menard, Pagano, et al. (2006) compared delusional and non-delusional variants in 191 subjects with BDD. Individuals with BDD and delusional disorder were similar to those with non-delusional BDD in terms of most variables, including most demographic features, BDD characteristics, most measures of functional impairment and quality of life, comorbidity, and family history. However, delusional subjects had significantly lower educational attainment, were more likely to have attempted suicide, had poorer social functioning on several measures, were more likely to have drug abuse or dependence, were less likely to be receiving mental health treatment, and had more severe BDD symptoms. However, when controlling for BDD symptom severity, the two groups differed only in terms of educational attainment. The conclusion from all the studies above was that the delusional and non-delusional variants of BDD have many more similarities than differences, although on several measures delusional subjects evidenced greater morbidity, which appeared to be accounted for by their more severe BDD symptoms.

We have no data from randomized controlled trials (RCTs) on whether BDD clients with or without a delusional disorder respond equally well to CBT. BDD clients are not just disturbed by what their appearance *is*, but by what it is *not* or what it *should be*. It appears, therefore, that the strength of their belief is merely an indicator of the severity of the disorder and there seems little justification for adding another diagnosis of a delusional disorder. If this logic were applied to other disorders like OCD or hypochondriacal disorder, then each diagnosis might require a comorbid delusional disorder. It is also questionable whether body image can be represented solely as a belief (Ben-Tovim et al., 1998). Body image is a complex interaction of beliefs, imagery, tactile sensation, and affect. The concept of a delusion is not an issue in other body image disorders such as anorexia nervosa. Such clients may well hold beliefs about how fat they feel with delusional conviction. Such considerations do not seem to have any advantage in routine clinical care other than alerting the clinician to increased difficulties in engagement. We describe a number of case vignettes at the end of this chapter to illustrate the discussion about diagnosis about the heterogeneity of symptoms within BDD.

Although the additional diagnosis of delusionality does not seem to be important in treatment, assessing for overvalued ideas regarding the importance of attractiveness on attaining certain goals, the strength of conviction about their own flaws is important, and has been found to be a predictor of treatment outcome with CBT (Neziroglu et al., 1996). For this reason we suggest using scales assessing overvalued ideation.

1.8   Making a Diagnosis in ICD-10

In ICD-10, the term BDD, or the older term "dysmorphophobia," is not separately classified but is subsumed under hypochondriacal disorder (World Health Organization, 1992). Although there is some overlap between the symptoms of hypochondriacal disorder and BDD, we believe there is greater merit in following DSM IV and separating the two disorders. Many clinicians outside the USA therefore "vote with their feet" and do not use the diagnosis of hypochondriacal disorder for BDD. The diagnostic criteria for hypochondriacal disorder in ICD-10 are shown in Table 1.2. Like DSM IV, the essential feature is a persistent preoccupation with the possibility of having one or more serious and progressive "physical" disorders, associated with persistent distress or handicap. There is sometimes true comorbidity where a client has both BDD as well as a fear or conviction about having a serious disease in another bodily part.

An important distinction in ICD-10 compared to DSM IV is that if the beliefs about being defective are considered delusional, then a client would receive an *alternative* diagnosis of "Other persistent delusional disorder" (F22.8) instead of hypochondriacal disorder. This is in contrast to DSM IV, which allows an *additional* diagnosis of delusional disorder to BDD. The ICD-10 diagnosis is a residual category for persistent delusional disorders that do not meet the criteria for delusional disorder (F22.0). They are disorders in which the delusion(s) are accompanied by persistent hallucinatory voices or by schizophrenic symptoms that do not justify a diagnosis of schizophrenia (F20.–) and include "Delusional dysmorphophobia." Delusional disorders that have lasted for less than three months should, however, be coded, at least temporarily, under F23 (Acute transient psychotic disorders).

Table 1.2: Diagnostic criteria for hypochondriacal disorder (F45.2) (ICD-10)

A. Either of the following must be present:
   1. persistent belief, of at least six months' duration, of the presence of a maximum of two serious physical diseases (of which at least one must be specifically named by the patient);
   2. persistent preoccupation with a presumed deformity or disfigurement (body dysmorphic disorder).
B. Preoccupation with the belief and the symptoms causes persistent distress or interference with personal functioning in daily living, and leads the patient to seek medical treatment or investigations (or equivalent help from local healers).
C. There is a persistent refusal to accept medical reassurance that there is no physical cause for the symptoms or physical abnormality. (Short-term acceptance of such reassurance, i.e. for a few weeks during or immediately after investigations, does not exclude this diagnosis.)
D. Most commonly used exclusion clause. The symptoms do not occur only during any of the schizophrenic and related disorders (F20–F29, particularly F22) or any of the mood [affective] disorders (F30–F39).

1.9 Differential Diagnosis of BDD and Comorbidity

Before discussing the differential diagnosis of BDD in DSM IV or ICD-10, we should note that although our classification of mental disorders has had clear benefits, there are also significant limitations. The benefits are that diagnoses are useful shorthand for communication with researchers and clinicians or for legal purposes. Clients and carers are also often relieved to receive a diagnosis (this is not always the case for clients with BDD). Diagnostic systems have undoubtedly assisted research for studying relatively homogeneous groups of clients in clinical trials, but have also generated a whole industry of studies on comorbidity and other associations. However, diagnostic systems also have significant limitations for a psychological approach to mental disorder. A structured clinical interview can make a diagnosis more reliable but not necessarily more valid. A diagnostic cake can be divided in many ways and has limited value in determining treatment or prognosis. There are many studies of comorbidity. This has resulted in a major criticism of the current diagnostic systems because of the high level of comorbidity and the lack of specificity for treatment. Making a diagnosis in DSM IV or ICD-10 is therefore just one way of organizing information and we shall be emphasizing the importance of a functional analysis and the relationship between disorders as well as highlighting the similarities in the behavioral and cognitive processes in BDD that cut across other diagnoses.

One of the diagnostic criteria for BDD is that the preoccupation must be with either an imagined defect or a slight physical anomaly. Clients with "moderate to severe" physical anomalies (e.g., facial burns, a port wine stain, or very small breast size) who have difficulty coping might receive another diagnosis, such as an adjustment disorder, or, if it is sufficiently severe, another disorder such as depressive episode. An adjustment disorder consists of clinically significant emotional distress or handicap that has developed within three months of an identifiable psychosocial stress such as a deformity. The diagnosis is "trumped" if the client meets the criteria for another specific Axis I diagnosis that better describes their symptoms, such as a depressive episode or even a "Not otherwise specified" category. For an adjustment disorder, the symptoms should also resolve within six months of the termination of the stressor although a chronic stressor (e.g., a disfigurement) that lasts more than six months and has enduring consequences is also recognized. The diagnosis is important as it bridges "normality" and pathology – for example, an adjustment disorder was diagnosed in 60% of burn patients (Perez Jimenez et al., 1994).

The boundaries of BDD and a minor or moderate physical anomaly are not always clear. The definition of a "minor physical anomaly" is somewhat subjective and there is a gray area between this and more noticeable or moderate "anomalies" which present to cosmetic surgeons and dermatologists. We are trying to improve this with an observer and subjective rated scale which measures how noticeable a defect is and how abnormal it is compared to others (see Body Image Questionnaire in Appendix 1) and therefore determining the discrepancy between the two. The severity of a physical defect is not always relevant to a psychiatric diagnosis as there are individuals with "moderate to severe" anomalies or a disfigurement who might have similar preoccupation, distress, and handicap to BDD although the large majority do not. A similar situation exists in health anxiety/hypochondriasis where a client with a "real" organic condition such as diabetes might have marked anxiety and preoccupation with, for example, his blood sugar, with constant checking and repeated reassurance-seeking. However, clients with moderate to severe physical disfigurement are more likely to experience intense curiosity, teasing, or staring by others. They may avoid public or social situations but check less. Further research is required to differentiate symptoms of BDD from individuals with moderate to severe physical anomalies who are not coping. In theory, some aspects of this treatment manual can be used for such a population, but additional modules may be required to prepare individuals for intense curiosity or teasing by strangers (e.g., assertiveness training and role-playing of being teased).

The diagnostic criteria in DSM IV state that the preoccupation must not be better accounted for by another mental disorder (e.g., dissatisfaction with body shape and size in anorexia nervosa). It is not always easy to separate a disorder that better accounts for symptoms of BDD; we discuss this under each of the diagnoses below. Comorbidity is the rule rather than the exception in BDD, although this may partly reflect the populations from which surveys are drawn. The data are from centers with a special interest in BDD which are likely to attract more severe cases. A large community survey is more likely to recruit those with less severity and comorbidity. There have been four surveys of treatment centers (Table 1.3). The most common current comorbid diagnoses are, in descending order, major depressive episode, social phobia, obsessive compulsive disorder, and alcohol or substance abuse. It is not known whether BDD has relatively higher levels of comorbidity compared to, say, other anxiety or somatoform disorders because such studies have not been done. In similar survey of clients presenting to an anxiety disorders clinic, Brown & Barlow (1992) found that the point prevalence rate of comorbidity was relatively high, with 50% of the participants with an anxiety disorder having an additional anxiety disorder or depression at the time of the assessment. This has been replicated across a whole range of other disorders presenting at treatment centers such as eating disorders (Schwalberg et al., 1992), bipolar disorder (Tamam & Ozpoyraz, 2002), or generalized anxiety disorder (Judd et al., 1998).

1.10 Affective Disorders

We have already noted that a diagnosis of BDD is often missed because clinicians do not ask about the symptoms or do not use a structured diagnostic interview. Clients are ashamed of being labeled as vain or narcissistic; it is more acceptable to present with symptoms of depression. Some European clinicians may also assume a diagnostic hierarchy whereby symptoms of BDD are regarded as a symptom of a depressive episode. Occasionally, a diagnosis of a major depressive episode might better account for the symptoms of BDD if the preoccupation is limited to mood-congruent ruminations involving appearance during a major depressive episode only. This becomes apparent in clients with a recurrent depression in which BDD is episodic and occurs at the same time as deterioration in mood. The distinction can be difficult because a depressive episode is frequently comorbid but typically develops *after the onset of symptoms of BDD* (Gunstad & Phillips, 2003).

Axis I current comorbidity rates in clients identified with BDD are shown in Table 1.3 and the lifetime rates in Table 1.4. Gunstad & Phillips (2003) have conducted the largest survey of comorbidity in a survey of 293 BDD patients and found a current rate of 59% with major depression and a lifetime rate of 76%. Veale et al. (1996) found a lower rate of major depressive disorder of 8% and dysthymia of 18%, although it is not entirely clear why.

Table 1.3: Axis 1 Current Comorbidity Rates

Study	N	Assessment instrument	Major depression	Bipolar disorder	Dysthymia	OCD	Social phobia	Eating disorder	Substance use disorder
Veale et al. (1996)	50	SCID-P (DSM III-R)	8%	–	18%	6%	16%	–	2%
Zimmerman & Mattia (1998)	16	SCID-P, DSM IV	69%	6%	19%	38%	69%	19%	6%
Gunstad & Phillips (2003)	293	SCID-P, DSM IV	58%	5%	×	25%	32%	4%	8%

Table 1.4: Axis 1 Lifetime Comorbidity Rates

Study	N	Assessment instrument	Major depression	Bipolar disorder	Dysthymia	OCD	Social phobia	Eating disorder	Substance use disorder
Hollander et al. (1993)	50	Clinical Interview (DSM III-R)	68%	8%	–	78%	12%	20%	22%
Perugi et al. (1997)	58	Semi-structured interview (DSM III-R)	41%	31%	–	41%	12%	22%	–
Phillips & Diaz (1997)	188	SCID-P (DSM III-R)	82%	7%	7%	30%	38%	10%	36%
Nirenberg et al. (2002)	28	SCID-P (DSM IV)	–	–	18%	14%	54%	21%	32%
Gunstad & Phillips (2003)	293	SCID-P (DSM IV)	76%	5%	6%	32%	37%	4%	28%

An additional diagnosis of depression appears to reflect the severity of BDD and perhaps a reason for seeking help. Although the rates of depression vary, it has always been the most common additional Axis I disorder. Treatment of depression usually has to be done in parallel with that of BDD. Many of the symptoms, such as avoidance of social activity and being withdrawn, overlap although there may be different motivations. When depression is severe, people avoid social activity or tackling problems because they have lost motivation and feel hopeless and become less worried about fears of negative evaluation.

With BDD and comorbid depression, it is particularly important to assess suicide risk. Suicide ideation and attempts appear to be especially high in BDD. A sense of hopelessness and suicidal ideation is more likely to occur when people with BDD believe that they are trapped and have exhausted all abilities to camouflage or alter their appearance. They may have just had cosmetic surgery and realize that all their hopes have been dashed after an unsatisfactory operation.

Beck recognized the link between concerns about appearance with depression in his original depression inventory (Beck et al., 1961). Item 14 asks a client to pick one of the following statements that best describes the way he has been feeling:

a) "I don't feel I look any worse than I used to" (score 0),
b) "I am worried that I am looking old and unattractive" (score 1),
c) "I feel there are permanent changes in my appearance that make me look unattractive" (score 2),
d) "I believe that I look ugly" (score 3).

This item has unfortunately been dropped from the Revised Version of the BDI-II (Beck et al., 1996) on psychometric grounds. The original version of the BDI was, however, a useful screening item for BDD clients presenting with depression. Oosthuizen et al. (1998) also developed a dysmorphic questionnaire and found that concerns about appearance were strongly correlated with cognitive items on the BDI.

1.11   Social Phobia

Someone with social phobia believes that they will *behave* in a way that is unacceptable and that this will lead to rejection, loss of worth or status, or failure to achieve important goals. This is confined to situations in which others will evaluate them negatively. The behavior includes being anxious, such as being seen to be sweating, shaking, or blushing. However, someone with BDD is more likely to believe they *look* unacceptable, whether in social or non-social situations. Confusion arises because people with BDD are often anxious and fear being evaluated negatively in social situations. A comorbid diagnosis of social phobia in BDD can only be made when there is a broader fear of one or more social and performance situations in which the person is exposed to unfamiliar people or to possible scrutiny by others and the individual fears that he will *act* in a way, or show anxiety symptoms, that will be humiliating or embarrassing. Thus a person with social phobia might fear he will go red or appear shaky in social situations, whilst an individual with BDD might fear that his skin is permanently red, which is ugly and distressing. Most surveys of BDD clients have found an additional current diagnosis of social phobia of 16–69% (Table 1.3) and a lifetime rate of 12–54% (Table 1.4). Although the prevalence varies, it is the second most common diagnosis in all studies after a major depressive episode. Coles et al. (2005) examined the differences between individuals with BDD with and without social phobia. They found that those with BDD with social phobia were less likely to be employed, more likely to report lifetime suicide ideation, and had poorer global social adjustment on one of two measures. They were somewhat less likely to experience remission of their BDD symptoms over one year follow-up, although this difference was not statistically significant. Although this study was conducted with a structured diagnostic interview, be aware that rates may be excessively high because the diagnosis may have been given due to avoidance of social situations because of appearance and a thorough evaluation of the reasons of the avoidance may not have been assessed.

Individuals presenting with social phobia may also be anxious about aspects of their appearance, but it may not be regarded as a preoccupation that is excessively distressing or handicapping. In two surveys of patients attending a clinic for anxiety disorders, the rates of BDD were highest among those diagnosed with social phobia at 12% in Wilhelm et al. (1997) and 13% in Brawman-Mintzer et al. (1995). In all case series and in the study reported by Gunstad Phillips (2003), the onset of social phobia *preceded* the onset of BDD by at least 10 years. This is in contrast to other comorbid disorders such as depression or OCD in which BDD usually develops first. This may have some developmental relevance.

1.12   Alcohol and Substance Misuse

BDD clients frequently misuse alcohol and illegal substances as a way of coping with distress and preoccupation. Comorbid current rates vary from 2% to 17%, but may be much higher in an inpatient setting (Grant et al., 2001). Grant et al. (2005) examined rates and clinical correlates of comorbid substance use in 176 consecutive subjects with BDD of whom 29.5% had lifetime substance abuse and 35.8% had a lifetime substance use disorder (SUD), most commonly, alcohol dependence (29.0%); and 17% (N = 30) had current substance abuse or dependence (9.1% reported current substance abuse, 9.7% reported current dependence). There were far more similarities than differences between subjects with a comorbid SUD and those without a SUD, although those with a lifetime SUD had a significantly higher rate of suicide attempts (p = 0.004).

Inevitably, alcohol and substances such as cannabis or stimulants increase paranoia and depressed mood and decrease motivation. Like other disorders, clients need help to stop drinking or using substances before BDD treatment is commenced (or at least done in parallel) as substances may interfere with therapy and cognitive and emotional processing.

1.13   Obsessive Compulsive Disorder

An additional diagnosis of obsessive compulsive disorder (OCD) is only given when the "obsessions" or "compulsions" are not restricted to concerns about appearance. Sometimes the symptoms overlap and there is gray area between the two. For example, a client may believe that his skin is defective through contamination and this is associated with washing compulsions or skin picking. A similar situation exists in clients preoccupied with perfection and symmetry, which may extend to their appearance. Typically, such clients do *not* believe their feature to be defective or ugly, but the preoccupation might be a need for the hair to be exactly symmetrical or their make-up to be perfect or "just right." Some of the older literature on OCD probably included clients with BDD and there are no diagnostic rules that determine whether such clients should be regarded as having OCD or BDD.

In surveys of clients with BDD, comorbid current rates of OCD are between 6% and 38% (Table 1.3) (Veale et al., 1996; Zimmerman & Mattia, 1998; Gunstad & Phillips, 2003) and lifetime rates from 14% to 78% (Table 1.4). In a study of 165 patients seeking treatment for an anxiety disorder, 3 of 40 (7.5%) OCD patients had a current diagnosis of BDD (Wilhelm et al., 1997). Other studies of OCD found that 12% of patients had a lifetime diagnosis of BDD (Simeon et al., 1995). Although age of onset is similar for BDD and OCD, the onset of BDD usually precedes OCD (Gunstad et al., 2003). One pattern of comorbidity of BDD and OCD is that the person experiences recurrent intrusive thoughts or images about a defect(s) which the person knows is absurd and the intrusions are regarded as egodystonic.

There are a number of group differences between individuals with OCD and BDD. Phillips et al. (1998) compared individuals with BDD (N = 53) with

OCD (N = 53), or both disorders (N = 33). They found that 14.5% (9 of 62) of subjects initially diagnosed with OCD had comorbid BDD. The two disorders did not differ significantly in terms of sex ratio; most other demographic, course, and impairment variables; illness severity; or lifetime frequency of most associated disorders in probands or first-degree relatives. However, individuals with BDD were less likely to be married and more likely to have had suicidal ideation or make a suicide attempt because of their disorder. They also had an earlier onset of major depression and higher lifetime rates of major depression, social phobia, and psychotic disorder diagnoses, as well as higher rates of substance use disorders in first-degree relatives. Phillips et al. (2007) reported on a larger study which compared subjects with OCD (N = 210), BDD (N = 45), and co-morbid BDD/OCD (N = 40). OCD and BDD did not significantly differ in terms of demographic features, age of OCD or BDD onset, illness duration, and many other variables. As in the previous study, subjects with BDD had significantly poorer insight than those with OCD and were more likely to be delusional. Subjects with BDD were also significantly more likely than those with OCD to have lifetime suicidal ideation, as well as lifetime major depressive disorder and a lifetime substance use disorder.

1.14 Eating Disorders

A common diagnostic dilemma for BDD is that of an eating disorder. BDD and eating disorders often share an altered body image and many other symptoms such as a low self-esteem or perfectionism. DSM IV states that a diagnosis of BDD should not be used if the patient's symptoms are best accounted for hierarchically by a diagnosis of an eating disorder. If, therefore, the preoccupation is predominantly focused on being "too fat" or overweight, it does not meet criteria for BDD.

There is a gray area between individuals with disordered eating who do not fulfill the criteria for anorexia or bulimia nervosa. Rosen et al. (1995a) describe a sample of BDD clients in whom an eating disorder was excluded using the Eating Disorders Examination (Cooper & Fairburn, 1987). Rosen et al.'s sample was all female and 38% were preoccupied with their weight and shape alone, and they were generally less handicapped and less socially avoidant than BDD clients described in most other centers. Such clients might still have periods of disordered eating or excessive exercise as a means of altering their body shape and weight. It is not known whether some of Rosen et al.'s sample would have fulfilled the later criterion for an Eating Disorder Not Otherwise Specified (EDNOS), which was not used in this study. The diagnosis of EDNOS is important as it has the largest prevalence of all eating disorders in the community (Fairburn & Harrison, 2003). To fulfill a diagnosis of EDNOS, the person fails to meet all the criteria for anorexia nervosa (e.g., if female, has regular menses) or of bulimia nervosa (e.g., binge eating and vomiting at a frequency of less than twice a week). The main criticism of the diagnosis of EDNOS is that different research groups may use slightly different criteria and it is difficult to establish the boundaries.

True comorbidity of BDD and eating disorder occurs when a client is preoccupied by imagined defects in his appearance unrelated to weight and shape. The comorbid current rates of an eating disorder in BDD vary from 0% to 19% (Table 1.3) and lifetime rates from 4% to 22.5% (Table 1.4). In the largest survey, Ruffolo et al. (2006) described 200 individuals with BDD and found that 32.5% had had a comorbid lifetime eating disorder (9% anorexia nervosa, 6.5% bulimia nervosa, 17.5% EDNOS). Those with a comorbid lifetime eating disorder were more likely to be female, less likely to be African American, had more comorbidity, and had significantly greater body image disturbance than those without a history of an eating disorder. There were no significant differences in BDD symptom severity, degree of delusionality, or suicidal ideation or attempts.

More interesting are the data reported by Grant et al. (2002), which indicate that 16 of 41 patients (39%) with anorexia nervosa were diagnosed with comorbid BDD unrelated to weight concerns. Therefore, preoccupation with a body part because it is "too fat" or because the body part is somehow affected by the patient's weight did not meet the criteria for BDD. The most common preoccupations in the study were (in descending order) with the nose, skin, hair, chin, lips, and eyes, which is virtually identical to BDD clients without anorexia. The patients with anorexia nervosa and BDD had significantly lower overall functioning and higher levels of delusionality than the anorexic patients without BDD, suggesting that the former had a more severe form of illness. Further research is required to replicate these findings in a larger sample of patients with anorexia and to investigate the prevalence of BDD in those diagnosed with bulimia nervosa and EDNOS. It is not known whether a diagnosis of BDD in an eating disorder is a poor prognostic factor and whether the symptoms alter when the eating disorder improves. In our experience, the diagnosis of BDD is rarely made by clinicians in eating disorder units and more attention needs to be focused on BDD aspects within that population. It is our experience that many eating disordered patients do have other body parts of concern and fulfill the criteria of BDD.

1.15   Psychogenic Excoriation

Psychogenic excoriation ("skin picking") and the differential diagnosis of various associated disorders are discussed in Chapter 5.

1.16 Trichotillomania

Like skin picking, hair pulling or body depilation can occur in BDD when an individual pulls hair from his skin as a response to a preoccupation with a "defect" to improve his appearance. This would be regarded as part of BDD and should be distinguished from trichotillomania, which is reinforced by tension reduction and a sense of gratification that usually occur with the hair pulling. Individuals may then become ashamed of the consequences of hair pulling and bald patches, which they strenuously try to cover. This is not usually BDD as they are not preoccupied with an imagined defect or minor psychical anomaly. It represents the shame that stems from an adjustment disorder or another Axis I disorder.

1.17 Olfactory Reference Syndrome

Olfactory reference syndrome (ORS) is sometimes regarded as part of BDD or obsessive compulsive spectrum disorder. ORS is not a recognized diagnosis in DSM IV or ICD-10 but is used to describe an individual who is preoccupied by their body odor or halitosis and feels persistent shame. They may be experiencing olfactory hallucinations or mental images. They may use a range of safety behaviors (e.g., excessive use of perfume) to mask the presumed odor. They frequently shower, brush their teeth, change their clothes, and ultimately avoid public and social situations where they think their body odor will be noticed. The degree of insight in ORS varies and has many similarities to BDD. Some patients are like someone with OCD with intrusive doubts and seeking frequent reassurance about their body odor. Others have a delusional disorder and often marked avoidance behavior. For further discussion of ORS and case reports, the reader is referred to Pryse-Phillips (1971), Lochner et al. (2001), and Suzuki et al. (2004). We have had a small number of BDD patients who are also preoccupied with their body odor, which blended easily with their preoccupation with aspects of their appearance. For example, if you believe you look hideous, it is not surprising if you also believe that you smell disgusting.

1.18 Schizophrenia and Persecutory Delusional Disorder

The differential diagnosis of BDD from schizophrenia is not usually an issue because of the presence of hallucinations, thought disorder, or more bizarre delusions in schizophrenia. Comorbidity is uncommon. Several authors (Traub et al. 1967; Chapman et al. 1978; Priebe & Rohricht, 2001) have described general distortions of body image in schizophrenia. Patients with schizophrenia may make dramatic changes to their appearance (e.g., bizarre use of make-up, sunglasses, or inappropriate clothes). These may be part of a command hallucination or delusion, or an attempt to retain their sense of identity. They may be inaccurate in their body size estimations feeling that parts of the body are unusually small or that their body size has changed. They can also experience symptoms of disembodiment, such as feeling they are no longer part of their body, feeling disintegrated or the body is torn apart.

Some clients with BDD may have extreme forms of delusions of reference and persecutory delusional disorder focused on others humiliating and laughing at them or being treated malevolently. This can be usually be treated in parallel with the approaches described in this book and finding an alternative explanation for the experience. This should, however, be differentiated from paranoid schizophrenia in which delusions and hallucinations are present.

1.19   Body Integrity Identity Disorder

BDD is sometimes confused with Body Integrity Identity Disorder (BIID) (previously known as "Amputee Identity Disorder," AID). This is not a recognized diagnosis in DSM IV or ICD-10, but is used to describe individuals who desire one or more digits or limbs to be amputated (Furth et al., 2000; Smith & Fisher, 2003; First, 2005). The term apotemnophilia has also been used, but this is strictly speaking a sexual fetish, whose adherents are known as "devotees." They have a special interest or a sexual desire for people who are disabled (Money et al., 1977).

Individuals with BIID feel that one or more limbs are not part of their "self" (a form of reverse "phantom limb") and that amputation will lead to them becoming more able-bodied. It is a preoccupation which derives not from a feeling of defectiveness or inadequacy but the expectation that they would be so much more comfortable if one or more limbs or digits were amputated. Prior to amputation, individuals with BIID may live as if they had a disability, when they are known as "pretenders." They may live with a wheelchair, crutches, or leg braces. In the face of opposition from surgeons, some individuals hasten amputation (e.g., chainsaw wound or shooting) or carry out self-amputation (e.g., on a rail track). Although such individuals are preoccupied with becoming disabled, they do not believe (as in BDD) their limbs to be defective or ugly, nor do they wish cosmetically to alter their limb. First (2005) interviewed 52 subjects (47 male, four female, one intersex) with BIID, of whom 17% (N = 9) had had an arm or leg amputated, with two-thirds using methods that put the subject at risk of death and one-third enlisting the support of a surgeon to amputate a healthy limb. The most common reason reported for wanting an amputation was the subject's feeling that it would correct a mismatch between the person's anatomy and sense of his true self (identity). None of the subjects was delusional. For all but one subject age at onset was during childhood or adolescence. No benefit occurred from psychotherapy or medication. The six subjects who had an amputation reported that following amputation they felt better and were no longer preoccupied by a desire for an amputation. Mr Robert Smith, an orthopedic surgeon in Scotland, conducted surgical amputation on two patients before the ethical committee stopped him doing further operations at his hospital. Fisher & Smith (2000) report in a letter that the patients experienced a better quality of life once the effort involved in seeking a solution was removed. This is unlike clients with BDD for whom cosmetic surgery is unpredictable (see Chapter 6).

BIID is therefore more akin to a gender identity disorder in which individuals feel that their genitalia do not belong to them and that they are trapped in a body of the wrong gender. There may be other variations of BIID concerning a desire for a disabled identity – for example, individuals who deliberately infect themselves with HIV (Morgan & Jones, 1993) or who have a compelling and persistent desire to be deaf (Veale, 2006). Such individuals feel that they are "a hearing person in a deaf person's body." There may also be a form of BIID in men who desire castration but not to change sex (Roberts et al., 2007). In summary, people with BIID appear to have in common an onset of desire in childhood or, at the latest, by early adolescence; and a sense that their fundamental identity will be "set right" by having the part of body removed or modified. A core feature is as much the desire for a particular identity (e.g., being an amputee, being a eunuch, being part of the deaf community) as the modification itself (First, personal communication). Patients with BIID or a desire to be disabled should not therefore be confused with those with BDD. There is a dedicated website for BIID (www.biid.org) and one by users (http://biid-info.org).

1.20 Body Modification or Self-mutilation

There is another group of individuals who are sometimes confused with BDD who modify or mutilate their body as a form of art. Alternatively, they may transform their body into an animal. Self-mutilation commonly occurs in young women, on the forearm with razors or other sharp implements. A number of studies have linked childhood adversity or abuse and especially borderline personality disorder with subsequent self-mutilation (for a more thorough discussion of self mutilation, see McVey-Noble et al., 2006). In the 1990s, self-mutilation developed into body piercing or tattooing partly from punk fashion and gay sadomasochism, which has now become mainstream. Decorative implants of various sorts are also popular, including some inserted under the skin. They include lobe stretching, ear scalpeling and tongue piercing, branding, scarification, and tongue splitting (wiki.bmezine.com). It now extends to circumcision (male or female); penis, scrotal, or labial stretching; glans splitting, and relocation of the urethra, either by the individual or a lay practitioner. Female genital mutilation is illegal in most Western countries unless it is conducted by a surgeon for physical or mental health reasons and sometimes a client may seek body modification on mental health grounds. For most people, body modification appears to be a lifestyle choice with an extensive subculture of sadomasochism. A few people who have modified their body might have BDD as a way of camouflaging their "defect" or distracting attention from it, but this has not been systematically studied.

The porn icon Lolo Ferrari, who died at the age of 37, was thought by some to have had BDD. She was a minor celebrity for having "the largest breasts in the world." She had 25 cosmetic operations in five years, especially on her bust, which gradually increased to a size 71". She looked like a freak, had difficulty breathing, and was unable to sleep on her front or back. She was a colorful but sad figure who made her name as a presenter on television shows. She is known to have had an unhappy childhood. She is thought to have committed suicide or may have been murdered by her husband and pimp, who was a transvestite and afraid of altering his own body. Her symptoms are, however, not typical of BDD and in many ways her behavior is an extreme version of body modification and self-mutilation, which was reinforced by male attention.

Another extreme version of body mutilation is "Orlan" who usually represents her modifying her body as "art." For one operation, Orlan had silicone implants put into her cheeks and forehead to give her "horns" or to make her more ugly and question the nature of beauty. The operations are videoed as "art" and parts of her body are then sold to the public. Examples of extreme body modification into an animal are "Tigerman" and "Lizardman" who can be viewed on the web by a search engine. No cosmetic surgeon will assist such individuals to transform their body and so such surgery is done without anesthetic by lay individuals. As far as we are aware, Orlan, Tigerman, Lizardman, or any other animals have not been psychiatrically evaluated. Such individuals might be regarded as highly eccentric or possibly personality disordered with beliefs akin to over-valued ideas. However, there is no evidence that they have BDD.

1.21   Koro

The Malayo-Indonesian term "Koro" and the Mandarin Chinese term "suo-yang" (Cantonese "suk-yang") is a syndrome that mainly occurs in Asia and to a lesser extent in Africa. It is also known as "genital retraction syndrome." It refers to the fear or belief that one's penis is shrinking or retracting into the body (Cheng, 1996; Chowdhury, 1998). Koro can also occur in populations without a Chinese influence as well as in women, when it refers to fears that their breasts and labia are shrinking. It is usually a transient state of acute anxiety and avoidance. The individual anticipates impotence, sterility, or even death. Moreover, the immediate family becomes convinced of the same outcome and may hold on to the sufferer's genitalia manually or with special instruments. Epidemics of Koro have been observed in Singapore, Thailand, and India precipitated by threats to security or even survival of the afflicted population. Some authors have suggested that Koro is a cultural variant of BDD, but the main differences is that in Koro others in the immediate family share the beliefs and usually it consists of a transient state of marked anxiety.

1.22   Personality Disorder

Three studies have used the same structured diagnostic interview of personality disorder in surveys of BDD clients (Table 1.5). Personality disorders were present in 57–100% of patients in the studies by Veale et al. (1996); Neziroglu et al. (1996), and Phillips and McElroy (2000). Cluster C (anxious or fearful) was the most common in all the studies. In descending order, avoidant, paranoid, obsessive compulsive, dependent, and borderline personality disorders were the most common. Neziroglu et al. (1996) found a higher rate (100%) than either Veale et al. (1996) or Phillips & McElroy (2000) and this may have been because the numbers were small (N = 17) and because of a higher rate of comorbid OCD (94%). There is often unreliability in the diagnosis of a personality disorder in the context of a chronic Axis I disorder. There are also often disagreements over whether a personality trait is enduring and persistent before the onset of a chronic disorder or whether it is developed after the disorder as a response.

The presence of a personality disorder generally reflects the severity of symptoms and, probably, a poorer prognosis. For example, Phillips & McElroy (2000) reported that those with a personality disorder had a significantly higher score on the Yale Brown Obsessive Compulsive Scale for BDD. They also found that they were unassertive on the Rathus Assertiveness Scale and the mean scores for all subjects were in the high range for neuroticism and in the low range for extraversion on the NEO-Five Factor Inventory. Scores were also in the low range for conscientiousness, the average range for openness to experience, and low–average range for agreeableness. In general, the presence of a personality disorder will make it more difficult to engage and treat patients with BDD. However, the number of personality disorders decreases

Table 1.5: Axis 2 – Current Comorbidity Rates

Study	N	Assessment instrument	At least one personality disorder	Avoidant	Paranoid	Obsessive compulsive	Borderline	Dependent
Veale et al. (1996)	50	SCID-II (DSM III-R)	72%	38%	38%	28%	6%	12%
Neziroglu et al. (1996)	17	SCID-II (DSM III-R)	100%	82%	53%	82%	76%	71%
Phillips & McElroy (2000)	74	SCID-II (DSM III-R)	57%	43%	14%	14%	8%	15%
Nirenberg et al. (2002)	28	SCID-II (DSM IV)	86%	50%	25%	39%	21%	29%

in responders after treatment with either CBT (Neziroglu et al., 1996) or pharmacotherapy with fluvoxamine (Phillips & McElroy 2000). This is probably due to the similarity of symptoms in some personality disorders and Axis I diagnoses. For example, once a client improves in symptoms of BDD and avoids less it is not surprising that the avoidant personality diagnosis disappears.

Lastly, Semiz et al. (2008) have investigated comorbidity of BDD in people with borderline personality disorder. BDD appeared to be extremely common in clients in whom BPD is their main problem. They found that 38 (54.3%) of 70 clients with BPD in a Turkish setting had BDD. Childhood traumatic experiences were significant predictors of diagnosis of BDD (77% correct) even when socio-demographic factors and severity of depressive symptoms were controlled for. However, many practitioners would probably regard a preoccupation with one's body image as just one part of disturbed self-identity in borderline personality disorder and not regard it as a separate problem. Furthermore, the symptoms of BDD in borderline personality are rarely fixed but are more variable and fluctuating in intensity than found in typical BDD. Treatment trials of BDD will therefore usually try to exclude people with BPD when BPD is regarded as the main problem.

Chapter 2

History of body dysmorphic disorder

Summary

This chapter reviews the history of body dysmorphic disorder (BDD). BDD was originally termed "dysmorphophobia" and we have reprinted an excerpt of the first description of it by an Italian psychiatrist, Enrico Morselli, in 1891. There are subsequent descriptions by Janet and Kraeplin. The most famous historical case of BDD is the Wolf Man, who was originally analyzed by Freud and subsequently by Brunswick. The latter clearly describes symptoms of BDD and the patient later describes his own behavioral program. The term body dysmorphic disorder was first used in DSM III-R in 1987 and has continued in DSM IV-R. The term "monosymptomatic hypochondriacal psychosis" is also disused and refers to a delusional disorder.

Sections

2.1   Dysmorphophobia

Historical and transcultural literature suggests that since classical times humans have considered their body and its appearance as a special object of aesthetic and symbolic inquiry (Maisonneuve & Bruchon-Schweitzer, 1981).

Body Dysmorphic Disorder: A Treatment Manual. David Veale and Fugen Neziroglu
© 2010 John Wiley & Sons, Ltd.

There has been much discussion about the normal and pathological development of attitudes and emotional reactions of individuals to their body. Sometimes, writers incorrectly named disorders or "complexes" after physically
deformed individuals. For example, Thersites was considered the ugliest Greek
in the Trojan War – he was cross-eyed and limped – but it is unclear whether
he was ever preoccupied with his ugliness (Stutte, 1962). Quasimodo Complex
was also suggested to depict a concern with physical deformity, but again there
is no evidence that a preoccupation actually existed (Masters & Greaves,
1987). Finally, during the late nineteenth century, worries and complaints over
an imagined deformity were named by Morselli (1891) as "dysmorphophobia."
The term was derived from the Greek word "dysmorfia," meaning a bad body
or unattractive. Dysmorfia first appeared in the *Histories of Herodotus*, referring to the myth of the "ugliest girl in Sparta" (Philippopoulos, 1979).

When Morselli first began to work on dysmorphophobia he had received
psychiatric training in a mental hospital, studied physical anthropology, started
lecturing at Turin University, written a book on suicide, founded a journal on
scientific philosophy, and begun a lucrative private practice. It was in private
practice that he began to see dysmporphophobic patients before he moved to
Genoa in 1890. In his article on dysmorphophobia, Morselli also described
"taphephobia" (an obsessional fear of being buried alive), a condition that
might now be regarded as part of obsessive compulsive disorder (OCD), as it
was characterized by frequent reassurance-seeking and checking the procedure that determines whether death had occurred. Jerome (2001) has translated the original article and we have quoted here with permission an excerpt
describing dysmorphophobia.

"As the result of some observations I have made in recent years, I propose to
add two new and previously undescribed varieties to the various forms of insanity with fixed ideas, whose underlying phenomenology is essentially phobic. The
two new terms I would like to put forth, following the nomenclature currently
accepted by leading clinicians, are dysmorphophobia and taphephobia.

The first condition consists of the sudden appearance and fixation in the
consciousness of the idea of one's own deformity; the individual fears that he has
become deformed (<u>dysmorphos</u>) or might become deformed, and experiences at
this thought a feeling of an inexpressible disaster. The second condition, taphephobia, consists of the sick person's being plagued, whenever he approaches a
dead body (taphe = grave), by a fear of the possibility of being buried alive, this
fear becoming the source of a terribly distressing anguish. It is not necessary for
me to give a very detailed description of these two new forms of rudimentary
paranoia I have discovered and named, since in so doing I would only be repeating descriptions that have long been available among the many and varied forms
of paranoia in books and the most important journals of psychiatry; instead,
I shall limit myself to making some general comments on the conditions. The

ideas of being ugly and of being buried whilst in a state of apparent death are not, in themselves, morbid; in fact, they occur to many people in perfect mental health, awakening however only the emotions normally felt when these two possibilities are contemplated. But, when one of these ideas occupies someone's attention repeatedly on the same day, and aggressively and persistently returns to monopolize his attention, refusing to remit by any conscious effort; and when in particular the emotion accompanying it becomes one of fear, distress, anxiety, and anguish, compelling the individual to modify his behavior and to act in a predetermined and fixed way, then the psychological phenomenon has gone beyond the bounds of normal, and may validly be considered to have entered the realm of psychopathology.

The dysmorphophobic, indeed, is a veritably unhappy individual, who in the midst of his daily affairs, in conversations, while reading, at table, in fact anywhere and at any hour of the day, is suddenly overcome by the fear of some deformity that might have developed in his body without his noticing it. He fears having or developing a compressed, flattened forehead, a ridiculous nose, crooked legs, etc., so that he constantly peers in the mirror, feels his forehead, measures the length of his nose, examines the tiniest defects in his skin, or measures the proportions of his trunk and the straightness of his limbs, and only after a certain period of time, having convinced himself that this has not happened, is able to free himself from the state of pain and anguish the attack put him in. But should no mirror be at hand, or should he be prevented from quieting his doubts in some way or other with rituals or movements of the most outlandish kinds, the way a rhypophobic who cannot get water to wash himself might, the attack does not end very quickly, but may reach a very painful intensity, even to the point of weeping and desperation."

For Morselli, dysmorphophobia was an obsessive idea and a sorrow about the deformity of the body and he classified it as a rudimentary paranoia or abortive monomania. It seems there was a double classification. At around the same time Kaan (1892) was studying fear of ugliness in his book on neurasthenia and obsession. Hartenberg (1901) also referred to dysmorphophobia in his book on timidity.

The next historical reference to "dysmorphophobia" was by the French psychiatrist Janet (1903), who described a woman who was housebound for five years. He considered the diagnosis to be part of an obsessive compulsive neurosis which he described as "l'obsession de la honte du corps" ("obsession of shame of the body"). His description includes the first possible use of behavior therapy, but without any shared formulation or negotiation of goals!

"This 38 years old lady presents with a ridiculous preoccupation: she believes she has a moustache. It is important to note that this patient's mother was authoritarian and expected a lot from her daughter who is weak, shy and ashamed of herself. Her upbringing was strict and she was so terrified of criticism that she attempted suicide many times. She is now married and experiencing problems with her neighbors who are argumentative: 'I fear my neighbors and I do not have the strength to argue with them.' 'How could I approach my neighbors with this hairy face, they would ridicule me and this will show I am inferior.' These thoughts are accompanied with anxiety crisis and agitation. She also imagines her neighbors shouting 'Hairy, hairy!' and becomes very distressed. This young lady has recovered rapidly, from a treatment dictated by her husband under our instruction. Treatment consisted of motivational and attention exercises to combat her shyness" (pp. 360–1).

In 1907, Dupré explained such fears as deriving from a disturbance of proprioceptive information. Korkina and Morozov (1979) point out that early in the century, Korsakov, Betcherev, and Suchanov had already reported similar clinical examples in the Russian literature. In 1912, Osipov (Korkina et al., 1979) introduced the term "dysmorphophobia" in Russia in describing a 27-year-old woman who believed that she was too big and the lower part of her face was deformed.

The term dysmorphophobia first came into the English literature probably with the translation of Tanzi's *Textbook of Mental Diseases* (1909) where Morselli was mentioned in the section on obsessive ideas. Kraepelin (1909), in his chapter on "Die Zwangsneurose", legitimized the term dysmorphophobia but did not mention Morselli, thus presenting the term as if he had coined it. He wrote:

"Some patients cannot get rid of the thought that there is something ridiculous or conspicuous about them. They think that they will attract the attention or ridicule of people they meet by an awkwardly formed nose, crooked legs or a disgusting smell, and make a nuisance of themselves (dysmorphophobia). While examining these patients, a physician may become acutely aware that it is extremely unpleasant for them to be looked at."

He classified dysmorphophobia as a compulsive neurosis.

2.2   The Wolf Man

Freud (1959), and subsequently Brunswick (1971), described the most famous case of BDD known as the "Wolf Man" who was preoccupied by imagined defects of his nose. The Wolf Man was a Russian aristocrat who had a recurrent dream of white wolves sitting staring at him from the bare branches of a tree outside his bedroom window in winter. The interpretation was that his nose represented his penis and that he desired to be castrated and made into a woman. The relevance of the dream to his symptoms is not clear to us as cognitive behavior therapists, but there is an excellent description of his psychopathology. Brunswick describes how by the time the Wolf Man came to her for analysis:

> "he neglected his daily life and work because he was engrossed, to the exclusion of all else, in the state of his nose. On the street he looked at himself in every shop window; he carried a pocket mirror, which he took out every few minutes. First he would powder his nose; a moment later he would inspect it and remove the powder. He would then examine the pores, to see if they were enlarging, to catch the hole, as it were, in its moment of growth and development. Then he would again powder his nose, put away the mirror, and a moment later begin the process anew. His life was centered on the little mirror in his pocket, and his fate depended on what it revealed or was about to reveal."

The maid who opened the door to his apartment was afraid of him because, as she said:

> "He always rushed past her like a lunatic to the long mirror in the poorly lighted reception hall. He would not sit down and wait like other patients, to be admitted to her office; he would incessantly walk up and down the small hall, taking out his mirror and examining his nose in this light and that. It was in this condition that he began his analysis."

There is an interesting postscript to this account as the Wolf Man himself described his experience of analysis with Freud and Brunswick (Obholzer, 1982). He constructed his own behavioral program of response prevention and wrote:

> "I gathered all my strength, stopped looking in the mirror, and somehow overcame these ideas in a few days. ... I took a stand against psychoanalysis and made a decision of my own. Stop thinking about your nose! It was much greater success than with Freud because I rejected transference."

If only response prevention was that easy for other people with BDD!

At least with this and other historical cases, we can be confident that BDD is not a phenomenon of modern society and its preoccupation with appearance. Other terms used in the 1900s to describe BDD include "dermatologic hypochondriasis" (Zaidens, 1950) and "beauty hypochondria" (Jahrreiss, 1930), which is chronicled by Phillips (1991).

2.3 American Diagnostic and Statistical Manual

Dysmorphophobia was first cited in the American psychiatric classification of DSM III in 1980 (American Psychiatric Association, 1980) as an example of an "atypical somatoform disorder" without any diagnostic criteria. The term "body dysmorphic disorder" was first used in DSM III-R in 1987 and has continued in DSM IV-R. The new term was justified on the grounds that there was no phobic avoidance of a physical defect. However, most people with BDD often exhibit some fear of negative evaluation or have a phobic avoidance of certain situations or activities that are anxiety-provoking. Several authors pointed out the problematic and confusing nature of the term "dysmorphophobia." Munro & Stewart (1991), for example, concluded that the "nomenclature is chaotic" and cited six contradictory uses in the literature. The term "dysmorphophobia" is now generally falling into disuse but is still sometimes used in the European literature, probably because ICD-10 subsumed "dysmorphophobia" as an example of hypochondriacal disorder and did not regard it as a separate diagnosis.

Symptoms of BDD may have been regarded as part of a depressive disorder in the past as part of a hierarchical classification. A good example is Beck (1969), who wrote in his treatise on depression that for patients who had severe symptoms,

> "The idea of personal unattractiveness becomes more fixed. The patient believes that he is ugly and repulsive looking. He expects other people to turn away from him in revulsion. One woman wore a veil and another turned her head whenever anybody approached her."

2.4   Monosymptomatic Hypochondriacal Psychosis

Another term used in the older European literature is "monosymptomatic hypochondriacal psychosis" (Riding & Munro, 1975). This was described as a single delusional belief of a somatic nature, usually in the absence of other prominent psychotic symptoms (Thomas, 1984). They included all somatic-type delusions of body odor, delusions of parasitic infestation, and delusions of defectiveness and ugliness. They were classified in DSM III as an atypical paranoid disorder or atypical psychosis. The delusional variant of BDD lives on in DSM IV-R as "Delusional Disorder Somatic-type," which can be diagnosed in addition to BDD. In ICD-10, the term now used is "Persistent Delusional Disorder, not otherwise specified" (F22.8). The non-delusional variant of BDD is classified in ICD-10 as hypochondriacal disorder (F45.2).

2.5   Contemporary Figures with BDD

Andy Warhol (1928–87) may have had BDD. The pop artist, who put Campbell soup cans and colored photographs of Marilyn Monroe in museums, was very self-conscious and preoccupied by the "redness" of his nose. In his autobiography, Warhol (1975) reveals, "I believe in low lights and trick mirrors. A person is entitled to the lighting they need" (p. 51).

"At one time, the way my nose looked really bothered me – it's always red – and I decided that I wanted to have it sanded ... I went to see the doctor and I think he thought he'd humor me, so he sanded it and when I walked out of St Luke's Hospital, I was the same underneath but had a bandage on. ... "If I didn't want to look so bad, I would want to look plain. That would be my next choice" (pp. 63, 69).

Carl Withers, who became his lover in 1952, confirmed in an interview: "he was incredibly self-conscious and had such a low opinion of his looks; it was a serious psychological block with him." Warhol's concern with his nose is reflected in one of his early works "Before and After," which is an advertisement for a rhinoplasty and can be seen in the Metropolitan Museum of Art in New York.

Franz Kafka (1883–1924) may have had BDD. His diaries tell us how he hated himself and his appearance:

"I didn't want any new clothes at all; because if I had to look ugly anyway, I wanted to at least be comfortable. I let the awful clothes affect even my posture, walked around with my back bowed, my shoulders drooping, my hands and arms all over the place. I was afraid of mirrors, because they showed an inescapable ugliness" (Brod, 1995).

Sylvia Plath (1932–63), the poet and novelist, is well known to have had depression and indeed committed suicide. However less well investigated is whether she might have had BDD. She was an attractive woman, but in her autobiography, Plath (2000) wrote:

"My face I know not. One day ugly as a frog the mirror blurts it back: thick-pored skin, coarse as sieve, exuding soft spots of pus, points of dirt, hard kernels of impurity – a coarse grating. No milk-drawn silk. Hair blued with oil-slick, nose crusted with hair and green or brown crusts. Eye-whites yellowed, corners crusted, ears a whorl of soft wax" (p. 306).

And later:

"I shiver, chilled, the grave-chill against the simple heat of my flesh: how did I get to be thick big, complete self, with the long-boned span of arm & leg, the scarred imperfect skin?" (p. 328).

Depression is also associated with a negative body image and this may have been the main problem rather than BDD.

Shirley Manson, the lead singer in the pop group "Garbage," states in a magazine interview that she had a history of BDD:

> "I always turned up five hours late because I'd be fussing about my hair and make-up. I would change into a million different outfits, and make them change the lighting a million times, I would spend two hours crying in the toilet – and whatever the result, I always thought I looked disgusting. I would look in the mirror every morning and be upset. I would get dressed and look in the mirror again, and be upset. It could be anything; I could be too fat, too thin, too flat chested. My hands were not long enough, my neck was too long. My tummy stuck out, my bum was too big. … It was driving me crazy and I was wasting energy – precious energy – that I should have been putting into my music or my family or friends."

BDD appears to be more stigmatized than other mental illnesses and is easily trivialized. The level of awareness of BDD is similar to that of depression in the 1970s. The knowledge that public figures can have BDD is helpful to some sufferers and increasing publicity in the media will help to reduce stigma. Ultimately, this should encourage more BDD sufferers to seek treatment at an earlier age.

Chapter 3

Epidemiology and presentation of BDD

Summary

There is a paucity of epidemiological data about BDD. The estimated prevalence from five community surveys is between 0.7% and 2.4% in the general population. However, BDD is probably under-reported to health practitioners because of the shame and stigma associated with it. The meager evidence that does exist suggests it is more common in adolescence and in young people. BDD may be less severe but more common in young women and overlap with a diagnosis of an "Eating Disorder (not otherwise specified)" (EDNOS). A higher prevalence of BDD has been found in psychiatric inpatients, in those with atypical depression, and in cosmetic surgery and dermatology settings. Few data exist on cultural influences on the prevalence of BDD. Surveys of BDD patients attending psychiatric clinics show they tend to have an equal sex incidence and to be single or separated. There are more similarities than differences between men and women in the site of their BDD concerns. In two follow-up studies, BDD appeared to be a chronic disorder with lower rates of recovery compared to depression and anxiety disorders.

Sections

Body Dysmorphic Disorder: A Treatment Manual. David Veale and Fugen Neziroglu
© 2010 John Wiley & Sons, Ltd.

3.1   Prevalence of BDD

Researchers into BDD may be forgiven for being slightly paranoid in wondering why BDD has never been included in any large catchment area surveys of psychiatric morbidity. There are hundreds of published studies on the incidence of schizophrenia, depression, or eating disorders in different settings. However, they have rarely included any question on the prevalence of BDD. The data on the prevalence of BDD in the community are lacking and we present below the little evidence that does exist. At first sight, the prevalence rate appears to vary from 0.7% (Faravelli et al., 1997) to 2.4% (Koran et al., 2008). The range reflects the heterogeneity of the different populations studied and the screening measures used. Another complication is that some participants with BDD may not reveal their symptoms on a screening questionnaire or at interview because of shame. Alternatively, they may refuse to participate in such studies. It is also important to exclude participants when an eating disorder better explains their body image symptoms or those who are just *dissatisfied* with their body – this may be as high as 60–70% in college populations (Biby, 1998). We discuss the relationship between eating disorders and BDD under comorbidity.

3.2   Community Surveys

Community surveys report a BDD prevalence of 0.7–2.4% (Faravelli et al., 1997; Otto et al., 2001; Rief et al., 2006; Koran et al., 2008; de Jongh et al., 2008). The rate may vary depending on the (a) sex ratio, (b) the diagnostic threshold and instrument used to measure BDD, (c) the culture, and (d) the survey method (e.g., telephone or face to face).

The first community survey of somatoform disorders found a one-year prevalence of BDD of 0.7% in Florence, Italy (Faravelli, et al., 1997), where 800 subjects were selected at random from a total sample of 4000 in a defined suburb. Of these, 673 were interviewed by four family doctors who were trained in the use of diagnostic criteria. BDD was identified in five cases (0.7%). BDD was about as common as somatoform pain disorder (0.6%) and somatization disorder (0.7%). BDD was less common than hypochondriasis

(4.5%) and undifferentiated somatoform disorder (13.4%). There are some anomalous findings in this study as all the individuals identified were women and most studies of BDD in psychiatric clinics have found an equal sex incidence. This study may therefore have underestimated the prevalence of BDD. Alternatively, the cases identified may have been mild and more commonly present in women.

Otto et al. (2001) conducted a survey of women aged 36–44 in the USA. They found a point prevalence rate for BDD of 0.7%. A sample of 4569 women completed a screening questionnaire, which resulted in a cohort of 976 women (318 with a past or present history of depression and 658 without). BDD was detected in eight participants in the cohort. It was significantly more common among individuals with a past or current history of depression or anxiety. They adjusted for the selection of women with depression to obtain an overall prevalence rate of 0.7%. Five of the eight reported onset of BDD between the ages of 11 and 14 and the other three reported onset in their thirties.

Rief et al. (2006) conducted a postal survey of 2552 out of 4152 selected participants aged 16–99 years in a nationwide survey in Germany. They estimated a point prevalence rate of BDD of 1.7% (CI 1.2–2.1%). The screening questionnaire has not however been validated against a clinical population and the sensitivity or specificity is not known. It is possible that a checklist on a self-report questionnaire will overestimate prevalence. However, the authors are to be commended as this is the largest epidemiological survey of BDD so far conducted. They found that BDD was more frequent in females (60%) than males (40%). They also reported higher rates of suicidal ideation (19% vs. 3%) and suicide attempts (7% vs. 1%) and more often a desire for cosmetic surgery in the individuals who did not meet criteria for BDD. BDD was associated with higher rates of unemployment, lower income, and lower rates of living with a partner.

Koran et al. (2008) conducted a household telephone survey by trained lay interviewers who screened 2048 individuals. The response rate was 56.3%. Respondents included a higher percentage of women and people >55 years than in the US adult population and a lower percentage of Hispanics. The estimated point prevalence of BDD among respondents was 2.4% (2.5% for women, 2.2% for men). The prevalence decreased after 44 years of age, and a larger proportion of BDD respondents were never married.

Lastly, de Jongh et al. (2008) approached 1522 Dutch adults (aged 16 and above) in public places of whom 60% (N = 906) agreed to participate in their survey; 27 had missing data, leaving a total of 879 participants. Their questionnaire followed the diagnostic interview schedule for BDD but has not been validated against a clinical interview (Van Rood et al. personal communication). They found a point prevalence rate of 1.5% (N = 13) fulfilling diagnostic criteria for BDD.

3.3 Adolescents and Young Adults

There have been five studies of the prevalence of BDD in adolescents and young adults, which have used various screening questionnaires. Rich et al. (1992) reported on the prevalence of BDD in psychology students with a mean age of 18.7 years and in university staff with mean age of 40.7 years. They studied 131 male undergraduates and 60 male staff of whom none had BDD. Among the 164 female undergraduates and 77 female staff, 9.7% and 3.9% respectively met the criteria for BDD. All participants underwent a structured diagnostic interview (Body Dysmorphic Disorder Examination – BDDE) (Rosen et al., 1995b). They note, however, that it was not possible to perform a thorough diagnostic evaluation and they cannot be certain that some subjects did not have an eating disorder. The study was never published but was used as part of the validation of the BDDE. The study is interesting because none of the 191 males had BDD and the female predominance might be accounted for by too loose criteria for BDD and the higher prevalence of disordered eating among the female population.

Mayville et al. (1999) used a sample of 464 ethnically diverse adolescents aged 14–19. They completed the Body Image Rating scale, which consists of 15 items in a Likert format that assesses body dissatisfaction. Thirteen participants (2.2%) met criteria for BDD of whom five (1.7%) were male and eight female (2.8%). A further 20 participants endorsed criteria for an eating disorder, which precluded a diagnosis of BDD. Body dissatisfaction was generally more common in girls than boys, and African Americans of both genders were less dissatisfied with their body than Caucasians, Asians, and Hispanics. The main weakness of this study is that the questionnaire was previously standardized on a sample of 269 college students and validated against the BDDE (self-report version) in a normal population. The screening questionnaire has not been validated against a diagnostic interview in people with BDD.

Biby (1998) screened undergraduate psychology students. The original sample included 83 females and 25 males (N = 108), but they excluded six students who had an eating disorder. They devised their own questionnaire and reported a prevalence of BDD of 13%. The strength of the study is the exclusion of subjects with eating disorders. The main weakness of this study is the relatively small number in the cohort, the preponderance of women, and the use of a non-validated questionnaire for BDD without any knowledge of the sensitivity or specificity of the questionnaire against a diagnostic interview. It is more likely that the screening questionnaire was identifying body dissatisfaction than BDD.

Bohne et al. (2002b) found the prevalence of BDD in German college students (average age 21) to be 5.3%. They used the BDDQ screening questionnaire (Dufresne Jr et al., 2001). Although the BDDQ has been validated in a psychiatric population, the main weakness is the lack of validation in a community sample.

Cansever et al. (2003) surveyed 420 female nursing college students in Turkey. A self-report questionnaire was used to screen for dissatisfaction with their appearance (43.8%); they were then interviewed by a psychiatrist, who diagnosed BDD in 4.8% of the total sample. Head/face areas and hips were the most common areas of concern.

Bartsch (2007) studied 619 Australian university students. Approximately two-thirds of the sample were concerned about an aspect of their appearance, with one third of these individuals preoccupied by this concern. Fourteen participants (2.3%) appeared to meet the criteria for BDD. Multiple regression analysis found that dysmorphic concern was predicted by self-esteem, depression, self-oriented perfectionism, socially prescribed perfectionism, and gender.

Taqui et al. (2008) used a screening questionnaire for BDD in 156 medical students in Pakistan, of whom 57.1% were female. A total of 78.8% reported dissatisfaction with some aspect of their appearance and 5.8% met the DSM IV criteria for BDD. BDD was more common in women compared to men in a ratio of 1.7. Regarding gender differences in body areas of concern, the top three reported as being of concern in male students were head hair (34.3%), being fat (32.8%), skin (14.9%), and nose (14.9%), whereas in females they were being fat (40.4%), skin (24.7%), and teeth (18%). Females were significantly more concerned about being fat ($p = 0.005$). Male students were significantly more concerned about being thin ($p = 0.01$) and about head hair ($p = 0.012$). Although the authors excluded students by asking whether they had a diagnosed eating disorder, they did not use a screening questionnaire.

It is recommended that future studies (a) clearly differentiate BDD from an eating disorder or determine if it is truly comorbid; (b) use a screening questionnaire that is validated against an interview in the relevant population; and (c) report the confidence interval. The data suggest that the prevalence of BDD is more common in adolescence and young people. During this time, BDD may be less severe but more common in women and overlap with subclinical eating disorders. BDD appears to become less common with age. The exceptions may be late onset BDD associated with a life crisis and a belief about the consequences of an ageing appearance or an onset after cosmetic surgery.

3.4   General Practice and Family Doctor Settings

The prevalence of BDD may be less common in general practice. Individuals with BDD may avoid going to their family doctor because of fears about being physically examined or because they avoid discussing their problem or only go direct to a dermatologist or cosmetic surgeon. Thus De Waal et al. (2004) conducted a prevalence study of somatoform disorders in 1046 consecutive patients aged 25–80 years in a Dutch general practice. They were screened with the SF-36 functional limitation questionnaire, the Hospital Anxiety and Depression Scale (HADS) (Zigmond & Snaith, 1983), and a physical symptom checklist (PSC). A high-risk sample was defined as anyone who scored 15 or more on the HADS or 5 or more on the PSC, which was 48% of the total sample. Of those defined as a high risk, 80% received a standardized diagnostic interview (Schedule for Clinical Assessment in Neuropsychiatry version 2.1). The prevalence of DSM IV anxiety disorders was 5.5%, depressive disorder 5.5%, and somatoform disorders 16.1%. The most common somatoform disorder was "undifferentiated somatoform disorder," with a prevalence of 13.1%. They had one or more unexplained physical symptom (e.g., fatigue, headache) that caused clinically significant distress or impairment. The important point of this study was that they found no cases of BDD. However, the study excluded anyone under the age of 25, where the majority of cases of BDD may occur, and none of the screening tools used enquires about symptoms of BDD. Assuming a few BDD patients passed the screen because of comorbid depression/anxiety, they were then interviewed with the WHO's Schedule for Clinical Assessment in Neuropsychiatry (SCAN). The SCAN interview is also inadequate for detecting BDD as there is only one question that asks whether their appearance seems to have *changed* recently.

Many people with BDD have experienced symptoms since childhood or adolescence. In future surveys, it may therefore be helpful to obtain screening information from family members. This may lead to a higher prevalence rate as clients may be too embarrassed to admit their problem to their GP or researcher.

3.5   Cosmetic Surgery Settings

There have been eight prospective surveys of BDD in a cosmetic surgery setting that suggest that BDD is relatively common in such settings with a prevalence of between 3% and 18%. The rate depends on the procedures offered at each clinic, the sex ratio, and the diagnostic threshold and instrument used to measure BDD. There are also difficulties in the diagnosis of BDD in a cosmetic setting and in deciding when the patient has a minor physical anomaly or when the concern becomes "markedly excessive." It is worth remembering that aesthetic cosmetic surgery is about enhancing a normal appearance and therefore many patients look perfectly "normal."

In the first study, Ishigooka et al. (1998) reported that in a sample of 415 patients (130 male, 285 female) between 1980 and 1997 in a Japanese state hospital, 15% had BDD, 8% had a depressive episode, and 4.1% were diagnosed with schizophrenia using ICD-10 criteria. A diagnosis of a mental disorder was more common in men (85/130) than in women (113/285). No outcome data were reported on their cosmetic surgery.

In a second study, Sarwer et al. (1998) saw 132 women of whom 100 completed a screening questionnaire for BDD (a response rate of 76%). They found that 5% of women had BDD. Of these, three were requesting a rhytidectomy, one a rhinoplasty, and one an abdominoplasty (a total of five). There were two other women (one requesting breast reduction, one laser resurfacing) whose defects were not regarded as "imagined or slight." They were, however, similar to people with BDD as they were significantly preoccupied and significantly distressed or handicapped by their defects. None of the seven patients was operated on at the clinic and so no outcome data are available.

Vindigni et al. (2002) reported that a staggering 53% of patients seeking cosmetic surgery were diagnosed with BDD. Of these, the majority (82%) were classified as mild, 10% were moderate, and 8% were severe. The mild cases had cosmetic surgery but no outcome data are available. The study raises a number of questions about the authors' interpretation of the diagnostic threshold. They assessed patients using a structured diagnostic instrument (SCID II 2.0 and MINIPLUS 5.0).

Aouizerate et al. (2003) reported on a study of 132 subjects (8 male, 124 female) who consulted one cosmetic surgeon over a six-month period at a university hospital in France. The plastic surgeon independently rated the location of the "defect" in subjects using a four-point defect severity scale (1 representing "minimal or no defect" and 4 "severe defect"). They were later interviewed using the BDD Diagnostic Module for DSM IV. Out of the 132 subjects, 30 were rated to have "minimal or no defect" of whom 12 (9.1% of the total) met the DSM IV criteria for BDD, and two (25%) were men. This study has some follow-up data after surgery (Tignol et al., 2007), which is discussed in Chapter 6.

Castle et al. (2004) conducted a survey of 137 patients attending the practices of two cosmetic physicians. Four subjects (2.9%) had a diagnosis of BDD. No follow-up data are available on the four subjects identified with BDD who had a cosmetic procedure. The cosmetic procedures offered included hair transplant, liposuction, botulin toxin injections, dermal filling, facial vein treatment, chemical peels, and micro-dermabrasion. The procedures offered may account for the slightly lower rate of BDD compared to other settings. Many more participants expressed over-concern with physical appearance and this accounted for a substantial amount of the variance in mood, social anxiety, and impairment in work and social functioning.

Veale et al. (2003) recruited patients seeking cosmetic rhinoplasty in the UK using a screening questionnaire for BDD (Phillips et al., 2005). They identified six out of 29 (20.7%) patients preoperatively as having possible BDD on the screening questionnaire (BDDQ), but in this pilot study it was not possible to validate the self-report screening questionnaire with an interview. The BDDQ was probably oversensitive in this population since all the patients identified were satisfied with their rhinoplasty. Our interpretation is that we identified a group of patients with subclinical or mild BDD. This study, and the one by Vindigni et al. (2002), suggest that mild BDD may be relatively common in cosmetic surgery clinics, and the diagnostic criteria for BDD may need tightening if the net is not to be cast too widely. Alternatively, the diagnosis of BDD by itself may not be a contraindication to surgery and additional factors such as an unrealistic psychosocial outcome may be more important.

Vulink et al. (2006) reported on the six-month prevalence of BDD in the plastic surgery outpatient clinic of a university medical center. A self-report BDD screening questionnaire was completed by 475 new patients. The plastic surgeon assessed the severity of the defect and 3.2% (95% CI: 1.7–4.7) of patients screened positive for BDD. No outcome data are available in the BDD patients.

Lastly, Bellino et al. (2003) investigated the relationship between personality disorders and dysmorphic symptoms in a group of 66 patients seeking cosmetic surgery. Assessment instruments included the Structured Clinical Interview for DSM IV, the Hamilton Depression and Anxiety Rating Scales, and the Yale-Brown Obsessive-Compulsive Scale modified for BDD (YBOCS-BDD). The 66 patients included 57 females (86%) and nine males (14%) and were planned to have corrections: blepharoplasty in 18 cases (28.12%), liposuction in 16 cases (25%), rhinoplasty in 12 cases (18.75%), abdominoplasty and otoplasty in eight cases each (12.5%), rhytidectomy in six cases (9.37%), and mastoplasty in four cases (6.25%), with some patients undergoing multiple surgical corrections. Previous cosmetic surgery interventions had been performed in 15 subjects (22.7%). Eight females and three males (total 16.6%, 95% CI = 7.6%–25.6%) met diagnostic criteria for BDD. An Axis II diagnosis was made in 35 subjects (53%). Common personality disorders were narcissistic and borderline (16.7% each), avoidant (12.1%), paranoid (9.1%), and schizotypal and obsessive-compulsive (7.6% each). A multiple regression analysis was performed using the YBOCS-BDD score as a continuous dependent variable. The severity of symptoms (YBOCS-BDD score) was related to two factors: the number of diagnostic criteria for schizotypal and paranoid personality disorders. No outcome data in the patients with BDD are available.

3.6   Dermatology Settings

The first survey of BDD in a dermatology clinic was undertaken in the USA. Phillips et al. (2000) found that 12% of patients were likely to have BDD. Of the 367 patients, 23.4% (N = 86) declined to participate, leaving a total of 268 patients who completed a modified version of the BDDQ. The authors note that many of the BDD patients were significantly handicapped. They were not specifically assessed for psychogenic excoriation. However, in another study, Phillips & Taub (1995) found that subjects who skin picked were more likely than those who did not skin pick to have received dermatological treatment.

A second study by Vulink et al. (2006) reported on the six-month prevalence of BDD in a dermatology outpatient clinic of a university medical center. A self-report BDD screening questionnaire was completed by 530 new patients. The dermatologist or cosmetic surgeon assessed patients for the severity of the defect and 8.5% (95% CI: 6.1–10.9) screened positive for BDD. There may be a difference in prevalence between the dermatology clinics in the UK and the USA. Not only is access to dermatology clinics easier in the USA, but they also perform greater number of cosmetic procedures. In the UK, family doctors are also more likely to manage dermatological problems.

A study in Turkey evaluated the prevalence of BDD in 159 patients with mild acne presenting to a dermatologist (Uzun et al., 2003) and found that 8.8% patients were diagnosed with BDD. Of these, three (21.4%) patients with acne and BDD also had concomitant psychiatric diagnoses. None of the patients had ever received any psychological or physical treatments. Bowe et al. (2007) also screened for BDD symptoms among patients with acne. They used a validated self-report questionnaire and an objective assessment of acne severity by a single observer. Rates of BDD ranged from 14.1% using more stringent criteria to assess acne severity to 21.1% using less stringent criteria. They had substantial distress and preoccupation related to their facial appearance. Two-fold increased odds of having BDD were seen in patients requiring systemic isotretinoin therapy. Individuals who excoriate (pick) their skin may also present to dermatologists. This is discussed in more detail in Chapter 5.

3.7   Dental Settings

Dental practitioners, maxillofacial surgeons, and orthodontists may have patients presenting with symptoms of BDD. There are, however, no prevalence studies of BDD in dental settings. They may present with "phantom bite" (preoccupation with their dental occlusion), believing that it is abnormal. This may, however, be viewed as a hypochondriacal disorder (Marbach, 1976, 1978;

Jagger & Korszun, 2004; Veale & Chapman, 2005). Others may be preoccupied by the ugliness of their teeth or dental decay (Cunningham et al., 1996; Kells et al., 1996) or an unattractive smile, lips, or expression which they are trying to correct by having their teeth altered. Maxillofacial surgeons may see patients who complain that the shape of their jaw is wrong or out of alignment (de Jongh & Adair, 2004) or that their cheeks are too hollow (Cunningham et al., 1996). The presentation of BDD in dental settings may be complicated by functional symptoms rather than aesthetic concerns. Alternatively, the patient may present with more functional symptoms as he she is aware that this may be more likely lead to a procedure, especially in public medicine. The most common form of cosmetic procedure in dental settings is probably teeth whitening or straightening. It would be interesting to look at orthodontal work in adults to see what percentage of patients fulfill criteria for BDD.

3.8   Psychiatric Settings

There have been four studies of BDD in a general psychiatric settings where clinicians would not normally ask about symptoms of BDD routinely. Zimmermann & Mattia (1998) found that of 500 referrals to a psychiatric outpatient clinic in the USA, none was diagnosed as having BDD when the clinicians used a routine, unstructured clinical interview. However, in a second sample of 500 outpatients, when a structured diagnostic interview was introduced (SCID for DSM IV), 3.2% (N = 16) were diagnosed as having BDD. Although it was not the patients' main reason for seeking treatment, the majority wanted treatment to address their BDD symptoms. Compared with patients without BDD, patients with BDD received significantly more current Axis I diagnoses, were more likely to be diagnosed with current OCD and social phobia, and were more functionally impaired.

Nirenberg et al. (2002) did a structured diagnostic interview of 350 outpatients with major depression who entered an anti-depressant treatment study and were evaluated with SCID-P and a diagnostic module for BDD. Of these, 28 subjects (8%) had a lifetime history of BDD and 23 (6.6%) had current BDD. The rate was higher in those with atypical depression compared to "typical" depression (14.4% vs. 5.1% for lifetime BDD; 11.6% vs. 4.1% for current BDD). BDD patients were also more likely to be diagnosed with social phobia, any eating disorder, and any somatoform disorder. Phillips et al. (1996) also identified 13.8% as fulfilling criteria for BDD in a series of 80 consecutive outpatients with "atypical depression."

In a study of adult inpatients, Grant et al. (2001) using the BDDQ screened 101 consecutive adult inpatients and 21 consecutive adolescent inpatients presenting for admission. Sixteen of the 122 (13.1%) were diagnosed as having

BDD. None of the subjects had been diagnosed as having BDD by their treating physician. All 16 subjects reported that they would not raise the issue with their physician unless specifically asked due to feelings of shame. This was true for the 13 out of the 16 patients who considered their preoccupation with their defect to be a "major problem" and the three who viewed it as their "biggest problem." Both of these studies underline the importance of routinely asking a screening question for BDD in psychiatric inpatients.

Conroy et al. (2008) conducted a similar study in 100 psychiatric inpatients. BDD was diagnosed in 16.0%. A high proportion of those with BDD reported that BDD symptoms contributed to suicidality. Patients revealed BDD symptoms to a mean of only 15.1% ± 33.7% lifetime mental health clinicians; only one out of the 16 (6.3%) reported symptoms to his current inpatient psychiatrist. Most did not disclose their symptoms due to embarrassment.

Dyl et al. (2006) assessed the prevalence and clinical correlates of BDD, any eating disorders (ED), or other clinically significant body image concerns in 208 consecutively admitted adolescent inpatients. Participants completed the Body Dysmorphic Disorder Questionnaire (BDDQ) and 6.7% (N = 14) met criteria for definite (N = 10) or probable (N = 4) BDD, 3.8% (N = 8) met criteria for an eating disorder, and 22.1% (N = 46) had clinically significant shape/weight concerns (SWC) that did not clearly meet criteria for BDD or an eating disorder. All three groups had significantly higher levels of depression than the no BDD/ED/SWC group. Only the SWC group scored significantly higher than the no BDD/ED/SWC group on measures of post-traumatic stress disorder (PTSD), dissociation, and sexual preoccupation/distress.

In another study of 900 consecutive referrals over seven years to an adult liaison psychiatry outpatient service in a UK hospital, only 2.2% (N = 20) were diagnosed as having BDD using ICD-10 criteria (Bass et al., 2002). Interestingly, all these referrals were from plastic surgeons; no referrals came from dermatologists. It is possible that some patients with BDD were referred to general psychiatrists in the same catchment area or that there is underreporting (similar to the studies in psychiatric settings).

Overall, these studies would strongly suggest that clinicians routinely ask about symptoms of BDD in patients presenting with depression, especially with atypical features, in adolescents and in inpatient settings.

3.9 Age and Gender Features

Surveys of BDD patients attending a psychiatric clinic tend to show an equal sex incidence among the single or separated (Neziroglu & Yaryura-Tobias, 1993a; Phillips et al., 1993; Phillips & Diaz, 1997). Rosen et al. (1995b) and Veale et al. (1996) found a greater preponderance of women, but this may be because of a referral bias. It is also possible that in the community, while more women are affected overall, a greater proportion experience milder symptoms. This was also the finding from the community prevalence studies. An analogous situation exists in social phobia where there is known to be an equal sex incidence in socially phobic patients attending a psychiatric clinic (Mannuzza et al., 1990), but in the community there is a ratio of 3:2 of women to men (Schneier et al., 1992). There are no significant gender differences regarding psychiatric treatment in terms of receipt of or response to psychopharmacological agents (Phillips & Diaz, 1997). Although the age of onset of BDD in adults is during late adolescence (Phillips, 1991), patients are usually diagnosed on average 15 years later (Veale et al., 1996; Phillips & Diaz, 1997).

Phillips, Menard et al. (2006) studied gender differences in 200 individuals with BDD and found more similarities than differences between men and women. The men were significantly older and more likely to be single and living alone. Men were more likely to be preoccupied by their genitals, body build, and thinning hair/balding; excessively lift weights; and have a substance use disorder. In contrast, women were more likely to be preoccupied by their skin, stomach, weight, breasts/chest, buttocks, thighs, legs, hips, toes, and excessive body/facial hair, and they were excessively concerned with more body areas. This probably represents the same feature in the general population and may represent an extreme variant of normal concerns about body image.

Women also performed more repetitive and safety behaviors, and were more likely to camouflage and use certain camouflaging techniques, mirror-check, change their clothes, pick their skin, and have an eating disorder. Men had slightly more severe symptoms of BDD as assessed by the Psychiatric Status Rating Scale for BDD and had poorer Global Assessment of Functioning Scale scores. They were less likely to be working because of psychopathology, and were more likely to be receiving disability benefit, including disability for BDD.

BDD is rarely studied in children and adolescents, although the clinical features appear similar to those in adults. It is not yet known if BDD that presents in childhood indicates a worse prognosis. Albertini & Phillips (1999) first described a series of 33 children and adolescents of whom 39% had been treated as a psychiatric inpatient and 21% had attempted suicide. The mean age of onset was 11.8 years. In the largest survey of adolescents, Phillips, Didie et al. (2006) compared 200 individuals with BDD (36 adolescents; 164 adults). Adolescents and adults were comparable on most variables, although adolescents had significantly more delusional BDD beliefs and a higher lifetime rate of suicide attempts. Adolescents experienced high rates and levels of impairment in school, work, and other aspects of psychosocial functioning. The handicap is different in a younger age group as it relates to poor concentration and grades at school, or stopping a sport when it is difficult to camouflage a "defective" feature. Eventually, the child may refuse to go to school or become housebound. BDD is often regarded as being on the obsessive compulsive spectrum, but the age of onset and presentation of BDD are significantly later than in OCD. There may also be a small subgroup of people with BDD who have a later onset, perhaps after a major loss or a cosmetic procedure.

3.10 Cultural Factors

Virtually no studies have examined prevalence or clinical features of BDD across cultures. Case reports and series suggest that the clinical features of BDD are generally the same around the world. It may be less prevalent in developing countries, but there may be under-reporting as individuals are more likely to attend traditional healers or surgeons (Al-Adawi, 2001).

Bohne et al. (2002a) found no differences between a German and an American population. In Japan, BDD is subsumed as part of social phobia and referred to as *taijin kyofusho*, which means the fear of offending or hurting others through one's improper or awkward social behavior, ugliness, or body odor.

3.11 Course of BDD

There are sparse data on the course or long-term outcome in BDD. If left untreated, it appears to be a chronic disorder which is continuous and persists for many years. Phillips et al. (1993) reported an average duration of 18.3 years (SD 13.1) and Veale et al. (1996) reported an average duration of 14.11 years (SD 15.38). Milder symptoms may appear episodic and deteriorate at times of stress. BDD is seen less commonly by middle age and rarely seen in the elderly, when presumably many of the symptoms have burnt out.

There are two follow-up studies reported by Phillips. In the first, Phillips et al. (2005) conducted a retrospective follow-up 95 outpatients with BDD treated in a clinical practice by a chart review. The mean duration of follow-up was 1.7 ± 1.1 years (range 0.5–6.4 years). Ratings were done at six-month intervals over the first four years of follow-up. The proportion of subjects who achieved full remission from BDD at the six-month and/or 12-month assessment was only 24.7%; the proportion who attained partial or full remission at six months and/or 12 months was 57.8%. After four years of follow-up, 58.2% had experienced full remission, and 83.8% had experienced partial or full remission, at one or more six-month assessment points. Of those subjects who attained partial or full remission at one or more assessment points, 28.6%

subsequently relapsed. Between baseline and the most recent assessment, BDD severity and functioning significantly improved: at the most recent assessment, 16.7% of subjects were in full remission, 37.8% were in partial remission, and 45.6% met full criteria for BDD. Greater severity of BDD symptoms and the presence of major depression or social phobia at baseline were associated with more severe BDD symptoms at the study end point. All subjects had received at least one medication trial, and 34.3% received some type of therapy during the follow-up period.

Because of the limitations of this study Phillips, Pagano et al. (2006) conducted a further naturalistic study over one year for 183 individuals with BDD. Relapse was defined as meeting full BDD criteria for at least two consecutive weeks after attaining partial or full remission from BDD. Over one year, the probability of full remission from BDD (defined as minimal or no BDD symptoms) was only 0.09, and the probability of partial remission (meeting less than full DSM IV criteria for at least eight consecutive weeks) was 0.21. Although 84.2% of the subjects received treatment during the one-year period, mean BDD severity scores during the year reflected full DSM IV criteria for BDD, and the mean proportion of time that the subjects met full BDD criteria was 80%. Among the subjects whose BDD symptoms partially or fully remitted, the probability of relapse was 0.15. The results suggest that BDD tends to be chronic and the likelihood of remission was lower than reported for mood disorders and most anxiety disorders in studies using similar methods.

3.12 Presentation of BDD

A one-year prevalence of 1–2% would make BDD a relatively common disorder (e.g., as common as schizophrenia or anorexia nervosa), but mental health professionals do not often diagnose and treat patients with BDD. It is a hidden disorder with many clients not seeking help and therefore mental health professionals are not confident enough to diagnose and treat it. BDD might therefore have a higher prevalence rate within the general population depending on the diagnostic threshold. Due mainly to shame it is under-reported and so under-diagnosed by health professionals. A client must pass several obstacles in the successful diagnosis and treatment of his BDD. First, there is a low level of awareness and stigma about BDD among the public or health professionals. There is increasing awareness about depression and other major psychiatric disorders but not of BDD. The second obstacle for clients is that when they do seek help they are more likely to present in a dermatological, cosmetic, or dental setting. When people with BDD finally seek help from a family doctor or mental health professional, they are often too ashamed to reveal their main symptoms and present with symptoms of depression, social phobia, or obsessive compulsive disorder (for which there is admittedly frequent comorbidity). Patients may be secretive because they may think they will be viewed as vain or narcissistic. When they are finally diagnosed (up to 15 years after the onset), they are often treated inappropriately with antipsychotic medication (Phillips, 1998). Alternatively, a therapist may have little experience in treating BDD clients or lack an effective treatment model. There is, therefore, an unmet need for the diagnosis and effective treatment of BDD. We hope this book will go some way in addressing this.

Chapter 4

Descriptive psychopathology of BDD

Summary

There is an enormous richness of phenomenology in BDD, which is not found
in standard textbooks of psychiatry or descriptive psychopathology. BDD, like
other body image disorders, has a complex interaction of beliefs, evaluations,
emotions, and behavioral reactions to self-views of one's appearance, including mental imagery and somatosensory changes (Cash, 1990; Ben-Tovim et
al., 1998). In this chapter we describe the phenomenology of BDD and introduce the terms that are used throughout this book. This chapter does not
generally take any theoretical approach on the development or maintenance
of the phenomenology described.

Sections

4.1 Body image
4.2 Mental imagery
4.3 Overvalued ideas and delusions
4.4 Ideas and delusions of self-reference
4.5 Beliefs and assumptions
4.6 Ruminations and meta-cognitions
4.7 Social anxiety, perfectionism, and shame
4.8 Safety-seeking behaviors and compulsions

4.1 Body Image

Before we describe the phenomenology of BDD in detail, we briefly describe
BDD in the context of body image disorders. Cash (1990) described how body

Body Dysmorphic Disorder: A Treatment Manual. David Veale and Fugen Neziroglu
© 2010 John Wiley & Sons, Ltd.

image can be studied either from an "outside view," for example, how external, objective attributes of physical appearance have an impact on human development and experience – this can be summed up as "How does what we look like 'on the outside' affect our lives?"; or an "inside view," or the impact of the internal subjective representation of physical appearance and bodily experience – this can be summed up as "The way we feel about our appearance." This is multidimensional and includes body-related self-perceptions, self-attitudes, imagery, thoughts, feelings, and behaviors. We focus predominantly on the "inside view," although very often behaviors in BDD, such as skin-picking or mirror-gazing, have a negative impact on the behavior of others, who may be critical or sarcastic. Research has frequently shown that an individual's subjective experience of body image has far more of an influence on quality of life than the objective or social "reality" of their appearance. Thus an individual who is extremely disfigured may have a good quality of life relative to their body image and another individual who is considered attractive may be significantly distressed. This is nowhere truer than in BDD where, by definition, individuals have a normal, "objective" appearance but may be extremely handicapped. The internal body image and external objective attributes of appearance are thus completely different constructs. This is counterintuitive to most people's experience and is probably a contributory factor to the stigma experienced by people with BDD.

There are two important concepts discussed by Cash on the psychopathology of body image that relate to beliefs.

Body image valence

Body image valence, or "body image investment" (Cash, 1990), is a measure of the *importance* attached to one's appearance. Thus it is possible to be dissatisfied with one's appearance but not to care about it. In this book we use the term "value" for the degree of importance of appearance as this uses a broader philosophical context concerning the importance attached to an attribute. For most people, appearance is part of a broader set of attributes that an individual holds to define their self. Individuals with BDD define their self almost exclusively through an *idealized value* about the importance of their appearance, which we discuss later in this chapter (Veale, 2002). Unfortunately, the term "value," as in "body image value," is used by other authors as referring to the evaluation or satisfaction with one's appearance (see below).

Body image value

Body image value in the body image literature is defined as the *evaluation* of one's body image (e.g., a rating of satisfaction or dissatisfaction) (Sarwer et al., 1998). As stated above, body image valence and value are not necessarily related. Thus, one person may be dissatisfied with a feature of his body but view his appearance as a small aspect of his identity, so that there is low level of distress or body-related behaviors. Another person may have a high degree of satisfaction with his appearance and view his appearance as a very important aspect of his identity, which makes the person vulnerable to distress if he feels he is under threat for being ugly as this will mean losing part of his identity and may have been reinforced in the past. A high level of valence in body image invariably occurs in BDD and must be present for BDD to develop. However, to reach the criteria for BDD an individual must have not only a high degree of body image valence but also a negative evaluation of body image and extreme distress. The components of body image valence and value in BDD are explored in sections 4.3 and 4.4 below.

4.2 Mental Imagery

Collins English Dictionary (1995) defines an image as "A mental representation of something (especially a visual object) not by direct perception but by memory or imagination." It can therefore encompass images, memories and dreams, and sensory qualities associated with any modality. It refers to an experience that resembles perceptual experience, but that occurs in the absence of the appropriate stimuli for the relevant perception (Thomas & Edward, 2001). It is the part of one's consciousness that has sensory qualities, as opposed to ones that are verbal or abstract (Horowitz, 1970). Mental imagery is therefore one aspect of body image and usually involves a visual modality (commonly called visualization or "seeing in the mind's eye"). However, imagery can also occur in other modalities such as tactile sensations. Mental images become "hallucinations" when they are externalized and have a compelling sense of reality, although the literature is not clear in differentiating between mental imagery which is a tactile sensation or hallucination.

Images can be divided into different types and categories. They may occur spontaneously, be deliberately generated, transformed, or suppressed. They may be reconstructions of past perceptual experiences or reflect present or future perspectives that are feared and may be literal or symbolic. Thus imagery often plays a role in both memory (Yates, 1966) and motivation (McMahon, 1973). Compared to verbal thoughts, images can provide direct access to a network of beliefs underlying emotional responses that may be difficult to identify through questioning alone (Hackmann & Hersen, 1998). Research examining the nature and meaning of imagery especially in anxiety disorders has increased in recent years. For example, clients with social phobia have been found to experience significantly more spontaneously occurring images in anxiety-provoking social situations than non-patient controls (Hackmann et al., 1998). These images are typically negative in content, involve seeing oneself from an observer perspective, and are perceived as at least partially distorted when considered after the event (Hackmann et al., 1998). The images of social phobics also appear to be recurrent and involve sensory components in a variety of modalities. Hackmann et al. (2000) found that bodily sensations occurred almost as often as visual ones. Importantly, these images were linked to particular memories close to the onset of the social phobia and were matched with regard to their sensory content in the various modalities. Similar findings have been reported in other disorders, such as health anxiety (Wells & Hackman, 1993). The evidence for the experience of imagery in BDD is a descriptive study that compared 18 BDD clients with 18 healthy controls using a semi-structured interview and questionnaires (Osman et al., 2004). BDD and controls were just as likely to experience spontaneous images of their appearance (Figure 4.1). However, people with BDD were more likely to rate the images as significantly more negative, recurrent, and vivid than normal controls. Images in people with BDD were more distorted and the "defective" features took up a greater proportion of the whole image. They typically reported visual images, that were sometimes associated with other sensory modalities (e.g., sensations of hunger or fatigue), and tactile sensations. Asking a client to draw an impression of him- or herself may dramatically convey to the clinician an experience of visual imagery that is difficult to describe in words. It may also provide an outcome measure after successful therapy. An example of a self-portrait from imagery is shown in Figures 4.1–4.3. Figure 4.1 is a self-portrait of a young woman before therapy, when she was preoccupied with multiple perceived defects. After successful

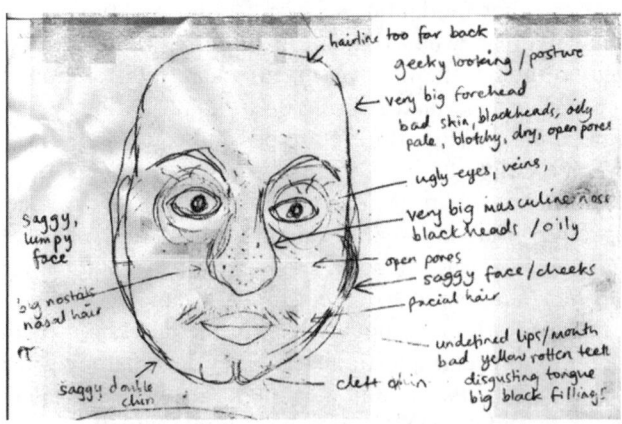

Figure 4.1   Client's self-portrait before therapy

Figure 4.2   Client's self-portrait after therapy

therapy her self-portrait (Figure 4.2) dramatically improved and this was consistent with her outcome scores.

Figure 4.3 is by a man with tactile sensations. He experienced a sensation of heaviness in his head and a picture in his mind looking like a "Mekon," which is abnormally large at the top of his head. Other clients describe tactile sensations such as burning, pain, or swelling sensations – for example, "Underneath my eyes are all swollen, my cheeks are puffy and round like a peach." Burning or scarring sensations are not uncommon and are distressing to clients. They may be a trigger to pick the skin to stop the sensation. Another person may experience a sensation of hotness on his face and this may trigger checking in the mirror to determine the degree of redness.

Of particular importance is that visual images in BDD are more likely to be viewed from an observer perspective compared to a field perspective, similar to a finding in social phobia (Hackmann et al., 1998). An observer perspective consists of the individual looking at himself from another person's perspective. An external perspective may add to its "authority" and increase the tendency to make internal attributions about an event. The

Figure 4.3   Self-portrait of client with tactile sensation

experience of mental imagery usually from an observer perspective is a core feature of BDD as it becomes fused with reality and may be associated with past aversive experiences. Some individuals do not report mental imagery or an impression of how they appear to others and experience only thoughts of being ugly or defective (from a field perspective). Whether a person experiences imagery or just thoughts, it may be experienced continuously and account for much of the preoccupation and encourage self-focused attention.

We have described how individuals with BDD often experience tactile or somatic sensations. These sensations may be further experienced (or misinterpreted) as depersonalization. This consists of an experience of unreality in which a client loses a feeling of familiarity he has for his inner world. An individual may preface his description by "as if" he was "hollow," or "like a puppet," "detached." The experience is intensely unpleasant and is usually recurrent and episodic, or may be continuous. When these symptoms are focused on a part of the body, it is termed "desomatization." Here the client may experience changes in size or quality of a body part, for example, feeling larger, taller, or smaller, heavier or lighter, or filled with a cotton wool. Some clients complain of a lack of ownership or detachment but are still able to make objective judgments and estimates ("It feels as if my legs do not belong to me, although I know they are attached to my body"). When symptoms of depersonalization, derealization, or desomatization are prominent, it is regarded as "depersonalization disorder." An example is a man who experienced himself as being excessively tall, towering above others as if he was in the trees. He walked with a stoop and avoided wearing heels. However, he knew that this was a personal experience that he was only six feet, and was not actually hugely taller than others. A culture-specific example of desomatization is "Koro" in which an individual experiences panic when he feels his penis is shrinking and fears that it will ultimately disappear.

The overlap between BDD and depersonalization disorder is sometimes blurred. In general, individuals with depersonalization disorder without BDD know that they do not have a bodily defect which can be seen by others. However, some BDD clients experience tactile sensations and desomatization. The experience of tactile sensations and desomatization may be used as evidence for the defect (in the same way that depersonalization may be used as evidence for going mad in a panic attack). An example of desomatization is a man with BDD who experienced numbness and a sensation of his mouth drooping to one side. At times he described the experience *as if* he had a Bell's palsy but on most occasions he was convinced that his mouth was defective and clearly visible to others. He was preoccupied with this defect and his doubts led him to repeatedly check his appearance in mirrors and against photographs, which led to further confusion.

4.3   Overvalued Ideas and Delusions

This section describes the phenomenology of overvalued ideas and delusions in BDD from a psychiatric perspective and how these overlap with negative automatic thoughts, beliefs, assumptions, and meta-cognitions derived from a cognitive behavioral perspective. Before discussing overvalued ideas in BDD, we should emphasize that there is a difference between the original description of overvalued ideas in the European literature and the current usage by many authors in the USA. We discuss the concept of overvalued ideas in detail because it is not covered very well in standard textbooks.

A delusion is defined in DSM IV as a false personal belief that is based on an incorrect inference about external reality. The degree of conviction may vary, but the belief is generally sustained in spite of what others believe and what constitutes incontrovertible proof to the contrary. Lastly, the belief is not one ordinarily accepted by other members of the person's culture or subculture. By contrast, an overvalued idea is defined as an unreasonable and sustained belief that is maintained with less than delusional intensity (i.e., the person is able is to acknowledge the possibility that the belief may or may not be true). Again, the belief is not one that is ordinarily accepted by other members of the person's culture or subculture (American Psychiatric Association, 1994). An overvalued idea has become shorthand for "poor insight" in the middle of a continuum of obsessional doubts to delusional certainty (Hollander & Hollander, 1993; Phillips & McElroy, 1993), which emphasizes the strength of a belief as one of the key criterion for an overvalued idea. Neziroglu et al. (1999) emphasize, however, that an overvalued idea includes both beliefs and values, and the importance of a lack of or very slight fluctuation in the strength of the conviction over time.

The older European concept of an overvalued idea is broader and discusses a number of dimensions other than the strength and abnormality of the belief (Jaspers, [1959] 1963; Hamilton, 1974; McKenna, 1984; Wernicke, 1900). This emphasizes the *preoccupation* in the individual's mental life, being *egosyntonic*, the way they develop in an *abnormal personality* and the *high degree of affect* when they are threatened. A cognitive behavioral model of overvalued ideas has been described by Veale (2002), who draws on the *philosophical* distinction between beliefs and values. A belief, or inference, is something thought to be true because of observation or evidence. It can often be subjected to empirical testing or logic to derive facts, which tend to be objective. By contrast, a value is something thought to be good or important to an individual. Hence strongly held values are the principles on which one will not yield and are not subject to empirical testing. Evaluations, or attitudes, are associated with values. They are a rating of an event or person on a scale of good to bad. In comparison to beliefs, values or evaluations are not subject to empirical testing. They are more difficult to measure or challenge because they are subjective and personal. In abnormal mental states, the evaluations are more extreme than normal ratings on a continuum of good to bad (or some variant, such as awfulness or evilness).

The division between beliefs and values is often confused and has had little impact in psychiatry or psychotherapies. More recently acceptance and commitment therapy has emphasized the role of acting in a valued direction in life, where a value guides like a compass. Thus goals in therapy are defined as actions in pursuit of values (e.g., being a good partner or a good father) as there are always actions that can be performed to be a better partner or father. These are different from achievable goals. The *values* that exist in an abnormal mental state are not usually described in psychopathology or cognitive theories but are related to evaluations. Cognitive theories usually describe *values* in the form of rules or demands (e.g., "I must be accepted by everyone all the time"). Such a rule would be related to valuing the importance of social acceptance. It is argued that overvalued ideas are beliefs that are associated with *idealized values*, which have developed into such overriding importance that they totally define the "self" or identity of the individual. Thus in BDD, the self is viewed as an "aesthetic object" because of the importance of appearance in defining the self.

A second characteristic of idealized values is the *rigidity* with which they are held. This is different from the conviction of an overvalued idea (the *belief*) that is described as being held extremely *strongly*. The emphasis on an idealized value is inflexibility. Such clients are unable to adapt to different circumstances and ignore the consequences of acting on their value. Individuals with BDD hold idealized values about the importance of appearance in defining their self and ignore the consequences of acting on such values.

Some values, such as perfectionism, cut across several disorders (e.g., in some clients with BDD, anorexia nervosa, and obsessive compulsive disorder). Also clients with the same disorder may hold variants of the same value. For example, for people with BDD who value the importance of appearance, some may value perfection or symmetry; others may value more the importance of social acceptance and desire for a "normal" appearance that allows them to blend in with others.

Diagnostic classifications and assessment tend to focus on the content of *beliefs*. For example, in BDD the idealized value (the importance of appearance) is crucial for the beliefs about appearance to have any significance (e.g., that one's "nose looks crooked and too red" is a belief that one's nose is being evaluated negatively). In the absence of the idealized value such beliefs hold little relevance for the person. In this book, we stick to the general convention of referring to the DSM IV definition of overvalued ideas as beliefs, and use the term "*idealized values*" for values which have developed into such overriding importance that they are excessively rigid and totally define the "self" or identity of the individual. Idealized values in body image are thus the same as an extreme level of "body image valence" (Sarwer et al., 1998) or "body image investment" (Cash, 1990), which is discussed in section 4.1 and make one extremely vulnerable to body image dissatisfaction. Thus a belief may be affect-driven as in the case of many individuals with BDD. Overvalued ideas have been assessed in BDD (Neziroglu et al., 1996) and found to be significantly high (McKay et al., 1997). A significantly high Overvalued Ideas Scale (OVIS) rate is suggested to be a primary reason for difficulty with treatment (Neziroglu et al., 2001).

The division between delusions and overvalued ideas in BDD is traditionally distinguished in DSM IV by the strength of conviction in the belief. Thus if a person believes that his skin is ugly when to the observer it is not, and there is the slightest element of doubt, then it is regarded as an overvalued idea. If the person holds the belief with 100% certainty and is completely convinced by it, it is regarded as a delusion. This determines whether BDD is classified with an additional diagnosis of a delusional disorder. A structured diagnostic interview such as the OVIS (Neziroglu et al., 1999) or the Brown Assessment of Beliefs (BABS) (Eisen et al., 1998) may be used to assess the strength of conviction of the belief. Part of the problem is that the instruments are being used to assess an aesthetic judgement, which may be more subjective. However, we also argue that it is important to assess the values in a client with BDD and the degree of importance that they attach to appearance.

Lambrou (2006) compared 50 BDD clients with two non-clinical control groups (50 art and design controls and 50 non-art and design controls). Participants were required to allocate a total of 100 points to a choice of the following 10 values: a) physical appearance, b) family, c) friends, d) health, e) academic/occupational success, f) religion, g) art, h) music, i) money, and j) scientific truth. They were asked to rate each value on degree of importance. Values that held no importance to them were rated as 0 and the total number of points allocated to all the values had to add up to 100. As predicted, BDD clients were significantly more likely to value physical appearance compared to art and design and non-art controls, as revealed by planned contrasts. There were no differences between the control groups. In relative terms, physical appearance was by far the most important value for BDD clients at a mean of 29%. This was followed by family (18%), friends (15%), and health (11%). By contrast, art and design controls and non-art controls rated appearance as only 9%. Physical appearance was ranked fifth by both control groups. The control groups were more likely to value relationships with family (art and design controls mean 22%; non-art controls mean 24%) and friends (art and design mean 18%; non-art controls 15%). Whether the importance of appearance developed before, during, or after the onset of BDD is an unanswered question as it may be a risk factor for the development of BDD or a consequence of experience of mental imagery and beliefs about being ugly. Furthermore, the value may even be ego-dystonic.

Another aspect of idealized value about appearance and an aesthetic identity is degree of self-objectification. This was used in the same study and three groups described above with the Self-Objectification Questionnaire (Fredrickson et al., 1998). This is a self-report questionnaire to assess the degree to which a person views himself in observable, appearance-based (objectified) terms as opposed to non-observable, competency-based (non-objectified) terms. It assesses concerns with appearance without any judgemental or evaluative component. Respondents are asked to rank-order a list of 10 body attributes by how important each one is to their physical self-concept. Half the attributes are based on physical appearance (physical attractiveness, sex appeal, weight, firm or sculpted muscles, and measurement) and half are based on physical competence (health, strength, physical coordination, energy level, and physical fitness). In this study (Lambrou, 2006), BDD clients also had significantly higher positive score on the self-objectification questionnaire relative to art and design controls Control groups did significantly differ in their scores.

These results suggest that individuals with BDD have more idealized values about the importance of appearance than non-psychiatric controls. Furthermore, they have become of such overriding importance that they define the "self" or identity of the individual in appearance-based (objectified) terms as opposed to competency-based (non-objectified) terms.

4.4 Ideas and Delusions of Self-reference

People with BDD often experience either ideas or delusions of self-reference depending on severity and degree of insight. Typically, clients believe that others are taking special notice of their defect. In a study of emotion recognition in BDD, Buhlmann et al. (2004) found that BDD patients misinterpreted emotional expressions as angry more frequently than people with OCD, or controls. Findings from a further study investigating emotion recognition (Buhlmann et al., 2006) indicate that BDD patients misinterpreted more emotional expressions as contemptuous or angry than controls in self-referent situations (i.e., when they imagined themselves in the situation), but not in other-referent situations (when they imagined another person in the situation). The authors suggest that ideas and delusions of reference may be related to a bias for misinterpreting other people's emotional expressions as negative. Perceiving others as rejecting may then reinforce a belief about being ugly.

4.5 Beliefs and Assumptions

In the previous section, we discussed the importance of distinguishing beliefs from values. In BDD, the beliefs (or negative thoughts) and evaluations are based on appraisals of one's appearance (which in turn may be associated with mental imagery). Beliefs and evaluations are like two sides of a coin. For example, someone with panic disorder might *believe* that feeling dizzy means that he will collapse and might *evaluate* the cost of collapsing as "absolutely terrible." An individual with BDD might experience a mental image viewed from an observer perspective of how he appears to others and *believe* that his skin is scarred and wrinkled. He might then evaluate his appearance as being as awful and ugly as the Elephant Man. Such evaluation depend on valuing the importance of appearance as it is possible for individuals even with a marked disfigurement not to value appearance and to focus their self on competency-based (non-objectified) terms.

In cognitive therapy models, various "core beliefs" and assumptions can be identified about the meaning of a defect in one's appearance. These personal meanings are traditionally identified through a "downward arrow technique." After eliciting the most dominant emotion associated with thinking about the defect, the therapist enquires about what is the most shameful (disgusting, anxiety-provoking) aspect about the defect. Thus a client who believed that his nose was too big and defective held an assumption that "If my appearance is defective, then I will end up unloved as I look like a crook." Another client who was excessively aware of flaws in her skin found them disgusting and thought of her skin as "dirty." Thus her core belief was that she was dirty and unloved. Veale et al. (1996) described 50 patients with BDD who strongly endorsed assumptions such as "If my appearance is defective, then I am worthless"; "If my appearance is defective, then I am inadequate"; "If I am unattractive, then I will be alone and isolated all my life." Geremia & Neziroglu (2001) found the following assumptions in BDD: "If I looked better, then my whole life would be better"; "Happiness comes from looking good"; "If there is one flaw in my overall appearance, then I feel unattractive"; "How I feel about my self as a person is usually related to how I feel about the way I look"; "If my [body part of concern] is unattractive or ugly, it means I look unattractive or ugly."

4.6   Ruminations and Meta-cognitions

Many people with BDD describe the preoccupation with their feature as being on their mind most of the time and intensely distressing. Little is known, however, about the cognitive processes involved in preoccupation in BDD. Mental imagery and thoughts about being ugly or defective represent an involuntary experience that is intrusive and distressing. Such experiences have a meaning (or meta-cognition) and a response that determines whether it will develop into a rumination and preoccupation. Meta-cognitive aspects of thoughts about appearance were studied in 22 people with BDD and a control group of 22 people with "normal concerns" regarding appearance (Holland et al., in submission). It was thought that the form of the rumination would follow a number of themes:

a)   About the past in which there is focus on "Why"-type questions – for example, "Why am I so ugly?"; "Why was I born looking too feminine"; "Why did I cut my eyebrows?".

b)   Reviewing past experiences ("post-mortems") – for example, reviewing the experience of being teased or bullied; how they last looked in the mirror; looking at old photos and thinking how much better they used to look, reviewing the reactions of others when they felt very self-conscious.

c) Planning how to cope with events in the future or "flash forwards" – for example, "Can I sit with my worst side of my face against the wall and not be in the light?"; "How will I deal with my friends seeing my blemishes?"; "How am I going to alter my appearance?".

d) Fantasy thinking – for example, "If only I had prettier, smoother skin"; "What will I be like when I have had cosmetic surgery?"

e) Worrying about the present or future which provokes anxiety – typically, "What if …?"-type questions, for example, "What if someone stares at me or calls me ugly?"

f) Self-attacking or punishing – for example, "You are so ugly that you should have been throttled at birth." This usually occurs when depression is more severe or when personality is more disturbed.

The content of thoughts about appearance was found to be similar in the two groups, but participants with BDD were found to endorse negative meta-cognitive beliefs significantly more strongly, to employ thought control strategies involving punishment significantly more frequently, and to report significantly lower frequency of social control (e.g., talking to other people about their worry).

Comparing one's feature against another's can also be viewed as a cognitive process which contributes to preoccupation and is discussed in section 4.8.

4.7   Social Anxiety, Perfectionism, and Shame

No discussion on phenomenology of BDD is complete without a discussion of shame, perfectionism, and social anxiety, and the way these relate to body image.

Body shame is a multifaceted experience with various components (Gilbert & Bailey, 2000):

a) A social or external evaluative component. The affect of shame elicited in social contexts is associated with thoughts about being inferior, defective, ugly, or bad: this is the belief that others are looking on the self with a condemning or contemptuous view for failing to reach an external standard or for having an unappealing appearance. The shame centers on the discrepancy between how a person thinks others view him and how he thinks he "should" be. This is referred to as external shame.

b) An internal self-evaluative component. This is the internal critic and global self-evaluation as being inferior, defective, ugly, or bad and a failure to achieve an internal standard or discrepancy between actual self and an ideal self. This is referred to as internal shame and is related to perfectionism when a person relentlessly pursues a personally demanding standard.

c) An emotional component. Various emotions are recruited, although the core emotion is regarded as self-disgust associated with social anxiety and anger when there is a feeling of humiliation.

d) A physiological component. Little is known about the pathophysiology of shame, although it is clearly related to a stressor response. In some cases it may involve heightened parasympathetic activity.

e) A behavioral component. This includes (i) avoidance and various safety-seeking behaviors within social situations described below; and (ii) a relentless pursuit of altering one's appearance according to a self-imposed standard.

Most people with BDD typically have a mixture of internal and external shame. However, not all clients are preoccupied by external shame and the negative evaluation of others. Thus a male client was preoccupied by the "flesh" on one side of his penis being flatter than on the other side. He had no avoidance behavior or concerns about his sexual performance or about what his girlfriend would think if she could see his penis was not symmetrical. He was more preoccupied by failing to achieve an internal aesthetic standard. He was extremely distressed because he was aware that the "problem" could not be rectified and was, as a result, significantly depressed and handicapped. At the other extreme, another male heterosexual client complained that his penis and testes were too small. He was aged 30 and had avoided virtually all intimate relationships because of his extreme anxiety and fear of rejection. When he once had intercourse, he did not allow his partner to see his genitals. In social situations, he would cross his legs so that his genital area could not be seen. It should be said that both clients had "normal"-sized and shaped genitals. However, the first client could be described as experiencing internal shame and the second external shame.

Individuals with BDD frequently report high levels of social anxiety and shame because of a fear of negative evaluation of their appearance by others (Phillips, 1991; Hollander et al., 1992; Phillips & McElroy, 1993). Veale et al. (2003) found that 107 participants with BDD scored approximately 1.5 standard deviations higher than non-clinical controls on both the Social Phobia Scale and the Social Interaction Scale. Pinto & Phillips (2005) examined social anxiety in 81 patients with BDD with the Social Avoidance and Distress Scale (SADS) (Watson & Friend, 1969) and measures of BDD symptomatology. They found that severity of symptoms on the SADS correlated with BDD severity scores. The mean baseline SADS score was 1.3 SD units higher than a non-clinical sample but similar to other anxiety disorders. This suggests that social anxiety is no greater in BDD than other anxiety disorders. However, the SADS is not necessarily a measure of social anxiety but of avoidance. Greater depressive symptoms as well as comorbid avoidant personality disorder (but not social phobia) were also associated with higher SADS scores.

Anson, Veale & de Silva (2003) conducted a study investigating concerns relating to negative evaluation of appearance by others, including the extent of such concerns relative to self-evaluative appearance concerns in individuals with BDD and healthy controls. Three components of appearance concern were explored, namely evaluation of appearance (self and perceived other) and the degree of importance and anxiety attached to these evaluations. A further aim of the study was to investigate the extent of concerns related to overall appearance relative to specific features of appearance in BDD and control participants. The above processes were explored using new self-completion scales, as well as the Fear of Negative Appearance Evaluation Scale (FNAE; Thomas et al., 1998) and the Multidimensional Body-Self Relations Questionnaire – Appearance Scales (MBSRQ-AS; Cash, 2000). The authors found that in addition to negative self-evaluation of overall and specific aspects of their appearance, BDD participants reported markedly negative perceptions of others' evaluations of their overall appearance and their specific body part of concern. Furthermore, their self-ratings of the most disliked body part did not differ significantly from their perceptions of ratings by the group of people whose opinion was most important to them. In addition, BDD participants reported high levels of importance and anxiety associated with self and perceived other views of both overall and specific aspects of their appearance, with no significant differences being observed in the level of importance or anxiety associated with their own view as compared to their perceptions of others' views of their appearance. These findings suggest that, in addition to self-evaluative appearance concerns, appearance-related social evaluative concerns are a central feature of the disorder.

The high degree of importance attached to others' views of appearance in BDD is in line with cognitive models and research in the field of body image disturbance (e.g., Cash, 1990; Thompson et al., 1999), and anxiety regarding perceived negative evaluation of appearance by others has been identified as a potential risk factor in the development of body image disturbance (Thomas et al., 1998; Thompson et al., 1999; Lundgren et al., 2004).

In terms of concerns relating to specific features, BDD participants' anxiety scores associated with their own view (but not others' views) were significantly higher for the most disliked body part as compared to overall appearance. There were no significant differences between importance scores for overall and specific appearance in the BDD group (self or perceived other). Healthy controls reported relatively high levels of self and perceived other evaluations of their overall appearance, and they also attached a relatively high degree of importance to these self- and other opinions of their overall appearance. However, they reported only mild to moderate levels of anxiety associated with both views of their overall appearance. In contrast, control participants reported relatively low self- and perceived other evaluations of their most disliked feature. However, unlike BDD participants, they attached significantly less importance to self- and other views of these features in comparison to self- and other views of their overall appearance, and they reported only mild to moderate anxiety scores relating to self- and other opinions of their most disliked feature.

These findings support models of BDD (e.g., Veale et al., 1996; Veale 2004; Wilhelm, 2006; Neziroglu et al., 2008) which propose that a core characteristic of BDD is an excessively high degree of importance attached to physical appearance in defining overall identity, accompanied by negative appraisal of appearance. The findings are also consistent with the theories emphasizing the disproportionate value accorded to appearance in comparison to other domains in defining the self in individuals with body image disturbance (e.g., Cash, 1990) and eating disorders (e.g., Fairburn et al., 1997; Fairburn et al., 2003). In line with clinical observations in the literature (Ladee, 1966; Phillips 1991; Phillips & McElroy, 1993; Veale et al., 1996; Wilhelm, 2006), these findings also suggest that in addition to the overvaluing of appearance as a whole, a crucial feature of BDD is the disproportionately high level of importance attached to specific body parts in defining overall appearance and, by extension, in shaping self-concept as a whole. Anson (2008) argued, however, that the findings from healthy control participants suggest that appearance-related anxiety and distress may be related to a combination of negative evaluation and high importance attached to overall appearance or particular body parts, and that the valuing of appearance is not necessarily a dysfunctional process, unless it is (a) very excessive, (b) to the exclusion of other characteristics, and /or (c) associated with negative appearance evaluation.

The role of social anxiety in BDD has also been explored with self-discrepancy theory (Veale et al., 2003), which proposes three basic domains of self-beliefs: (a) the *actual self* – the individual's representation of the attributes that someone (self or significant other) believes the individual actually possesses; (b) the *ideal self* – the individual's representation of the attributes that someone (self or significant other) would ideally hope the individual to possess; and (c) the *should or ought self* – the individual's representation of the attributes that someone (self or significant other) believes the individual ought as a sense of duty or moral obligation to possess. The *ideal* and *should* selves are referred to as self-guides. It is assumed that a discrepancy between the actual self and the self-guides determines the individual's vulnerability to negative emotional states (Higgins, 1987). For example, in a self-actual/self-ideal discrepancy, the individual is vulnerable to dejection-related emotions (e.g., depression, internal shame), resulting from the appraisal that his hopes and aspirations are unfulfilled with the absence of positive reinforcement. In a self-actual/self-should discrepancy, the individual is vulnerable to anxiety resulting from the appraisal that one has been unable to fulfill one's responsibilities and is therefore liable for punishment (the anticipated presence of negative outcomes seen in social phobia). Veale et al. (2003) explored the role of self-discrepancy theory in 72 BDD patients and 42 controls who completed a modified version of the Selves Questionnaire (Higgins et al., 1986) requiring them to list and rate physical characteristics according to the following standpoints: (a) self-actual; (b) self-ideal; (c) self-should; (d) other-actual; and (e) other-ideal. Compared to controls, BDD patients displayed significantly greater discrepancies between their self-actual and both their self-ideal and self-should. There were no significant discrepancies in BDD patients compared to controls, however, between their self-actual and other-actual or other-ideal domains. What is not known from this study is whether the discrepancy is because self-actual is excessively low or the self-ideal or self-should is excessively high (or whether both are abnormal). The results suggest that individuals with BDD are more concerned with a failure to achieve their own aesthetic standard than with being punished for failing to achieve the ideals of others. The difference between self-ideal and self-should is also not clear when it is related to appearance as opposed to a moral responsibility.

Related to internal shame is the concept of perfectionism, which is the tendency to set high standards and to evaluate one's self in an overly critical manner (Frost et al., 1990). Hewitt & Flett (2002) differentiated the dimension of self-oriented perfectionism, which is characterized by a striving for perfection and unrealistic self-standards with a focus on flaws in oneself. They contrasted other-oriented perfectionism (perfectionist expectations of others) and socially prescribed perfectionism (a belief that others had expectations of perfection of one's self). Self-oriented perfectionism is more likely to occur in depression (Hewitt & Flett, 1991). Shafran et al. (2002) extended the definition of self-oriented perfectionism to "clinical perfectionism," which they define as "The over-dependence of self-evaluation on the determined pursuit of personally demanding, self-imposed, standards in at least one highly salient domain, despite adverse consequences." An example is anorexia nervosa where there are clear adverse consequences. Standards are not necessarily objectively high but the individuals are striving to attain a personally demanding standard. Sherry & Vriend (2009) found that perfectionism was correlated with body dissatisfaction in a non-clinical sample. Specific sub-scales concerning mistakes, doubts about actions, and parental criticism were all elevated in women with body dissatisfaction. This is a non-specific finding as the scale is also elevated in other disorders, such as OCD and social anxiety.

Sherry & Vriend (2009) examined the relationship between a neurotic self-presentational style involving an extreme need to conceal perceived imperfections from others and symptoms of body image disturbance. Findings from both a community and a university sample indicated that non-display of imperfection (i.e., concerns over behavioral displays of imperfections to others) predicted body image disturbance beyond self-imposed perfectionist expectations rather than striving to achieve perfection. They suggest that individuals with body image disturbance (and therefore BDD) are characterized by a strong need to avoid appearing imperfect to others.

Lambrou (2006) measured shame in 50 individuals with BDD and 50 controls using the Experience of Shame scale (Andrews et al., 2002). Individuals with BDD had significantly higher scores compared to healthy controls. The total was significantly higher in the BDD group (mean 74.5, SD 17.1) relative to a control group (mean 44.7, SD 10.5). There were also significant group differences for all the sub-scales of characterological shame, behavioral shame, and bodily shame. In a structural equation analysis, body shame also mediated the relationship between body image and BDD symptomatology and between self-consciousness and BDD symptomatology.

In the same study, individuals with BDD had significantly higher scores on the disgust sensitivity scale (Haidt et al., 1994) (mean 58.8, SD 18.0) compared to controls (mean 48.6, SD 15.0). Lastly, individuals with BDD were significantly more self-conscious on the Self-Consciousness scale (Fenigstein et al., 1975) (mean 70.1, SD 9.8) compared to healthy controls (mean 49.8, SD 13.9). They also differed on all three sub-scales (private self-consciousness; public self-conscious; social anxiety). Lambrou (2006) also measured perfectionism on the Multidimensional Perfectionism scale (Frost et al., 1990). BDD patients had significantly higher perfectionism scores (mean 114.6, SD 21.1) compared to art and design controls (mean 96.2, SD 21.4) and non-art controls (mean 95.4, SD 17.3). Of the six sub-scales, three revealed group differences (concern over mistakes; parental criticism; and doubts about actions), but not on the other three scales (personal standards; parental expectations; and organization).

Clinically, some individuals appear to have little or no social evaluative concerns at all and would still be distressed and looking in mirrors if they were alone on a desert island and no one was evaluating them – that is, they predominantly experience internal shame because of their extreme self-evaluation of ugliness and their inability to achieve an acceptable aesthetic standard for themselves. Some individuals have almost exclusively social evaluative concerns and believe they would have no symptoms of BDD in the hypothetical situation of being left alone on a desert island or knowing for certain that others are not evaluating them. They experience external shame and are more concerned with avoiding punishment and rejection by others. In our opinion they are generally easier to treat through various behavioral experiments or exposure to test out their beliefs. However, most people with BDD experience both internal and external shame and regard social evaluative concerns as an additional burden. They would be less distressed in a hypothetical situation of being left alone on a desert island. This reflects the heterogeneity and complexity of BDD and the importance of an individual formulation in treatment planning.

4.8   Safety-seeking Behaviors and Compulsions

BDD is classified by some as being on the spectrum of obsessive compulsive disorder (OCD) (Hollander & Hollander, 1993; Neziroglu et al., 1993; Yaryura-Tobias & Neziroglu, 1997a) although this needs to be tested (McKay & Neziroglu, in press). This is because of the possible similarity in phenomenology, family history, pathophysiology, and treatment response but with other distinct symptoms. Many of the behaviors in BDD, such as mirror-checking, were originally conceptualized as "compulsions," defined as a repetitive behavior or mental act that the person feels driven to perform. In OCD, compulsions are largely involuntary, repetitive, and seldom resisted. The aim of a compulsion is usually to feel "comfortable" or "just right" (Richards & Salkovskis, 1995; Neziroglu et al., 1996). Compulsive behaviors can generally be divided into those aimed at verification and those aimed at restitution ("putting right").

The term "safety-seeking behaviors" is used to refer to any action that aims to prevent a catastrophe in a feared situation and reduce harm (Salkovskis, 1985). Safety-seeking behaviors therefore include a broad range of responses, including escape.

The behavior is not what defines a safety-seeking behavior, but the behavior together with the intention of making oneself safe. This specifically prevents people from discovering that the things that they fear do not happen. An example of a within situation safety-seeking behavior might be someone with BDD who, in a social situation, may focus his attention on the way he feels, keep his head down, have poor eye contact, and not reveal personal information to reduce threat of eye gaze because of the risk of being humiliated. These behaviors are also described as "submissive behaviors" in the evolutionary psychology literature (Gilbert & Miles, 2002).

Safety-seeking behaviors are different from compulsions in that the former refer to behaviors that one performs to avoid aversive experiences. Compulsions are behaviors that one performs to *undo* an aversive experience. Thus safety seeking behaviors are preventative (they appear to prevent negative outcomes) whereas compulsions are restorative (restoring homeostasis by taking away the negative outcome, e.g., feeling anxious). Thus safety-seeking behaviors are not necessarily repetitive (i.e., come one after the other) and individuals do not necessarily use criteria of feeling comfortable or "just right" to terminate them. For example, a person with BDD might briefly check his appearance in a mirror to reduce uncertainty about his look and return half an hour later for another look. Classically, someone with OCD continues washing his hands or checks a door lock until he feels "comfortable" or "just right." People with BDD have a myriad of safety-seeking or compulsive behaviors which we describe below, some of which may use the termination criteria of feeling "right" or "comfortable." The frequency of the behaviors described are taken from surveys done by Phillips & Diaz (1997), which had a sample of 188 BDD patients, by Perugi et al. (1997), which had a sample of 58 patients, and by Lambrou (2006), which had a sample of 50 patients.

Behaviors in BDD can be broadly categorized as responses which aim to:

a)   Restore or enhance a feature (restitution) (e.g., a cosmetic procedure). The cognitive form of restitution is "neutralizing," which is defined as any voluntary or effortful mental action done to prevent or minimize harm by putting it right (e.g., self-reassurance or saying a phrase).
b)   Avoid, camouflage, or distract attention from a feature (e.g., the excessive use of make-up). The cognitive form of avoidance is to try to avoid experiencing aversive thoughts, images, and feelings by distraction or suppression.
c)   Verify one's appearance or the impression one is giving to others (e.g., mirror-checking). The cognitive form of verification is to verify one's image by checking against one's internal image.

Some actions, such as mirror-gazing, may overlap different categories – for example, a person may be using make-up (to camouflage their skin) and trying to verify exactly how she looks. Mirror-gazing might also be both a safety-seeking and a compulsive behavior at different times depending on its function.

Restoring or camouflaging

Cosmetic procedure
Seeking a cosmetic procedure is one of the biggest safety-seeking behaviors in BDD. The goal is to alter the feature permanently – hence the desire for cosmetic or dermatological procedures, hair transplants, dental or orthodontic treatment. Others may perform DIY surgery. Alternatively, they may spend an inordinate amount of time researching cosmetic products or procedures, trying the latest beauty products, or having further opinions with a cosmetic

surgeon or dermatologist. They may perform "mental cosmetic surgery" in front of a mirror or in their mind's eye and fantasize about how they will look. We discuss cosmetic procedures in BDD in more detail in Chapter 6. A huge problem for many people with BDD who proceed with cosmetic procedures is that they are not satisfied with the outcome. Indeed, some feel substantially worse, blaming themselves or the surgeon for having a procedure that they believe has worsened their appearance.

Make-up
A quarter (25%) of men and over half (56%) of women with BDD (Phillips & Diaz., 1997) or in general (65%) (Neziroglu et al., 1996) may use excessive make-up or a cover stick specifically to camouflage their skin. This in turn requires further mirror-gazing to check whether the make-up is "working" or needs retouching. When men use overt make-up in our society, it may attract attention and derision. For some men, this is less embarrassing than not camouflaging themselves. Note that some female clients may avoid using make-up (which they would normally use), believing it will direct attention to them or because it will involve having to use the mirror, or because it is not recommended for a dermatological treatment.

Skin behaviors
Clients preoccupied by their skin may be cleaning it excessively with a variety of soaps and cleansers in an attempt to improve or camouflage it. They may be using cover-up sticks for spots and blemishes or, more often, not use make-up because of fears of clogging the pores. Others may be bleaching their skin, using facial peels, scrubs, or saunas, avoiding sun exposure, excessively shaving, cutting, or tweezing. An interesting question to ask is how much your client spends on skin and beauty products each week and to monitor this at monthly intervals. Skin-picking is described in more details in Chapter 5. This includes picking, squeezing, or pressing blemishes on skin. This usually has a mixture of compulsive and impulsive features.

Tanning
Phillips et al. (2006) describe the use of tanning in BDD. They compared 200 subjects with BDD to assess the prevalence of BDD-related tanning. This was defined as darkening of one's skin by direct exposure to sunlight or artificial light, which was motivated by a desire to improve a perceived appearance defect. A quarter (25%) (95% CI, 19.0–31.0%) of subjects reported BDD-related tanning. Among tanners, the skin was the most common body area of concern (84%). Half (52%) of tanners had received dermatologic treatment, which was usually ineffective for BDD symptoms. Tanners were more likely than non-tanners to compulsively pick their skin.

Hair
Hair was used to camouflage a feature in 56% of the sample in Phillips & Diaz (1997). This is often characterized by a curtain hanging on either side of the face and looking down. Others may wear a wig. Excessive grooming was described in 44% (Phillips et al., 1997). This might involve excessive combing of one's hair or cutting one's hair excessively until it feels "right" (a compulsion). Others may avoid touching their hair or have difficulty in getting their hair cut by somebody else as this might involve looking in the mirror for a prolonged period. Others preoccupied by the loss of hair may use topical medication to promote hair growth. They may believe salvation will eventually come and life can start again when their hair looks right.

Clothes
Hats, especially baseball caps and woolly hats, and scarves may be worn to hide one's face or reduce eye contact (13% in women, 35% in men) (Phillips et al., 1997). The summer season is often more difficult as a client has less opportunity to use hats and scarves. Others are frequently looking for the "just right" outfit or change their clothes several times before they leave the house. We have also known a non-Islamic client with BDD to obtain a *burqua* over the Internet to provide complete anonymity when she went out.

Hands and objects
Phillips et al. (1997) found 41% of men and 24% of women reporting using their hands to cover their feature. Alternatively, individuals may cover their feature with an object such as a newspaper, book, or file.

Size and shape behaviors

Those who are preoccupied by some aspect of their weight or shape may use a variety of strategies, which are seen in eating disorders. There is often frequent checking in mirrors or pinching the skin. When seated, the thighs may be raised to prevent them appearing flabby. They may exercise excessively, body build, take steroids, diet pills, or laxatives, or use padding. They may restrict the amount or type of food they eat to alter their shape or reduce weight. Interestingly, such strategies may also be used for other areas of the body (e.g., reducing the perceived chubbiness of the face). Others may eat or exercise more in an attempt to increase their bulk or body shape as they may feel they are not masculine enough. Pope et al. (2005) reviewed the histories of 63 men with BDD. They compared 14 men with muscle dysmorphia (a pathological preoccupation with muscularity) with 49 comparisons without muscle dysmorphia. They were matched in terms of demographic features, BDD severity, delusionality, and a number of non-muscle-related body parts of concern.

Those with muscle dysmorphia were more likely to have attempted suicide, have a poorer quality of life, and have a higher frequency of substance use disorder and anabolic steroid abuse.

Padding
Women may pad their bra to enlarge their breast size or men may use padding over the genital area. Individuals preoccupied by body shape or men preoccupied by their genital size may wear loose-fitting clothing. One woman would wear up to seven layers of clothing to cover up being "revoltingly skinny."

Avoidance and distracting attention away from a feature

Avoidance behaviors
Direct avoidance of various activities or situations often occurs. The most common avoidance is of social and public situations, such as going out with friends or meeting new people, and appears to be an attempt to avoid negative evaluation. Many people with BDD avoid sexual intimacy or will only have an intimate relationship in the dark or whilst wearing make-up. Some people with BDD may avoid wearing certain colors or types of clothing; others avoid public changing rooms and hairdressers, avoid looking at photos and mirrors, or avoid a certain posture. Others avoid having a medical examination or treatment because they are too ashamed to reveal their defect; this may be a reason for not obtaining cosmetic surgery. One patient told us that the only reason they had not committed suicide was that their body would then be on view to the mortuary attendants.

Mirror avoidance
Avoiding mirror and reflection occurred in 30% in a sample of BDD patients (Phillips et al., 1997). Veale & Riley (2001) found that some reported finding mirror-gazing too time-consuming or distressing and had deliberately avoided all mirrors at certain times. This is similar to the mirror avoidance seen in anorexia nervosa (Norris, 1984). Two-thirds (67%) of our BDD patients reported that they selectively avoided only certain mirrors compared to 14% of controls. There are four types of selective avoidance of mirrors in BDD patients. The first type is of looking at a specific "defect" in the mirror. An example was a client who was preoccupied with the ugliness of his nose, so that he would only use a hand mirror when combing his hair, holding it above the line of his nose so that he avoided seeing it.

The second type of selective avoidance is of specific mirrors – for example, two clients reported avoiding mirrors that they regarded as "bad" or "unsafe" (they were associated with a bad image and feeling distressed in the past) and only checked in "good" or "safe" mirrors. Other clients reported only using mirrors that they trusted as being in the "right" light or if they were tilted correctly, as other mirrors or lights were too distressing. The third type of selective avoidance is only using mirrors in private but avoiding mirrors or reflective surfaces in public or social situations to prevent themselves from feeling upset. The fourth type of selective avoidance is to use only a mirror that is obscured – for example, one that is cracked, dusty, or dirty so that a clear reflection could not be seen. Another client reported looking in a mirror with soap on her face so she did not see her skin. Lastly, some clients may oscillate between avoidance and gazing – for example, a client who picked his skin would remain housebound checking his skin many times during a week to see if his skin had healed. When he was satisfied that he could go out, he would then avoid mirrors until the urge to check in the mirror and pick his skin would overcome him and the cycle would be repeated. In general, the function of mirror avoidance is usually to avoid aversive thoughts and feelings or to prevent a lengthy check. Note that avoiding mirrors is different from resisting the urge to check when it is still possible to use a mirror functionally and not in response to an urge.

Avoidance by altering posture or part of the body
In social situations 60% of men and 42% of women (Phillips & Diaz 1997) change their posture to avoid being seen in a certain way or at a particular angle. Examples include only showing the "best side"; not showing their profile and looking straight ahead or at 45 degrees (depending on the beliefs about which side appears best); always sitting with their back against the wall or head down; and avoiding eye contact. A client preoccupied by his thighs may sit with his toes on the floor to avoid his thighs spreading on the chair. Occasionally, a client might sit with his back to us during an interview, a process which is somewhat distracting.

BDD clients sometimes create an unusual feature such as a tattoo or a piercing that is designed to distract attention from their perceived defect. An example is a woman who shaved her hair and had a ring pierced on one eyebrow to distract attention away from a perceived defect on the skin by her mouth. Such behaviors are less common in BDD as most clients do not want to direct any attention to themselves. Interestingly, such behaviors often make the person less attractive and actually increase attention to the individual. Some may use more subtle ways of distracting attention such as a piece of jewelry or a particular item of clothing. An excessive amount of time may thus be spent choosing or trying on clothes in the morning as a way of camouflaging and distracting attention from a particular feature.

Verifying a feature
The majority of the clients engage in mirror-checking, checking reflective surfaces, and body-checking or measuring a feature. Many clients will report

monitoring bodily sensations in the area of their body that they are concerned about to ascertain size or shape, especially if they cannot easily check their appearance in other ways. This extends to monitoring the picture in their mind or impression of themselves, especially in social and public situations.

Mirror-gazing

Surveys have found that 80–90% of people with BDD mirror-gaze (Veale et al., 1996; Perugi et al., 1997; Phillips et al., 1997). Gazing and checking in mirrors include a myriad of other reflective surfaces, from shop windows and car mirrors to cutlery or the surface of the water in a pond. Inevitably, such reflections provide a distorted image.

Veale & Riley (2001) studied 52 patients with BDD who reported mirror-gazing to be a feature of their problem compared to 55 non-psychiatric controls. Subjects were given a self-report mirror-gazing questionnaire for the feelings that they had in front of a mirror during the past month. BDD patients were more likely than controls to endorse all the beliefs listed below, except that the controls were more interested in making themselves look presentable:

a) trying to hide my defects or enhance my appearance by the use of make-up;
b) combing or styling my hair;
c) trying to make my skin smooth by picking or squeezing spots;
d) plucking or removing hairs or shaving;
e) comparing what I see in the mirror with an image that I have in my mind;
f) trying to see something different in the mirror;
g) feeling the skin with my fingers;
h) practicing the best face to pull or show in public;
i) measuring parts of my face.

BDD patients also spontaneously reported that they were more likely to use the mirror if they were feeling depressed. Overall, BDD patients retained some insight into their behavior. They were more likely than controls to agree with the statements: "Looking in a mirror so often and for so long distorts my judgement about how attractive I am" and "Every mirror I look in I see a different image."

For long mirror checks, BDD patients did the same proportion of activities (in percentage terms) as controls in front of mirrors for: (a) applying make-up; (b) combing or styling their hair; (c) picking their spots; and (d) feeling their skin with their fingers. The controls were more likely to use a mirror for removing hairs or shaving. BDD patients were more likely (a) to compare what they see in front of a mirror with an image in their mind of how they think they should ideally look; or (b) to try to see something different in the mirror. For short checks BDD patients were more likely than controls to use the mirror (a) for checking their make-up, (b) practicing the best position or face to pull or show in public; and (c) compare what they see in front of a mirror with an image in their mind of how they think they would ideally look. Controls were more likely to use a mirror in a short session for shaving. BDD patients listed a range of other behaviors that they engaged in whilst in front of the mirror. These included "washing rituals"; "combing my eyebrows"; "studying my eyes, hair, and skin to observe the effect of stress on the aging process"; "pulling my features or squashing my nose to see how I'd look if I had plastic surgery"; "pulling ugly faces to prove how disgusting I am"; or "trying to permanently fix my image mentally."

BDD patients rated themselves retrospectively as significantly more distressed than controls before any gazing. For long mirror sessions, the BDD patients continued to be more distressed than controls after mirror-gazing. Lastly, they experienced a greater degree of distress if they resisted gazing in the mirror compared to controls.

The overall difference in distress before and after mirror-gazing was calculated for the BDD patients. After a long session in front of the mirror, BDD subjects overall experienced a significant increase in distress (18.5%). The overall difference in distress before and after resisting an urge to gaze for a long session was also calculated from the visual analog scales of the BDD patients. After resisting an urge to gaze, patients reported only a slight but non-significant increase in distress (5.9%) (this is in contrast to the belief prior to mirror-gazing that resisting looking in the mirror would make them feel worse). A number of patients reported significant handicap from mirror-gazing from being very late for appointments to having caused a road traffic accident after gazing in a car mirror.

BDD patients are more likely than controls to focus their attention on an internal impression or feeling (rather than on their external reflection in the mirror) but not for a short check. BDD patients were also more likely to focus their attention on specific parts of their appearance during a long session (rather than the whole of their appearance). Patients were significantly more likely to use a series of mirrors with different profiles (52.4%) compared to controls (6.7%). Both BDD patients and controls admitted to using shop windows. However, BDD patients spontaneously reported using a wide variety of reflective surfaces, including car mirrors, windows or bumpers on vehicles, cutlery, fish knifes, TV screens, reflective table tops, glass watch faces, washroom taps, or the back of CDs. The motivation for mirror-gazing is complex, but usually includes (a) the hope that one will look different from one's body image; (b) a need to reduce uncertainty and to know exactly how one looks; and (c) a lack of confidence in one's memory of how one looked during the last check. Whilst looking in the mirror may satisfy this urge in the short term, it will increase self-consciousness and thus distress and handicap.

Lighting is also often reported as important in mirror-checking. Clients often only use certain mirrors in the house which they perceive as giving themselves a better image. One of us (Neziroglu) has reported on several clients who did not move from their apartments because of the "superb" lighting.

Verifying by taking a photo
Some people with BDD may repeatedly check their feature by taking a photograph. This can be done by camera-phone or digital camera with an instant result that can be destroyed. They are more likely to avoid having a digital or analog photo taken by somebody else (as they cannot destroy it if they wish) or let a photographic shop see the photos when they are processed. Others may repeatedly compare their current feature with an old photo of how they used to be (before they aged, had an accident, or had cosmetic surgery that went wrong).

Verifying by an internal mirror
Internal mirror-checking one's appearance can occur when an individual examines how he looks. He experiences a picture in his mind and this may have the same effect as checking in the mirror in which an individual activates a chain of events as well as the emotional bias in his rating of his own appearance and others' rating of him. An internal mirror has the advantage of being available at all times. Unfortunately, it has a major disadvantage in being an unreliable representation of his appearance.

Verifying a feature directly (without a reflective surface)
If the feature is not on one's face, then the person is likely to check his feature directly without the need for a mirror. The function is usually similar to that of mirror-gazing, i.e., to reduce uncertainty.

Verifying with one's fingers or measuring
Another way of monitoring one's appearance is to check the size or contour of a feature (usually the skin) with one's fingers or by pinching it. Some may repeatedly measure their feature with their fingers or with a ruler, or weigh themselves. Others may doodle or regularly draw their image. The motivation is again usually to reduce uncertainty.

Comparing
Comparing one's defect with others' was reported in 90% of the sample of BDD patients (Phillips & Diaz, 1997). The target comparator is usually the same feature in an individual of the same sex in real life or those in the media (e.g., on television or in a magazine). People with BDD may constantly look

at old photos and compare their current flaw with the way the feature looked in the past. As a consequence of social comparison or looking at photos, BDD patients may seek surgery or try to alter their appearance. If they cannot do that satisfactorily, they may avoid the situation where the comparisons occur. Anson et al. (in submission), examined the role of appearance comparison with the Body Comparison scale (Fisher et al., 2002). BDD patients with facial concerns reported that they compared their facial features to those of others significantly more frequently than healthy controls. Initial results indicate that BDD clients report high levels of appearance comparison. It most commonly involves comparison of the feature the client perceives as defective to the same feature in people of the same sex, particularly those considered attractive in terms of the this feature.

Reassurance-seeking

Reassurance-seeking occurred in 47% of Phillips & Diaz's (1997) sample. Reassurance-seeking is usually in response to doubts – for example, about whether a defect has gotten worse or whether a feature is adequately camouflaged (e.g., by make-up). More often reassurance-seeking in BDD refers to trying to convince others how unattractive a feature is and becoming angry when they don't agree.

Because of the heterogeneity of the disorder, the presentation in these domains may differ. Heterogeneity in the function also exists in the behaviors that are chosen – for example, two people may be preoccupied with blemishes on their facial skin: one may pick his skin with the aim of reducing bumps and making it smooth, while the other may avoid touching his skin because of a fear of damaging it. Understanding the phenomenology and function of the response is an important aspect of developing any psychological understanding of the problem.

Chapter 5

Psychogenic excoriation

Summary

Psychogenic excoriation consists of excessive scratching, picking, gouging, lancing, digging, rubbing, or squeezing of normal skin or skin with minor surface irregularities (Arnold et al., 2001). It causes significant distress and handicap and may lead to visible disfigurement and chronic infections. It may be a symptom of BDD when it is in response to a preoccupation with either an imagined defect on the skin or minor surface irregularities. Psychogenic excoriation may also be a symptom of obsessive compulsive disorder (OCD) (when it is related to reducing anxiety and responsibility for harm, such as contamination from under the skin) and borderline personality disorder (when it has more impulsive features with the function of reducing tension). The evidence base for treating psychogenic excoriation (either pharmacotherapy or a psychological therapy) is tiny. There is one randomized controlled trial (RCT) of fluoxetine and several case reports on the benefit of selective serotonin reuptake inhibitors (SSRIs) for psychogenic excoriation. There are two case reports on the benefit of anti-psychotic drugs (pimozide and olanzapine) and an opiate antagonist (naltrexone). There is only case report for cognitive behavior therapy (CBT) in the treatment of psychogenic excoriation and no RCTs. CBT for psychogenic excoriation consists of a contextual functional analysis of the behavior, followed by self-monitoring and habit reversal.

Sections

Body Dysmorphic Disorder: A Treatment Manual. David Veale and Fugen Neziroglu
© 2010 John Wiley & Sons, Ltd.

5.1   Introduction

Psychogenic excoriation is characterized by excessive scratching, picking, gouging, lancing, digging, rubbing or squeezing of normal skin or skin with minor surface irregularities (Arnold et al., 2001). Skin lesions range from red patches, swelling, blisters, and denuded areas to crusts, cuts, burns, and scars. Lesions are often in bizarre shapes with irregular outlines in a linear or geometric pattern and usually clearly demarcated from surrounding normal skin. They are usually found on sites that are readily accessible to the client's hands, e.g., face, neck, hands, arms, or legs. They may be produced by a variety of mechanical or chemical means, including fingernails, sharp or blunt objects, lighted cigarettes, and caustic chemicals. Psychogenic excoriation causes significant distress and handicap and may lead to marked scarring, infections, and visible disfigurement.

Psychogenic excoriation was first described in the 1800s by Brocq, who termed it "acne excoriée" (Bach & Bach, 1993). This referred to excoriation of minor or nonexistent acne lesions. Since then, it has been described under a variety of different names, including "pathological skin picking," "neurotic excoriation," "compulsive skin picking," "self-injurious skin picking," or "dermatotillomania." The term "excoriation" is used by Arnold et al. (2001) and in this book since this is the term often used in the dermatological literature and it encompasses a broader range of behaviors than skin picking alone. "Psychogenic" is used because it implies a psychological or psychiatric cause (as opposed to a medical condition). We have reviewed psychogenic excoriation as a separate chapter because it is a symptom of a number of different disorders, including BDD, OCD, and borderline personality disorder (BPD), and because the psychological treatment is different from that of BDD without psychogenic excoriation.

5.2   Differential Diagnosis

Psychogenic excoriation occurs when a client admits to the self-inflicted nature of the lesions but cannot resist their actions and is seeking treatment. The terms dermatitis factitia and artefacta are often used interchangeably in the dermatological literature (Kalivas, 2003). Indeed, it may be hard for a doctor to distinguish them from natural disease, particularly if the lesions inflicted mimic those with a pathological cause. Psychogenic excoriation should be differentiated from:

a) Dermatitis factitia (a factitious disorder in DSM IV) in which skin lesions are produced by the individual's own actions "for secondary gain," but the individual denies their self-inflicted nature (if, e.g., they are seeking compensation or an insurance claim). The factitious nature of skin lesions can also occur in Munchausen's by proxy, when lesions are inflicted on a child to try to convince a doctor that the child requires medical treatment.
b) Dermatitis artefacta also occurs when the skin lesions are self-inflicted but the patient may or may not be willing to admit to it and he does not necessarily seek treatment for it. He may be indifferent to the lesions or how they occurred. There is a marked female preponderance.

When dermatitis factitia or artefacta is suspected, dermatologists are advised to avoid direct confrontation. Doctors should provide supportive care of the skin lesions with cleansing and application of topical antibiotics if needed, as well as occlusive dressings to prevent access to the lesion. Doctors are encouraged to validate the client's distress in an empathic and non-judgemental manner. This may lead to engagement in which psychological understanding of the problem issues may be accepted – for example, the client may be being physically or sexually abused and is not ready to reveal the context. Referral to a therapist may be refused and limited progress can be made in CBT.

A minority of clients may excoriate their skin in response to tactile hallucinations (from stimulant abuse), to sensations such as pruritus, or to an underlying dermatological condition which clearly accounts for the behavior. Alternatively, they may meet criteria for an undifferentiated somatoform disorder (e.g., idiopathic pruritus), if the skin sensations cannot be explained by a known medical condition or are in excess of what could be expected from a specific medical condition (Arnold et al., 1998). Patients with a medical condition differ from those who have psychogenic excoriation as the latter have psychiatric comorbidity. Calikusu et al. (2003) compared 31 patients with psychogenic excoriation and 31 patients with urticaria in a dermatology clinic. All subjects were interviewed using the Structured Clinical Interview for DSM III-R (SCID-I) and also completed symptom questionnaires. Current major depressive syndrome was present in 58% of the psychogenic excoriation group as compared to 6.5% of the control group. In the psychogenic excoriation group, 45.2% had OCD, while the rate was only 3.7% in the control group.

The psychogenic excoriation group also scored significantly higher on the Beck Depression Inventory, Hamilton Anxiety Rating Scale (HARS), and Yale-Brown Obsessive Compulsive Scale (YBOCS).

Psychogenic excoriation is not a recognized diagnosis in DSM IV or ICD-10, but it is classified in the former as "Impulse Control Disorders not otherwise specified." In ICD-10, it is classified as "Other Habit and Impulse Disorders" (F63.8) for persistent repeated maladaptive behaviors that are not secondary to a recognized psychiatric syndrome and in which there is repeated failure to resist impulses to carry out the behaviors. It thus includes psychogenic excoriation, onchyophagia (compulsive nail biting); compulsive nose picking, compulsive biting of the inside of the cheek, and lip-biting.

Psychogenic excoriation is typically a symptom of BDD, OCD, or BPD or a stereotypic movement disorder (e.g., Prader-Willi syndrome) (Stein & Simeon, 1999). For the diagnosis of BDD, there should be a preoccupation with the skin and the excoriation should be in response to an imagined defect on the skin or minor surface irregularities. Here the intended aim for the excoriation is to improve appearance. However, over time, repeated excoriation often leads to skin "defects," such as scarring and other complications, and it is often difficult to determine whether a "slight defect" existed before the picking began. Phillips & Taub (1995) note the limitations of this definition as many clients may have poor or no insight about when the excoriation began. They suggest interviewing a close relative or asking to view a photograph of the skin before the picking began to determine the nature of the "defect." Once skin excoriation has started, it may develop into a more automatic and impulsive pattern of behavior and the original reason for picking may be forgotten. Such situations were first described in case reports or case series by Zaidens (1951a; 1951b), Krupp (1977), and Phillips & McElroy (1992).

Psychogenic excoriation can also occur in BPD when such individuals may act impulsively to reduce tension. It can also occur in OCD when the intended aim is to reduce harm, such as to remove contaminants from under the skin. The distinction between the different underlying diagnoses (whether the excoriation is related to BDD, OCD or BPD) may be artificial because there is frequent co-morbidity and the original diagnosis may alter with the passage of time. The underlying diagnosis is also less relevant in a good functional analysis of the behavior.

5.3   Self-injurious Behaviors

Psychogenic excoriation can also viewed in the wider context of self-injurious behaviors (SIBs). SIBs are defined as deliberate infliction of direct physical harm to one's body without any intent to die as a consequence of the behavior

(Simeon et al., 2001). Favazza et al. (1995) and Simeon et al. (2001) have classified SIBs phenomenologically and found them to be consistent with the proposed operational criteria for psychogenic excoriation and its subtypes (Arnold et al., 2001) (Table 5.1).

1. Stereotypic SIBs are repetitive, seemingly driven, and nonfunctional motor behaviors (e.g., body rocking, head banging, mouthing of objects, self-biting, skin picking, self-hitting or rectal gouging). They are typically seen in severe learning disability syndromes such as Prader-Willi syndrome. Alternatively, the behavior may be associated with Tourette's syndrome. The repetitive movements usually increase with stress, frustration, or boredom. This type of skin excoriation is not seen in BDD.

Table 5.1: Proposed diagnostic criteria for psychogenic excoriation reproduced from (Arnold et al., 2001)

A. Maladaptive skin excoriation (e.g., scratching, picking, gouging, lancing, digging, rubbing or squeezing skin) or maladaptive preoccupation with skin excoriation as indicated by at least one of the following:

B. (i) preoccupation with skin excoriation and/or recurrent impulses to excoriate the skin that is/are experienced as irresistible, intrusive and/or senseless

C. (ii) recurrent excoriation of the skin resulting in noticeable skin damage
(ii) The preoccupation, impulses or behaviors associated with skin excoriation cause marked distress, are time-consuming, significantly interfere with social or occupational activities, or result in medical problems (e.g., infections).
(iii) The disturbance is not better accounted for by another mental disorder and is not due to a general medical condition.

Subtypes

Compulsive Type

Skin excoriation is performed to avoid increased anxiety or to prevent a dreaded event or situation and/or is elicited by an obsession (e.g., obsession about contamination of the skin). It is performed in full awareness. It is associated with some resistance to performing the behavior. There is some insight into its senselessness or harmfulness.

Impulsive Type

Skin excoriation is associated with arousal, pleasure or reduction of tension.
It is performed at times with minimal awareness (e.g., automatically).
It is associated with little resistance to performing the behavior.
There is little insight into its senselessness or harmfulness.

Mixed Type

Skin excoriation with both compulsive and impulsive features.

---

2. Compulsive SIBs (e.g., skin excoriation, hair-pulling, nail-biting). Here, the skin excoriation is reinforced as it prevents increased anxiety or a feared event (e.g., the skin being defective as in BDD) or an obsession (e.g., contamination of the skin). The individual is generally fully conscious of his behavior and may have some resistance to performing it. The individual usually has insight into the senselessness or harmfulness of his behavior. This is the most common presentation of psychogenic excoriation in BDD when it is in response to a minor skin irregularity. In OCD, the excoriation also has predominantly compulsive features, but in response to a fear of contamination or feeling anxious.

3. Impulsive SIBs (skin-cutting, skin picking or burning) are typically seen in a borderline personality disorder or in the context of severe trauma and dissociative states. Here the primary function of the skin picking is a means of emotional regulation. It is associated with mounting tension and after the behavior there is decreased arousal, gratification or a reduction of tension. It is often associated with minimal awareness (e.g., automatically) but can also be intentionally planned. Compared to compulsive SIBs, the individual usually has less insight into its senselessness or harmfulness. Clients with BDD may sometimes start with a compulsive type of excoriation but then develop mixed compulsive-impulsive symptoms (see Table 5.1).

4. Major SIBs tend to be isolated events and consists of severe or life-threatening tissue damage (e.g., self-castration, enucleation, or, less commonly, self-amputation, e.g., of a limb or ear). They mainly occur in young psychotic men or older males with psychotic depression, usually in the context of command auditory hallucinations or delusions of guilt. Psychogenic excoriation is not normally part of major SIBs.

5.4   Relationship of Psychogenic Excoriation with OCD

Trichotillomania and other self-injurious behaviors are currently classified in DSM IV as impulse control disorders. Stein & Hollander (1992) have suggested that psychogenic excoriation, trichotillomania, and other forms of self-injurious behaviors should be classified under a separate diagnosis as obsessive-compulsive-related disorders. Others regard behaviors such as psychogenic excoriation, nail-biting, trichotillomania, mouth-chewing and lip-biting, onchyophagia, and compulsive nose-picking as "Body Focused Repetitive Behaviors" (Teng et al., 2002; Penzel, 2003).

Lochner et al. (2002) compared the phenomenological similarities and differences between two groups of patients with psychogenic excoriation or trichotillomania. Both groups were very similar in demographics, psychiatric comorbidity, and personality dimensions. Dissociative symptoms were more common in trichotillomania than in psychogenic excoriation. These data support the idea that there is some overlap between the two conditions.

Arnold et al. (1998) conducted a survey of 34 patients with psychogenic excoriation recruited from a dermatology clinic and by advertisement. They were mostly women with a mean age of onset of 38 years and a chronic course. They all met diagnostic criteria for at least one comorbid psychiatric diagnosis, with a mood disorder being the most common. Most subjects experienced mounting tension before excoriation and relief afterwards as in impulse control disorders. About one third had BDD and a minority had OCD.

Wilhelm et al. (1999) conducted a survey of 31 patients with psychogenic excoriation. The mean age of onset was 15 and the duration of the illness was 21 years. The most common Axis I diagnosis was OCD (52%), followed by an affective disorder (48%), alcohol abuse/dependence (39%), illicit substance abuse (26%), BDD (32%), eating disorder (28%), and social phobia (23%); 72% met criteria for at least one personality disorder. The most common were obsessive compulsive personality disorder (48%) (N = 15), borderline personality disorder (26%) (N = 8), avoidant 23% (N = 7), dependent 10% (N = 3), and others 18% (N = 6).

Neziroglu et al. (2008) conducted a survey of skin picking in 36 participants who were recruited from a clinic population and via an advertisement in the *Obsessive Compulsive Foundation Newsletter*. Participants had a mean age of 37.9 years and 72% were female. All the participants reported a history of at least one current or past psychiatric diagnosis. Eighty-nine per cent of participants had an anxiety disorder, with 63% reporting OCD, 11% reporting BDD, and 14% reporting generalized anxiety disorder (GAD); 31% of the participants had a mood disorder, 11% had an eating disorder, and 9% had a diagnosis of borderline personality disorder.

5.5 Handicap in Psychogenic Excoriation

Whatever the diagnosis, psychogenic excoriation causes significant distress and handicap, with secondary problems of shame and embarrassment. There is likely to be avoidance of activities that involve exposure of the skin to others, such as in intimacy, sexual activity, or sports. Many clients attempt to camouflage themselves with cosmetics, clothing, or bandages to cover the damage. Some may become housebound or suicidal. Physical complications include redness of the skin, bleeding, infections, ulcers, permanent discoloration, and disfiguring scarring. This is turns leads to more scabs or imperfections which become a further target for excoriation making a vicious circle. Infections are the most common problems encountered with any picking behavior (Neziroglu et al., 2008).

5.6   Epidemiology

The prevalence of psychogenic excoriation is unknown and the following data (unless otherwise stated) refer to psychogenic excoriation in general and not just BDD. Psychogenic excoriation has been reported to occur in about 2% of dermatological settings (Griesemer, 1978). Phillips et al. (2000) found that 12.9% of patients in a dermatology setting had BDD, but it is not known what proportion had psychogenic excoriation as their main problem. Keuthen et al. (2000) found a prevalence of 4.9% of psychogenic excoriation with severe tissue damage and significant distress, as well as impairment, amongst 105 college psychology students. Seventy-eight percent endorsed some skin picking behavior, and 78 students (95.1%) had noticeable tissue damage without impairments or distress, categorized as mild to moderate skin picking. These individuals were compared to a clinical sample of 31 individuals with severe skin picking. They differed in the amount of time spent, areas picked, and implements used. Furthermore, higher tension before picking, higher satisfaction during picking, and higher levels of shame after picking also differentiated the severe from the non-severe pickers. Likewise, higher rates of depression and anxiety were reported in the individuals with severe picking. The authors concluded that skin picking as a symptom does not discriminate clinical from non-clinical populations.

Bohne et al. (2002) reported on a German student population (N = 133) with 91.7% (N = 122) reporting occasional excoriation, 57.9% reported recurrent skin picking, but only 8.3% engaged in skin picking for more than 30 minutes each day. Six students (4.6%) had significant impairment from recurrent, self-injurious excoriation.

The mean age of onset in all the studies was from 15 to 45 (Gupta et al., 1986; Simeon et al., 1997; Arnold et al., 1998; Wilhelm et al., 1999) and the mean duration of excoriation was between 5 and 21 years. Most studies have found a female to male ratio of about 8:1, although this may reflect differences in treatment-seeking.

5.7   Psychopathology

Only one study has surveyed excoriation in individuals with BDD (rather than excoriation across different disorders). Phillips & Taub (1995) found that 33 out of 123 (26.8%) of BDD patients excoriated their skin habitually. Individuals with BDD who excoriated were more likely than those who did not excoriate to have developed defects in the appearance of the skin and to have received dermatological treatment. Excoriators were also more likely to use specific safety behaviors, such as excessive grooming and camouflaging of the skin than non-excoriators. Skin concerns in those who excoriated usually involved nonexistent or minimal acne, scars, scabs, "large" pores, "bumps," "small black dots," "white dots," "ugly things," or other supposed imperfections, or dirt, pus, or "impurities" under their skin. They often excoriated for several hours each day (in some cases for up to 12 hours), usually in front of a mirror. Many patients used their hands to pick, pinch, or squeeze or used implements such as tweezers, needles, pins, razor blades, staple removers, or knives. A few excoriated other people's skin as well. Dermatological treatment was required in several cases because some subjects excoriated to the point where they caused severe damage or induced infection.

Wilhelm et al. (1999) conducted a survey of 31 subjects (described in section 5.4) who picked more than one body area. The face was the most frequent site, followed (in descending order) by the back, neck, scalp, ears, chest, cuticles, arms, and legs. The most frequent targets for excoriation were pimples and scabs (87% each), red, swollen, or infected areas (52%), mosquito bites (48%), and scars (42%); 52% reported excoriating healthy skin. Excoriation tended to be worse in the evenings and, for women, premenstrually or during menstruation. The most common trigger was looking at or touching the skin when they were home alone. Subjects rated their emotions before, during, and after excoriation. Shame, guilt, and pain increased after excoriation. Tension and feeling "mesmerized" decreased.

Arnold et al. (1998) described a sample of 34 adults, most of whom were women. The mean age at onset was 38 years and the excoriation a chronic course. Subjects excoriated multiple sites, most frequently the face. The behavior caused substantial distress and dysfunction. All 34 subjects met criteria for at least one comorbid psychiatric disorder, with a mood disorder the most common. Family histories were notable for depressive disorders and psychoactive substance use disorders. Most subjects experienced mounting tension before and relief after excoriation as in impulse control disorders. A minority of subjects excoriated skin as part of OCD. Body dysmorphic disorder with preoccupation about the skin's appearance precipitated excoriation in about a third of subjects.

Deckersbach et al. (2002) described a group of students who primarily squeezed (85%) and scratched (77.4%) the skin, with a primary focus on the face (94.7%) and cuticles (52.6%). About 20% (N = 26) ate the picked tissue.

Neziroglu et al. (2008) conducted a survey of psychogenic excoriation in 40 participants with a range of psychiatric disorders (predominantly OCD, depression, and BDD). Participants reported multiple target areas for skin picking. Of these, the most common was the face (68%, 27 of 40), with cuticles (50%, 20 of 40) being the second most common target area. Picking was also frequently reported for the torso (back, 32%, 13 of 40; chest, 25%, 10 of 40) and limbs (arms, 35%, 14 of 40; legs 30%, 12 of 40). Other target areas included the neck (30%, 12 of 40), scalp (25%, 10 of 40), and ears (20%, 8 of 40). Nineteen participants (48%) reported picking in more idiosyncratic areas such as their feet and elbows.

While the majority of participants (95%, 38 of 40) utilized their fingers and/or fingernails, some also used implements to facilitate their picking. The most common included tweezers (52%, 21 of 40), pins (32%, 13 of 40), and razors (5%, 2 of 40). In addition to using standard implements, 32% of participants (13 of 40) reported using "other" implements (i.e., anything that was available at the time). The triggers that can precipitate an episode of skin picking were emotional, perceptual, tactile, or environmental. Emotional triggers, such as general anxiety, were reported by every participant. Typical emotional triggers included general stress (95%, 38 of 40), interpersonal rejection (20%, 8 of 40), a sense of emptiness (42%, 17 of 40), and teasing (18%, 7 of 40). Perceptual triggers were reported by most of the participants, with general skin imperfections reported by 80% of participants (32 of 40). Imperfections included such things as pimples and scabs (75%, 30 of 40), scars (25%, 10 of 40), mosquito bites (18%, 7 of 40), and other, idiosyncratic, observed imperfections (40%, 16 of 40). Additional perceptual triggers included the perception of asymmetry in one's skin (35%, 14 of 40) and overall dissatisfaction with skin appearance (60%, 24 of 40). Thirteen participants (32%) reported picking even at sites with no imperfections (i.e., healthy skin). Tactile triggers included itchiness (40%, 16 of 40), sensations such as something underneath the surface of the skin (32%, 13 of 40), and the "right feeling" sensation (40%, 16 of 40). The most common environmental trigger was mirror-checking (52%, 21 of 40). Many participants (50%, 20 of 40) also described anticipatory social anxiety as a trigger.

Most participants reported that their skin picking episodes took place when they were alone at home and stated that they were aware of it and attempted self-restraint: 74% (17 participants) indicated that they were aware of their skin picking at the start of an episode more than half of the time, 13% (3 of 23) were aware half of the time, and 13% (3 of 23) were aware less than half of the time. Skin picking episodes typically lasted anything from less than five minutes to up to three hours. As a result of skin picking, the majority of individuals experienced clinically significant interference in their daily functioning and lives. The vast majority were significantly distressed. Ten participants (43%) found their symptoms to be disturbing but manageable, seven (30%) found the symptoms to be very distressing, and three (13%) described constant and disabling distress in relation to their symptoms.

As a result of skin picking, 58% of participants (11 of 19) experienced a moderate degree of tissue damage. Mild tissue damage was reported by 26% (five of 19), and severe tissue damage was reported by 5% (one of 19); 11% (two of 19) reported no damage at all. Numerous dermatological complications were reported. Infection was the most common occurrence (18%, six of 33). Bleeding (6%, two of 33) and inflammation (3%, one of 33) were also reported. For some individuals with particularly severe forms of skin picking, corrective surgery was necessary (6%, two of 33). Moreover, 38% of participants (nine of 24) had sought some sort of other professional help, including visiting their general practitioner or internist. In general, participants generally reported that they did not obtain significant relief from their negative emotions after picking. After excoriation, individuals report a significant increase in the intensity of feelings of physical pain, guilt, and shame. They experienced a significant decrease in intensity of their sense of satisfaction, and tension after picking. There was no significant change in their sense of control over the situation or their feelings of being mesmerized.

5.8 Neurobiological Models

One neurobiological model of psychogenic excoriation is that of a repetitive behavior which has evolved phylogenetically. Skin excoriation is present in all mammals and may present itself in dogs as "canine acral lick," a self-inflicted disorder caused by continued licking, biting, and/or scratching the skin (Rapoport et al., 1992). Another animal model in birds is compulsive feather-picking (Grindlinger & Ramsay, 1991). Like skin excoriation, it appears to be triggered by boredom, confinement, loneliness, or provoked by local irritation (similar to humans). One hypothesis is that body-focused repetitive behaviors may be an attempt by genetically prone individuals to regulate an internal state of stimulatory balance (Penzel, 2003). Thus examining and picking provides both visual and tactile stimulation to relieve states of under-arousal (e.g., boredom, inactivity) and over-arousal (e.g., anxiety, depression).

Psychogenic excoriation similar to hair-pulling can also be regarded as inappropriate grooming behavior (Graybiel, 1998). Some episodes of excoriation can be done in an highly automated manner, associated with an impaired ability to inhibit the motor response similar to OCD and trichotillomania (Chamberlain et al., 2006). In terms of learning theory, impulse control disorders seem to involve positive reinforcement similar to addictive disorders. This in contrast to behaviors performed to reduce anxiety that involve negative reinforcement. The nucleus accumbens and serotonergic circuits may therefore play an important role.

There may also be abnormal opiate receptor sensitivity in individuals with stereotypic self-injurious behaviors. Frecska & Arato (2002) used fentanyl-induced prolactin response as an opiate receptor sensitivity test in patients with stereotypic movement disorder who manifested skin excoriation. Healthy volunteers and trichotillomanic patients were used as comparison groups. Those with skin excoriation, but not trichotillomania or healthy volunteers, showed significantly increased responses, which suggests the involvement of endogenous opiates in the pathophysiology of stereotypic SIB.

5.9   Evidence for Pharmacotherapy

The evidence base for the treatment of psychogenic excoriation (BDD or not) by either CBT or pharmacotherapy is extremely small. The studies which have been published are hampered by the lack of information on related comorbidity, chronicity, or whether the symptoms were predominantly compulsive, impulsive, or mixed. Furthermore, RCTs and case series of BDD usually include cases with and without psychogenic excoriation and are not separately reported.

In theory, fluoxetine might be helpful for those whose psychogenic excoriation is related to over-arousal. There has been one RCT of fluoxetine in psychogenic excoriation with a range of diagnoses (Simeon et al., 1997). There were 21 participants in whom one had panic disorder, two had social phobia, three had a simple phobia, three had OCD, four had GAD, two had major depressive episodes, five had dysthymia, and one had somatization disorder. They were *excluded* if they had BDD. There was a flexible dosing schedule of up to 80 mg (mean 55 mg) for 10 weeks in 21 patients in a double-blind placebo-controlled trial. There was a significant reduction in the frequency of excoriation compared to placebo according to two out of three outcome measures for the completer analysis and one of the three outcomes for the intention to treat. There was no relationship between reduction in excoriation and changes in measures of depression, anxiety, or obsessive compulsive symptoms. The study is difficult to interpret because of the small numbers and may be less relevant to those with BDD. However fluoxetine has demonstrated efficacy in those with BDD (Phillips et al., 2002).

There has also been one open label study of fluoxetine (Bloch et al., 2000) and several case reports (Stout, 1990; Gupta & Gupta, 1993; Stein et al., 1993; Phillips et al., 1995; Vittorio & Phillips, 1997). Other case reports of SSRIs include sertraline (Kalivas et al., 1996), fluvoxamine (Arnold et al., 1999; O'Sullivan et al., 1999), paroxetine, (Biondi et al., 2000), and clomipramine (Gupta et al., 1986). There are also two case reports in which SSRI treatment may have induced or aggravated skin excoriation (Denys et al., 2003). This has also been observed by one of the authors (DV): when a patient with chronic psychogenic excoriation stopped taking fluoxetine after many years, there was significant improvement and she ceased picking.

Little is known about the long-term efficacy of SSRI in psychogenic excoriation, the use of an SSRI in adolescents with psychogenic excoriation, or whether there is a higher rate of relapse when the person discontinues the drug (that is similar to SSRIs in OCD).

There are case reports describing the benefit of pimozide in two patients with psychogenic excoriation (Duke, 1983). In theory, a neuroleptic in a low dose might be useful. The dose was initially 4 mg a day and both patients improved after a month. Olanzapine has also been described in three case reports (Garnis-Jones et al., 2000; Gupta & Gupta, 2000; Blanch et al., 2004). Of the three cases one was a non-delusional patient (dose up to 7.5 mg daily); the second patient experienced improvements on 2.5 mg a day along with isotretoin for facial acne; and the third also improved on a low dosage. Lienemann & Walker (1989), describe the use of an opiate antagonist (naltrexone) at 50 mg per day. It reduced the frequency and pruritus in a patient who had no response to prednisolone.

5.10   Evidence for Cognitive Behavior Therapy

There are no RCTs of CBT for psychogenic excoriation. There are a number of case reports, but most of the individuals did not report whether they also had BDD. Rosenbaum & Ayllon (1981) first described the use of habit reversal in four individuals whose scratching had aggravated their "neurodermatitis" (a condition that begins with minor infection or skin lesion, which produces itching and subsequent scratching). Habit reversal includes multiple components: self-monitoring to increase awareness, competing response training, and stimulus control. We describe habit reversal in detail in Chapter 21.

Kent & Drummond (1989) described the use of habit reversal in one case of "acne excoriée," in which the person picked real or imagined acneiform lesions, resulting in worsening of acne. Twohig & Woods (2001) describe the successful use of a simplified habit reversal in two male patients with psychogenic excoriation but without any significant comorbid psychiatric disorder. Deckersbach et al. (2002) reported the use of habit reversal and other components of cognitive restructuring in two out three patients with psychiatric comorbidity. One case had BDD alone, one had dysthymia, attention deficit disorder and BDD, and one had no other current comorbidity. They noted that "habit-like" excoriation appeared to respond better to habit reversal than when excoriation functioned to regulate intense emotion.

There are two cases of "acne excoriée" treated with pulsed laser irradiation and "cognitive psychodynamic therapy" (Bowes & Alster, 2004). No details are provided on the psychological intervention, although "basic" behavior modification techniques were used (e.g., avoidance of unnecessary situations of conflict and removal of mirrors from the house). The second individual had comorbid OCD and depression, which was treated with venlafaxine. She was "counselled" to avoid the affected areas and treated with laser scar revision.

Twohig & Woods (2006) evaluated the effectiveness of a version of acceptance and commitment therapy (ACT) for chronic skin picking. Self-monitoring of skin picking showed that four of the five participants reached near-zero levels of picking at post-treatment, but these gains were not fully maintained for three of the four participants at follow-up. The findings of the self-reported skin picking were generally corroborated by ratings of photographs of the damaged areas and by ratings on a validated measure of skin picking severity. All participants rated the intervention as socially acceptable, and reductions were found on measures of anxiety, depression, and experiential avoidance for most participants as a result of the intervention.

O'Connor (2005) has developed a model for reducing tics, which emphasises muscle discrimination, tension reduction and sensori-motor exposure. This model could also be applied to skin-picking.

From the above, it is clear that much needs to be researched on CBT for psychogenic excoriation. The evidence for habit reversal has come from other impulse and habit disorders such a trichotillomania (Azrin et al., 1980).

It may be helpful to differentiate patients with BDD from other patients such as OCD or BPD in RCTs because the treatment and prognosis may be different. It is also important to do a functional analysis (e.g., patients in whom the excoriation is driven by emotional regulation or has become like a habit disorder) and investigate the motivation and in what contexts the behavior occurs in those with a habit disorder and those with BDD.

Chapter 6

Psychological aspects of cosmetic procedures

Summary

No book about BDD could fail to review the evidence for cosmetic surgery and the context in which individuals seek help from cosmetic practitioners. There has been a marked increase in the number of cosmetic procedures performed over the past decade. However, there have been very few studies on the psychosocial benefits of cosmetic procedures and there are no prospective studies to determine risk factors for dissatisfaction. The majority of individuals who have cosmetic procedures do not have BDD and are generally satisfied with the outcome. However, in individuals with BDD the outcome is unpredictable. Retrospective studies of cosmetic procedures in people with BDD attending a psychiatric clinic are that some clients may be satisfied with the cosmetic procedure, but most experience an exacerbation of or no change in BDD symptoms, and only a minority report improvement. The majority of people with BDD seen in mental health services are either dissatisfied with the procedure or the preoccupation transfers to a different part of the body. One small, prospective study found that although people with BDD may be satisfied with the procedure, their symptoms of BDD (preoccupation, distress, and handicap) persist as the preoccupation shifts to another feature.

Sections

6.1 Cosmetic procedures
6.2 Psychosocial outcomes
6.3 Psychiatric contraindications to surgery

Body Dysmorphic Disorder: A Treatment Manual. David Veale and Fugen Neziroglu
© 2010 John Wiley & Sons, Ltd.

6.1   Cosmetic Procedures

In the USA, a total of 2.1 million cosmetic procedures were performed in 2000; this had increased to 10.2 million in 2008 (The American Society for Aesthetic Plastic, 2008). The number of cosmetic *surgical* procedures had however increased from 0.92 million in 1997 to 1.76 in the same period. The top five surgical procedures are now mammoplasty augmentation or lift, liposuction, cosmetic eyelid surgery, rhinoplasty, and abdominoplasty. Men represented 8% of the total. The top five procedures for them were liposuction, rhinoplasty, eyelid surgery, breast reduction, and hair transplantation. The increase in popularity of cosmetic procedures and beauty products partly reflects the financial prosperity of the population, coupled with widespread dissatisfaction with appearance and body image. We have previously stressed that body dissatisfaction is not the same as BDD. The latter can be conceptualized as at the extreme end of a continuum of body dissatisfaction or body shame. Furthermore, for the vast majority of people, seeking a cosmetic procedure does not imply psychopathology. However, many people with BDD are attracted to cosmetic procedures as being the solution to their problems and it is for this reason that we focus our attention on it in this chapter.

6.2   Psychosocial Outcomes

Sarwer et al. (1998) and Castle et al. (2002) reviewed the literature on psychosocial outcomes after cosmetic surgery for all patients (not identified as BDD). They found only 36 longitudinal studies of varying design and quality over the past 50 years. Most were investigations of patients undergoing a specific procedure (e.g., rhinoplasty) and the follow-up period ranged from post-operative to 10 years after the procedure (in one study). Only 11 studies included a control group. Overall, most patients were satisfied with the results of the surgery and felt more self-confident after it. However, many of the studies had methodological problems, such as the absence of blind raters or valid assessment measures. However, surgeons' headaches and claims for negligence arise from the minority of patients who are dissatisfied with their outcomes. There is a paucity of good quality, large, prospective studies on predictors of dissatisfaction and poor psychosocial outcome. Putative factors associated with poor outcome include being male, young, suffering from depression or anxiety, and having a personality disorder (Castle et al., 2002). Other authors have suggested that the nature and degree of surgical change ("type-change" procedures, e.g., rhinoplasty) are more difficult to adjust to than "restorative" procedures (e.g., rhytidectomy) (Sarwer et al., 1998). The extent of changes in sensation following the procedure (a feeling of skin-tightening after a rhytidectomy or loss of nipple sensation after breast augmentation) may also influence outcome, with greater sensory disturbances lessening the chances of good adjustment (Pruzinsky & Borkovec, 1990).

Lastly, the client's expectation of outcome appears to be important: a distinction may be drawn between expectations regarding the self (e.g., improvement of body image and self-confidence) and expectations relating to external factors (e.g., a client's wish to please his or her partner). The latter might be associated with lower levels of satisfaction. However, it should be emphasized that these putative factors have not been properly evaluated in any prospective studies.

6.3   Psychiatric Contraindications to Surgery

Cosmetic surgery is usually contraindicated in three groups of clients. The first group consists of clients with psychosis, mania, or severe depression, who lack capacity or whose judgement about the need for surgery may be impaired. They may have systematized delusions or command hallucinations about cosmetic surgery or the surgeon. This, fortunately, is rare and will never be a subject of a controlled trial.

The second group in whom cosmetic surgery might be contraindicated are those with eating disorders, who might be attracted to procedures such as liposuction or abdominoplasty. However, there are no data to guide the clinician. Screening for a history of bulimia would be important if only because of the possibility of electrolyte imbalance and cardiac arrhythmias during surgery. In addition, there may be an expectation that surgery will enable them to stop bingeing or purging and this certainly may not be the case. There are no prevalence studies of people with eating disorders presenting in a cosmetic surgery clinic or prospective outcome studies in clients with eating disorders. There is likely to be a publishing bias of negative case reports. McIntosh et al. (1994) described two women who had breast augmentation. After CBT, they regretted having surgery and became more concerned about the possible health risks of the implants. Yates et al. (1988) report two cases (both women) of eating disorders. In the first, breast augmentation provided a decrease in symptoms of bulimia for about three months. The other woman had a chin and nose reconstruction. She experienced a remission of her eating disorder for about a month. Both appeared pleased with the results of their surgery but disappointed with the recurrence of their eating disorder. Lastly, Losee et al. (1997) reported improvements in several patients with symptoms of eating disorder with breast reduction, but not in all.

The third group in whom cosmetic surgery is usually contraindicated is those with a diagnosis of BDD. Many clients with BDD seek repeated consultations with surgeons but do not necessarily proceed with surgery, either due to lack of money or for other personal reasons. Many clients like to seek the reassurance of surgeons that their problem feature exists and that it could be corrected. Alternatively, they may spend hours researching clinics or surgeons on the Internet.

Some studies have looked at postoperative outcome in individuals with minimal deformity who have undergone cosmetic surgery. Some of these early studies implied that those with minimal deformity may have had BDD, although preoperatively no formal diagnosis was made. Hay & Heather (1973) studied patients with varying degrees of deformity and concluded that even patients with minor defects could benefit from surgery. Similarly, Connolly & Gibson (1978) studied 187 patients 15 years after rhinoplasty and found that patients may feel better about themselves. Thomas (1990) stated the decision to operate on a patient of normal appearance is hazardous. His opinion was that dissatisfaction with appearance will continue and further requests for cosmetic surgery will be made.

There are four retrospective studies of cosmetic surgery in BDD patients attending a psychiatric clinic. The first was by Phillips et al. (1993) who reported on eight patients who had between them undergone 25 plastic or dental surgery procedures. Only two procedures led to an improvement or remission of symptoms, while 20 procedures resulted in an exacerbation of symptoms. Phillips et al. (1997) reported, in an extended sample of 188 BDD patients, that 131 patients sought and 109 received surgical, dermatological, or other medical treatments; of these 83% reported an exacerbation of or no change in BDD symptoms. The most common outcome following surgery was no change in overall BDD severity (58%) and no change in the concern with the treated body part (48.3%). More patients worsened in overall BDD severity (24.3%) than improved (17.4%). However, in terms of the treated body part, more patients reported a decrease (34.5%) than an increase (17.2%) in concern. This discrepancy may be attributable to the expectation that improvement of the affected body part would lead to satisfaction. However, patients often note that some change in the affected part is not sufficient for them to look precisely the way they want. Therefore, it is likely that satisfaction with improving a "defect" is not sufficient to change the evaluation of their appearance and their emotional biases. This disappointment, and the loss of hope in surgery as a means to improve their appearance, led to a worsening of their preoccupation.

Yaryura-Tobias & Neziroglu (1997b) initially reported that of the patients who refused CBT or medication and pursued surgery, 50% improved minimally but enough to accept treatment. They suggested that their self-perception and overvalued ideas may have been altered enough to enter treatment. Recently, one of the authors (FN) has noticed that there is a two-pronged phenomenon: the client who believes that the surgery has improved the appearance of the defect but nevertheless experiences an exacerbation of symptoms of BDD without transferring focus to a different body part. A possible explanation may be that the appearance does improve slightly but not to the extent the client wanted and therefore further despair sets in. There is no alternative but to pursue more surgery but the client is now quite skeptical and does not believe this will accomplish his goal. This may explain the two initial discrepant findings of Phillips & Yaryura-Tobias and Neziroglu. Both may be correct, and may have assessed two different aspects of the surgery as noted above.

Veale et al. (1996) reported that in a series of 50 BDD patients in the UK, 26% had obtained one or more cosmetic operations but no outcome data were collected. Later, Veale et al. (2003) reported on 25 BDD patients in the UK at the time of psychiatric assessment prior to cosmetic surgery. Patients were asked to rate their degree of satisfaction with the outcome of each procedure; any change in the overall amount of time and distress they experienced thinking about their appearance after the operation; and any change in the overall degree of handicap in relation to their occupational and social life after the operation. They reported that 76% of these were dissatisfied postoperatively having received (between them) 46 procedures. Many had taken out loans or borrowed money from relatives for private surgery. Three patients (12%) claimed that they were not preoccupied by their appearance prior to the surgery and that their symptoms of BDD developed only after surgery, which, they believed, had been done badly. This is similar to Freud's Wolf Man (Brunswick, 1928), who became obsessed with a minimal scar after a cyst had been removed. This is the experience of both authors: i.e., surgery may be a trigger for the development of BDD. It is very hard to determine retrospectively whether the patients had minimal symptoms of BDD, which were fully manifested after surgery, or whether it elicited the onset of BDD. Some operations, such as rhinoplasty, appear to be associated with greater dissatisfaction. The nose is also the most common location for complaint by BDD patients. Most of the patients in the Veale (2000) study had multiple concerns about their appearance and reported that after 50% of the procedures the preoccupation transferred to another area of their body. When patients were dissatisfied with their operation, they often felt guilty or angry with themselves or at the surgeon for having made their appearance worse, thus further fuelling their depression and a failure to achieve their ideal. This in turn tended to increase mirror-gazing and craving for more surgery. Six patients (24%) rated themselves satisfied with their procedure (defined as a rating of 7–10). Four of these patients went on to have one or more further procedures or were dissatisfied with another area of their body but did not have further surgery. Mammaplasty and pinnaplasty (ear pinning) tended to have relatively higher satisfaction ratings. These operations are usually unambiguous in that patients can describe the problem that concerns them and their desired outcome, and the cosmetic surgeon can understand their expectations.

One weakness of these studies is that there is no control group of normal or psychiatric patients who have undergone cosmetic surgery but do not have BDD. However, the majority of individuals (who do not have BDD) are satisfied with cosmetic surgery, and their self-esteem and other psychological measures will improve (Klassen et al, 1996; Harris & Carr, 2001). The main weaknesses of these studies are that the data are retrospective and there is a selection bias of patients in favor of treatment failures. Theoretically, mental health practitioners will not see BDD patients who are satisfied with their cosmetic surgery and whose symptoms of BDD improve. It is, however, difficult to conduct large prospective studies that identify clients with BDD before surgery and then follow them up. Tignol et al. (2007) did evaluate the effect of cosmetic surgery in 30 patients with a minimal defect in appearance (of whom 12 had BDD and 18 non-BDD) five years after their request for cosmetic surgery. Of the 30, it was possible to re-evaluate 24 (80%) by telephone interview (10 with BDD and 14 non-BDD). Seven participants with BDD had undergone cosmetic surgery vs. eight non-BDD. Patient satisfaction with the surgery was high in both groups. Nevertheless at follow-up, six of the seven operated BDD patients still had a diagnosis of BDD and exhibited higher levels of handicap and psychiatric comorbidity compared to people without BDD. Five of the six BDD patients at follow-up were preoccupied with a new body site. There was a slight but non-significant decline in disability scales after surgery. Moreover, three non-BDD patients had developed BDD after surgery. Patient satisfaction with surgery may contribute to explaining why some plastic surgeons continue to operate. At this stage, it is not known what factors might predict satisfaction in BDD patients who undergo cosmetic surgery and in whom the preoccupation does not transfer to another part of the body.

6.4   Cosmetic Phalloplasty

Cosmetic phalloplasty deserves special mention as there are a number of papers by surgeons who describe "penile dysmorphic disorder." Penile augmentation is becoming an increasingly popular procedure. Li et al. (2006) reported on 42 men, of whom 27 (64%) had "penile dysmorphic disorder," who underwent division of the penile suspensory ligament. Their preoperative penile stretched length (a good indicator of erect length) was 11.5 cm, which is in the normal range (the mean being 13 cm). The mean increase in length was only 1 cm. In some patients who persevere with postoperative stretching exercises as much as 3 cm gain can be achieved. Some had a small degree of penile shortening, which can usually be prevented by the addition of a spacer to prevent reattachment. However, the satisfaction rate in those with penile dysmorphic disorder was 27% and 54% requested further surgery. The satisfaction in those with congenital micropenis, penile carcinoma, and trauma was much higher, although the number of patients was much smaller. One complication of division of the penile suspensory ligament is of decreased angle of elevation of the erect penis and sexual dysfunction. It is unfortunate that the authors did not do more comprehensive measures of psychosocial outcome as it is unclear who is likely to be satisfied with this procedure.

Other surgeons report good results with penile girth enhancement. Spyropoulos et al. (2005) reported on 11 out of 28 "psychosomatically normal men (25–35 years) who presented complaining of penile dysmorphophobia," who had (a) penile lengthening (suprapubic skin advancement – ligamentolysis) (N = 5); (b) penile lengthening and shaft thickening (free dermal fat graft shaft coverage) (N = 3); and (c) panniculectomy – suprapubic lipectomy and penile lengthening (N = 2). The mean penile length gain (flaccid–stretched penis) was 1.6 cm (1–2.3 cm), the mean circumference gain was 2.3 cm at the base and 2.6 cm subcoronaly. Significant (20%–53%) sexual self-esteem and functioning improvement were reported by the majority (91%) of patients.

Perovic et al. (2006) operated on 204 men (mean age 26) with "penile dysmorphic disorder" and previous failed surgery for penile girth enhancement. A total of 84 randomly selected patients were followed 1–5 years postoperatively (median 24 months). The gain in girth ranged from 1.9 to 4.1 cm (mean 3.15 cm). Postoperative complications occurred in three. The procedure was judged by patients on a scale of 1–5: the best mark (5) was given by 44.05%, very good (4) by 36.90%, good (3) by 19.05% and only one patient gave the mark 2, judging general penile appearance as dissatisfactory. Mean score was 4.25. These and other studies in urology literature would have benefited from psychiatric and psychological evaluation pre- and postoperatively as it is not clear whether they necessarily satisfied criteria for BDD pre- or postoperatively or what psychosocial outcomes occurred in the long term, especially in Perovic et al.'s (2006) study.

6.5   Cosmetic Vaginoplasty

Whereas some men want bigger penises, some women are distressed by the size, shape, or proportion of their labia being too big. However, labia and clitoral size and shape vary enormously among women (Lloyd et al., 2005). In response to the lack of knowledge about size and shape of the vagina, a body sculptor has tried to educate the public by creating vaginal molds and displaying them *en masse* (www.brightonbodycasting.com/design-a-vagina.php).

Labiaplasty is becoming increasingly common, with the incidence in the National Health Service (NHS) in the UK, doubling between 1998–9 and 2004–5 (Liao & Creighton, 2007). No studies have been done on the prevalence in BDD in women seeking labiaplasty. In this regard it may be important for cosmetic gynecologists to define when the degree of protrusion or hypertrophy of the labia minora is no longer a minor defect (which would exclude a diagnosis of BDD). One of the authors (FN) has seen several women seeking labiaplasty in recent years because of her affiliation with gynecologists. Most of the women had either bulkiness or a slight protrusion of their labia, but were not abnormal in size. Because it is not appropriate for mental health professionals to assess the size or shape of the labia of women, the clinician must rely on a gynecologist or family doctor who has examined the patient.

Labiaplasty may be requested for predominantly functional reasons (e.g., because of complaints that the labia rub on the clothes). They may not wear panties because they believe their labia "get stuck" between the seams or their underwear does not fit them properly. Alternatively, they may complain that their labia become trapped inside the vagina when they have sexual intercourse. Labiaplasty may also be requested for cosmetic reasons (e.g., being excessively self-conscious about their appearance in changing rooms or during intimacy). Women may request flat vulvas with no protrusion beyond the labia majora, similar to the prepubescent aesthetic that is seen in advertisements (Liao & Creighton, 2007). Cartwright & Cardozo (2008) note that labiaplasty is often not justified on medical grounds and is being performed without adequate evidence of safety or psychosocial benefit. Liao & Creighton (2007) highlight the lack of an evidence base on psychosocial outcome. In addition, although the decision to have surgery always has a strong psychosocial basis, women seeking such surgery may tailor their reasons for doing so. This makes audit information on patient satisfaction or psychosocial benefits difficult to collect (Bramwell et al., 2007). In one qualitative study of the experience of labiaplasty (Bramwell et al., 2007), participants described feeling weird or abnormal. The motivation for labia reduction was to appear "normal" and to improve their sex life. It was found that their expectations of the outcome of surgery on their sex lives were not all fulfilled, resulting in a second operation in two cases. Some patients seeking labiaplasty may have BDD, although a preoccupation with the size or shape of the labia being abnormal or too big genitalia in women is an uncommon presentation in psychiatric clinics.

6.6   Identifying BDD in Cosmetic Surgery Settings

In Chapter 3 we reviewed six surveys of BDD in a cosmetic surgery setting which suggest that the prevalence rate is between 3% and 18%. The rate depends on the procedures offered at each clinic, the sex ratio, the diagnostic threshold, and the instrument used to measure BDD.

There may be difficulties in the diagnosis of BDD in a cosmetic clinic and in deciding when the patient has a "minor physical anomaly" or when it becomes a more significant "anomaly" and when the concern becomes "markedly excessive." It is worth remembering that aesthetic cosmetic surgery is about enhancing a normal appearance, so most patients will look perfectly "normal." Alternatively, a surgeon may describe the appearance in medical jargon, when it is still part of a normal variation. However, patients will latch on to this as if it were a medical diagnosis in order to "prove" that they do have an abnormal appearance. The major unanswered questions are what predicts satisfaction with cosmetic surgery in BDD patients and when symptoms of BDD improve. One of the authors (DV) has examined the differences between 23 individuals without BDD in a cosmetic surgery clinic who were satisfied with their rhinoplasty and 16 patients in a psychiatric clinic diagnosed with BDD (Veale et al., 2003). The BDD patients were selected if they craved rhinoplasty but for various reasons had not obtained it (e.g., they could not afford it or feared the operation would fail). The BDD group was significantly younger than the rhinoplasty patients but there was no significant difference in sex. As expected, BDD patients had higher scores on YBOCS-BDD (Phillips et al., 1997) and anxiety and depression on the HAD scales (Zigmond & Snaith, 1983). BDD patients were more distressed and reported much greater interference in their social and occupational functioning and in intimate relationships because of their nose. They were more socially anxious, tended to avoid situations, checked their nose in mirrors, or felt it with their fingers and believed that cosmetic surgery would significantly alter their life (e.g., help them to obtain a new partner or job). BDD patients were significantly more likely to be dissatisfied with other areas of their body. They were also likely to have attempted DIY surgery. In summary, BDD patients who desire cosmetic rhinoplasty are a quite different population from those patients who obtain routine cosmetic rhinoplasty. This study provides a number of clues that are useful in the development of a screening questionnaire or structured interview to assist cosmetic surgeons to identify individuals with BDD who are unsuitable for cosmetic surgery. However good a questionnaire or interview, patients may be economical with the truth, and even when a surgeon identifies possible symptoms of BDD, they may not agree to a referral to a mental health practitioner and may merely take themselves to another surgeon. More research is required to enable practitioners to identify BDD patients and to explain when cosmetic surgery can be indicated in BDD in a prospective outcome study.

In the USA, a patient made an unsuccessful claim against her surgeon on the grounds that he should have refrained from operating on her in view of her BDD (Kaplan, 2000). Such cases may well increase and it is very important to document the recommendations to the patient and surgeon and ensure they both receive written communications.

In summary, we have very few data to support the efficacy of cosmetic procedures in BDD. Most retrospective studies seem to suggest dissatisfaction and worsening or shifting of BDD symptoms. Even when satisfaction with the surgery is expressed, patients remain preoccupied with their specific defects. In a few cases when the desired outcome is unambiguous (e.g., mammaplasty) or when patients do not expect any significant change in their symptoms of BDD and psychosocial situation, satisfaction with surgery may also be expressed, but once again this does not mean a reduction in BDD symptoms. Where there are multiple concerns, the preoccupation is often likely to transfer to a different area of the body. At worst cosmetic surgery leads to dissatisfaction, and symptoms of BDD may intensify. Rarely, dissatisfied patients with BDD resort to harassment and violence against a surgeon (Lucas, 2002). In a survey of plastic surgeons in the USA, 41% claimed that a BDD patient had threatened them legally and/or physically (Sarwer, 2002). A prospective study of BDD patients undergoing different cosmetic procedures with long-term follow-up is required to determine long-term effects and to assess whether some patients eventually become satisfied after several operations.

6.7　Do-it-Yourself Surgery

Do-it-yourself (DIY) surgery is an attempt by the patient to alter their appearance drastically by their own hand. Veale (2000) reported on eight BDD patients who, either in desperation at being turned down for cosmetic surgery or because they could not afford it, had performed DIY surgery. The procedures were often associated with many hours of mirror-gazing and intense disgust at their perceived defect. DIY surgery is best viewed as an extreme safety-seeking behavior that aims to alter the appearance. DIY surgery has a poor psychological outcome in so far as nearly all the patients in the Veale study were dissatisfied with the outcome and found their symptoms of BDD had exacerbated. It reflects the extreme measures that some patients feel driven to take.

A few examples from Veale (2000) and others are described below:

1. A young man was preoccupied by his skin, which he believed was "too loose." He had consulted a cosmetic surgeon who had turned down his request for a facelift. In desperation, he used a staple gun on both sides of his face to try to keep his skin taut. The staples fell out after 10 minutes and he narrowly missed damaging his facial nerve.
2. A man who was preoccupied with the appearance of his chin said that, as an adolescent, he had deliberately cycled into the back of a lorry in an attempt to fracture his jaw so that it could be reset in the way that he wanted. At the last moment, he decided against the plan, dropped his head, cut his forehead and fractured his skull, necessitating five weeks of inpatient treatment.
3. A woman reported striking her nose with a hammer in an attempt to reduce a bump. She later obtained funding for a rhinoplasty.
4. A man dissatisfied with his drooping eyelids would try to lift them by holding his lashes up to his eyebrows for hours.
5. A woman preoccupied by "lines" on her knee and wrinkles on her face repeatedly used an iron to remove her lines resulting in significant burns. She experienced an impulse to use the iron, which she found difficult to resist.

There are also reports of injection of paraffin and Vaseline into the penis and even the use of a high pressure grease-gun injection (Kalsi et al., 2002). Phillips (1996a) reported on a man who cut open his nose with a razor blade and attempted to replace his nose cartilage with chicken cartilage to obtain the desired shape. Other unpublished or less dramatic examples of DIY surgery include an adolescent unhappy with her nose who spent hours pulling it from side to side, using tweezers to get the corners just right, and banging the bridge of her nose with her hands. Virtually all cases reported are dissatisfied with the results of their attempts at DIY surgery, which, like most safety behaviors, lead to an increase in preoccupation, distress, and symptoms, such as checking. Some of the DIY procedures required formal surgery to rectify the injuries. Not all DIY procedures are as drastic. Some patients may tape their noses or eyelashes up, or their ears back, and some may use a clothes peg to pinch their nose to make the nasal passages smaller. The intention is the same, but the procedures vary.

Other symptoms of BDD such as psychogenic excoriation (Chapter 5) (Phillips & Taub, 1995) can also be construed as attempts to change appearance by one's own hand (e.g., "to make it perfectly smooth"). Invariably, such practices worsen the appearance and may then justify dermatological or cosmetic surgery. O'Sullivan et al. (1999) describe a patient who attempted to remove skin irregularities, eventually becoming preoccupied with a skin imperfection on her neck. The patient used tweezers to create a defect through her dermis, subcuticular tissue, and neck musculature exposing the carotid artery.

6.8　Dermatological Procedures

In the dermatology literature, BDD is found to be common but underdiagnosed (Koblenzer, 1992; Hanes, 1995). Many seek dermatological treatment for years and pressure the dermatologist to keep prescribing unsuitable treatments despite a poor response. In a study of 268 dermatology patients, approximately 12% screened positive for BDD (Phillips et al., 2000). Patients were most frequently concerned with elasticity, coloring, and/or presence of perceived imperfections of their skin such as acne, scars, moles, or cellulite. Skin picking is also common in BDD patients who seek dermatological treatment. The picking behavior itself often creates problems, even when they did not exist before. Cotterill (1981) described 28 patients with "dermatological non-disease," a group of patients who present with dermatological symptoms but with no objective dermatological pathology. He reported that these patients often have BDD and depression, and the areas of concern are usually the face, tongue, scalp, and perineum. High rates of suicidal ideation and suicide are evident in this dermatological population (Cotterill, 1981; Cotterill & Cunliffe, 1997) (as it is within BDD). The fact that many BDD patients seek a dermatological solution does not mean they benefit from it. They may skip from one dermatologist to another, always seeking an answer to an irresolvable problem. Often the initial visit may have been due to a mild skin problem, which then triggered many more visits. The degree of distress, preoccupation, and cause in impairment of functioning is disproportionate to the original problem. In the largest sample of BDD patients 50% sought dermatological treatment and 38% received some form of intervention (Phillips & Diaz, 1997). Again, we have even fewer data on the efficacy of dermatological treatment and we tell patients that a diagnosis of BDD makes the outcome unpredictable. In very few cases dermatological treatment may lead to some satisfaction or decrease of symptoms of BDD, but whether this is because of the dermatological procedure is unclear. It is the opinion of the authors that many dermatologists make the patients even more obsessional. They give them precise routines to perform while applying various creams and this leads to further mirror-checking and obsessions. Some examples of suggestions given by dermatologists that increased obsessionality are:

- Make sure you use only white towels because the dye can aggravate your condition.
- You need to put the creams on with extremely clean hands.
- You may use sanitizers before the application.
- Keep your hands and face very clean, wash your hands and face often.
- Eat only these precise foods so your face is not oily; etc.

Clinical aspects of assessment and therapy for patients requesting a cosmetic or dermatological procedure are discussed in Chapter 15.

Chapter 7

Risk factors in the development of BDD

Summary

An understanding of how BDD develops is largely unknown. BDD is very under-researched compared to other psychiatric disorders, including other body image problems such as eating disorders. Putative risk factors include genes, temperament, childhood adversity, a past history of dermatological disorder or other physical stigmata, homosexuality in men, aesthetic sensitivity, and parental interaction styles. Many of the risk factors are not specific to BDD and remain very speculative. The exception to this in BDD may be aesthetic sensitivity. This is discussed in the context of the psychology of beauty. Potential risk factors are likely to be additive and interact with a biological vulnerability, which then leads to the final common pathway. In this regard it will be important first to define the various phenotypes before investigating their interaction with putative genetic factors. Much further research is required to determine whether the onset of BDD can be prevented, delayed, or mitigated.

Sections

Body Dysmorphic Disorder: A Treatment Manual. David Veale and Fugen Neziroglu
© 2010 John Wiley & Sons, Ltd.

7.1   OCD Spectrum Disorder

To date very limited data are available regarding risk factors for the development and onset of BDD. One of the most important challenges for any epidemiological investigation in this area is distinguishing between risk factors that are specific to BDD and those that predispose to other disorders. BDD is regarded by some as being on the OCD spectrum (Hollander, 1993; Neziroglu & Yaryura-Tobias, 1993a) or of affective disorders (Phillips et al., 1995) because of the similarity in phenomenology and reported comorbidity (Phillips, 1996b; Veale, Boocock, et al., 1996).

BDD and about a third of the diagnoses in DSM IV are described as part of an obsessive compulsive spectrum disorder (OCSD) (Hollander, 1993; Neziroglu & Yaryura-Tobias, 1993a). The spectrum is divided into three broad clusters. The first cluster is a preoccupation with bodily appearance or sensations and includes BDD, hypochondriasis, depersonalization, and anorexia nervosa. These disorders are mainly characterized by intrusive thoughts that are difficult to resist, compulsive behaviors, and difficulties in engaging clients in treatment. There is a high degree of comorbidity with OCD for many of these disorders. This cluster contains some evidence for a specific treatment response to serotonin reuptake inhibitors (SRIs) for BDD. Some of the disorders may also respond to CBT, but there is no evidence that this is a treatment-specific response.

The second cluster is impulse control disorders and includes pathological gambling, kleptomania, sexual compulsions, pyromania, trichotillomania, and self-injurious behavior. Compulsive and impulsive behaviors have a common characteristic: an inability to inhibit repetitive behavior. Whereas compulsions are associated with risk avoidance and a reduction in anxiety, impulsive behaviors are associated with risk-seeking and maximizing pleasure, arousal, or gratification, at least in the short term. There is some evidence that SRIs improve compulsive behaviors after a time-lag, but there is a high rate of relapse when the medication is discontinued. Impulsive disorders may respond to a wider variety of medications including SRIs, with a more rapid response than compulsions, which then decrease over time. CBT is generally more effective at reducing compulsive rather than impulsive behaviors, although the latter are under-researched.

The third cluster of OCSDs includes neurological conditions such as autism, Asperger's syndrome, trichotillomania, simple tics, Tourette's syndrome, encephalitis lethargica, Huntingdon's chorea, and Sydenham's chorea. Again, there is frequent comorbidity with OCD. This cluster includes OCD from an abnormal immune response from Group A beta-haemolytic streptococci in which antibodies bind to the basal ganglia; OCD as a consequence of encaphilitis lethargica; or as part of Tourette's disorder. There is limited evidence for the efficacy of pharmacotherapy or behavior therapy in these conditions, except for tics and Tourette's syndrome.

Neziroglu & Yaryura-Tobias (1993a), Hollander (1993), and others have argued that OCSDs share many features with OCD. These include:

a) Symptom profile: the pattern of repetitive thoughts, urges or behaviors.
b) Associated features: evidence from demographics, family history, comorbidity, and clinical course.
c) Neurobiology: evidence from pharmacological challenge studies, neuroimaging, and immune factors.
d) Aetiology: evidence from genetics and environmental factors.
e) Treatment: a specific response to SRI medications.

Evidence for inclusion of each disorder in an OCSD with these criteria can be argued to a greater or less degree. However, the clinical utility and evidence are limited even in conditions such as BDD and hypochondriasis, which have a stronger argument for a closer relationship with OCD. Conditions such as pedophilia and sexual compulsions have weak evidence for a close relationship with OCD. For example, clients with BDD have a high degree of comorbidity with OCD, whilst those with sexual compulsions do not. Both BDD and pedophilia may have recurrent intrusive thoughts and repetitive behaviors. People with BDD have difficulty in resisting their "compulsive" behaviors (such as mirror-checking), which is similar to OCD. However, a pedophile does not usually wish to inhibit his impulsive behavior.

Recently, the inclusion of any of these being a part of the OCD spectrum or more specifically a subtype of OCD has been called to attention (McKay & Neziroglu, in press). McKay & Neziroglu (in press) assert that it is impossible to make a determination of whether a particular disorder belongs within the spectrum merely by studying phenomenology and treatment response and argue that it is important to do taxometric studies using statistical equivalence and cluster analysis to make such determinations. Phenomenological and treatment-response analyses do not provide sufficient evidence for inclusion or exclusion into a diagnostic category.

7.2   Risk Factors

From the previous discussion on OCS disorders and high levels of comorbidity with depression, a study on risk factors ideally needs to include both non-clinical controls and those with depression and OCD. The onset of BDD is usually in adolescence and therefore particular attention will need to be given to risk factors preceding onset. For example, not all individuals who experience being teased about their appearance develop BDD. One aim of future research will therefore be to determine which factors, or combination of factors, predict future persistence of extreme self-consciousness so that interventions may be devised for those at risk. We review some of the hypothesized risk factors, especially during childhood and adolescence. A diathesis stress model is assumed as with the development of any disorder. Thus individuals who have a biological predisposition may develop a disorder given the right environmental conditions.

7.3   Genetic Factors

BDD, like most psychiatric disorders, is very likely to have a genetic predisposition to its development. Family history data suggest that 6–10% of first-degree family members have BDD (Richter et al., 2004). Bienvenu et al. (2000) investigated the relationship of OCD to putative OCD "spectrum disorders." They compared 80 cases with OCD and 73 control probands as well as 343 cases and 300 control first-degree relatives. They found that BDD, hypochondriasis, any eating disorder, or any habit disorder (but not impulse control disorder such as pyromania, kleptomania or pathological gambling) occurred more frequently in the case probands with OCD compared to controls. The lifetime prevalence of BDD occurred more frequently in case relatives (4% in case relatives compared to 1% of controls) whether or not probands had the same diagnosis. The adjusted odds ratio for the lifetime prevalence of BDD was six times greater in the first-degree relatives with OCD compared to control relatives. Although most of the other spectrum disorders were slightly more common in case relatives than in control relatives, there were no differences in groups with eating disorders or impulse control disorders other than those involving grooming behaviors. They note that other psychiatric disorders such as generalized anxiety disorder appear to be more substantially related to the familial OCD spectrum than many OCD spectrum disorders. The limitations of the study are that only probands with OCD were identified and that no data were collected on the frequency of other psychiatric disorders (to disconfirm a link with OCS disorders). Furthermore the low prevalence of some the disorders of interest limited the ability to detect differences. However, the study does provide evidence of a modest familial association between OCD and relatives having BDD, with 7% of BDD patients having a first-degree relative with OCD.

The only genetic investigation so far is by Richter et al. (2004), who compared the alleles of genes. They found an association between Y-aminobutryic acid (GABA A-Y2) gene and comorbid BDD-OCD but not OCD alone. There was also a trend towards association with the serotonin transporter polymorphism (5-HTTPRL) short allele.

In future, both twin and adoption studies are required to determine the role of specific genes. In this regard it will be important to define the various phenotypes such as perfectionism, extreme self-consciousness, or skin-picking, each of which may have an additive effect. Such an approach has been especially helpful in eating disorders research (Bulik, Devlin et al., 2003; Bulick, Sullivan et al., 2003).

7.4 Temperament

Temperament is the interaction between biological predispositions and the experiences one has with the environment (Prior, 1992). Temperamental traits are known to be dependent on social contexts (Mills et al., 1993; Rubin et al., 1999). Elliot & Thrash (2002) have suggested that there are two broad temperaments, termed approach and avoidance. The latter is characterized by general sensitivity to negative or undesirable (punishment) stimuli. This is supported by factor analysis. Similarly, the temperamental construct of behavioral inhibition refers to a constellation of behaviors such as uneasiness, wariness, lower threshold to autonomic nervous system arousal, and avoidance of novel situations (Garcia-Coll et al., 1984). According to several studies, adolescents who report a history of behavioral inhibition are more likely to develop social anxiety symptoms (Hayward et al., 1998; Mick & Telch, 1998; Schwartz et al., 1999). Of note is that individuals with BDD and comorbid social phobia report that the onset of social phobia *preceded* that of BDD (Gunstad & Phillips, 2003), which suggest a common pathway. Furthermore, the most common personality disorder in BDD is avoidant and such individuals will tend to avoid intimacy and close interpersonal relationships. Further investigation is required to determine the factors that make a child who is social phobic subsequently develop BDD. In summary, an avoidant temperament, with shyness, extreme self-consciousness, or an anxiety, all of which may be partly genetically determined, may be a risk factor for the development of BDD. There is some evidence on the role of temperamental factors in BDD but not in any prospective cohort study to determine whether they are the cause or effect.

7.5   Childhood Adversity

Childhood adversity such as teasing or bullying about appearance or compe-tence, poor peer relationships, social isolation, insecure attachments, lack of support in the family, or sexual abuse may all be non-specific factors in the development of BDD. There is some evidence that repeated childhood adver-sity such as bullying and emotional abuse can be internalized as negative self-criticism. This is *associated* with changes in brain functioning, such as decreased activity of the serotonergic system and increases in cortisol produc-tion (Gilbert & Bailey, 2000).

Osman et al. (2004) found that 15 (88.33%) BDD patients and two (13.3%) control participants identified their images to be closely *associated* with a particular memory during adolescence. Typical themes include being teased and bullied at school for at least a third of the time (e.g., "I was 10 years old and never got on with this boy in school. I remember one day I asked him why he didn't like me and he said 'it's because you're ugly'").

Sexual and emotional abuse appear to be significantly more prevalent in BDD as compared to OCD and controls (Neziroglu et al., 2006) They com-pared 50 OCD and 50 BDD patients and found that significantly more BDD patients (38%) reported abuse as compared to OCD patients (14%). This was predominantly emotional abuse in 14 (28%) BDD and one (2%) OCD indi-viduals. Sexual abuse occurred in 11 (22%) with BDD and three (6%) with OCD, and physical abuse in seven (14%) with BDD and four (8%) with OCD. It appears that almost 25% of the BDD patients experienced emotional or sexual abuse or both. Most of this abuse is perpetrated by male relatives and fathers. They discuss their findings in terms of bodily shame often seen in sexual abuse. Body shame has been linked to early sexual and physical abuse.

Didie et al. (2006) examined the prevalence and clinical associations of childhood abuse and neglect in BDD. Seventy-five subjects (69.3% female, mean age = 35.4 ± 12.0) with BDD completed the Childhood Trauma Question-naire and were interviewed, but there was no control group. Of these 78.7% reported a history of childhood maltreatment: emotional neglect (68.0%), emotional abuse (56.0%), physical abuse (34.7%), physical neglect (33.3%), and sexual abuse (28.0%); and 40% reported severe maltreatment. Among females (N = 52) the severity of reported abuse and neglect was much higher than norms for a health maintenance organization sample of women. Severity of sexual abuse or adversity did not predict current BDD severity in a simulta-neous multiple regression analysis with age and current treatment status.

Andrews (1995; 1997) conducted lengthy interviews that covered attitudes and current or past life experiences. In the study with young women, early abuse was associated with disordered eating and bulimia. In a study with older women, body shame mediated the relationship between early abuse and episodes of chronic or recurrent depression. In the absence of bodily shame, there was no relationship between early abuse and chronic or recurrent depression. In the study by Osman et al. (2004) sexual abuse was linked in 11% of the childhood images, a finding similar to Neziroglu et al.'s (2006). For example, a patient reported that at the age of 15 she felt pretty. However, during a rape she looked in a mirror and saw her face putrefying and decaying and this image from an observer perspective remained with her and became her view of herself.

Insecure attachments and poor parental bonding during childhood may be relevant in the development of BDD. Lambrou (2006) found that on the Insecure Attachment Scale (Livesley et al., 1989; 1992) BDD patients scored significantly higher (mean 47.2, SD 16) than non-psychiatric controls (mean 32.5, SD 10.6). Similarly, Phillips (2001) found that BDD patients as a group had poor parental care scores on the Parental Bonding Instrument compared to published norms. It is not known whether the parental bonding or insecure attachment is perceived or actual, nor whether it is of greater frequency than in other psychiatric populations. There is some evidence that an insecure attachment is an underlying dimension which is mediated through other variables such as body shame and self-consciousness (Lambrou, 2006).

7.6 History of Dermatological or Other Physical Stigmata

Childhood adversity may include being teased about a dermatological disorder (e.g., acne) or other physical stigmata as an adolescent. Such stigmata may be either minor or noticeable and may have attracted teasing. However, the stigmata are usually long since resolved as an adult but the imagery of their previous appearance and associated teasing remains.

Buhlmann et al. (2007) have investigated the role of perceived teasing experiences in a small pilot study of BDD (N = 16) and healthy controls (N = 17). They found that BDD patients reported more appearance-related than competency-related teasing than did controls. There was no psychiatric control group and no difference between the BDD patients and healthy controls for the effect of teasing. What is not known is whether teasing may be a search for meaning after the problem has developed or whether this is a factor in the development of BDD.

Even if no teasing occurs clients often report that they first experienced a change in their body image with the advent of physical stigmata such as acne. Some people with BDD remember being found attractive before acne developed. Equally, social withdrawal due to the negative self-image may have led others to distance themselves from the client rather than the acne being found abhorrent. Other physical stigmata may be height, chubbiness, thinness of legs, etc., which remain in the mind of the client. Yaryura-Tobias, Neziroglu & Torres-Gallegos (2002) suggest that tactile sensations may act as a trigger as clients may report facial tightness and tingling that may trigger urges to check in mirrors.

7.7   Sexual Identity

Young homosexual men may be at a greater risk of BDD, perhaps because of an increased pressure to look attractive within the gay community. There may be other communities with similar societal or cultural pressures that lead to an increased incidence of BDD. However, there are no epidemiological studies on the frequency of homosexuality on BDD. Lambrou et al. (2006) found in a series of 50 individuals with BDD in comparison to 50 non-clinical controls that there was no significant difference in sexual orientation. However, there were only 18 males with BDD and this would be underpowered for such comparisons.

7.8   Sociocultural Factors

As noted in Chapter 3 on epidemiology, virtually no studies have examined prevalence or clinical features of BDD across cultures. Some cultures such as in South America or the Philippines appear to value the importance of appearance and have higher rates of cosmetic surgery. Thus increased pressure for beauty would increase the prevalence of BDD in such cultures.

At the other extreme Islamic states might protect some women against the development of mild BDD as a veil would ensure that such women do not reveal themselves other than to their husband or family. Arab cultures do not value physical attractiveness as much as in the West (Al-Adawi et al., 2001). They believe that beauty may make certain individuals vulnerable to the evil eye and misfortune is blamed on envy (Helman, 1990).

Other cultural aspects and the meaning of certain features may be relevant in individual cases. For example, MacGregor (1981) describes a Puerto Rican woman who was intensely distressed by a small facial scar sustained in an accident. The relevance was that in her ethnic group, a scar was inflicted for punishment for adultery.

7.9   Parental Interactional Styles

Some clients with BDD report that their parents directly or indirectly gave more importance to attractiveness than is normal. They may remember their parents commenting on various body parts of actors or actresses on TV, their own physical characteristics, or characteristics of their friends as compared to themselves. It may also be that people with BDD are more prone to recall such information. Although there is no current study to evaluate perceived family criticism of appearance, one of the authors (FN) has conducted a pilot survey of BDD clients which indicates that familiar modeling and values are significant.

7.10 Aestheticality

The putative risk factors described above are not specific to BDD and remain very speculative. Potential risk factors are likely to be additive and interact with genetic predispositions. In this regard it will be important first to define the various phenotypes before investigating their interaction with putative genetic factors. One risk factor, aesthetic sensitivity, may be more specific to BDD. Aesthetic sensitivity is defined as awareness and appreciation of beauty and harmony.

Being more aesthetically sensitive would be an attribute like being musical, which varies among individuals. However, before discussing the role of aesthetic sensitivity, we need to discuss the broader construct of the psychology of beauty. There is very limited research in beauty and aesthetic perception other than body weight and shape. It has been neglected perhaps because aesthetic perception is regarded as too subjective ("Beauty is in the eye of the beholder") and often defined by the consensus of a group of experts or of a particular culture. Nevertheless, it seems that there are some universal rules about beauty, especially at the extreme ends of attractiveness, as well as individual or cultural variations. We tend to value beauty because it may confer other qualities, which have no other physical markers. Evolutionary psychology holds that attractiveness is important for reproduction and social acceptance; and some individuals might idealize the importance of attractiveness, which can then become a factor in the development of BDD. Perceptions of physical attractiveness have some biological bases, which include a preference for symmetry, averageness, and the exaggeration of secondary sexual characteristics (Etcoff, 1999; Thornhill & Gangestad, 2000).

7.11 Symmetry

One feature of attractiveness is bilateral symmetry (Gombrich, 1984; Zebrowitz et al., 1996). Darwinian theories of beauty predict that sexual selection favors traits that advertise resistance to infections and healthy genes (thus ensuring reproductive capacity) (Thornhill & Gangestad, 1993). Exposure to parasites, pollutants, and extreme temperatures all serve to decrease bilateral symmetry, known as fluctuating asymmetry (Gangestad et al., 1994). For example, male Japanese scorpion flies with the most symmetrical wings have been shown to obtain the most mates; similar biases can be found in other animals (Concar, 1995). A male swallow's chances of finding a mate can be ruined by making their tails less symmetrical (Moller, 1993). In humans, women with evenly matched breasts were found to be more fertile than less evenly endowed matched control group of women (Moller et al., 1995). They also found that symmetry correlated positively with self-reported age at first copulation and number of lifetime partners (Thornhill & Gangestad 1994). Enhancing facial symmetry increases attractiveness ratings for both male and female faces (Perrett et al., 1998; Rhodes et al., 1999). In summary, animals and humans may seek symmetry, perhaps because it advertises biological quality and serves to attract individuals to partners resistant to developmental disruptions and the absence of infections.

The need for symmetry and precision in objects or activities is a recognized symptom in OCD usually associated with ordering, hoarding, repeating, and counting compulsions (Baer, 1994). The symptoms in BDD are very similar to Janet's description of OCD patients who were tormented by an inner sense of imperfection and felt that their actions were never achieved to their satisfaction (Pitman, 1987). In some people with BDD, the need for symmetry and order may be focused on appearance rather than on an object or activity. This is occasionally an overt symptom of the client who complains of a lack of symmetry in some aspect of their appearance. Alternatively, there may be a covert wish for symmetry that clients are unable to articulate but may be possible to demonstrate empirically in an experimental setting.

7.12   Averageness

Langlois & Roggman (1987) suggest that averageness predicts attractiveness. The averaging process also eliminates fluctuating asymmetry, but Rhodes et al. (1999) found that averageness remained attractive in perfectly symmetrical faces. Symons (1987) argues that averageness is attractive because natural selection has a stabilizing effect on facial features so that average traits are functionally optimal (e.g., an average-sized nose is best for breathing) and therefore averageness is associated with good phenotypic condition. However, average faces may not be optimally attractive because many attractive features are non-average, such as exaggerated secondary sexual characteristics.

7.13 Secondary Sexual Characteristics

The size of secondary sexual characteristics that develop during puberty are also important in ratings of attractiveness (Thornhill & Grammer 1994). Jaws, chins, and cheekbones are examples of secondary sexual traits which are enlarged by testosterone during puberty in men and largeness of these features are considered by women as sexually attractive perhaps because of advertised immunocompetence. Female attractiveness, on the other hand, is correlated with the opposite: small jaw, chin, and cheekbones (Johnston & Frankin, 1993). However, although Rhodes et al. (2000) found exaggerated female traits were attractive in female faces, exaggerated female traits were also more attractive in male faces, corroborating findings by Perrett et al. (1998). Rhodes et al.'s and Perrett et al.'s results are particularly significant because there is stronger evidence that sex-typical traits advertise health and immunocompetence in males than females (Thornhill & Moller, 1997).

7.14 Attractiveness

Although the physical cues that determine physical attractiveness are difficult to specify precisely, the assertion that physical attractiveness has important interpersonal and social advantages has been consistently shown. Several studies have demonstrated the benefits of being attractive (or of not being ugly). For example, for students assigned to a blind date, only one factor predicted satisfaction with their date: their physical attractiveness (Walster et al., 1966). In addition, social psychologists have repeatedly demonstrated that people are susceptible to the "what is beautiful is good" stereotype, responding more positively to more attractive individuals than less attractive individuals. For example, mental acuity, interpersonal skills, employability, and moral goodness are all associated with beautiful individuals (Dion et al., 1972; Webster & Driskell, 1983). Attractive individuals are liked more as friends (Dion & Berscheid, 1974) and as sexual partners (Kaats & Davis, 1970). Conversely, a negative stereotype prevails for the physically unattractive (Lacey & Birtchnell, 1986). For instance, jurors were found to set greater fines for less attractive defendants (Downs & Lyons, 1991). People therefore value beauty because it may confer other qualities, which have no physical markers. Evolutionary psychology might argue that because attractiveness is important for reproduction and social acceptance, some individuals will idealize the importance of attractiveness for survival and it will be a factor in the development of BDD. Alternatively, it could be that idealizing the importance of appearance is a consequence of developing BDD. This means that appearance may only become important when a person views him- or herself to be ugly and deformed.

Cash (1990) reviewed the literature on the social consequences of attractiveness and suggests that attractive individuals experience greater encouragement and reinforcement of socially competent behavioral repertoires. By contrast, less attractive individuals experience less responsive social encounters, which discourages the development of competent social skills and self-concept. Physical attractiveness may therefore predispose an individual to any mental disorder and this has been examined in schizophrenia (Napoleon et al., 1980; Archer & Cash, 1985). Thus a strategy of self-monitoring, camouflaging, and enhancing one's appearance is a survival strategy.

7.15   Aestheticality and BDD

The discussion about attractiveness and beauty leads to a number of possible factors in the etiology of BDD. The first is that individuals with BDD are more aesthetically sensitive than the rest of the population (Veale, Gournay et al., 1996; Veale et al., 2002; Veale & Lambrou, 2002). It could be that people with BDD are more aware of subtle differences in facial asymmetry or the size of secondary sexual facial characteristics or are better at evaluating harmony and balance in appearance. This is linked to the concept of "aestheticality" as proposed by Harris (1982). He has argued that individuals seeking cosmetic surgery are more aesthetically sensitive (an attribute, like being musical, which varies in different individuals). The earliest indication that individuals with BDD may be more aesthetically sensitive comes from a study which found that BDD patients as compared to other psychiatric patients were more likely to have had an education or occupation in art and design (Veale et al., 2002): 20% of BDD patients had such an education or occupation compared to 4% in the depressed group, 3% in the OCD group, and 0% in the PTSD group. We do not have any evidence for a causal relationship between BDD and an occupation or education in art and design. Phillips & Menard (2004), however, examined a sample of BDD patients and found that the proportion who were currently employed as artists was approximately twice that of the general population. Although the rate of 1.4% was notably lower than the rate of 20% in the sample in the UK, they cannot be directly compared since Veale et al. (2002) used a much a broader definition of a higher education, training, or an occupation in art and design. Furthermore, Veale et al. used a lifetime definition rather than current occupation. Lambrou (2006) repeated the study in a new sample of 50 patients with BDD and found 22% of BDD patients with an education, occupation, or training in art and design compared to none in 50 healthy controls. This is remarkably similar to the original study, which reported 20% of BDD patients had an education or training in art and design. The onset of BDD is usually gradual during adolescence and an interest in art and design may be a contributory factor to the development of the disorder in some patients. Individuals might develop a more critical eye and appreciation of aesthetics, which is then applied to their own appearance. An alternative explanation is that individuals with BDD have a selection bias for an interest in aesthetics, which is linked to the desire to alter their appearance.

Lambrou (2006) suggests that aesthetic sensitivity has three components: a) perceptual sensitivity (the ability to differentiate variations in aesthetic proportions); b) emotional sensitivity (the degree of emotion experienced when presented with beauty or ugliness); and c) evaluative (aesthetic values, standards and identity). Each of these factors will now be considered in more detail.

For increased aesthetic sensitivity in perception, BDD patients might be more aware of subtle differences in their own facial asymmetry or better at evaluating harmony in appearance. Alternatively, they may have a disorder of perception. Research in eating disorders began with the theory that patients have a disorder of perception. Thus Yaryura-Tobias et al. (2002a) conducted a pilot study on perception on three groups (BDD, OCD, and a non-psychiatric control group) to investigate whether there are abnormalities of perception. There were 30 participants (10 in each group) who were asked to make changes to a computerized image of their face. The participannts were instructed to directly modify or not modify the face according to the way they believed it to be. The experimenter in fact distorted none of the images presented to the participant. They were also tested on Wisconsin Card Sorting Test and the Perceptual Organization factor (picture completion, block design, and matrix reasoning subtests) of the Wechsler Adult Intelligence Scale (WAIS). The three groups did not differ in their scaled scores on the three perceptual organization subtests of the WAIS or on the total number of errors in the Wisconsin Card Sorting Test. None of the 10 participants in the control group altered their photos, but five out of 10 participants in the BDD group made changes and four out of 10 participants in the OCD group made changes. Results indicated a difference between the two patient groups and the control group. The authors suggest that the results support a perceptual defect in some cases of BDD and the need for symmetry and perfectionism by patients with BDD and OCD. However, the apparent perceptual distortion may represent a nonspecific response by someone with a psychiatric disorder to please the experimenter. Furthermore, the method employs a technique that measures the ability to create or re-create an image rather than accuracy of perception. As will be seen from subsequent studies, it is the emotional bias and memory of an image that may be distorted, rather than the perception. For this reason, Yaryura-Tobias and colleagues are currently collecting data where two images of the individual are presented simultaneously. They are asked to identify when they note a difference between the two images. This is a more direct way of measuring perception. In addition, Yaryura-Tobias and Neziroglu are looking at the way BDD, OCD, and controls perceive not only their own face but those of others as well.

The evidence against a distorted perception comes from a number of studies. Jerome (1992) found that patients on a waiting list for cosmetic rhinoplasty (but not necessarily diagnosed as with BDD) were *more* accurate than healthy controls in estimating the size of their nose from memory. However, they also spent more time gazing in the mirror and this may explain why they are more accurate. Thomas & Goldberg (1995) also found evidence of an *enhanced* accuracy for BDD patients in assessing facial proportions. They compared three groups (BDD, healthy controls, and cosmetic surgery patients) who were presented with a facial image on a monitor screen. Their facial image had been distorted by either an increase (125%) or a reduction (75%) in width. Participants were instructed to turn the knob on the camera until their appearance resembled the image they saw when they look in a mirror. The BDD were more accurate in their ability to estimate the width of their facial image compared to the controls or the cosmetic surgery group (which is not necessarily the same as accuracy in perception as they are comparing against their memory of their appearance).

Lambrou (2006) compared 50 BDD patients to two non-clinical control groups: 50 art and design controls and 50 non-art controls. To investigate the three possible components of aesthetic sensitivity, a digital photograph of the participant was manipulated using computer graphic techniques to create a symmetry continuum. Participants were presented with the continuum on a computer and were required to select and rate the images representing their actual self, ideal self, idea of a perfect, most physically attractive, most pleasure, and most disgust. Using the same methodology as the self-image condition, symmetry continua were created for a standardized male and female face to explore whether any trends translate to faces in general. A building was also included to represent the general surroundings as a control condition.

The results were that BDD and art and design controls were better at identifying the more attractive and perfect image (for their own face, the other face, or for the building) compared to non-art controls. The BDD group were more accurate in identifying their actual face compared to both art and design and non-art controls. Both art and design and non-art controls had a positive bias in choosing a more attractive image of themselves, whilst BDD patient had a slight negative bias. Perceptual accuracy was not related to the frequency of checking in the mirror. BDD and both controls were no different in the accuracy of recognition of another person's actual face or building. BDD patients did not express a higher aesthetic for their ideal self – the self-discrepancy (self actual-ideal) was accounted for by the increased accuracy of the actual self rather than striving for an unrealistic ideal. However, it is possible that BDD patients process their faces differently by focusing on specific features they consider to be ugly and ignoring the more attractive features or looking at themselves as a whole. Thus Jansen et al. (2005) found that when viewing their own bodies, healthy controls focus more on their self-identified beautiful body parts and less on their self-identified ugly parts. Eating disordered patients do the exact opposite.

The findings of Lambrou (2006) are consistent with those of Pittenger & Baskett (1984). They found that students significantly overestimated the attractiveness of their own faces compared to the mean rating of others. Furthermore Jansen et al. (2006) found that eating disordered patients rated their appearance more realistically than healthy controls, who rated themselves as significantly more attractive than a community sample who rated them.

These studies suggest that overestimating personal attractiveness is important for psychological health. The findings suggest that patients with BDD have lost their "rose-tinted glasses" and the positive bias in their rating of their own attractiveness. They are able to identify symmetry and more readily identify any flaw or imperfection they may possess.

Harris (1982) suggests that a consequence of increased aestheticality is that an individual reacts with greater emotional response to beauty or ugliness. By definition BDD clients will rate their own faces as less attractive compared to the rating of the rest of the population. When rating their own face or body, the emotional response may be a mixture of shame, disgust, depression, hatred, and anxiety, depending on the context. The emotional response is crucial to our understanding of BDD as clients will often only "face the world" or terminate behaviors such as mirror-checking when the BDD client feels "comfortable" or "just right" (similar to compulsions observed in OCD clients).

Lambrou's (2006) study comparing 50 patients with BDD with 50 art and design students and 50 healthy controls (described above) found BDD patients were biased in their emotional processing. Compared to both healthy controls and art and design groups, the BDD group was negatively biased, responding with lower levels of pleasure when presented with their attractive faces and higher levels of disgust when viewing the unattractive versions of their face. This negative emotional processing applies exclusively to their own face but not to others' faces and buildings.

Do people with BDD set themselves unrealistic aesthetic standards which are impossible to achieve? Veale et al. (2003) explored this with self-discrepancy theory. BDD patients were found to be predominantly disturbed by a discrepancy in their ability to achieve their own aesthetic standard rather than not achieving the ideals of others. They are therefore more like depressed patients, who fail to achieve their ideal or experience internal shame, than social phobic or bulimic patients, who experience external shame and are more concerned with the avoidance of punishment by the perceived demands of others. However, the situation is complex as some BDD patients appear to be more like social phobic patients and in our experience easier to treat (a similar situation exists in eating disorders where patients with bulimia tend to be easier to treat than patients with anorexia). In the same study, BDD patients were not expressing a higher aesthetic standard of beauty compared to the two control groups. The crucial determining factor for BDD patients and potentially the source of the disturbance in their appearance appears to be that a discrepancy exists between their actual and ideal self, rather than them possessing an unrealistic ideal.

The emotional bias identified may be related to an idealized value about the degree of importance that one attaches to attractiveness and the degree of identification of these values with the self (Veale, 2002). In this regard, threats to the self are likely to be associated with increased emotional response. One would predict that BDD patients value attractiveness more than the rest of the population. Wilhelm et al. (2001) found that BDD patients rated attractive faces as more attractive compared to normal controls and OCD patients. Interestingly, one might predict that BDD patients would be more averse to unattractive faces, but there was no difference between BDD and OCD patients and healthy controls in their rating of neutral and unattractive faces. There may be greater emotional response to beauty or ugliness in BDD (an emotional rather than a perceptual phenomenon). If this is the case, then it may be related to idealized values about the degree of importance that one attaches to attractiveness (Veale, 2002). In Lambrou's (2006) study the BDD group were more likely to overvalue the importance of appearance and self-objectify compared to both controls groups. These aesthetic evaluations may interact with aesthetic perceptions and emotions to predispose them to the disorder. Preliminary results, therefore, suggest that people with BDD are more aesthetically sensitive than the general population. However, at present it is unclear whether high aesthetic sensitivity predisposes an individual to BDD as a risk factor for its development and/or a consequence of developing of BDD and whether it is a maintaining factor.

Chapter 8

Neurobiological aspects of BDD

Summary

BDD, like any other mental disorder, develops in the context of a biological vulnerability and a genetic predisposition. This is discussed in the Chapter 7. There are rare cases of organic disorder described in the literature that mimic BDD. Brain insults that deplete serotonin or block serotonin receptors also exacerbate symptoms of BDD in vulnerable individuals. There have been few neuroimaging and neuropsychological studies in BDD which have led to a description of the neuro-anatomical correlates of BDD and suggestions for future research.

Sections

8.1   Neuro-anatomical circuits
8.2   "Organic" BDD
8.3   Obsessive compulsive spectrum models of BDD
8.4   Neuroimaging in BDD
8.5   Neuropsychological Testing in BDD
8.6   The role of serotonin in BDD and OCSD
8.7   Neurobiological models of BDD

8.1   Neuro-anatomical Circuits

The neural correlates of body image may involve the visual perception of images of the body in the extra-striate body area (EBA) located in the occipito-temporal cortex (Downing et al., 2001). The representation of one's body map or schema is also found in neural circuits involving the right parietal

Body Dysmorphic Disorder: A Treatment Manual. David Veale and Fugen Neziroglu
© 2010 John Wiley & Sons, Ltd.

cortex and connections to the thalamus (McGlynn & Schacter, 1989). Of relevance to BDD is that the face is represented in the inferior occipital gyrus, left fusiform gyrus, superior temporal sulcus, hippocampus, amygdala, right inferior frontal gyrus, and orbitofrontal cortex, especially in the right hemisphere (Boesiger et al., 2005). An event such as looking at one's own face in a mirror would activate impulses from the retina via the temporal-parieto-occipital junction, and to the right supra-marginal gyrus (part of the inferior parietal lobule); right inferior occipital gyrus to the right inferior frontal gyrus and left fusiform gyrus (which subsumes the extra-striate body area). Further circuits would be linked to the limbic structures such as amgydala and insula (for emotional processing including disgust and aversion to visual perception). There are further circuits linking the superior temporal sulcus, which is responsible for memory and body image and links with the dorso-lateral prefrontal cortex, which is important for attention, memory, and judgement (Feusner et al., 2008).

Lesions in the optic pathway and primary visual area of the occipital cortex would cause contralateral hemianopsia. Lesions in the secondary visual area would result in an inability to interpret visual impulses. Lesions in the somatosensory cortex are associated with loss of perception or reception; lesions in the non-dominant (right) temporal lobe are linked to deficits in visual field defects, mood and body image disorders; lesions in the parietal lobe can cause deficits in the integration of information, sensory ataxia, general loss of awareness, apathy, faulty sensory impulse recognition, a distortion of body image, mood abnormalities, and an inability to interpret spatial relationships (Yaryura-Tobias & Nezioglu, 1997; Yaryura-Tobias et al., 2002).

8.2   "Organic" BDD

Virtually all psychiatric disorders can be mimicked by an organic brain disorder. There are a few case reports of BDD presenting as an organic brain disorder or a drug-induced state. Such cases are rare and in general their symptoms tend to be atypical – for example, symptoms may be more bizarre or people may retain full insight into the nature of their symptoms.

"Organic" BDD is reported in a number of inflammatory diseases. Salib (1988) reported a 21-year-old man presenting with symptoms of BDD who had subacute sclerosing panencephalitis. The patient was preoccupied with his ears, which he believed had become smaller, and that one foot was bigger than the other; he had other concerns too about his appearance. Gabbay et al. (2003) reported on a 24-year-old male with childhood onset insulin-dependent diabetes mellitus who developed BDD at age 21 following an inflammatory brain disease of unknown origin. In the acute phase, he experienced an expressive aphasia, memory deficits, and complex seizures. About six weeks later, he became preoccupied with his nose, experienced delusional ideas of reference, constantly checked in mirrors, and was socially avoidant. Neuroimaging studies found mild atrophy in the left fronto-temporal region, particularly in the temporal lobe.

Sverd et al. (1997) published three cases of pediatric autoimmune neuropsychiatric disorder (PANDAS) associated with a streptococcal infections, in which there were a presumed autoimmune antibodies on the basal ganglia. They experienced schizophrenia-like disorder with symptoms of BDD and Tourette's syndrome. Mathew (2001) reported on a variant of PANDAS and BDD and suggested that somato-sensory triggers were antecedents to the onset of BDD. And Gabbay et al. (2003) reported on two cases of BDD triggered by an illness. The first patient developed Bell's palsy at the age of 15; despite eventual resolution of the palsy, he complained of facial deformity and avoided social contact. Another patient developed ulcerative colitis, which was followed by a belief that his skin was deformed and dry. The authors speculated that inflammatory mediators or cytokines might alter the neurochemistry and suppress the serotonergic system.

Temporal lobectomy often produces visual field defects; mood disorders and non-dominant (right) temporal lesions can lead to disorders of body image (Trimble, 1988). Naga et al. (2004) reported on 10 patients (including two with BDD) who developed somatoform disorders after anterior temporal lobectomy, especially on the right. Therefore, right temporal lobe lesions may be associated with "organic" BDD and depressed mood. Other evidence on the role of the temporal lobe comes from brain imaging studies, which are discussed later in this chapter.

An abnormality in the somatosensory cortex may exist in some cases of BDD (Yaryura-Tobias et al., 2002). They suggest that several psychiatric and neurological conditions exhibit symptomatology similar to BDD. Individuals with BDD often experience tactile sensations (facial tightness or tingling). Khelmani-Patel (personal communication) has suggested that these act as a trigger for mirror-gazing and other symptoms of BDD. The alternative explanation is that these are normal physiological sensations which are magnified through the process of selective attention and are then misinterpreted as evidence of a defect similar to that seen in health anxiety. A dysfunction in the somatosensory cortex could be associated with such tactile symptoms. This is based on the observation that several rare body image disorders can occur as a result of neurological insults to these and other circuits. These include anosognosia, prosopagnosia, and autotopagnosia (or body image agnosia). *Anosognosia* is the inability to recognize impaired bodily functioning, such as a paralysis, leading to neglect of one side of the body (e.g., shaving only one side of the face or not using the sleeve of one side of a garment). This usually results from lesions such as a cerebrovascular accident in the right hemisphere of the brain. *Prosopagnosia* (face agnosia) is a form of visual agnosia characterized by an inability to recognize familiar faces or even one's own face in a mirror. Thus an individual with prosopagnosia recognizes that he is looking at a face but is unable to identify or recognize an individual face, even though he may exhibit the appropriate emotional reaction. Classical prosopagnosia occurs as a result of bilateral damage to the medio-inferior occipital lobes along the medio-ventral surfaces of the temporal lobes. The converse is true in Capgras syndrome, which often develops after a head injury. Here, an individual can recognize a face but has no emotional reaction. He therefore misinterprets the individual as a "double" or "impostor" (Andreasen et al., 1977). *Autotopagnosia* (body image agnosia) is characterized by an inability to localize or orient correctly different parts of the body. Individuals are able to dress appropriately and use their body normally. They are able to identify others' body parts but cannot talk about their own bodies or relate to their own body parts. Autotopagnosia is usually caused by a lesion in the parietal part of the posterior thalamic radiations in the right hemisphere. Inter-parietal syndrome can also present with agnosia, aphasia, and corporal misperception. Lesions in the left inferior parietal region can cause Gerstman's syndrome, manifested by finger agnosia, right and left disorientation, difficulty with object naming, dyscalculia, and dysgraphia.

8.3   Obsessive Compulsive Spectrum Models of BDD

Neurobiological models of obsessive compulsive and spectrum models start with the observation that animals show innate or fixed patterns of behavior such as grooming rituals (e.g., licking of the face or paws in cats). These fixed patterns of behavior often occur inappropriately at times of stress and are located in the basal ganglia. For example, a dog under stress may compulsively lick its paws excessively until they become painful and raw, a condition called "acral lick dermatitis." These abnormal grooming behaviors may reduce when the animal is given a serotonin reuptake inhibitor (e.g., clomipraimine). Humans also have innate and fixed patterns of behavior, including washing and grooming, which stem from the basal ganglia and will be activated at times of stress. Some types of BDD seem to consist of excessive grooming behaviors (e.g., skin picking, hair brushing) which occur excessively or inappropriately and begin at times of stress.

Neurobiological theories of obsessive compulsive spectrum disorders (OCSDs) are associated with activation of specific fronto-subcortical circuits, especially the orbitofrontal cortex, with less consistent involvement of the anterior cingulate gyrus, striatum, thalamus, lateral frontal and temporal cortices, amygdala, and insula (Mataix-Coles & van den Heuvel, 2006). The effect is to increase inhibition of the thalamus and decreased excitation of the prefrontal cortex.

8.4 Neuroimaging in BDD

There are three neuroimaging and three neuropsychological studies in BDD, the results of which are inconsistent and nonspecific, mainly because of small sample sizes.

In the first study, Rauch et al. (2003) studied regional brain volumes in eight women with BDD and eight matched controls using magnetic resonance imaging (MRI). They found that individuals with BDD had significant asymmetry (leftward shift) in the caudate nucleus of the basal ganglia compared to healthy controls, and overall increased white (but not gray) matter volume. A reduced hippocampal volume (e.g., found in people with affective disorders) was not found in the BDD group.

In the second study, Carey et al. (2004) reported on single photon emission computed tomography (SPECT) brain scans undertaken on six BDD patients (four males and two females, age range 19–63). Two subjects had comorbid depression and one had comorbid OCD excluded. They were free of medication for a month. They found widespread deficits in parieto-occipital temporal and frontal regions. Abnormalities in parietal circuits might be consistent with an abnormal perception of body image in BDD. The authors acknowledged their conclusions were limited by the small sample size, comorbidity, lack of healthy controls, and the absence of structural imaging data. It is not possible to determine whether any structural or functional abnormalities on neuroimaging are a consequence of BDD or an association with a comorbid symptom.

Feusner et al. (2007) studied 12 subjects with BDD and 13 matched controls with fMRI while performing matching tasks of face stimuli. Stimuli were neutral-expression photographs of others' faces which were unaltered, altered to include only high spatial frequency visual information, or altered to include only low spatial frequency visual information. Subjects with BDD showed greater left hemisphere activity relative to controls, particularly in lateral prefrontal cortex and lateral temporal lobe regions for all face tasks (and dorsal anterior cingulate activity for the low spatial frequency task). Controls showed left-sided prefrontal and dorsal anterior cingulate activity only for the high spatial frequency task. The BDD group also showed an abnormal activation of amygdalae. This suggests that people with BDD are different from controls in visually processing others' faces. The predominance of left-sided activity for low spatial frequency and normal faces suggests detail encoding and analysis in a piecemeal manner rather than holistic processing, a pattern that was found in controls only for high spatial frequency faces. Clinically, people with BDD are likely to be scrutinizing and comparing another person's features with their own and this would be associated with detailed encoding and analysis. Future studies are needed to investigate processing of one's own face.

It is also worth considering evidence of brain responses to line drawings of underweight, normal weight, and overweight female bodies to fMRI in women with another body image disorder (e.g., bulimia nervosa, anorexia nervosa) or healthy controls (Downing et al., 2001). In the three groups, the lateral fusiform gyrus, inferior parietal cortex, and lateral prefrontal cortex were activated in response to body shapes compared with the control condition (drawings of houses). The responses in the lateral fusiform gyrus (which subsumes the previously identified extra-striate body area and includes areas previously identified as responsive to faces more than to inanimate objects in the inferior parietal cortex) were less strong in patients with eating disorders compared with healthy control subjects. The patients with eating disorders rated the body shapes as more aversive than did healthy women. In the group with eating disorders, the aversion ratings correlated positively with activity in the right medial apical prefrontal cortex. Thus processing of female body shapes engages a distributed neural network, parts of which are underactive in women with eating disorders.

8.5   Neuropsychological Testing in BDD

Two neuropsychological studies have investigated executive functioning in BDD (Hanes, 1998; Deckersbach et al., 2000; Laniti & Neziroglu, in submission). Other neuropsychological studies of perception are described in Chapter 7. Hanes (1998) used neuropsychological measures of executive memory and motor function. BDD patients (N = 14) were compared to OCD patients (N = 10), patients with schizophrenia (N = 14), and normal controls (N = 24). Results suggested normal performance on measures of memory and motor function in BDD patients. BDD patients, however, performed worse than controls on the two non-verbal tests of executive function (ability to plan on the Tower of London and response inhibition on the Stroop task), but not the verbal fluency test. There was no difference on the Rey Complex Figure Test and Rey Auditory Verbal Learning Task, which are more typically characterized by memory and visuospatial measures. The overall performance of the BDD and OCD groups on the neuropsychological measures was similar, while the group with schizophrenia had a wider spectrum of deficits. The overall conclusion is that BDD and OCD patients are more easily distracted by neutral stimuli on two tests of executive function. This is a nonspecific finding which can be found across several psychiatric disorders not just OCSDs; it is discussed below.

Deckersbach et al. (2000) describe a study using the Rey-Osterrieth Complex Figure Test (RCFT) (non-verbal memory) and the California Verbal Learning Test (CVLT) (verbal memory) in 17 BDD patients and 17 matched healthy controls. Post-hoc analyses revealed that BDD patients and controls did not differ in their copy accuracy. BDD patients recalled less of the figure than controls on the immediate recall condition. On the CVLT, BDD patients demonstrated slowed learning compared to controls and were significantly less able than controls to discriminate between previously presented words and distractors on the recognition task. BDD patients did not display problems in storing information once learned. Multiple regression analyses revealed that group differences in free recall from verbal and nonverbal memory were statistically mediated by deficits in organizational strategies in the BDD patients. BDD patients tended to focus on details rather than recalling the overall organization and properties of any visual stimuli or verbal information. Limitations of the study include small sample size, an exclusively female sample, and the absence of any other group with a psychiatric disorder as a direct comparison.

Laniti & Neziroglu (2008) used the Wisconsin Card Sorting Test (computer version 4), the Delis Kaplan Executive Function System Sorting Test (D-KEFS), D-KEFS Trail-Making Test, D-KEFS Verbal Fluency Test. D-KEFS Design Fluency Test, D-KEFS Color Word Interference Test, K-KEFS Tower Test, three subtests of the Wechsler Adult Intelligence Scale III (picture completion, block design, object assembly), the comprehensive test of visual functioning, Hooper Visual Organization Test, and Benton Facial Recognition Test. Participants with BDD and OCD had equivalent levels of symptom severity and insight into their clinical condition. Their levels of depression and anxiety were also equivalent, but significantly higher compared to the normal controls. The two clinical groups further endorsed significantly higher levels of perfectionism than the normal controls; participants with BDD also had significantly lower self-esteem compared to participants with OCD and the control groups. Therefore, the two disorders had a similar clinical presentation. However, the clinical groups did not exhibit poorer executive functioning relative to controls as measured by the tests administered. In terms of the visual spatial assessment, the three groups displayed equivalent visuospatial abilities. However, performance on the comprehensive test of visual functioning showed that the OCD group had significantly more impaired visuospatial orientation, visual memory, and fine motor coordination compared to participants with BDD and the normal controls.

In summary, one study found that BDD patients tended to focus on details rather than recalling the overall organization and properties, which may turn out to be more specific to BDD (Deckersbach et al., 2000). Two of the studies suggest that BDD patients have attentional deficits and are easily distracted by neutral stimuli. The most prosaic explanation from these studies is that increased distractibility is a function of the individual scanning of the environment for any stimulus or threat that is relevant to their concerns. Alternatively, heightened distractibility may represent a more trait-like vulnerability to a psychiatric disorder which is independent of the patient's concerns (Harvey et al., 2004). Attentional deficits of this sort are therefore nonspecific to BDD.

8.6   The Role of Serotonin in BDD and OCSD

Veale et al. (2003) believes that the concept of OCSD has been pharmacologically driven and has little to say about response to psychological treatments. It is frequently acknowledged that models of etiology should be not be influenced by treatment response. One of the differences about OCD is that patients respond preferentially to a serotonin reuptake inhibitor (SRI) compared to noradrenergic reuptake inhibitor (NRI) (e.g., desipramine). This is in contrast to depression, in which patients respond equally well to an SRI or an NRI. Hence it was hypothesized that OCSDs will also preferentially respond to SRIs compared to NRIs. OCSD are characterized by a paucity of RCTs, but there is one in BDD that demonstrates a slight preferential response to an SRI (clomipramine) over an NRI (desipramine) (Hollander et al., 1999). This study is discussed in more detail in Chapter 12. It is a nonspecific finding as other anxiety disorders (but not depression) will preferentially respond to an SRI compared to an NRI. However, many psychiatric disorders (and not just OCSD) have an association with an abnormal brain scan and serotonergic activity and can be viewed as a response rather than a cause.

Evidence for a role in serotonergic system in BDD comes from a variety of sources. There are three case studies that demonstrate that brain insults that interfere in serotonergic function exacerbate symptoms of BDD.

a) Five-hydroxy-tyryptophan (5-HT) is an essential amino acid and precursor to serotonin. Dietary depletion of tryptophan (Barr et al., 1992) exacerbated symptoms of BDD in a woman who had been treated with clomipramine (a potent SRI).

b) Chlorophenylpiperazine (m-CPP), a serotonin antagonist, but not a placebo led to an increase in symptoms of BDD (Hollander et al., 1994). In another study, the onset of BDD symptoms occurred following chronic abuse of cyproheptadine, a serotonin receptor antagonist (Craven & Rodin, 1987).

c) The 5-HT$_2$ agonist psilocybin temporarily reduced symptoms of BDD in a single case report (Hanes, 1996).

Exacerbation of psychiatric symptoms after depletion of tryptophan or use of serotonergic receptor antagonists are nonspecific findings in a wide range of psychiatric disorders. An abnormal serotonergic response is part of the theoretical basis for the use of SRIs in BDD. Furthermore, Marazziti et al. (1999) reported that platelet 5-HT transporter binding density was significantly lower in BDD, OCD, tic disorders, and impulse-control disorders, compared to controls.

8.7 Neurobiological Models of BDD

Etiology cannot be inferred from treatment response and neuroimaging. Differences in brain function do not necessarily indicate that a dysfunction in specific circuits *causes* BDD. Mataix-Coles & van den Heuvel (2006) acknowledge that neuroimaging tools should be regarded as correlational techniques which allow researchers to understand the neurophysiological basis of OCSDs, but not necessarily their cause.

An alternative hypothesis to an "abnormal" serotonergic function or dysfunction in certain regions in BDD is that it is a normal response to anxiety. Alternatively, there may be another spurious variable that causes both phenomena (Whiteside et al., 2004). Thus individuals with BDD may have a normal or even exaggerated inhibitory response in the fronto-striatal circuits, the function of which is to reduce anxiety. The serotonergic system may not, therefore, be relevant to the development of BDD but a consequence of an overloaded system that is trying to stabilize. The beneficial effect of serotonin SRIs may be related to several mechanisms, including enhancing inhibitory serotonergic pathways in the amygdala and insula and in the basal ganglia. An SRI does not therefore correct a "defect," but enhances an inhibitory pathway. Not surprisingly, there is a high level of relapse or exacerbation of symptoms if the SRI is discontinued.

Mataix-Coles & van den Heuvel (2006) also argue that current models of OCSD fail to recognize the heterogeneity of OCD. On the basis of various neuroimaging studies, they suggest that patients with OCD with prominent washing and contamination or hoarding are phenomenologically and neurobiologically closer to limbic disorders (noticeably the involvement of the amygdala and paralimbic brain regions). They suggest that patients who have a need for symmetry/order and checking symptoms are closer to fronto-striatal spectrum of disorders with noticeable involvement of the sensorimotor cortico-striato-thalamic loops. BDD fits more with this model, but being a body image problem, especially around the face, neuroimaging studies should examine correlates in inferior occipital gyrus, fusiform gyrus, inferior frontal gyrus, inferior parietal lobule, mesial temporal structures (including the parahippocampal gyrus and amygdala), tempero-parieto-occicipital junction, and superior temporal sulcus, especially in the right hemisphere. For a more detailed discussion on a proposed neuroanatomical model of BDD, see Saxena & Feusner (2006) and Feusner et al. (2008). Like OCD, there is heterogeneity in BDD and the experience of neuroimaging in OCD is that there may be no single pattern of neurophysiological response.

In summary, the evidence for a neurobiological understanding for BDD is in its infancy and is not yet able to inform treatment. BDD, like any other mental disorder, develops in the context of a biological vulnerability and a genetic predisposition. There are a few rare cases of an organic disorder or brain insults that precipitate symptoms of BDD. Brain insults that deplete serotonin or block serotonin receptors will also exacerbate symptoms of BDD in vulnerable individuals. Neurobiological correlates do not necessarily indicate that a dysfunction in specific circuits *causes* BDD; rather, they are a tool for investigating the neurophysiological correlates of BDD.

Chapter 9

Learning theory models of BDD

Summary

A two-factor model based on learning theory is described for the acquisition and maintenance of Body Dysmorphic Disorder (BDD). Recently, there have been many cognitive behavioral theories proposed for various disorders. These theories often explain the possible mechanisms involved in a disorder and at best why certain processes and behaviors are maintained, but not necessarily how and why they develop. Theories for the development of BDD have been suggested by Veale (2004) and Neziroglu (2004; Neziroglu et al., 2004). Although these two models are specific to BDD, this chapter discusses it from a social learning theory perspective, a diathesis stress model, and field perspective. It emphasizes evaluative, operant, and relational frame conditioning in the acquisition and maintenance of BDD symptoms.

Sections

9.1   Acquisition and Maintenance of Behavior

A two-factor model (Dollard & Miller, 1950) has been adapted for the acquisition and maintenance of BDD (Neziroglu et al., 2004). Although the etiology

---

Body Dysmorphic Disorder: A Treatment Manual. David Veale and Fugen Neziroglu
© 2010 John Wiley & Sons, Ltd.

of BDD is unknown, several models exist which attempt to explain this disorder. Models are structures or frameworks based on hypotheses as to how a particular disorder initially develops, expands, and is ultimately maintained (Rabinowitz et al., 2007; Neziroglu, Khemlani-Patel et al., 2009). Models are important because they ultimately guide research aimed at developing efficacious treatments (Neziroglu et al., 2004; Rabinowitz et al., 2007; Neziroglu, Khemlani-Patel et al., 2009). Current models of BDD include the notion of aesthetic sensitivity and self as an aesthetic object (Veale et al., 2002), social learning and conditioning (Neziroglu, 2004; Neziroglu et al., 2008), neurobiological (Yaryura-Tobias, Neziroglu, Chang et al., 2002; Yaryura-Tobias, Neziroglu & Torres-Gallegos, 2002; Saxena & Feusner, 2006; Feusner et al., 2008), and neuroanatomical (Rauch et al., 2003). Below we discuss a cognitive behavioral model based on learning and conditioning to explain the development and maintenance of BDD. The key components of the CBT model for BDD are show in Figure 9.1 and include: a) a biological predisposition; b) initial operant conditioning; c) social learning; d) classical/evaluative conditioning; e) rela-

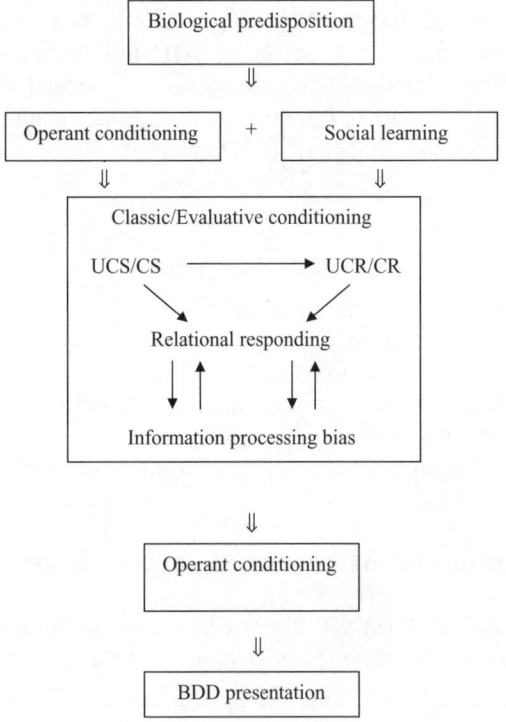

Figure 9.1 Behavioral acquisition and maintenance model for BDD

tional responding; and f) secondary operant conditioning (Nezioglu et al., 2004; 2008). In Chapter 10 the cognitive behavioral model based on self as an aesthetic object is discussed.

9.2   Biological Predisposition

The learning model begins with the premise that some individuals are genetically predisposed to develop a disorder of a particular class in times of stress. Individuals may be predisposed to develop a single class of disorders or be multiply disposed to develop several classes of disorders. This is in keeping with the diathesis-stress model regarding mental disorders in general. It should be noted that simply having a biological disposition to a disorder does not necessarily predict one will develop a specific disorder. Instead, it is more likely that the development of BDD is the result of an interaction of several factors, with biological predispositions representing an important prerequisite. Examples of biological predispositions include genetic factors, visual processing problems, somatosensory problems, and changes in neuroanatomical/neurochemical circuitry (Nezioglu, 2004; Nezioglu et al., 2004). Also, individuals with BDD may temperamentally be high in disgust sensitivity – in other words, they are more inclined to react with disgust to various disgust elicitors (e.g., hygiene, sex, body envelope violations, sympathetic magic, animals, death, foods); for a review of disgust sensitivity see Rozin & Fallon (1987). Preliminary evidence of higher levels of disgust reactivity in BDD patients and the habituation of disgust in these patients support the assertion that disgust is a salient emotional factor in BDD (Nezioglu, Hickey et al., 2009).

9.3   Childhood Reinforcement History

It is hypothesized that the process of operant conditioning coupled with social learning results in the development of values and beliefs about attractiveness, as well as a sense of the self's value being conditionally based on body image (Nezioglu et al., 2004). This is similar to Cash's (1997, 2002) general CBT model of body image disturbance which discusses the importance of how historical factors (cultural socialization, interpersonal experiences, physical characteristics, and personality attributes) develop body image perception and attitudes (e.g., body satisfaction and investment in one's body image). The over-importance and/or sensitivity about attractiveness serves as a potential risk factor to the development of BDD and lays down the framework for the specific beliefs, assumptions, and values that are developed (Wilhelm & Nezioglu, 2002).

Early experiences which positively reinforce an individual for appearance may play an important role in BDD development. In clinical interviews with individuals with BDD, Neziroglu et al. (2004) reported that for a significant number of BDD patients, appearance was one of, if not the most, salient factors reinforced during their childhood. These experiences may function to reinforce in the child a sense that appearance is ultimately important to the exclusion of behavior (e.g., comments such as "Wow! You are the tallest kid on the team," or, "You were wonderful on stage and you looked so good," rather than "You played the flute so well during the school concert"). Although not all BDD patients were positively and/or intermittently reinforced for their overall general appearance, many were reinforced as children or adolescents for a particular body part, height, cuteness, poise, and weight or body shape. Often, patients with BDD report being in the "attractive" crowd in school, early dating success, and other childhood and adolescent experiences where the importance of appearance is highlighted and exaggerated.

Early life experiences need not be positive to have an impact. Research has also demonstrated that BDD patients report a significantly greater incidence of emotional and sexual abuse (Didie et al., 2006; Neziroglu et al., 2006). Many patients also report that other kinds of trauma, such as car accidents, resulting in scars or skin conditions (acne or psoriasis) impacted their appearance resulting in unnecessary attention on appearance. Negative early experiences (images of negative experiences, teasing, neglect, bullying, etc.) may function to prepare the individual for the negative affect he feels when observing body parts in later life (Phillips, 1996a; Zimmermann & Mattia, 1999; Osman et al., 2004). These experiences may also build core beliefs regarding the value of attractiveness.

Social learning

Vicarious learning occurs by observing others being reinforced for a particular behavior. One can learn that physical attractiveness leads to rewards. This is perhaps most salient in the media and popular culture. It is difficult (if not impossible) to find an unattractive lead female television or movie character win "Prince Charming." If she is initially unattractive, her appearance goes through a radical transformation before she wins her prize. Not only are children and adolescents taught that physical attractiveness is necessary for success, they are also bombarded by advertisements for cosmetic products to achieve this goal.

Besides the individual's sociocultural environment, one's immediate environment can provide numerous learning opportunities. Family members may be over-concerned about their own appearance or may make frequent comments about the appearance of others. This type of vicarious learning gives the individual further confirmation that appearance is an important trait valued in society.

Although many models of body image include the above-mentioned social learning factors, a true etiological model must explain how these factors intersect with respect to the development of a particular illness. How might these factors combine and interact to form the symptomatology necessary for BDD?

9.4   Symptom Development through Classic Conditioning

With predisposition factors in place, the next aspect of the CBT model of BDD is aimed at explaining the acquisition and maintenance of actual BDD symptomatology. BDD development is formulated to be a function of classical or evaluative conditioning. Evaluative conditioning is similar to classic (Pavlovian) conditioning, with the latter referring to conditioning of physiological responses and the former to conditioning of liking or disliking of stimuli. In the case of BDD, negative events involving one's physical appearance, such as being teased, abused, acne, or early puberty, may serve as unconditioned stimuli (UCS) and cause an unconditioned emotional response (UCR), such as anxiety, depression, disgust, or shame. The UCS are evaluated to be negative or unpleasant and therefore anything paired with them is also evaluated to be negative. An example would be a person who is teased (UCS) and this evokes a negative affect and then a word (CS: "small") or body part (CS: "shoulder") is evaluated to be negative as well. According to evaluative conditioning, any previously neutral body part or word (relational responding to the word "small") can take on the same valence (negative reaction) as the UCS. Consequently, when the patient either purposely (e.g., mirror-checking) or indirectly (e.g., passing a reflective surface, intrusive thought) is exposed to his body part of concern the negative emotional response is elicited. Not only is the CS evaluated negatively but it evokes the same response as the UCS (e.g., shame or disgust).

Information processing/development of the belief system based on relational frame theory

Conditioning and early experiences begin to shape an individual's cognitions and emotions, but because human beings have the capacity for language, it plays a significant role in strengthening and developing appearance-related beliefs. Conditioning and learning in humans is mediated by language. Relational frame theory (Hayes et al., 2001) highlights the role of language and its impact on human emotions and cognitions, and how it potentially results in the suffering of human beings. A full review of the tenets of relational frame theory is beyond the scope of this chapter, so we shall focus on three of the main premises we believe relate to BDD.

Bidirectional stimulus relations

Only for humans does a word and the actual item or event enter into a bidirectional stimulus relation wherein each can equally stand for the other (e.g., the word "cookie" and the actual cookie are equal). For humans, because of our ability to use language, we do not need to see a cookie in order to anticipate getting one. Simply hearing the word "cookie" is a powerful enough stimulus. The word "cookie" and the actual food are equally powerful reinforcers. Animals also require a direct experience with an object for learning to occur; they learn about events that predict the onset of something (e.g., show a cookie, say "cookie," and a dog salivates). Our ability to use language allows us to learn about things, even though we may never have experienced a particular event. For example, a child can learn that touching a hot stove will burn without having direct experience of a hot stove. In addition, for animals, the order in which the word "cookie" is said and the presentation of the actual cookie are important. The word has to be said before the object is shown in order for the animal to learn that the word and the object are the same. In humans, however, the word "cookie" could be said either before or after the child eats the cookie. Once the child learns that word, similar reinforcers can be taught so that both can elicit the thought even though the child may not have had direct experience with the second stimulus. For example, we can teach a child that a cookie is similar to a muffin and eventually both words, "cookie" and "muffin," will elicit the thought of a cookie and muffin, even though the child has never seen a muffin. Humans can learn after the fact, in other words, they are taught once an event has occurred, whereas other animals need to have the event precede the onset of the response. This bidirectionality is the most important defining feature of human language and cognition and explains why evaluative conditioning can occur and why arbitrary associations can be made.

Relational frames

Another important feature of human language and cognition involves the emergence of complex networks of related events. The ability to think relationally allows us not only to make predictions, similar to other animals via classic conditioning, but our mind allows us to generate various other relations. Relational responding is established during early language training by teaching relational frames (e.g., learning things that are "similar"; learning temporal and causal relations – "before and after," "if … then"; comparative and evaluative – "better than," "bigger than," etc.). Relational frame theory seeks to explain the generative nature of language and cognitions. It draws from both classic (Pavlovian) and operant (Skinnerian) conditioning to explain various thoughts and emotions.

Language aids classic conditioning. For example, a child could learn that having a pimple (UCS) makes her feel (UCR: disgust) – and later any blemish (CS) elicits – disgust (CR). The word "pimple" has a similar meaning to "blemish," "acne," "bumps on face," or "unsmooth face" and thus those similar words alone can elicit the same negative affect (classical conditioning via relational frame of coordination or similarity). Words that connote similar concepts conjure up the same thoughts. This is why a person with BDD may respond with negative affect to any events or words that remind him of a similar situation. If at one point he had a disgust reaction to a pimple, then anything similar to it can elicit the same reaction merely by thinking about it, even if it no longer exists. If one had been teased about having a big head, then one may think of the word "big" and have a negative feeling and any similar associated body part (hairline/hair) can elicit the same response.

Arbitrary and non-arbitrary connections
Relational frame theory (Hayes et al., 2001) also suggests that language enables us to make arbitrary and non-arbitrary connections among events and therefore develop certain beliefs based on these associations. In other words, due to language, we think about the future, make plans, and are able to evaluate and compare outcomes. Relational frame theory suggests that we use language as a way to make connections that may or may not be factual. Perhaps in the case of BDD, humans make arbitrary associations between appearance, social success, and/or undesirable human traits. For example, a child may hear an adult or peer make a comment about a child who is difficult to invite over to the house because she is bossy. However, at the same time the parents may comment that this child is cute and pretty and what a shame she is so difficult. The child may learn that people will put up with unpleasantness (bossiness) if the person is pretty, and thus attractiveness is important. In short, people will accept unpleasantness from good-looking people. The child may in fact start comparing herself with her friend to see if she is just as pretty or prettier in order for people to accept her as well.

In addition to language and cognitions eliciting emotions, thoughts can take on meaning. For example, if you think of a plate, you may have a neutral response, but if you think of a plate that has fallen into the toilet bowel and later sanitized, you may have a disgust reaction to it. Between the time a thought or an event occurs and you make an association with it (i.e., during the evaluative or classic conditioning process), certain thoughts are formulated. Thus, due to language, we make arbitrary associations in our minds and have certain emotional responses to those thoughts. As early as 22–27 months, infants are able to combine all relationships among events even if they are not specifically taught each relationship (Lipkens et al., 1993). As soon as we are able to think, we arbitrarily *relate* events that may co-occur. As stated above, evaluative conditioning is similar to classic (Pavlovian) conditioning, but our use of language allows for some differences. It is not within the scope of this chapter to discuss similarities and dissimilarities between the two, but for a review, see de Houwer et al. (2001). For the most part, the two have been used interchangeably in the psychological literature, with classic conditioning used more often.

Therefore, there may be either direct conditioning of the CS and UCS occurring or conditioning via the mediation of language. As the CS is paired with the CR, a set of cognitions is strengthened. Information is processed at this time, and a set of beliefs initially introduced through early life experiences continues to be reinforced. These beliefs may center on thoughts such as: "If I am attractive, I will be more likely to obtain what I want"; "Being attractive is the most important thing in the world"; "I need to be noticed"; "Life is not worth living unless I am attractive," etc. It is also during this time that attention is drawn to the perceived defective body part. Selective attention to the defective part leads to more focus on the defect and thus a strengthening of the conditioning process. It is believed that cognitions take on importance as a result of this conditioning process. As you break up the conditioning later, the belief in the cognitions may lessen, although this needs to be tested. One may need to challenge the cognitions separately because they become functionally autonomous even when the behavior and mood change. In other words, the person is able to go out, feel less negative emotionally, and interact with others, even if they were not able to do so previously, but still retain the belief that they are unattractive (though possibly to a lesser degree).

9.5   Higher-order Conditioning

BDD symptoms secondary to the patient's primary concern may be accounted for by higher-order conditioning; that is, the patient observes himself in the mirror and believes that the shape of his ears causes him to look disgusting. Then, he turns his attention to the hairline around his ears and, not surprisingly, continues to feel disgust. From this point on, the BDD sufferer may display disgust when examining this area of his hairline. If such phenomena occur due to higher-order conditioning, it follows that these secondary concerns would be of secondary importance to the patient, in that higher-order conditioned stimuli produce less of a conditioned response than lower-ordered conditioned stimuli (Neziroglu et al., 2004).

Higher-order conditioning may be direct or through relational framing. For example, initially a child is taught to see an object, then hear its name, and then say its name. Later, the child can hear the name and point to the object. Once the object–word and word–object relation is explicitly trained (relational training) derived relational responding emerges. If a child is taught "This is your nose, mouth, ear," then the child can identify the facial part when asked "Where is your nose, mouth, and ear?" even in the absence of differential reinforcement for doing so. This derived, arbitrarily applicable relation is referred to as "relational frame" and it is brought under the control of contextual cues through a process of differential reinforcement. After the history of reinforcement a derived relation emerges without reinforcement. As human beings we can generalize to novel situations without direct reinforcement of these situations by using what we have learned in the past. Thus, if a person has a disgust reaction to pimples and then equates pimples with blemishes, elevations on the skin, or redness, or any other arbitrary relation, then those new events (facial aspects) can elicit the same response. This is similar to higher-order conditioning, whereby the CS is paired with another CS and thus evokes the same response.

9.6   Maintenance of Symptoms through Operant Conditioning

Once acquisition has been established and beliefs, assumptions, and values developed it is hypothesized that secondary operant conditioning in the form of negative reinforcement serves to maintain the maladaptive behaviors and cognitions seen in individuals with BDD (Neziroglu et al., 2004; 2008). More specifically, similar to the role of compulsive behavior seen in OCD, in BDD the compulsive or avoidance behaviors serve to reduce short-term distress by "taking away" the negative emotional reaction (negative reinforcement) triggered by either an intrusive thought or coming into contact with the perceived flaw. In other words, BDD patients engage in behaviors such as camouflaging, reassurance-seeking, mirror-checking or mirror-avoiding, or excessive grooming in an attempt to reduce disgust, anxiety, or negative feelings in general. The avoidance or compulsive behaviors are negatively reinforcing and thus likely to be used repeatedly in similar situations. Unfortunately, this behavior interferes with the patient staying in the situation long enough to "habituate" to the associated distress, as well as challenge faulty beliefs.

BDD patients can be roughly divided into two types: mirror-checkers and mirror-avoiders. Mirror-checkers often spend hours each day scrutinizing their image in reflective surfaces, checking their appearance, and evaluating the degree of their physical flaw and its potential for a catastrophic effect on their lives. They may also endlessly attempt to fix their appearance in order to hide it; this may occur through camouflaging or DIY surgery. Mirror-avoiders, on the other hand, consistently go out of their way to avoid seeing their reflection (e.g., removing reflective items from their home, covering bathroom mirrors, etc.). Mirror-avoiders report fearing the sight of their "deformed" image. In either case, the BDD patient's behavior serves to reduce anxiety and uncertainty. For mirror-checkers, the checking compulsion allows them briefly to escape the feelings of anxiety associated with the thought "Do I look hideous?" Or "Have I changed since I last looked at myself?" It also allows them an opportunity to engage in the camouflage compulsion. For mirror-avoiders, not checking allows one to avoid the possibility of seeing the "deformity." In either case, the BDD patient's behavior serves to reduce *temporarily* the patient's anxiety regarding his appearance. Because such behaviors function to reduce anxiety, they are maintained by the principle of negative reinforcement and become more likely to occur in the future. In addition, at times the individual may like the way he looks more than he did the previous time. This may be due to different lighting, his particular mood state, a different mirror, or expectations of how he ought to look. In addition, many patients feel uncertain about their appearance. This is due to the different images they obtain at different times depending on the variables above. By looking at the mirror they gain certainty of how they look; the reduction in doubting is also reinforcing and thus leads to further mirror-checking. Thus mirror-checking may be reinforced in the hope that each time their appearance will appear better and/or to reduce uncertainty. Also the discrepancy between what they see in the mirror (actual self) and what they hope to see (idealized self) may lead to further mirror-checking or mirror-avoidance. Most mirror-avoiders used to be mirror-checkers but became discouraged because they consistently saw a negative image. The variable ratio reinforcement may have changed to consistent punishment (the image was consistently negative).

In Chapter 8 we discuss a neurobiological understanding in which some BDD patients may have a perceptual problem located in the somatosensory strip of the parietal lobe. If this is the case, the image seen in the mirror may, in fact, appear distorted and is certainly unreliable. A separate hypothesis is that BDD patients experience cognitive dissonance (Festinger, 1954) when viewing of their own image; that is, the patient sees his own image and feels abject horror (due to previously classically conditioned experiences) but accidentally attributes these feelings to his image rather than to past experiences (e.g., "If I feel this bad looking at my own image, it must be because my nose *really is* crooked").

Nevertheless, BDD patients typically report that, on occasion, their appearance is acceptable. If this is so, BDD patients are reinforced for checking their own appearance on a variable ratio schedule. This may explain the difficulty BDD patients often experience in engaging in response prevention (i.e., not engaging in compulsive behaviors), as variable ratio schedules of reinforcement are particularly strong. We have thus offered a behavioral acquisition and maintenance theory, which needs to be investigated further. Although parts of the theory have been established to date, there are many aspects that need to be teased out and studied. Some of the proposed behavioral treatment strategies are based on the model above.

In summary, the cognitive behavioral model based on learning theory suggests that a biological predisposition paired with early learning experiences (through both direct reinforcement of attractiveness as well as social learning) make individuals vulnerable to classic and evaluative conditioning experiences, which can lead to BDD symptomatology. Also, relational frame theory may help us explain how certain associations are made. In other words, some pairings are arbitrary and not clearly identified; it is a matter of how events are associated based on the learning experience of the person. Ultimately, BDD behaviors are maintained via negative reinforcement. There is support for cognitive behavioral techniques as well as pharmacological interventions to reduce BDD symptoms and their associated distress (Neziroglu & Khemlani-Patel, 2002; 2003; Neziroglu et al., 2008). Repeated exposures to the conditioned beliefs, behaviors, and emotions while preventing the learned avoidance and escape behaviors are the main behavioral components of treatment. Cognitive therapy is then used to challenge the helpfulness of the processes of ruminating and idealized values placed on appearance that have been learned and reinforced in childhood and adolescence.

Chapter 10

A cognitive behavioral model of BDD

Summary

This chapter describes a cognitive behavioral model of BDD, which seeks to explain the maintenance of BDD symptoms. The model is developed from previous publications (Veale, 2004; Veale et al., 1996; Neziroglu et al., 2008) and summarizes more recent evidence. The core of the model is the experience of the self as an aesthetic object. This is an excessive, self-focused attention on an image (or "felt" impression) from an observer perspective, which becomes fused with past experiences. This in turn activates the assumptions about the importance of one's appearance in defining the self and the various ways of responding, namely avoidance and safety-seeking behaviors, ruminating, and comparing. The clinical implications of the model are described.

Sections

10.1   Introduction

There are many cognitive behavioral models for different disorders, which broadly focus on the factors that maintain symptoms (rather than the

Body Dysmorphic Disorder: A Treatment Manual. David Veale and Fugen Neziroglu
© 2010 John Wiley & Sons, Ltd.

development) of a disorder since it is thought they are more likely to lead to advances in therapy. Stice (2002) provides a useful definition of a causal maintenance factor if it predicts symptom persistence over time vs. remission among initially symptomatic individuals and results in symptom expression or suppression, respectively. Thus the various components can be evaluated empirically to determine if a factor will lead to an increase or decrease in symptoms. In addition to a focus on maintenance factors, a successful model will have various characteristics:

a) It will need to be clinically relevant and be able to guide the strategies to use in therapy, which are evaluated in controlled trials.
b) An idiosyncratic version of a model will need to be understood by a client. It should assist in the process of engagement and provide an alternative explanation for an individual with BDD so he can do various behavioral experiments to determine whether it best explains his experience.
c) It should clearly distinguish between the *processes* (represented by the arrows in Figure 10.1) and the *outcomes* (represented by boxes). Traditionally, cognitive therapy has focused on helping a client to question the content within the box. More recent developments have focused on the cognitive processes (e.g., selective attention, rumination) and the beliefs about such processes (or meta-cognitions, e.g., the positive beliefs or motivation for ruminating).

For each component of the model, we discuss the theory, evidence, and therapeutic implications. The model described has some overlap with a cognitive behavioral model of body image developed by Cash et al. (2002), which was most commonly applied to dissatisfaction for body weight and shape in a non-psychiatric population. There are similarities in the model for BDD with that of social phobia (Clark et al., 1995), OCD (Salkovskis, 1999), and health anxiety (Warwick & Salkovskis, 1990), whose influence we acknowledge. However, a model for BDD needs to incorporate features that are unique to BDD. One such feature is the relationship with a representation of one's appearance (e.g., reflective surfaces such as mirrors or old photographs, which may act as an external trigger for the symptoms). Although the model describes a discrete process, it is probable that the process is permanently "switched on" in many individuals with BDD and accounts for an aggravation of symptoms.

10.2   The Self as an Aesthetic Object

The cycle begins (or is aggravated by) an event or a trigger, which can be broadly described as a representation of a person's appearance. Examples of external events include looking in a mirror or seeing a picture of one's self. Examples of internal events include a somatic sensation (e.g., feeling puffiness under the eyes) or an intrusive thought (e.g., "Why is my nose crooked?") (Figure 10.1). Such triggers are thought to activate a *process* of self-focused attention. The *outcome* is the "self as an aesthetic object." It consists of extreme self-consciousness and being excessively aware of one's body image from an

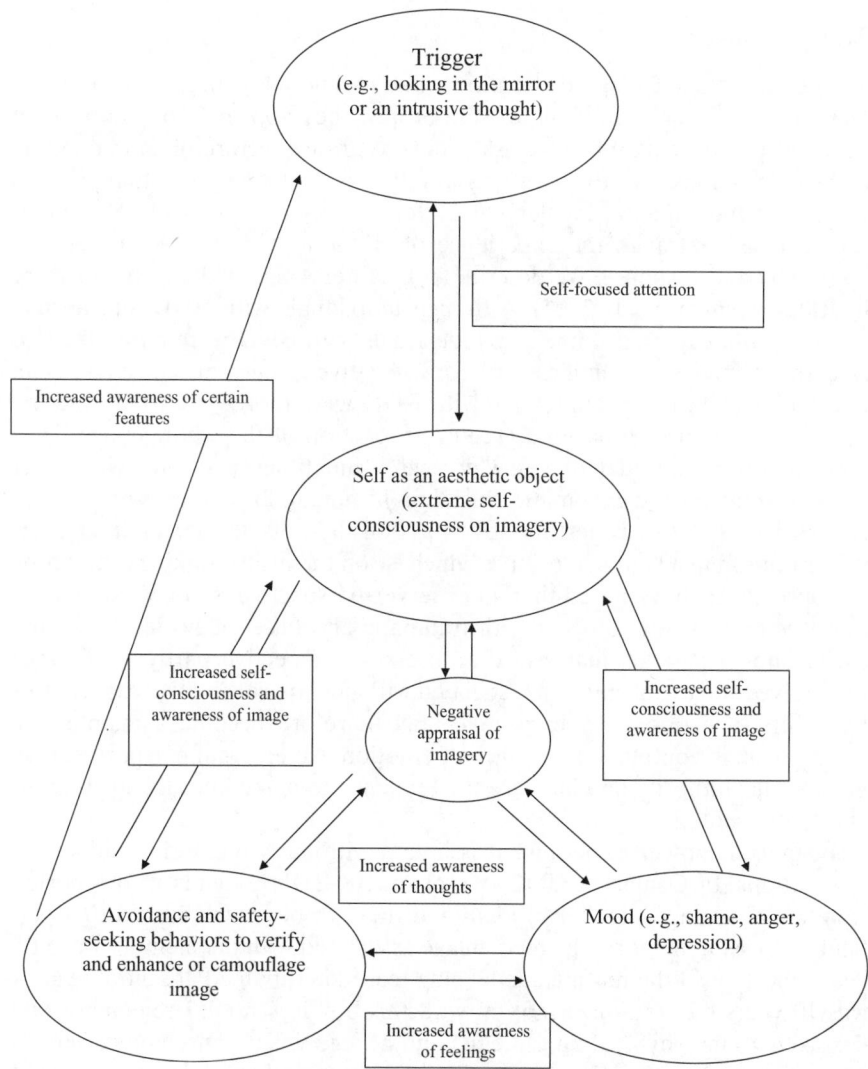

Figure 10.1   CBT Model of BDD

observer perspective. This becomes fused with past aversive experiences and provides an impression of how the self appears to others. We discuss the main components of the self as an aesthetic object in terms of (a) mental imagery, (b) self-focused attention and cognitive fusion, (c) beliefs about the importance of self-focused attention, and (d) the lack of a self-serving bias. However, each of these components acts with the others to create an experience of the self as an aesthetic object.

Mental imagery

The outcome of self-focused attention is that individuals with BDD experience mental imagery or a "felt" impression of how they appear to others from an observer perspective. When we ask clients to draw a picture of an impression of how they look to others, our assumption is that they are attempting to reproduce their mental imagery or a "felt impression" of their self. This is regarded as central to the experience of BDD as it drives the subsequent appraisals and response. We describe in Chapter 4 the evidence for imagery in BDD (Osman et al., 2004). Although individuals with BDD and normal controls both experience imagery, individuals with BDD were more likely to rate their images as significantly more negative, recurrent, and vivid than normal controls. Images in people with BDD were more "distorted" and the "defective" features took up a greater proportion of the whole image. They typically reported visual images, which were sometimes associated with other sensory modalities (e.g., somatic sensations) from an observer perspective. An observer perspective is best described as "on the outside looking in at yourself" rather than a field perspective, which is "on the inside looking out." Stopa & Spurr (2003) have noted that an observer perspective is not abnormal *per se* but is more likely to occur with traumatic and false memories. BDD and social phobic patients may use the observer perspective partly to distance themselves and avoid emotion associated with negative evaluative experiences by others. The observer perspective may therefore become a maintaining factor through continued avoidance of emotion. An external perspective may increase its authority and increase the tendency to make internal attributions about an event.

Imagery is powerful because it is linked with early memories and verbal associations. In Osman et al. (2004), of the 18 BDD patients who reported spontaneous images, 15 (88%) identified these to be closely linked to a particular stressful memory. The median age associated with the memory was 11.5 years and typical themes included: being teased and bullied at school (e.g., "I was 10 years old and never got on with this boy in school. I remember one day asking him why he didn't like me and he said 'it's because you're ugly'") and self-consciousness about appearance changes during adolescence (e.g., "I was very tall for my age and I remember queuing in the playground after break-time one day and seeing my reflection in the hall window. My whole face and body seemed out of proportion and I was about two heads taller than everyone else"). Inspection of the themes suggested that all the early memories could be placed in one, or both, of these two categories. A small number were linked to sexual trauma. Of the 15 control participants who reported spontaneous images, only two (13%) identified these to be closely linked to a particular memory. The median age associated with this memory was 13 years. Significantly more BDD patients reported a particular memory associated with their images than control participants. It is these aversive memories that have become fused with the felt impression or imagery of the self.

Self-focused attention

When anxious, a person can be in one of two possible modes: an orienting mode or a defense mode (Mogg & Bradley, 1998). In the orienting mode, a person scans the environment for threat and may be more sensitive or hyper-vigilant to danger signals. Thus, in BDD a person may be comparing his appearance with others' to determine his social standing in relation to others. When a threat is imminent, such as being physically close to a person who is perceived as more attractive, the person will switch into defense mode. This involves a readiness to carry out some form of safety-seeking behavior that protects the individual (the "fight or flight" reaction). A person may attempt to escape from the situation or camouflage himself. In this mode, attention may be directed towards the source of safety (e.g., an escape route) and avoiding the threat (e.g., being self-focused, keeping the head down and avoiding eye contact).

Selective attention is the process of selecting certain portions of information from the vast amount confronting us at any given moment for further processing and to guide the individual's behavior. Self-focused attention is one type of selective attention that results in awareness of self-referent, internally-generated information (Ingram, 1990). Self-referent information can include a wide range of stimuli from an awareness of sensations, thoughts, images, or emotions from past memories that influence the self in the present.

We have noted that a person with BDD is excessively self-focused and fused with aversive imagery, verbal associations, and memories. The next process occurs when this internal experience becomes fused with reality. The term "fusion" has slightly different meanings – for example, "thought action fusion" in OCD refers to the idea that thinking something means one will act on it (Harvey et al., 2004) or thoughts can be fused with events or objects. However "cognitive fusion" refers to the fusion of internal events with past experiences (Hayes et al., 1999). Cognitive fusion then occurs when the dominance of certain aversive images and verbal functions are treated as truth and they organize behaviors (e.g., escape, avoidance, control). This is partly related to selective attention since, in a limited bandwidth, a person's reality is generated by the focus of attention. The phenomenon is not specific to BDD and an increase in self-focused attention is generally associated with increased psychopathology and handicap (Woodruff-Borden et al., 2001). With increasing psychopathology, the flexibility to switch attention easily may be lost. Thus, a subtype of social phobia may only experience self-focused attention in specific social situations (e.g., speaking to a group). By contrast, someone with BDD tends to experience self-focused attention in both social and non-social situations. When a person is excessively self-focused, it prevents accurate observations in social situations of others' reactions, so preventing disconfirmation of fears of negative evaluation; it also contaminates their environment and a person might *appear* to lack social skills. This in turn generates a negative reaction in others, which an individual experiences as a negative reaction to his appearance.

When an individual is alone, less attention is focused on tasks and the environment and there are usually difficulties in concentration. In severe cases, attentional capacity may be taken over by the constructed image and negative appraisal. Furthermore, the system may be so rigid that it is unable to switch to any external information about one's appearance. In less severe cases, there appears to be some attentional capacity for external information so that the image may be less stable and associated with doubts about how the person appears to others. In this case, the individual may feel driven by a need to know exactly how he looks. The person might be rewarded only with certainty whilst he is looking in a mirror and focusing on what he sees (rather than with an impression of how he looks). However, the longer a person with BDD looks in a mirror, the more self-focused he becomes, the worse he feels, and the more it reinforces his view of being ugly and defective. When there is no external reflection available, clients seem to use their image or "felt impression" as an internal mirror and way of checking how they look. The unintended consequences are to create further doubt and preoccupation, and at times confusion about how their appearance might alter from day to day or hour to hour. However, this might occur in the context of change in self-focused attention, mood changes, and occasional reinforcement of feeling better in a particular light or a "good" mirror when there is less self-focused attention. Hence a client may believe that in every mirror he looks at, he sees a different image (Veale & Riley, 2001). The process of selective attention also appears to be focused on specific features of an image leading to a heightened awareness and relative magnification of certain aspects, which has the effect of magnifying certain features.

Further evidence on the role of selective attention in BDD is provided by Anson et al. (2003). In this study, 42 BDD patients, all of whom had face-related concerns, were compared to 43 healthy controls using a modified dot probe task developed by Mansell et al. (1999). This was based on the original dot probe paradigm designed by MacLeod et al. (1986). In Mansell et al.'s study, high and low socially anxious individuals (without BDD) were briefly presented with pairs of pictures comprising a face and a household object under conditions of either anticipatory social-evaluative threat or no threat. The faces were negative, neutral, or positive in emotional expression. Each face–object pair was followed by one of two letters in a location corresponding to the centre of one of the pictures (i.e., the face or the object), and participants had to indicate as quickly as possible which letter they were shown. It is assumed that subjects would show a faster response to letters that followed the location of the picture to which they were attending. Mansell et al. (1999) found that subjects with high social anxiety, unlike those with low social anxiety, showed an attentional bias away from emotional (negative and positive) faces, but only when tested under conditions of anticipatory social threat. Chen et al. (2002) used the same task with patients diagnosed with social phobia, although they did not include a threat condition. The authors found that socially phobic subjects directed their attention away from the faces, irrespective of emotional expression, whilst controls showed no attentional bias. Chen et al. (2002) argued that the results of their study and Mansell et al.'s (1999) were consistent with a model of social phobia by Clark et al. (1995), which stresses the role of self-focused attention and reduced processing of external social cues in maintaining social anxiety.

In Anson's (2008) study of BDD the anticipatory threat condition was modified to include a BDD threat and no threat condition. The threat condition involved an appearance-related social-evaluative threat, in which subjects were informed that their head/face area would be video-recorded for five minutes and that they would then observe volunteers watching the video, but would not watch it themselves (the video recording did not actually take place). The authors found that in the absence of threat, BDD subjects showed a marked attentional bias towards the faces (regardless of whether these were negative, neutral, or positive), as compared to the controls, who did not show an attentional preference. However, under conditions of anticipatory BDD threat, neither the BDD subjects nor the controls displayed any attentional bias towards/away from the faces. One explanation for the findings is that under conditions of no threat, BDD patients were attending to faces as a result of appearance comparison processes. Anson et al. (in submission) suggest that when exposed to pictures consisting of face–object pairs, in the absence of direct appearance-related threat, people with BDD would be likely to show a greater tendency than people without BDD to direct their attention to the faces. Two potential explanations are suggested for the absence of an attentional preference for faces when anticipating a BDD-relevant threat:

activation of appearance-related social-evaluative anxiety; and intensification of distress resulting from appearance comparison.

Drawing from the social phobia model (Clark et al., 1995), the default state for many people with BDD is a shift of attention to being self-focused to monitor and check the appearance of themselves from their image. The presence of others (or indeed a reflective surface) will induce the process of appearance comparison, and switching between their own image and that of another face or their own reflection. Under conditions of BDD-related social-evaluative threat, individuals with BDD may perceive faces as threatening in terms of potential negative evaluation, leading to a suppression of the tendency to process the faces. However, the suggested general underlying tendency of BDD patients to attend to faces may account for the finding that, even under threat, attention does not shift to such a degree as to lead to them actually directing their attention away from the faces. The alternative explanation for absence of attention to faces under threat is that attention to faces may be affected by appearance comparison processes.

Meta-cognitions about self-focused attention

Positive beliefs about the process of self-focused attention in BDD are not documented and are being explored in a current study. Self-focused attention is a safety-seeking behavior as clients report that their motivation is to check on how they appear to others, similar to checking in a mirror. Thus, whilst their attention is directed towards their self, they are verifying exactly how they look and how vulnerable they are, and mentally preparing themselves for future threats.

Self-serving bias

Another form of selective attention occurs when attention is self-focused on a picture of their self and they may then experience an increase in depth from excessive vigilance. Individuals with BDD appear to have lost their self-serving bias (or "rose-tinted glasses") in ratings of attractiveness for their self. Jansen et al. (2006) first identified this phenomenon in patients with eating disorders. Eating-disordered individuals and controls were asked to rate their own torsos. They were then rated by two community panels who rated the torsos of eating symptomatic individuals as less attractive. Contrary to the eating symptomatic patients, the control group showed a strong positively biased perception of their attractiveness, contrary to the eating-disordered individuals, i.e., they rated their own bodies as far more attractive than others rated them. The study suggests that the problem in eating disorders is not a distorted body image but a lack of a self-serving body image bias (or the loss of rose-tinted glasses). Furthermore, Jansen et al. (2005) found that when viewing their own bodies, healthy controls focus more on their self-identified beautiful body parts and less on their self-identified ugly parts.

These studies have not been replicated in BDD. However, Lambrou's (2006) data (described in Chapter 7) are consistent with this finding. In this study, 50 BDD patients were compared with two non-clinical control groups: 50 art and design students and 50 non-art controls. A digital photograph of the participants was manipulated using a computer graphics technique to create a symmetry continuum. Presented with a continuum on their computer, participants were required to select and rate images representing their actual self, another person's face, and a building. BDD individuals were similar to the art and design controls and both groups were superior to non-art controls and had a greater understanding of aesthetic proportions and a superior accuracy in their self-estimations. The assumption is that under experimental conditions, individuals with BDD and art and design controls can switch attention to focus on a photo of their self, another person, or a building and come to a "better" aesthetic judgement than non-art controls. Furthermore, people with BDD are likely to selectively attend to those features that they consider to be ugly and less on those that are attractive. In other words, they not only are more accurate in their self-evaluations but also lack the self-serving bias to compensate or override the accuracy, thus experiencing a pronounced self-depreciation of their appearance.

All this has significant implications for therapy. First, a discussion of the role of imagery and self-focused attention, the link with early experiences, and the lack of a self-serving bias will assist in the process of engagement and validating the experience of BDD. It should be possible to *validate* in part a client's experience by describing the loss of "rose-tinted glasses" and how people without BDD tend to rate themselves as more attractive than they are. Furthermore, a person with BDD may be more aesthetically sensitive about his appearance and attend more to the less attractive parts of his appearance than the more attractive parts. However, this also brings several costs and a therapist can discuss the experience of being excessively self-focused and losing one's rose-tinted glasses as being the problem. This may lead to a discussion about the way perception is constructed. The outcome is that perception is not just an image on the back of the retina that is faithfully reproduced, but a more complex phenomenon influenced by "ghosts from the past" and an excessive, self-focused attention which interacts with the way a person thinks and feels.

The second implication for therapy is that, when assessing clients, more negative self-beliefs can be accessed via images and from earlier memories than via verbal thoughts (Osman et al., 2004). Third, there are a number of techniques for modifying the meaning of the image by historical reviews or rescripting an image, especially for teasing, bullying, and sexual trauma

(Hackmann & Hersen, 1998; Arntz & Weertman, 1999) or the beliefs about the imagery (Layden et al., 1993; Smucker et al., 1995), which we discuss in Chapter 16. Thus the strategy is to develop a different relationship with their image so that it is no longer regarded as a truthful reproduction but just a "picture in one's mind" that has been constructed over time. The model is complex, but starts to assist in the process of engagement in a psychological understanding of the problem which starts to make sense for people with BDD.

Lastly, the model suggests that techniques that help to train individuals to increase the degree of attention away from self-referent information towards tasks or the environment will be of assistance. This strategy has been described for social anxiety (Bogels et al., 1997; Clark, 2001) or health anxiety (Wells, 1990). The principle of increasing attention on a task such as shaving or combing one's hair can also be applied to mirror retraining (Veale & Riley, 2001) or routine activities such as walking down a street and becoming more aware of the environment from a field perspective.

10.3 Negative Appraisal of Body Image

Individuals with BDD appraise and aesthetically judge their body image negatively in a process of automatically activating assumptions and values about the importance of appearance. In BDD, appearance has become over-identified with the self and at the center of a "personal domain" (Veale, 2002). The term "personal domain" was first used by Beck (1976) to describe the way a person attaches meaning to events or objects around them. At the center of a personal domain are a person's characteristics, physical attributes, goals, and values. Clustered around are the animate and inanimate objects in which he has an investment (e.g., family, friends, and possessions). An idealized value occurs when one of the values develops into such overriding importance that it defines the "self" or identity of the individual or becomes the very center of a personal domain. The idealized value in BDD is usually the importance of the appearance of certain features, but other values may include social acceptance, perfectionism, symmetry, or youth. Such values will reinforce processing of the self as an aesthetic object, and in social situations as a social object (Clark et al., 1995). Without these idealized values, it might be possible to adapt to a body image in the way that some individuals with a disfigurement may accept themselves and become less self-conscious (Lansdown et al., 1997). The conditional assumptions and rules about one's appearance will be driven by the values about the importance of appearance to one's identity. Typical assumptions include: "If I am unattractive, then life is not worth living"; "If I am defective, then I will be alone all my life"; or "I can only do something when I feel comfortable about my appearance" (Veale et al., 1996). Geremia

& Neziroglu (2001) have noted other assumptions such as "If I looked better, then my whole life will be better"; "How I feel about myself as a person is related to how I feel about how I look." Typical core beliefs that are activated are based on a) being a failure or generally inadequate, b) being worthless, c) being ugly, repulsive, or abnormal, d) being unlovable or unacceptable, and e) being rejected by others and being alone for the rest of one's life (Osman et al., 2004). Most of the assumptions are not specific to BDD but are common in depression, anxiety, and personality disorders.

In common with other mood disorders, such appraisals will contribute to the bias towards beliefs that are confirmatory. For example, compliments are easily dismissed in a process of "discounting the positive." Examples include: "They are saying it to be nice to me" or "They have to love me however ugly I am because they are my parents." Alternatively, neutral comments may be turned into negative and be self-referential. The model predicts that activation of the negative appraisals will have a negative feedback and will increase self-focused attention on the individuals image and preoccupation.

What is not known is whether the importance of appearance and the assumptions about a defect have developed before or after the experience of mental imagery. In other words, in the absence of mental imagery of appearing defective and believing it to be true, would the person hold such beliefs and assumptions? Or have such assumptions developed as a consequence of the mental imagery and do they subside once the person no longer views such imagery as true or is no longer preoccupied and distressed by such imagery? This might partly depend on how chronic the problem is, in that dysfunctional attitudes and beliefs may be reinforced over time.

Therapeutic implications of negative appraisals

The *content* of the negative appraisals and evaluations such as being ugly and defective are generally ignored in therapy as they are relatively fixed and fused with the mental imagery. The strategy is to develop a different relationship with one's thoughts and images. Later in therapy, one can help clients question the meaning or the rigidity of the values about the importance of appearance in defining the self (Lazarus et al., 1977; Dryden, 1998; Veale, 2002). Reverse role-play has also been used to strengthen an alternative belief in which clients can practice arguing the case for their alternative belief whilst the therapist argues the case for the old beliefs or values (Cromarty & Marks, 1995). Clinical experience suggests that examining assumptions and values about the importance of appearance are best used later in therapy when an individual is engaged in the model, is in the process of giving up safety behaviors, and has become more functional (see Chapter 20). Examining the process of their thinking in terms of their ruminative style and appearance comparisons better helps many clients. Individuals compare themselves with others and engage in upward comparisons or choose inappropriate comparison targets with unrealistic ideals.

10.4   Rumination and Appearance Comparison

Another vicious cycle in maintaining preoccupation and distress in BDD is the process of appearance comparison and rumination. The outcome of such processes tends to be further evaluations and appraisals and this is highlighted more in Chapter 16.

Appearance comparison

Individuals with BDD excessively compare the feature they perceive as defective to others' features. They especially choose individuals of the same sex who are more attractive. This appearance comparison is common in body image disorders and body dissatisfaction. This refers to comparison of one's appearance to that of others, either in social or public settings, or when viewing media images. Theories of social comparison (Festinger, 1954) or social ranking (Allan & Gilbert, 1995) have been applied to body dissatisfaction. Heinberg & Thompson (1992) and Thompson et al. (1992) suggest that the more the individual makes comparisons, the greater the body dissatisfaction, particularly if comparisons are made with targets who are considered more attractive. Heinberg & Thompson (1992) describe appearance comparison behaviors in relation to the target of comparison. They describe "upward" (as opposed to "downward"') comparison, involving comparison targets considered more attractive, and "particularistic" (as opposed to "universalistic") comparison, involving comparison on the basis of specific factors such as characteristics of comparison target (e.g., age, gender) and specific body features that are considered relevant in terms of comparison processes. Cash (1991) uses the term "unfair to compare" to describe a cognitive error involving biased appearance comparison, in which people selectively compare themselves with people whom they regard as being attractive in terms of the features they are concerned about in themselves. Anson et al. (in submission) examine the role of appearance comparison with the Body Comparison Scale (Fisher et al., 2002). Preliminary results indicate that individuals with BDD report high levels of appearance comparison. BDD patients with facial concerns, for example, reported that they compared their facial features with those of other people of the same sex (particularly those considered attractive in terms of this feature) significantly more frequently than healthy controls did. Not surprisingly clients usually feel worse and are more preoccupied with their feature after making the comparison. Results from the study by Anson et al. suggest that immediately after BDD patients make comparisons of their appearance with others (particularly others of the same sex) they usually rate themselves as less attractive than their comparison targets and feel more distressed about their appearance. Thompson et al. (1991) found that the tendency to make comparisons with others in terms of physical appearance is related to body dissatisfaction, and Heinberg & Thompson (1992) suggest that the comparison process in itself may be threatening.

On the basis of the above, it is proposed that in situations where BDD patients are already experiencing heightened concerns about their appearance (which could be due to negative self-evaluation or perceptions of social-evaluative threat), the distressing effects of appearance comparison may be intensified, leading to reduced attention to the comparison targets (i.e. people's faces or other body parts) in order to mitigate anxiety. Appearance comparison is a core factor in the development and maintenance of body image problems (Stormer & Thompson, 1996). In BDD, it is hypothesized that selective attention to mental imagery and specific features prevents BDD patients from obtaining a representative or accurate view of the appearance of others. In addition, this process is likely to contribute to excessive focus on overall and specific features of appearance and the resultant mental imagery. These factors are proposed to maintain negative beliefs and exaggerated ideals relating to appearance in terms of both self-evaluation and perceived evaluation by others, and exaggerated beliefs about the importance of overall appearance and specific features in terms of identity. In addition, appearance comparison may contribute to anxiety and distress in social and public situations and this is explored below.

In summary, the appearance comparison appears to be on specific features regarded as defective. Those who view their feature as very unattractive may desire to blend in with an average. A minority who view their feature as average may desire an unrealistic standard or perfectionism. When looking in a mirror the comparison may be with the constructed image. Alternatively, the comparisons may be with an old photo of himself or a picture in the media. In social situations, the comparison is usually of peers the same age and sex. Appearance comparisons are another factor that maintains distorted negative appraisals and self-focused attention on imagery in a negative feedback loop. Furthermore, the attention is often selective and unrepresentative and likely to interfere with the processing of other external information. The implications of the model are that therapy involves resisting the frequent comparison and rating of one's appearance against others. In this regard, it will be important to conduct a functional analysis about the immediate and unintended consequences of comparing and to determine the beliefs about helpfulness of comparing.

Rumination

Individuals with BDD use effortful cognitive strategies such as mentally planning, monitoring, fantasizing (e.g., "If only I hadn't been born this way"), or
self-attacking in response to thoughts. They are trying to solve the wrong
problem by responding to intrusive thoughts and doubts (e.g., "Why did I have
the surgery done?"). Rumination may have an immediate consequence of
avoidance by inhibiting aversive imagery or thoughts about being ugly and is
therefore reinforcing. However, the strategy has an unintended consequence
of maintaining preoccupation and distress.

Holland et al. (in submission) describe a study comparing 22 people with
BDD and 22 people with "normal concerns" regarding appearance (14 females
and eight males in each group). Amongst other scales, they were compared
with the Metacognitions Questionnaire (MCQ; Cartwright-Hatton & Wells,
1997) and the Thought Control Questionnaire (TCQ; Wells & Davies, 1994)
and a structured interview to determine their strategy in response to their
worries (distraction, social control, worry, punishment, and reappraisal). The
content of thoughts about appearance was broadly similar in people with BDD
and people with "normal concerns" regarding appearance. However, people
with BDD were significantly more likely to report experiencing future-
oriented thoughts than people with "normal concerns." People with BDD
also endorsed negative meta-cognitive beliefs regarding both uncontrollability
and danger and the responsibility, superstition, and punishment associated
with thoughts about appearance more strongly than people with "normal
concerns." People with BDD also reported employing more punishment
strategies, while the "normal concerns" group employed more social control
strategies.

Self-attacking and punishment in response to thoughts and images are very
destructive and another feedback loop in which engagement and trying to
solve the appraisals and evaluations of one's appearance further contribute to
the preoccupation and distress. Chapter 18 describes a functional analysis of
these processes and a method of determining the beliefs about self-attacking
and rumination. This then leads to ceasing ruminating and non-engagement
with intrusive thoughts and feelings. In those who are self-attacking, we recommend the use of compassionate mind training (Gilbert, 2005).

10.5   Emotion

Emotions in BDD are complex and depend on the exact appraisal of the
situation and event and subsequent behavior. The emotions include: a)
internal shame (or self-disgust) when the individual compares and ranks his

appearance as lower than others; b) external shame and anticipatory social anxiety based on judgements about how others are likely to scrutinize, humiliate, or reject him; c) depression and hopelessness at the person's failure to reach his aesthetic standard, perhaps living in social isolation, interpersonal conflicts and deficits in relationships; d) anger and frustration with oneself for damaging his appearance (e.g., DIY surgery, skin-picking), others not understanding or agreeing with their concerns, not having enough money to pay for cosmetic surgery, or not obtaining satisfaction in cosmetic surgery; and e) guilt and shame at damaging one's appearance either oneself or by seeking cosmetic surgery. With the prominence of hopelessness and shame, it is not surprising that there is a high degree of comorbidity with depression and risk of suicide (Phillips et al., 1993; Veale et al., 1996). As in other areas, there is a negative feedback loop, as increases in emotional arousal will tend to increase the frequency or severity of negative appraisal of one's body image and increase self-focused attention. Symptoms of arousal are not normally specifically targeted in CBT, but any strategy that improves mood or increases tolerance to negative states would theoretically decrease preoccupation and negative appraisal.

10.6   Avoidance and Safety-seeking Behaviors

Escape and avoidance behaviors refer to a way of responding to situations or activities that trigger aversive imagery and beliefs or as a way of avoiding the experience of aversive thoughts, images, or emotions. It may include direct suppression of emotion (e.g., use of substances) or thought suppression. Clients typically avoid a wide range of social and public situations or certain reflective surfaces knowing that they will be more self-conscious and distressed. This behavior therefore becomes reinforcing and maintains the distress and preoccupation.

There are also many safety-seeking behaviors in situations that are anxiety-provoking which aim to reduce the risk of danger, including escape and repetitive and non-repetitive behaviors (Salkovskis, 1991; Salkovskis et al., 1996). These are known from an evolutionary psychology perspective as "submissive behaviors" (Allan & Gilbert, 1997; Gilbert & Bailey, 2000). It is assumed that such learnt behaviors may have been adaptive in the past in certain contexts. They may also be termed "defense mechanisms" and have the aim or effect of reducing social threat and gaining or maintaining social rank. Thus interpersonal factors are also relevant and include positive and negative responses elicited from friends and family.

Being excessively self-conscious with mental imagery of a defective appearance is highly aversive. Individuals will try to avoid such feelings or use various safety-seeking behaviors that aim to reduce self-consciousness. Traditionally, safety behaviors for all anxiety disorders are actions within situations designed to prevent feared catastrophes. The essence of a submissive behavior in a social situation is damage-limiting self-presentations (Gilbert & Bailey, 2000) rather than acquisitive ones.

Safety-seeking or submissive behaviors in BDD are often idiosyncratic and have personal meaning to the individual. Thus one woman may be using excessive make-up to camouflage facial skin, while another woman may be avoiding using make-up in the belief that it will draw attention to her. They are generally adapted by the individual to:

a) Restore, alter, or enhance a feature (restitution) – for example a cosmetic procedure. The cognitive form of restitution is "neutralizing," which is defined as any voluntary or effortful mental action done to prevent or minimize harm by putting it right (e.g., self-reassurance or saying a phrase). It more commonly occurs in OCD, but less is known about such cognitive responses in BDD.

b) Avoid, camouflage, or distract attention from a feature (e.g., by the use of excessive make-up). The cognitive form of avoidance is to try to avoid experiencing aversive thoughts, images and feelings by distraction or suppression.

c) Verify one's appearance or the impression one is giving to others (e.g., mirror-checking). Here the aim is to reduce uncertainty or distress about a feature. The cognitive form of verification is to verify one's image by checking against one's internal image or compare it against another person's. This may be repeated with the aim of feeling "comfortable" or "just right."

Various safety-seeking behaviors are described in the Chapter 4 and examples are given below:

a) A man who tore up all photos of himself to prevent thinking about his appearance or the "wrong" impression that he was giving to others. He did not want to look at himself or he did not want others to look at him (avoidance).

b) A man who had had three rhinoplasties to alter his nose but was now preoccupied by mentally planning how to restore scarring from the first operation (restitution).

c) A woman who spent time using various beauty treatments to camouflage her face, which she believed to have numerous lines and scars (avoidance).

d) A woman who shaved off all the hair on her head and had a large tattoo to distract attention in public from a "flaw" on her nose (avoidance).

e) A man preoccupied with his nose, who stood in front of a mirror and performed mental cosmetic surgery on his nose until he felt "comfortable" and able to know what he looked like (verification). This is similar to a compulsive washing or checking in OCD as the person is using problematic criteria for the termination of a compulsion, i.e., feeling "comfortable" or "absolutely sure" (Richards et al., 1995) or the "right feeling" (Yaryura-Tobias & Neziroglu, 1997a).

The importance for the model is that there is another negative feedback loop. Escape and safety behaviors may briefly decrease distress or uncertainty but have the unintended consequence of increasing self-consciousness, preoccupation, and negative appraisal. Furthermore, safety-seeking behaviors: a) involve enormous mental effort and attention, which means less capacity for external information; b) often lead to yet more monitoring (e.g., mirror-checking to determine if the camouflage is "working"); c) may objectively make one's appearance worse (e.g., skin-picking); and d) increase others' attention to one's appearance (e.g., a person holding up their hand to their face).

In clinical practice, an idiosyncratic version of the model is drawn up with the client which focuses on a specific episode of increased worry about one's appearance (e.g., a person looking in a mirror in the hope that he does not look as bad as he thinks he does in his mental image). A behavioral experiment may be constructed to determine the effect of the safety-seeking behavior on the degree of preoccupation, self-consciousness, and negative appraisal. Suffice to say all safety behaviors are a major maintenance factor in the preoccupation and distress of BDD and much creativity may be required to help clients give up their safety behaviors. Similarly, clients will require exposure to situations avoided without their safety behaviors and with maximum attention on tasks (rather than the self).

10.7 Conclusion

The cognitive behavioral model of BDD is driven by the experience of excessive self-focused attention on an image or felt impression of the self, which fuses past memories with the present. This in turn activates assumptions of the importance of one's appearance in defining the self and the various ways of responding (i.e., avoidance and safety-seeking behaviors, ruminating, and comparing). The following chapters describe how each of these factors may be reversed.

Chapter 11

Evidence for cognitive behavior therapy in BDD

Summary

There is a paucity of evidence for psychological treatments in BDD. There are two randomized controlled trials (RCTs) comparing cognitive behavior therapy (CBT) against a waiting list; one RCT of adding cognitive therapy to exposure and response prevention (E&RP) and several case-controlled studies of E&RP or CBT. The two RCTs of CBT have demonstrated that CBT is better than no treatment in BDD. There are no RCTs of any psychological therapies in adolescents with BDD and there are only a few case reports of E&RP or CBT in adolescents. Little is known about the optimal duration, frequency of sessions of CBT, or the effect of discontinuation of CBT and relapse prevention. Furthermore, since the original pilot studies, the model for the maintenance of BDD has been updated, and no treatment studies have examined the latest findings. There are only case reports for CBT in the treatment of psychogenic excoriation and no RCTs. CBT for psychogenic excoriation consists of a contextual functional analysis of the behavior, followed by self-monitoring and habit reversal. A variety of RCTs, therefore, need to be conducted. The priorities are a) to compare CBT against a nonspecific psychological therapy; b) to compare the effectiveness of a SSRI vs. CBT or a combination of the two; c) to determine the effectiveness of CBT in children and adolescents with BDD; d) to determine the effectiveness of CBT in psychogenic excoriation; and e) to determine the durability of CBT and prognostic variables after treatment.

Sections

11.1   Randomized controlled trials of CBT for BDD in adults
11.2   Case control studies of CBT for BDD in adults

Body Dysmorphic Disorder: A Treatment Manual. David Veale and Fugen Neziroglu
© 2010 John Wiley & Sons, Ltd.

11.3   CBT in children and adolescents with BDD
11.4   CBT for psychogenic excoriation
11.5   CBT or pharmacotherapy for BDD?
11.6   Clinical guidelines
11.7   Future research

11.1   Randomized Controlled Trials of CBT for BDD in Adults

This chapter reviews the evidence for behavior and/or cognitive therapy, or a combination of the approaches in BDD. Two RCTs have been conducted with CBT in adults (Rosen et al., 1995a; Veale et al., 1996). A meta-analysis of these studies in BDD and treatment guidelines has also been published in the UK (National Collaborating Centre for Mental Health, 2006). A meta-analysis of the RCTs and various case series and a comparison of the effect size of CBT and pharmacotherapy have also been published (Williams et al., 2006).

The meta-analysis of RCTs found evidence suggesting a difference favoring CBT over a waiting list control on reducing BDD symptoms as measured by the Body Dysmorphic Disorder Examination (BDDE) (N = 2; N = 73; SMD = –2.35; 95% CI, –2.96 to –1.73) (See Figure 11.1). Only one of the two

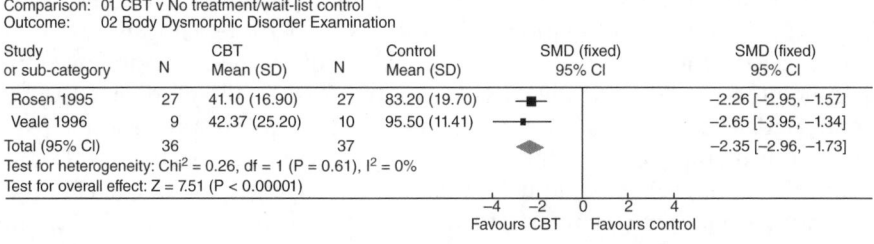

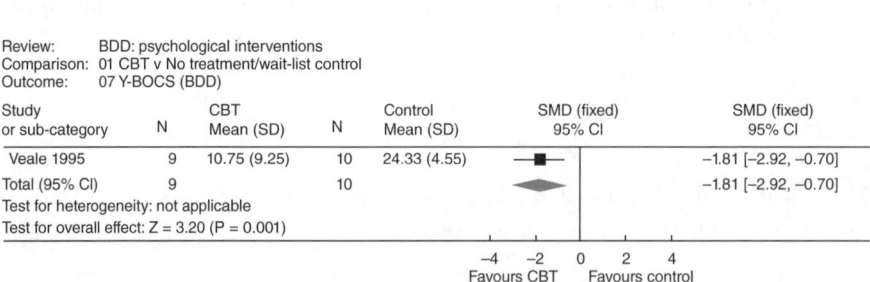

Figure 11.1   RCT of CBT for BDD (Rosen et al., 1995; Veale et al., 1996)

studies (Veale, et al., 1996) used the Yale-Brown Obsessive Compulsive Scale modified for BDD (YBOCS-BDD), which has been used in pharmacotherapy trials. There is limited evidence suggesting a difference favoring CBT over waiting list controls on reducing BDD symptoms as measured by the YBOCS-BDD (N = 1; N = 19; SMD = −1.81; 95% CI, −2.92 to −0.7). There is also limited evidence suggesting reducing depressive symptoms as measured by the Montgomery Asberg Depression rating Scale (MADRS) (N = 1; N = 19; SMD = −1.53; 95% CI, −2.58 to −0.47).

These two studies are now briefly described. Rosen et al. (1995a) conducted an RCT of group CBT in 54 participants with BDD. Results indicated that 81.5% of the 27 patients were clinically improved after treatment. Treatment involved a small group format for an eight-week period. Therapy sessions consisted of education about causation and treatment of BDD, constructing a hierarchy of distressing aspects of their appearance, homework assignments involving exposure to anxiety-provoking situations and preventing body checking behaviors, as well as keeping a body image diary. The participants in this study were different from those described in other centers, as they were less severely handicapped, they were all female, and the most common preoccupation was their weight and shape. However, they did not have a diagnosable eating disorder.

Veale et al. (1996) conducted the second RCT of CBT in 19 participants, who were predominantly female but more severely handicapped than those in the Rosen et al. study. Participants were randomly allocated to either 12 sessions of individual CBT by three different therapists or a waiting list control over 12 weeks. Seven out of the nine treated patients were rated as having either absent or a subclinical BDD at the end of the trial. In contrast, all the patients on the waiting list were rated as having a disorder in the clinical range at the end of the trial. Therapy focused on helping the individual to have a good psychological understanding of the factors that maintained the symptoms, behavioral experiments to test an alternative theory, exposure to situations avoided, and dropping of excessive safety behaviors and rituals.

Khemlani-Patel (2001) conducted an RCT, but because of the small sample size, it was not included in the meta-analysis. She investigated whether the addition of cognitive therapy would increase the efficacy of exposure and response prevention by targeting affective symptoms and decreasing overvalued ideation. Patients were randomly assigned to one of two treatment conditions: combined cognitive behavioral therapy or behavioral only therapy. A total of 10 participants with a primary diagnosis of BDD participated. Treatment was conducted for a total of eight weeks preceded by a two-week baseline. Participants in the combination group received four weeks' cognitive therapy followed by four weeks' exposure and response prevention; the other group received eight weeks' exposure and response prevention only. All sessions were 90 minutes in duration three times a week. Results indicate that all participants, regardless of treatment condition, demonstrated statistically significant improvement on symptom and affective measures. Improvement on symptom measures and decrease in overvalued ideation were clinically significant. Available follow-up data at six weeks post-treatment indicate that gains were maintained. Results suggest that exposure and response prevention alone may be just as effective as a combined approach in targeting BDD symptoms. A short-term structured treatment protocol, therefore, may be beneficial when conducted intensively. Due to the small sample size, however, results should be evaluated with caution.

11.2   Case Control Studies of CBT for BDD in Adults

We provide a brief narrative review of other case control studies and case reports on the use of CBT, which is summarized in Neziroglu & Khemlani-Patel (2002) and Williams et al. (2006). We highlight some of the better controlled studies.

Neziroglu & Yaryura-Tobias (1993b) reported on E&RP and cognitive therapy focused solely on BDD. The participants were not on medication and various standardized assessment measures were utilized. Patients received either weekly or daily 90-minute sessions for 4–12 weeks. Most of the session was spent on E&RP, with 20–30 minutes at the end of each session for cognitive therapy. One of the patients dropped out and the other four showed significant improvement on observer-based measures. Obsessing for less than one hour a day was the criterion for improvement. Results suggest that intensive sessions, more than once a week, seem to provide the greatest gains.

Neziroglu et al. (1996) found exposure and response prevention and cognitive therapy to be effective in 12 out of 17 patients with comorbid Axis II diagnoses using intensive 90-minute sessions five times a week for four weeks. All the participants met criteria for at least one personality disorder, and 13 out of the 17 had four or more. Treatment consisted of 60 minutes' E&RP and 30 minutes' cognitive therapy. No relationship between treatment response and number of personality disorders was found. However, the number of personality disorders decreased as patients improved with CBT.

McKay et al. (1997) conducted a maintenance follow-up program involving exposure and response prevention for individuals with BDD after CBT. The maintenance phase consisted of a psycho-education session following treatment to explain relapse and management of a lapse. Patients were contacted twice a week for assessment with all measures for a total of six months. All subjects were assessed at follow-up and all had remained symptom-free. Patients in the maintenance group, however, had continued to improve on measures of anxiety and depression and showed significantly lower levels of anxiety and depression at follow-up. McKay (1999) followed up these patients two years later and noted that treatment gains were maintained.

Cognitive behavioral group therapy has been shown to lead to significant improvement in both BDD and depressive symptoms (Wilhelm et al., 1999). Participants in this study received weekly 90-minute group sessions which included psycho-education, self-monitoring, cognitive restructuring, exposure, response prevention, and scheduling of pleasant events and achievement-oriented activities.

Geremia & Neziroglu (2001) systematically investigated a trial of cognitive restructuring. Four individuals with BDD were treated in a single-subject multiple baseline design in which each patient served as his own control. Treatment consisted of seven weeks of 75-minute sessions twice a week for cognitive treatment, followed by three weeks' follow-up data-gathering. Results indicated that cognitive therapy resulted in statistically significant reductions in obsessions in three out of the four patients. Three out of the four patients also showed statistically significant reductions in dissatisfaction with body parts, depression, and anxiety. Minimal improvement was seen with overvalued ideation. The authors note that prior to treatment patients may still be susceptible to setbacks when encountering distressing situations, such as negative comments about their physical appearance. In this study, no behavioral assignments were given. The authors suggest that the addition of behavior therapy may enhance treatment efficacy.

There are case reports of behavior therapy with or without medication, including Munjack (1978), Solyom et al. (1985), Marks & Mishan (1988), Vitello & de Leon (1990), Watts (1990), Gomez Perez et al. (1994), and Campisi (1995). There are also case reports of CBT by Schmidt & Harrington (1995) and Neziroglu et al. (1996); and descriptions of reverse role-play to behavior therapy by Newell & Shrubb (1994) and Cromarty & Marks (1995). Brown et al. (1997) describe the use of eye movement desensitization and reprocessing (EMDR, a form of CBT which can include imagery rescripting) in seven cases of BDD. However, there are no data such as changes on YBOCS-BDD. Lastly, there are two case reports of psychodynamic therapy (Philippopoulos, 1979; Bloch & Glue, 1988).

11.3 CBT in Children and Adolescents with BDD

There are no RCTs of any psychological interventions in children and adolescents with BDD. There is one successful case report of behavior therapy (Braddock, 1982); one successful case report of behavior therapy combined with an anti-depressant (doxepine) (Sobanski & Schmidt, 2000);

one of multiple treatment modalities (psychodynamic therapy, CBT, family therapy, and medication) by Horowitz et al. (2002); and one case report of psychodynamic therapy (Philippopoulos, 1979).

11.4   CBT for Psychogenic Excoriation

Chapter 5 discusses some of the difficulties in the "diagnosis" of psychogenic excoriation and its comorbidity with BDD, OCD, and BPD. Existing RCTs and case series of CBT for BDD would have included some cases of psychogenic excoriation. In future, it may be more useful to differentiate RCTs as BDD with or without psychogenic excoriation as the treatment is different (e.g. self-monitoring, functional analysis, and habit reversal in psychogenic excoriation) and to report on the functional analysis (e.g., patients in whom the excoriation is driven by emotional regulation or has become more like habit).

There are no RCTs of CBT for psychogenic excoriation. There are a number of case reports for which most of the subjects did not have BDD. Rosenbaum & Ayllon (1981) first described the use of habit reversal in four individuals whose scratching had aggravated their neurodermatitis (a condition that begins with a minor infection or skin lesion that produces itching and subsequent scratching) and who would not have had psychogenic excoriation. Habit reversal includes multiple components: self-monitoring to increase awareness, competing response training, and stimulus control.

Kent & Drummond (1989) described the use of habit reversal in one case of "acne excoriée," in which the person picked real or imagined acneiform lesions, resulting in worsening of acne. Twohig & Woods (2001) describe the successful use of a simplified habit reversal in two male patients with psychogenic excoriation but without any significant comorbid psychiatric disorder. And Deckersbach et al. (2002) reported the use of habit reversal and other components of cognitive restructuring in two out of three patients with psychiatric comorbidity. One case had BDD alone, one had dysthymia, attention deficit disorder, and BDD, and the third had no other current comorbidity. They noted that "habit-like" excoriation appeared to respond better to habit reversal than when excoriation functioned to regulate intense emotion.

There are two cases of acne excoriée treated with pulsed laser irradiation and "cognitive psychodynamic therapy" (Bowes & Alster, 2004). No details are provided on the psychological intervention, although "basic" behavior modification techniques were used (e.g., avoidance of unnecessary situations of conflict and removal of mirrors from the house). The second individual had comorbid OCD and depression, which was also treated with a serotonin-norepinephrine reuptake inhibitor (venlafaxine). She was "counseled" to avoid the affected areas and treated with laser scar revision.

From this, it is clear that much needs to be researched for CBT for psychogenic excoriation. It is also important to define clearly the population under study as the main problem is BDD rather than BPD or OCD.

11.5 CBT or Pharmacotherapy for BDD?

The evidence for pharmacotherapy in BDD is evaluated in Chapter 12. Evidence from RCTs in pharmacotherapy favors the use of selective serotonergic reuptake inhibitors (SSRIs). There are no controlled trials that compare CBT with a SSRI or a combination of the two. Whether monotherapy or a combined approach is more efficacious needs to be studied, but so far there is no evidence that a combined approach in moderate to severe BDD is unhelpful or less efficacious.

Williams et al. (2006) compared relative effectiveness of CBT and SSRI alone from RCTs and case series. The weighted mean effect size, $M_d = +0.92$ for the eight pharmacotherapy outcomes trials, while the mean effect size, $M_d = +1.63$ for the 15 studies with psychological intervention outcomes. There was a significant difference in effect sizes between outcomes from pharmacotherapy trials and outcomes from psychological interventions. When the psychological interventions were subdivided into CBT and behavior therapy, it was found that CBT had increased $M_d = +1.78$, nearly double the effect size of pharmacotherapy. Great caution should be used, however, in interpreting such findings as the selection of subjects may significantly influence the outcome. Several studies had patients who were already taking medication, albeit on a stable dose. The only studies to be included in most evidence-based guidelines will be randomized controlled trials and as yet there are no head-to-head RCTs that compare CBT and an SSRI. Therefore, Williams et al.'s (2006) meta-analysis needs to be interpreted with great caution because of possible selection bias.

11.6 Clinical Guidelines

On the basis of the meta-analysis and a narrative review, the National Institute of Health and Clinical Excellence (NICE) in the UK has produced clinical guidelines for the treatment of OCD and BDD (National Collaborating Centre for Mental Health, 2006). It recommends that individuals with BDD with mild functional impairment should be offered a course of CBT which addresses key features of BDD. If there is moderate functional impairment, individuals with BDD should be offered the choice of a course of an SSRI or more intensive individual CBT. Individuals with BDD with severe functional impairment should be offered combined treatment with an SSRI and CBT. Those with more severe symptoms should have an increased frequency of sessions or a more intensive program on a residential unit or as inpatients.

11.7   Future Research

In conclusion, the evidence for psychological treatment in BDD is minimal and research is still in its infancy. There is a paucity of RCTs and most of the publications consist of case studies or have been conducted without a treatment manual. Earlier case reports have not used diagnostic criteria for BDD and some studies have not controlled for use of medication. Despite this, there is some evidence for the effectiveness of CBT in BDD and that it holds the most promise in similar disorders. Further research is required to determine:

a)   the specificity of CBT compared to a credible psychological therapy;
b)   the effectiveness of CBT in children and adolescents with BDD;
c)   the effectiveness in individuals with psychogenic excoriation who require different strategies;
d)   the intensity, with optimal frequency and duration of CBT;
e)   the relative effectiveness of individual or group therapy;
f)   the durability of the effects of CBT in the long term and relapse prevention;
g)   the effectiveness of CBT compared to an SSRI anti-depressant, and combined;
h)   the cost-effectiveness in comparison to medication;
i)   the effectiveness of "third-wave" CBT, such as acceptance and commitment therapy (Hayes et al., 1999);
j)   which components of the treatment are especially effective;
k)   prognostic variables, such as strength of belief, comorbidity of depression, and readiness for change.

Chapter 12

Evidence for pharmacotherapy in BDD

Summary

This chapter reviews the use of pharmacotherapy in BDD and for psychogenic excoriation. Two RCTs and several open label case series have been conducted on SSRIs or clomipramine in BDD. The evidence for adults with BDD, including those with an additional diagnosis of a delusional disorder, favors a serotonin reuptake inhibitor (SRI). One RCT has been conducted with pimozide as an augmentation strategy to an SSRI in BDD compared to placebo augmentation, which found it to be ineffective. Open label case reports suggest augmentation strategies such as adding clomipramine to citalopram or adding buspirone to an SSRI. No continuation, maintenance, or discontinuation studies of an SRI have been reported. The evidence base for pharmacotherapy for psychogenic excoriation is tiny. There is one RCT of fluoxetine and several case reports on the benefit of SSRIs for psychogenic excoriation. There are two case reports on the benefit of anti-psychotic drugs (pimozide and olanzapine) and an opiate antagonist (naltrexone). No evidence exists for the use of ECT or psychosurgery in BDD. As yet, there are no published RCTs of an SSRI in adolescents with BDD or its delusional variant. Case series suggest that adolescents with BDD may also benefit from an SSRI in the same way as an adult with BDD.

Sections

12.1   Randomized controlled trials in adults with BDD
12.2   Open label studies of anti-depressants in adults with BDD
12.3   Open label studies in adolescents with BDD
12.4   Open label studies of anti-psychotic drugs in adults with BDD

Body Dysmorphic Disorder: A Treatment Manual. David Veale and Fugen Neziroglu
© 2010 John Wiley & Sons, Ltd.

12.1   Randomized Controlled Trials in Adults with BDD

There have been three RCTs of pharmacotherapy in adults with BDD. Treatment guidelines based for pharmacotherapy on the following data have also been provided in the UK (National Collaborating Centre for Mental Health et al., 2004). Phillips & Hollander (2008) also provide a review of all the controlled and open label pharmacotherapy studies conducted to date. In the first RCT, Phillips et al. (2002) entered 74 adults with BDD or its delusional variant into the study. Sixty-seven were randomized to either fluoxetine (40–80 mg a day) (N = 34) or placebo (N = 33) for 12 weeks. Twelve patients (37.5%) in the fluoxetine group and 15 patients (46.9%) in the placebo group were delusional at baseline. Fluoxetine was superior to a placebo on YBOCS-BDD. Benefits began at week 8 and continued at weeks 10 and 12. The baseline YBOCS-BDD in the fluoxetine group was 31.5, reducing to 21.0 at 12 weeks. The mean change from baseline in the YBOCS-BDD total score was more than twice as large with fluoxetine as with placebo treatment (35% vs. 14% decrease). The response rate on the YBOCS-BDD to fluoxetine was 53% (18/24) vs. 18% (6/53) to placebo. The treatment effect size was modest (f = 0.35; 95% CI, 0.22–0.48; d equivalent = 0.70). Delusional patients at baseline were as likely as those of non-delusional patients at baseline to respond to fluoxetine (50% [six out of 12] vs. 55% [11 out of 20]). In contrast, no delusional patients responded to the placebo (0% [0 out of 15] vs. 35% [6 six out of 17]). The effect was independent of comorbid diagnoses of OCD or depression.

There has been one randomized double-blind crossover trial comparing clomipramine with desipramine (Hollander et al., 1999). Forty participants with BDD or its delusional variant were entered and 29 were entered into a two-week, single-blind run-in, followed by eight weeks of clomipramine or eight weeks of desipramine, which was then crossed over. Clomipramine is a potent SRI and tricyclic anti-depressant. Desipramine is a potent noradrenergic reuptake inhibitor and tricyclic. The two drugs are equally effective in the treatment of depression, but clomipramine has been found to be more effective than desipramine in OCD (Goodman et al., 1990) and other anxiety disorders. In the first eight weeks of the clomipramine arm, the YBOCS-BDD decreased from approximately 23 at baseline to 16.2 (SD 8.7) at eight weeks, a reduction of 25% on the main outcome scale. Only the relationship between baseline and endpoint (16 weeks) is reported. Clomipramine was more effective in individuals with an additional diagnosis of delusional disorder. Treatment efficacy was not influenced by comorbidity of OCD, depression, or social phobia. There are limitations to this trial, including a lack of a placebo arm, a maintenance phase after the crossover, and potential carry-over effects, which are inherent in any crossover design. There is some evidence that the response may have been greater if a higher dose of clomipramine (mean 138 mg/day) was used and for a longer duration (at least 12 weeks).

Phillips (2005) has conducted an RCT of pimozide augmentation of an SSRI. Twenty-eight people with BDD or its delusional variant who had failed to respond to fluoxetine participated in an eight-week double-blind study of fluoxetine with pimozide (up to 10 mg) or fluoxetine with a placebo. Pimozide was no more effective than the placebo: 18.2% of subjects responded to pimozide and 17.6% to the placebo. Delusionality did not decrease significantly more with pimozide than with the placebo. Possible explanations of the lack of efficacy include the study's low power and the modest mean pimozide dose. Furthermore, SRI augmentation studies in OCD with an antipsychotic have found higher response rates in patients with a tic disorder or schizotypal personality disorder. No BDD participant in this study had either diagnosis.

12.2 Open Label Studies of Anti-depressants in Adults with BDD

SSRIs other than fluoxetine may theoretically be of benefit and there are four open label studies of SSRIs in adults with BDD: two of fluvoxamine (Perugi et al., 1996; Phillips et al., 1998), one of citalopram (Phillips & Najjar, 2003) and one of clomipramine (Hollander et al., 1989).

Hollander et al. (1989) first reported on a case series of five participants with BDD, who all responded to either clomipramine or fluoxetine. Four of the five patients had failed to respond previously to drugs that had some serotonergic action, including tricyclics, trazodone and lithium.

Perugi et al. (1996) entered 15 participants with BDD into an open label trial lasting 10 weeks. The average dose was 208 mg (range 100–300 mg). They did not use the YBOCS-BDD as an outcome measure, but reported a 60%

reduction over 12 weeks on symptom scores, with 10 out of the 15 participants responding on the Clinical Global Impression scale.

Phillips et al. (1998) entered 30 participants with BDD who received fluvoxamine over 16 weeks. The average dose was 238.8 mg (range 50–300 mg). The YBOCS-BDD decreased from 31.1 (SD 5.4) at baseline to 16.9 (SD 11.8) at 16 weeks, a 45% reduction on the main outcome measure; 63% of participants responded (defined as 30% decrease or more on the YBOCS-BDD). Fluvoxamine was as effective in participants with an additional diagnosis of delusional disorders as without.

Phillips & Najjar (2003) entered 15 participants with BDD or its delusional variant in an open label study of citalopram over 12 weeks. The average dose was 51.3 mg (range 10–60 mg). The YBOCS-BDD decreased from 30.7 (SD 4.9) at baseline to 15.3 (SD 10.6) at 12 weeks, a 50% reduction on the main outcome measure; 73.3% of participants responded (defined as 30% decrease or more on the YBOCS-BDD). Citalopram was as effective in participants with an additional diagnosis of delusional disorders as without.

Phillips (1996d) conducted a retrospective case review of 130 patients who had 316 treatment trials of which 42% of 65 SRI trials had led to an improvement on the Clinical Global Impression scale, compared to 30% of 23 trials with a monoamine oxidase inhibitor (MAOI) and 15% of 48 trials with a non-SRI tricyclic drug.

No continuation, maintenance, or discontinuation studies of an SRI have been reported. Expert opinion and clinical experience suggest that, like OCD, there may be further small gains with an SRI after 12 weeks' treatment. Furthermore, like OCD, there is likely to be a high rate of relapse on discontinuation of an SRI (Phillips et al., 2001).

There are case reports on the benefit of sertraline in BDD (el-Khatib & Dickey, 1995); two cases with intravenous clomipramine (Pallanti & Koran, 1996); and two case reports of the benefit of an MAOI: tranlcypromine (Jenike, 1984); and a combination of phenelzine, trimipramine, and perphenazine (Phillips, 1991). Other case reports indicate improvement on the YBOCS-BDD on clomipramine, fluoxetine, and pimozide combined with CBT (Neziroglu & Yaryura-Tobias, 1993a).

12.3   Open Label Studies in Adolescents with BDD

There are no published RCTs of anti-depressants in adolescents with BDD, although there is one ongoing study in the USA with fluoxetine. Albertini & Phillips (1999) reported on 33 children and adolescents with BDD of whom 10 out of 19 (53%) treated with an SRI improved on the Clinical Global Impression scale. Non-SRI medications in eight trials were ineffective. There is one case report on clomipramine in an adolescent with BDD with delusional disorder (Sondheimer, 1988) and one case report of doxepine and behavior therapy in an adolescent with BDD (Sobanski & Schmidt, 2000).

12.4   Open Label Studies of Anti-psychotic Drugs in Adults with BDD

Psychiatrists, especially in Europe, have traditionally treated BDD with an anti-psychotic, specifically pimozide in delusional disorder. Riding & Munro (1975) first described the benefit of pimozide in individuals with delusional disorder. The case series included cases of delusions of infestation, delusions of body odor, and dysmorphic delusions. The popularity of pimozide has since declined, probably because of concerns about its toxicity and having to perform an ECG prior to its administration. However, psychiatrists continue to prescribe other anti-psychotic drugs, either as monotherapy or as an adjunct for BDD without any evidence base.

The first negative case series was by Phillips (1996d), who reported a retrospective survey of medication trials. She found that only 3% of 83 trials of an anti-psychotic were of any benefit in BDD. Grant et al. (2001) described a case report of olanzapine for BDD without delusional disorder. The individual fulfilled diagnostic criteria for BDD, alcohol dependence, and bipolar II disorder. At the end of three weeks, the patient reported no preoccupation with her appearance and no longer met criteria for BDD.

12.5   SSRI Switching or Augmentation Studies

In individuals with BDD who fail to respond to an SSRI, or who demonstrate a partial response, are often switched to another SSRI or augmented with another drug. Phillips et al. (2001) reported that of those individuals who failed to respond to an adequate SRI trial, 42.9% (N = six out of 14) responded to at least one subsequent adequate SRI trial and 43.5% (N = 10 out of 23) of subsequent SRI trials received by these subjects were effective. Among responders to an initial SRI, and who were then treated with a different SRI, improvement was reported in 92.3% (N = 12 out of 13) of subsequent trials.

Phillips et al. (2001) report on an open label series of buspirone (also extended from Phillips, 1996c) in a chart review of patients who failed to respond to an SRI alone or had only a partial response. Buspirone was added after an adequate trial of an SRI and was successful in 33.3% of trials (N = 12 out of 36). This was lower than in the previous smaller study (Phillips, 1996c).

The mean dose was 56.5 mg (range 30–80 mg daily) and was as effective in delusional as non-delusional cases.

12.6   Pharmacotherapy for Psychogenic Excoriation

Chapter 5 reviews some of the difficulties in the "diagnosis" of psychogenic excoriation and comorbidity with BDD, OCD, or BPD. The evidence base for the treatment of psychogenic excoriation (BDD or not) by pharmacotherapy is extremely small. The published studies are hampered by the lack of information on related comorbidity, chronicity, or whether the symptoms were predominantly compulsive, impulsive, or mixed. Furthermore, RCTs and case series of BDD usually include cases with and without psychogenic excoriation and are not separately reported.

There has been one RCT of fluoxetine in psychogenic excoriation with a range of diagnoses (Simeon et al., 1997). There were 21 participants of whom one had panic disorder, two had social phobia, three had a simple phobia, three had OCD, four had generalized anxiety disorder, two had major depressive episode, five had dysthymia, and one had somatization disorder. They were *excluded* if they had BDD. There was a flexible dosing schedule of up to 80 mg (mean 55 mg) for 10 weeks in 21 patients in a double-blind placebo controlled trial. There was a significant reduction in the frequency of excoriation compared to placebo according to two out of three outcome measures for the completer analysis and one of three outcomes for the intention to treat. There was no relationship between reduction in excoriation and changes in measures of depression, anxiety, or obsessive compulsive symptoms. The study is difficult to interpret because of the small numbers and may be less relevant to those with BDD. However, fluoxetine has demonstrated efficacy in those with BDD generally (Phillips et al., 2002).

There has been one open label study of fluoxetine (Bloch et al., 2000) and several case reports (Stout, 1990; Gupta & Gupta, 1993; Stein et al., 1993; Phillips & Taub, 1995; Vittorio & Phillips, 1997). Other case reports of SSRIs include that of sertraline (Kalivas et al., 1996), fluvoxamine (Arnold et al., 1999; O'Sullivan et al., 1999), paroxetine (Biondi et al., 2000), and clomipramine (Gupta et al., 1986). There are also two case reports in which SSRI treatment may have induced or aggravated skin excoriation (Denys et al., 2003). One of us (DV) has also noticed that discontinuing an SSRI after several years has led to an improvement in psychogenic excoriation. Little is known about the long-term efficacy of an SSRI in psychogenic excoriation, the use of an SSRI in adolescents with psychogenic excoriation, or whether there is a higher rate of relapse when the person discontinues the drug (that is similar to SSRIs in OCD).

There are case reports describing the benefit of pimozide in two patients with psychogenic excoriation (Duke, 1983). The dose was initially 4 mg a day, and both patients improved after a month. Olanzapine has also been described in three case reports (Garnis-Jones et al., 2000; Gupta & Gupta, 2000; Blanch et al., 2004) which describe how olanzapine was effective in a non-delusional patient (dose up to 7.5 mg daily), who had reduced urges to engage in excoriation. A second patient experienced improvements on 2.5 mg a day in combination with isotretoin for facial acne. Lienemann & Walker (1989) describe the use of an opiate antagonist, naltrexone, at 50 mg per day. It reduced the frequency and pruritus in a patient who had no response to a steroid (prednisolone).

12.7 Inositol

Fux et al. (1996) conducted a double-blind placebo controlled study on high-dose inositol (part of the vitamin B complex) in OCD. Inositol was found to have a significant effect on the symptoms of OCD in 13 out of 13 patients and might therefore be relevant for treating BDD.

12.8 SSRI Augmentation of CBT for BDD

As yet there are no controlled trials comparing CBT with an SSRI, or a combination of the two, for BDD. Whether monotherapy with an SSRI or a combined approach is more effective in the long term needs to be studied, but there is no evidence yet that a combined approach in moderate to severe BDD is unhelpful. Indeed, maintaining a stable mood and reducing self-consciousness may have a synergistic benefit. There are some practical questions about using combined CBT in the long term. For example, if a person has had an exceptionally good response to an SSRI, they may relapse on discontinuation without having learnt skills in CBT.

Another possibility is the use of D-cycloserine to enhance CBT. This has shown some promise in augmenting CBT for some phobias and OCD (Wilhelm et al., 2008). D-cycloserine is thought to work cooperatively with the glutamate released through synaptic activity associated with CBT. It is believed that D-cycloserine activates the endogenous glycine receptor site of the N–methyl-D-aspartate (NMDA)-glutamate receptor while CBT activates the glutamate site at the same time. It is believed NMDA is the critical nerve cell involved in short-term learning and memory. It plays an important role in extinction learning, such as that purported to take place during exposure-based therapy. Future research should test the efficacy of D-cycloserine and exposure to social situations in BDD since it has been found to be efficacious in social anxiety.

Several case reports and small clinical trials suggest support for the therapeutic use of specific glutamatergic agents (e.g., memantine, N-acetylcysteine, riluzole, topiramate, glycine) in OCD and these could also be investigated in BDD with or without CBT.

12.9   Electroconvulsive therapy in BDD

There are seven published case reports of electroconvulsive therapy (ECT). Phillips (1991) reported that six of these did not respond. In the literature there is one case report indicating ECT to be successful (Carroll et al., 1994). In another report, Phillips (1996d) notes that in her retrospective chart review none of the eight ECT trials was successful in her patients. ECT is therefore not generally recommended in BDD.

12.10   Psychosurgery in BDD

Phillips (2002) notes one published case report and two personal communications describing benefit in three individuals with BDD (modified leucotomy in one, capsulotomy in one, and bilateral anterior cingulotomy and subcaudate tractotomy in one) and no benefit in two individuals (both received anterior capsulotomy). There is no evidence for the benefit of deep brain stimulation. Psychosurgery and deep brain stimulation are not therefore recommended in treatment of refractory BDD and should be considered as experimental procedures.

12.11   Further Research

At the time of writing, a search of the ISRCTN Register and ClinicalTrials. gov website and personal communications revealed that there are three ongoing RCTs for pharmacotherapy in BDD. These include the evaluation of a) levetiracetam (an anti-convulsant) vs. placebo (NCT00265109); b) fluoxetine vs. placebo in adolescents aged 10–17 (NCT00245635); and c) escitalopram (an SSRI) vs. placebo (NCT00149799).

Further research in pharmacotherapy for BDD needs to be prioritized for:

a)   children and adolescents with BDD;
b)   individuals with psychogenic excoriation who may represent a separate variant of BDD;

c) the optimal dose, duration, and long-term use of SSRIs in BDD and cost- effectiveness;
d) the effect of discontinuation of SSRIs on symptoms of BDD;
e) the clinical effectiveness and cost-effectiveness of an SSRI in comparison to CBT and in combination with CBT;
f) the effect of CBT augmented by D-cycloserine;
g) the effectiveness of a SSRI in combination with a low dose atypical antipsychotic drug.

Part B
Assessment and Therapy

Chapter 13

Assessment

Summary

This chapter describes an assessment, which is the basis for developing a formulation. A formulation is a psychological understanding of the factors that are maintaining the preoccupation and extreme self-consciousness in BDD. The chapter also describes the use of standard assessment scales in BDD which can be used for outcome measures. Assessment also provides you and your client with a reference point of "how things are now" to refer to as therapy progresses.

Although we have described two distinct modules that follow one another (assessment and engagement in the Chapter 14) you will need to be flexible and return to them at different points in therapy. Engagement follows much more easily when the client feels understood and can see the connection between his (mental and behavioral) actions and the maintenance of his preoccupation and distress. We normally encourage at least two assessment sessions and weaving sessions on engagement into this as some individuals will otherwise drop out. For example, for an individual with poor insight who has been coerced into seeing you by a relative, you might want to skip the assessment scales in the first session and focus on engagement, hopefully returning later to complete the assessment. When there is comorbidity and complexity in symptoms, more time is required to complete an assessment and formulation. Part of your assessment will be to determine the level of insight or ability to engage in a mutual understanding of the problem and the goals. This can occur informally when you determine how receptive the individual is to an alternative formulation and formally by scales such as the Over Valued Ideas Scale (OVIS) (Neziroglu et al., 1999) or the Brown Assessment of Beliefs Scale (BABS) (Eisen et al., 1998).

Body Dysmorphic Disorder: A Treatment Manual. David Veale and Fugen Neziroglu
© 2010 John Wiley & Sons, Ltd.

Sections

13.1   Structure for Sessions

Different formats are available for assessment. The diagnosis may be made in the initial assessment when various outcome scales can be used. Assessment for CBT and the development of a formulation will usually consist of two 1-hour sessions or three or four 45-minute sessions. This will depend on you and the attention span of your client. Investing this time is important because many BDD clients are anxious about being viewed as vain or ugly, or suspicious that they are being tricked into believing that they have a psychological problem because no one truly understands their real concerns about their appearance. Investing time to develop a good therapeutic relationship with your client will help him build trust and feel more able to disclose his beliefs and worries. It's particularly important during the assessment phase that you hold an "enquiring mind" rather than challenging your client's experience about his appearance. Research centers require a structured diagnostic screening interview and this inevitably takes longer. Many individuals with BDD feel ashamed and fear that they are viewed as vain. It therefore takes them a long time to trust the therapist before they are able to divulge information. It may also be helpful to interview family members, who may provide more information than the individual does, especially if he lacks insight and does not believe he has a psychological problem. Similarly, it may be important to obtain collateral information from other mental health practitioners, dermatologists, or surgeons who have seen the individual. However, many individuals will not reveal the details of surgeons or dermatologists they have consulted, fearing that an offer of cosmetic procedure may then be withdrawn.

13.2 What's the Agenda?

Always clarify the nature of the referral. Was there an entourage of relatives in the waiting room who have brought your client under protest to you? Determine whether your client has made the appointment himself and come willingly or whether he is there under pressure from, say, a relative. Or was he referred to you by a cosmetic surgeon or dermatologist who will not operate without your approval? Some people with BDD feel very pessimistic about change as they believe that they have been sent for psychiatric assessment as a last resort because no one can help with their appearance or dare agree with them as to how ugly they look. Explore with your client what he would hope for by the end of your consultation. The standard question "Why have you sought help now?" or "How do you feel about seeing me?" is often helpful to understand ambivalence if your client has been sent to you under pressure and important in making a judgement about his willingness to change.

13.3 Diagnosis and Comorbidity

We discuss comorbidity and differential diagnosis in Chapter 1. A research clinic will conduct a structured diagnostic interview, but clinicians in non-research facilities should at least assess for the presence of a major depressive episode, social phobia, OCD, eating disorder, and substance abuse as these are the most common comorbid Axis I diagnoses.

The "magic wand" question ("If I had a magic wand and was able to take away your preoccupation and distress with your appearance, do you think you would still be sufficiently depressed to seek treatment for it?") is often helpful to determine whether a comorbid condition is the main problem. It is often helpful to explore the chronology of symptoms ("Which symptoms came first?") and the severity ("Which symptoms cause you more distress and interference in your life?").

The diagnosis of a delusional disorder can be assessed formally by measuring the strength of beliefs, either by OVIS or BABS, which are described below. Personality disorder is also common and, as a minimum, try to exclude avoidant, paranoid, obsessive compulsive, and borderline personality disorders (BPD) as these are the most common Axis II disorders in BDD (Neziroglu et al., 1996). Where BPD is regarded as the main problem there is an argument for this to be treated first.

We shall assume that you have established a diagnosis of BDD (see Chapter 1) and that this is your client's main problem. A standard history of BDD should include the following.

13.4   Development of Appearance Concerns

A standard history should include the development of the problem to determine how old your client was when he began to be preoccupied about his appearance and when it became a significant problem. The individual may report a gradual onset of symptoms of BDD so that it did not become significantly handicapping until more recently. Quite often the feature that a person is preoccupied with will be different earlier in life than it is currently. For example, a person might have been very ashamed about his nose as an adolescent but more concerned about his hair in recent years.

Determine the relevant critical events and risk factors for the development of BDD such as sexual abuse, a critical parent, a history of teasing, or an education in art or design. Was appearance reinforced as important by parents or peers? Was there a specific trigger to the development of the preoccupation? Triggers are often best evoked by discussing imagery. Try to determine the onset of when your client first experienced a picture in his mind (or felt impression) of his feature. These are often accessed from an earlier period and are highly pertinent. The history is extremely important in making a developmental formulation and how memories and past associations and appraisals are influencing the present. A good developmental formulation will greatly assist in engagement of a psychological understanding of the problem.

13.5   Features Disliked

Clarify the features that your client dislikes and the degree of concern for each area. Ask what features he dislikes most, in what way he dislikes each feature, and, if relevant, or if he won the lottery, how he would like it changed by any cosmetic procedure.

When there are multiple areas of preoccupation it is often helpful to identify the main areas and to determine the percentage of preoccupation on each feature, ensuring that the total adds up to 100% (this can also be done as a pie chart). For example, an individual might say that her nose accounts for about 60% of her preoccupation, hair 30%, breast size 4%, tummy 2%, thighs 2%, and facial skin 2%. Here the nose and hair are the main preoccupation and concern, while the rest of the body is fairly irrelevant. However, if your client does not engage with treatment and returns later, has a cosmetic procedure, or is successful in therapy but relapses, then it is often interesting to note how the main area of preoccupation may change.

Some individuals do not have specific features they dislike but just feel that they are ugly. Some may indicate that they believe their individual features are not too bad, but that they just don't fit together properly. Alternatively, a man may feel he looks too feminine (or a woman that she looks too masculine). Less commonly, people describe concerns about not looking right for acceptance in a cultural or family group.

Some individuals may feel that their features change during the day or that their features look worse at particular times. In this case, it is helpful to explore whether your client thinks the feature actually changes or whether it changes according to other factors such as mood or focus of attention. The uncertainty of exactly how an individual looks and the hope he may look better than how he feels, is often the motivation for mirror-gazing.

13.6   General Observation

Much can be gleaned from your general observation before you even start your consultation. None of the following attires or behaviors is in itself "wrong," but the context and function are important. The most obvious observation is that of camouflaging a body part. Other behaviors may be to distract attention from a feature or a consequence of picking. For example:

- Is your client wearing any specific attire like dark glasses on a cloudy day, a baseball cap, or a scarf, baggy clothes, or long coat in warm weather?
- Is the person wearing a wig, a burqua, or a veil when it is inappropriate to do so?
- Is the person covering his face with his hand?
- Does the person have long hair with which they hide their face?
- Is the person heavily made up or excessively tanned?
- Is the person's head shaved (e.g., to avoid combing his hair ritualistically)?
- Has the individual had any body piercing or a tattoo or wear a very revealing dress to distract attention from a feature?
- Is the person sitting in a particular way to show his "best" side?
- Does the person find it difficult to make eye contact and tend to look down?
- Are there scars from skin-picking?
- Does she have unusually thin eyebrows from plucking?

- Does she have an unusual hairstyle?
- Does she sit in a particular way (e.g., on their toes to avoid their thighs looking fatter when seated).
- Does he cover his mouth?

If your client confirms your observation about a particular attire or behavior, always ask about its purpose (e.g., "Do you do this to improve or camouflage your [name of feature]?" or "Is this to distract attention away from your [name of feature]?") and add it to the list of safety-seeking behaviors as this may help strengthen your understanding.

You usually need to view the feature(s) considered defective or ugly without any camouflage such as make-up or clothing. If appropriate, ask permission to view the feature without the camouflage at a closer distance or with a magnifying mirror. If you cannot view the feature because your client refuses to remove an item of clothing or make-up or it is inappropriate, it can be difficult to make a judgement about how noticeable it is or how abnormal the feature is in comparison to others.

Unless you are medically qualified and have a chaperon(e) it may be inappropriate for you to examine some areas of your client's body. Of particular difficulty is men complaining of small or abnormal genitalia and trying to decide what is normal. Wessells et al. (1996) conducted a survey of 80 men and found that the mean flaccid length was 8.8 cm, stretched length 12.4 cm and erect length 12.9 cm. Neither client age nor flaccid length accurately predicted erectile length. Stretched length most closely correlated with erect length. They suggest a flaccid length of less than 4 cm or stretched or erect length of less than 7.5 cm were in the small range.

A similar situation exists in women who request cosmetic labiaplasty. Liao & Creighton (2007) report that their clients uniformly wanted their vulvas to be flat, with no protrusion beyond the labia majora, similar to the prepubescent aesthetic featured in advertisements. Lloyd et al. (2005) have reported on dimensions of female genitalia based on 50 pre-menopausal women. Labial and clitoral size and shape, vaginal length, urethral position, color, rugosity, and symmetry varied greatly; there is no "normal" size or shape. However, it is unusual for clients with BDD to present with complaints of labia size as their main problem.

In most cases of BDD it is possible to obtain either corroborative evidence about the feature from a relative or a medical practitioner who has examined the client. In an attempt to make the definition of minor physical anomaly more reliable, especially in cosmetic surgery settings, we have used a rating scale of how abnormal or noticeable a feature is and compare it to the client's assessment. It is then easier to assess the discrepancy between the two ratings (see Body Image Questionnaire in Appendix 1).

13.7 Functionality of the Defect

Assessing whether the feature is functioning normally can be important as questions about function can sometimes arise in concerns about breathing or being able to smile or chew food. Sometimes the impaired functioning is associated with pain or a somatic sensation (e.g., a tingling or the sensation of a facial palsy). There are many other somatosensory sensations that may be misinterpreted (e.g., a sensation of swelling under the eyes; a bump beneath the skin; a burning sensation; feeling "squidgy" or doughy; a feeling of one's lip being pulled to one side; or a sensation of an abnormal dental occlusion [also known as phantom bite]) (Jagger & Korszun, 2004; Veale & Chapman, 2005). Clients may monitor such sensations carefully, which will tend to amplify their awareness.

If a client complains about the size and shape of his genitalia this will necessitate enquiring about his sexual experiences and any associated problems of erectile dysfunction or premature ejaculation. You should enquire whether your client is concerned about the size of his penis when it is erect, non-erect, or both, and the context (e.g., when he is with a partner or alone). One would also ask whether the preoccupation extended to the size or shape of his scrotum and testes. In women, one would want to know whether a preoccupation with their genitalia was associated with sexual difficulties, avoidance of some sexual practices, or restrictions in lifestyle. Where sexual dysfunction or avoidance of relationships is prominent, it may be more appropriate to treat such clients in a sexual dysfunction clinic.

13.8 Imagery

Imagery refers to an experience that resembles perceptual experience, but which occurs in the absence of the appropriate stimuli for the relevant perception. Visual imagery is colloquially called visualization, or "seeing in the mind's eye," but it can be in the form of a sensation on the body ("as though something is touching you"). Images may be associated with bodily sensations such as fatigue or other modalities such as smell. Assessing imagery is an important step in understanding BDD as it is frequently from an observer perspective. What is seen in the mind's eye is then assumed to be what others view. Chapter 19 discusses working with images and includes a detailed structured interview.

We often find it clinically helpful to ask our clients to draw or paint a portrait "from the picture in your mind or an impression that you have of your face or body that distresses you." They can choose which medium to use. Even clients who are not artistic can convey much more this way than using words to the clinician. More interesting is the change in self-portrait that can occur after therapy. Figure drawings are, however, regarded by some as an invalid measure of body image (Radika et al., 2002).

Assessing selective attention

One way of measuring attention is to consider how it can broadly be divided between self, tasks, and the environment. Attention in healthy individuals tends to be focused predominantly on tasks (e.g., 80%), and a small proportion (e.g., 10%) on both the environment and the self. BDD clients focus excessively on the self (e.g., 70%) with less attention directed on tasks (e.g., 20%) and the environment (e.g., 10%). Self-consciousness can be enhanced in even healthy controls by mirror-gazing, which is an aversive experience. At the assessment, it is helpful to identify how self-focused the client is and whether this varies in different contexts. The therapist can ask:

> "What percentage of your attention is on the picture in your mind (or felt sense of your appearance) and what percentage is on tasks and the environment?"

Imagery and past experiences

Imagery may be linked with past aversive experiences so it is important to look for associations between early memories and the subsequently related images. These are especially helpful in making a developmental formulation. Sometimes these images may be associated with experiences of being teased or bullied, or a specific trauma such as abuse. It is important to elicit these memories, either within the assessment or during the course of therapy when they are associated with a high degree of anxiety and have been avoided. Chapter 19 discusses strategies for altering imagery. You can ask:

I'd like you to stick with the picture/impression and how you feel ... [prompt]:
- What is the earliest recollection of having the experience reflected in the picture (or impression)?
- How old were you?
- What was happening in your life at that time?
- Is there a particular memory from that time that seems to be closely linked to the image? (Or are there any particular memories that you'd prefer not to think about it because they are too painful?)
- If so, do you think you could evoke it in your mind now and describe it to me? (Where were you? Who were you with? What were you doing?)
- Can you see anything in the memory?

- Are there any other sensations in the memory? For example, do you notice any sensations or feelings inside your body? Do you notice any sensations of smell? Or are you touching anything in the memory? Are you performing any actions within the memory?
- How similar is the memory compared with the spontaneous image/impression?

The memories associated with intrusive imagery can be especially helpful in adding to the developmental formulation.

13.9 Assumptions and Beliefs about the Feature(s)

A cognitive behavioral model assumes that the "felt" body image activates idealized values about the importance of appearance in defining the self and assumptions about appearance and that the product is a negative appraisal and ratings of ugliness ("the way you feel about your appearance") and meanings (e.g., "I'll be alone all my life").

Assumptions and beliefs about one's appearance are best evoked by deriving them from the images as these are often accessed from an earlier timeframe. If the person denies experiencing images, then an alternative question might be:

What goes through your mind when you think about your appearance or see yourself in the mirror?

Suitable questions for exploring assumptions and beliefs are based on a standard "downward arrow" technique:

Let's assume for the moment that the image/impression/thoughts you had about yourself is correct:
- What's the most distressing aspect about this image/impression?
- If that were true, what would be so bad or distressing about it?
- What would that mean about you (using a belief rating of 0–100)?
- What would it mean about other people?
- What would that mean about the world?
- Why do you worry so much about it?
- How do you think your world would be different?
- Do these assumptions reflect your current views?
- To what extent does you feature define who you are in your identity?

The most common assumption about being ugly or defective is of being alone or unloved. Other common beliefs are the awfulness of being average or inferior, unnoticed, not standing out, not getting the best position in a job setting, of being of less worth than others, of being subjected to relationships or things that are unfair. However, individuals with BDD will often just feel grotesque and want not to feel that way. For these clients it is not the consequences of being flawed but rather the discomfort or disgust caused by their appearance.

Many clients ask whether it isn't true that attractive people are more rewarded in life. Some may in fact be familiar with the social psychology literature which shows that attractive people have been found to get higher salaries, better positions, even have lost items returned more frequently. Although this is true, the majority of people are in the average range of attractiveness and therefore the findings really apply only to people who are on the very low and upper end of the continuum. In other words, people who are exceptionally attractive are the ones who enjoy these benefits as compared to those who are on the low end. However, most people compete with people on the average range where the differences in appearance are not great, so these social psychology findings are not applicable.

Internal shame and perfectionism

Internal shame or self-disgust refers to failing to achieve an aesthetic standard. In the purest form, a person may state that he has no concerns about what others think of him. However, most clients have some degree of external shame and fears of negative evaluation by others. It is for this reason that they avoid certain situations and people. The self-disgust is largely unavoidable because one cannot strip oneself of one's external appearance. Unlike other anxiety or various mood triggers, our bodies are inescapable.

Some individuals may be trying to achieve an unrealistic aesthetic standard, while for most there is a discrepancy between how they actually see themselves and how they would like to be or how they think they can fit in with others. If there are perfectionist attitudes, try to determine whether this is an over-compensatory strategy (e.g., to prevent others humiliating or rejecting them). Does he finish some behaviors with problematic criteria such as feeling "right" or "comfortable"? In this case, try to explore the goals that have not been achieved; the cost of trying to achieve them; the feared consequences of not achieving them; whether he thinks that the standards are unrealistic; and the criteria he uses for deciding whether he has achieved perfection. This will need to be tied to a discussion of long-term goals and valued directions in life.

External shame

External shame refers to the fear of negative evaluation by others. You can explore this by asking:

"If you knew for certain that other people did not think your appearance was flawed, do you think your preoccupation and distress would a) remain the same, b) be slightly better, or c) be much better?" (Anson, personal communication).

An alternative question to explore concerning the fear of negative evaluation is:

"If you were alone on a desert island and had a guarantee there was no one else on the island and no prospect of being rescued, do you think your preoccupation and distress about your appearance would a) remain the same, b) be slightly better, or c) be much better?"

Many individuals with BDD report that they would still be preoccupied and distressed if they knew for certain no one else was evaluating them, but that the degree of self-consciousness and distress would improve anything from slightly to much better. Social anxiety is thus usually a burden in addition to internal shame.

When your client has a fear of negative evaluation about his appearance, you will also need to assess whether the fear is focused not only on his appearance but also on other aspects of the self (e.g., his competence or intelligence) and whether the latter amounts to an additional diagnosis of social phobia. A good question to ask is:

"If you knew for certain that other people did not think your appearance was flawed, would you still be anxious about people rating you negatively or being critical of you for other reasons? If yes: What do you think they would be rating badly other than your appearance? For example, would you be anxious about eating or talking in front of others? Are you worried you may say something stupid?

Can you estimate what percentage of your anxiety in social situations is about your appearance and what percentage is for other reasons?"

13.10 Ruminating and Comparing

Preoccupation in BDD can take the form of one's own image and beliefs about being ugly or defective and/or it can be reviewing and doubting one's felt impression of how a defect looks. This may lead to comparing the feature with another person's or an old photo of oneself. When a person is overwhelmed, he may respond by avoidance or suppression of the thoughts and images of his appearance. If clients have very low self-esteem and are more personality disordered, they often attack themselves (e.g., "You are so ugly and stupid, you shouldn't even have been born"). BDD clients, and especially depressed clients, often ruminate on "Why" questions: "Why am I so ugly?", "Why was I bullied as a child for having buck teeth?" Such questions do not, of course, have any answers and serve no useful function other than to make the person feel worse and even more preoccupied.

Worries about future events are usually more anxiety-based. They commonly consist of "What if ... ?" questions – for example, for a woman, "What if someone sees my moustache?" Alternatively, a client may ruminate or dream about the surgery he is planning. Beliefs *about* cognitive processes such as ruminating and comparing are called "meta-cognitions." They are important to assess in order to understand the function of the process and to set up behavioral experiments. A common belief is that such processes are helpful in making the person mentally prepared.

The following semi-structured interview is simplified and extended from that used by Holland (2006) and is designed to assess the nature of preoccupation and ruminations in BDD. A fuller discussion on ruminations is found in Chapter 18.

I would like you to think about some of the times when you were worrying or preoccupied about your appearance or your feature. When I use the word "preoccupied," I mean thinking a lot about your appearance.

What usually goes through your mind when you are preoccupied with your appearance? (If no: Try to think back to a specific time when you were preoccupied with your appearance.)

a) *Self-attacking*
When you are preoccupied by your appearance, do you criticize or attack yourself? Can you tell me a little about those self-critical thoughts and what you tell yourself?
Does it feel as you have a bully inside you?
What do you do in response to these thoughts/your bully?
Do you feel as if self-attacking/bullying can protect you or keep you safe?
Are there any unintended consequences of bullying yourself?

b) *Past ruminations*
Do you think about an embarrassing or humiliating experience in the past and/or what you could have done differently?
(Do you often think "If only ..."? For example, "If only I had done something differently" Can you give me some examples?)
(Do you ask yourself "Why" questions? For example, "Why was I born this way?" Can you give me some examples?)

Do you try to answer these sorts of questions?
Do you feel as if trying to find the answer can prevent something bad happening or help you know where you stand?
Are there any unintended consequences to answering these questions?
Do you ruminate about the way you used to look?
(If yes, do you think that your different life was due to the way you looked then?)

c) *Worry about the future*
Do you worry about potential problems in the future?
Do you ask yourself "What if" questions?
(Can you tell me a little about those worries?)
(Do you worry about what other people might think about your appearance?)
(Can you tell me a little about what you think other people might think?)
Do you try to solve these sorts of worries?
Do you feel as if trying to find the solution to your worry can prepare you for the event, or is there another reason?
Are there any unintended consequences of trying to solve potential problems?

d) *Mental planning*
Do you think or dream about ways you could change the way you look?
(Can you tell me a little about those thoughts about changing the way you look?)
Are there any consequences of dreaming about how you will change your appearance?
(What effect does dreaming about how you will change your appearance have on your preoccupation and distress about your appearance?)
Do you envisage a different sort of life for yourself?

f) *Others*
When you are preoccupied with your appearance, is there anything else you think about that has not been covered?
(Can you tell me a little about the thoughts you have about this?)
In which of the areas we have discussed do you spend most of your time thinking?

g) *Comparing*
People with BDD frequently compare their "defect" against others. Try to specify the main target for comparison according to sex, attractiveness, age, or specific features:
Do you compare your appearance to others?
Do you compare just the feature(s) that concerns you or the whole of yourself?
Who do you choose to compare against – people of the opposite sex; people who are the same age; people who are more attractive than you?
Do you compare it against a picture in your mind?
Do you compare it against how you used to look, to the way other people look, or to how you would like to look?

Do you feel as if comparing can protect you or keep you safe?

Are there any unintended consequences of comparing?

(What effect does comparing have on your preoccupation and distress about your appearance?)

13.11   Mood

Mood changes in BDD are complex and the initial assessment should focus specifically on the severity of depression and suicide risk. Clients are also likely to experience significant anxiety, disgust, and shame as they evaluate their body image. There are frequent mood swings so, for example, after mirror-gazing, some might feel angry or more depressed because nothing has changed since the last time they checked, or feel guilty for time spent in front of a mirror. Try to determine the dominant emotion and link this to specific examples – typically a person with BDD feels continuously down in mood and experiences episodic anxiety in social and public situations.

13.12   Safety-seeking Behaviors

Most safety-seeking behaviors in BDD are aimed at a) altering or camouflaging the feature (e.g., excessive make-up or cosmetic surgery), b) monitoring any deterioration or how the person appears to others (this includes mirror-checking or feeling the feature with one's fingers), and c) providing a distraction to the feature. The checklist in the Body Image Questionnaire in Appendix 1 can assist in identifying the behaviors that usually need to stop during therapy. They can also assist in making a global rating of "compulsive" behaviors for the Yale-Brown Obsessive Compulsive Scale modified for BDD (YBOCS-BDD) (see below). However, note that many of the behaviors rated are not strictly repeated or "compulsive," which is why we prefer to term them as "safety-seeking behaviors."

An assessment would clarify the frequency and handicap of the behavior and a functional analysis would determine a) the context in which the behavior occurs, b) a detailed description of the behavior or cognitive process in chronological sequence, and c) the consequences on the person's self-consciousness, mood, and activity level. An example of a functional analysis is mirror-gazing. The context may be situations when the person is about to be exposed to public view and going to check their appearance in a mirror. The act of looking in the mirror may have an immediate consequence of reduced anxiety and increased certainty of how exactly the person looks. The assumption about this process is that "If I know exactly how I look, then I can mentally prepare myself for being humiliated." As the person continues to look in the mirror and becomes more self-focused, the unintended consequences are of feeling more depressed and more self-consciousness and a desire to avoid public situations.

It is often helpful for clients to describe a typical day and to focus on the length of time some activities, such as grooming and applying make-up, take. When clients are depressed, it is also helpful to ask them to complete an activity schedule and complete a broader assessment of avoidance behaviors. We discuss this further in Chapter 22.

Some features will lead to specific questions about particular safety-seeking behaviors. For example, if the client has significant concerns with his hair, you will want to know whether he combs it in a special way. Does he have to repeatedly comb or adjust his hair? What effect is he seeking (e.g., is it to make his hair smooth, straight, to feel "just so" or symmetrical)? What criterion does he use to complete adjusting his hair? Does he repeatedly cut his hair? How often? Who does it? Does he use any particular hair lotions, restorer, or colorants?

When someone is preoccupied with "excessive body hair" he may feel he has to repeatedly shave or cut his beard more than most men. You would enquire about frequency and about from which parts of the body he removes hair. A functional analysis will require you to determine the context, the sequence of behavior for removing the hair (e.g., shaving, plucking), and the immediate and unintended consequences of removing the hair. There may also be different aims and consequences for removing hair from different areas of the body.

13.13   Past Cosmetic Procedures

A cosmetic procedure is a major safety-seeking behavior which is usually designed to solve the problem once and for all. Enquire about your client's past experiences of cosmetic or dermatological procedures or whether he has tried to alter his appearance himself (DIY surgery). Was he satisfied or dissatisfied with each procedure? What effect did each procedure have on his preoccupation and distress? Did it get worse, stay the same, or get better? Did he think his appearance was made worse and if so, is he angry with the surgeon or does he feel guilt or regret for making it worse?

Alternatively, is your client planning a procedure in the future and if so, how serious is his plan? Many clients just dream about surgery or conduct mental cosmetic surgery in front of a mirror and imagine how they will look after surgery. Others have not seen a surgeon but collect brochures or information about procedures from the Internet. If there is no specific plan for a cosmetic procedure, ask what stops him. If money is an obstacle, what would he do if he won the lottery?

Assessment and advice on cosmetic procedures are discussed in Chapter 15. A specific scale for assessing expectations about surgery is provided in the Body Image Questionnaire in Appendix 1. This is currently being used in a prospective study of cosmetic procedures which may be helpful for exploring some of the issues. Suffice to say at this stage we would not normally advise taking a client on for CBT if he has a specific plan for surgery during therapy. However, many clients go from one surgeon to another without undertaking the procedure. If surgery is going to be performed, do a cost–benefit analysis (see Appendix 2) and if you believe it is unlikely to be helpful, it may be better to start therapy after the procedure.

13.14   Avoidance Behavior

The form in Appendix 1 in the Body Image Questionnaire can be used to assess avoidance behavior and then to develop a hierarchy for exposure or behavioral experiments. It is designed for clients to add their own situations or activities that they avoid. Some body parts will lead you to enquire about specific situations. For example, a man worried about the size of his non-erect penis might avoid public urinals. If he is worried about his erect penis, then he may avoid sexual relationships or ensure his partner does not see his penis (a somewhat tricky maneuver). A woman worried by the size and shape of her thighs will almost certainly avoid wearing certain clothes (e.g. a short skirt). Avoidance of some activities (e.g., swimming) might occur for different reasons in different people. For example, the person might avoid swimming because they do not want to ruin their make-up. Another might be avoiding it because it involves revealing their body. Another person preoccupied by their hair might be avoiding and camouflaging themselves by using a hat and scarf in the winter but be fairly housebound in the summer. The last item on the YBOCS-BDD (described below) can be used to make a global rating of severity of avoidance behavior.

Avoidance of social situations may be related to social anxiety or depression and necessitates enquiring about the context and meaning of the situation. For social anxiety, would your client feel more anxious if he were with an individual or group of people? Would it make a difference if a) he was with a person who was more attractive? b) male or female? c) about the same age, (d) strangers, someone he doesn't know that well, or a friend? Avoidance behavior may also be related to depression. Your client may be avoiding answering the phone in case it is an invitation to go out and he lacks motivation and can't be bothered. The role of avoidance in depression is explored in Chapter 22.

13.15   Past Treatments for BDD

Many people with BDD feel misunderstood and have not revealed their symptoms to other health practitioners. It is useful to explore this in the first session and ask about whether he has ever sought help for the BDD with his family doctor or other mental health practitioner. Alternatively, he may have sought help for other symptoms such as depression and not mentioned his main problem because of shame and the type of treatment that is likely to be offered.

It is surprising how often clients do not know the type of therapy they have received in the past. If they received CBT, enquire about what they were taught, what it consisted of, and whether there was any homework. Find out what aspects of a therapy helped and what did not, and whether it had any overall effect on symptoms of BDD.

13.16   Assessment Scales

There are a number of specific scales that are used to assess a client with BDD. A structured diagnostic interview for the diagnosis of BDD is discussed in Chapter 1. We shall review here outcome measures and scales that assist in a better understanding of the client's problem to assist in the formulation.

Neziroglu Henrikson (unpublished) have developed a Body Dysmorphic Disorder Interview Scale. It consists of four parts: 1) Body Dysmorphic Screening Questions to determine if one may have BDD; 2) Assessment of Specific Body Parts and Concerns; 3) Assessment of Specific Thoughts Associated with the Area of Concern; and 4) Assessment of Specific Safety Behaviors. This is an interactive scale and can be accessed on www.bio-behavioral.com. Some of the specific beliefs and assumptions have been gathered from Veale et al. (1996) and Geremia & Neziroglu (2001); many more have been added to address those specific to different body parts. The beliefs have been gathered over the course of treating many BDD clients. There are a number of specific outcome scales for BDD which are described below.

Symptom outcome scales

For clinical practice, you are advised to choose one outcome scale to measure the severity of symptoms during and after therapy. For an observer rated scale, we would recommend YBOCS-BDD as this provides ease of comparison with other studies.

Yale-Brown Obsessive Compulsive Scale Modified for BDD
The YBOCS-BDD (Phillips et al., 1997) has become the gold standard for assessing the severity of BDD as well as the outcome of treatment in

randomized controlled trials. Like the YBOCS for OCD, we have reservations about it for various reasons (explained below). It is reproduced by permission of the authors in Appendix 1.

The YBOCS-BDD is a clinician-rated 12-item instrument comprising five questions on preoccupations, five on compulsive behaviors, one on insight, and one on avoidance. More specifically, it assesses time occupied by preoccupations with the perceived defect in appearance, interference in functioning, distress, resistance, and control. Similar constructs are assessed for compulsive behaviors. Similar to the YBOCS for OCD, each item on the YBOCS-BDD is measured on a five-point Likert scale, with higher scores denoting increased psychopathology. Scores on this 12-item scale range from 0 to 48. Scores above 24 are usually required for entry into a clinical trial.

The YBOCS-BDD has been shown to have good inter-rater reliability, test–retest reliability, and internal consistency; it has also been shown to be sensitive to change. While it was developed as a measure of the severity of BDD symptoms, rather than as a diagnostic tool, it should be noted that the scale's first three items reflect the DSM IV diagnostic criteria for BDD. The advantage of the YBOCS-BDD is that it assists in comparing clients across studies. It is based on the YBOCS and is therefore theoretically bound to a model of an obsessive compulsive spectrum disorder.

One disadvantage of the YBOCS-BDD is that measures of avoidance have less weighting than those of obsessions and compulsions, as there is only one item for avoidance. There are also difficulties in some items, for example, resistance to thoughts (described below). However, the degree of avoidance of activities is included in the interference items for both preoccupations and compulsive behaviors. Also note that the YBOCS for OCD is normally reported as a 10-item scale whereas YBOCS-BDD is a 12-item scale.

Defining the thoughts about the body defect

An importance difference between the YBOCS-BDD and YBOCS for OCD is that the thoughts about the body defect combine the rating for both the stimulus (e.g., "My skin is marked and blotchy so that I am ugly and deformed") and the cognitive response (e.g., ruminations such as "Why I am so ugly? If only I'd had a clear skin; if only I had enough money for laser treatment"). In OCD the ruminations would be rated under the compulsions.

Rating the time occupied by thoughts about body defect

The first item asks about the amount of time occupied by thoughts about a defect or flaw. It is important to rate only how much time reported is in the "forefront" of their mind, rather than being background "awareness."

Rating resistance to thoughts about body defect

The item asks "How much of an effort do you make to resist these thoughts? How often do you try to disregard them or turn your attention away from these thoughts?" You are asked to rate the effort made to resist such thoughts, not the success or failure in actually controlling them. At one end of the continuum, if the client reports that he always makes an effort to resist or the symptoms are so minimal he doesn't need to actively resist, then he scores 0. At the other end of the spectrum, if he completely and willingly yields to all such thoughts, then he scores 4.

Many clinicians find that the item on resistance to thoughts about defects is problematic to rate in OCD, especially after CBT, and this is equally true in BDD. For example, Woody et al. (1995) assessed YBOCS in 54 patients with OCD. They found consistency of the items was acceptable but was improved by deletion of the items concerning resistance to obsessions and compulsions. Analyses of new items assessing avoidance and the duration of obsession-free and compulsion-free intervals indicated that only the avoidance rating added meaningfully to the full-scale score. Woody et al. recommended deletion of the resistance items and inclusion of the avoidance item to yield a revised nine-item YBOCS total score for OCD. Deletion of the resistance item could theoretically be done for YBOCS-BDD.

The item on resistance can be problematic if, after CBT, the client has been taught to willingly accept intrusive thoughts and not to engage or respond to them with any form of mental activity but to focus more on what he does in the real world. We would interpret this as scoring 0 on the resistance item. Phillips (personal communication) has found that both resistance items (for preoccupations and compulsive behaviors) are positively correlated with the other items, although the correlation of the resistance items with the other scale items is lower than that for the other scale items. In addition, resistance does increase with successful treatment. Rating resistance to compulsive behaviors has more face validity than resistance to intrusive thoughts.

Rating avoidance item

The item asks you to rate the degree to which the client tries to avoid things such as social interaction or work-related activities. You are asked not to include avoidance of mirrors or avoidance of compulsive behaviors as well as the degree of experiential avoidance of thoughts and emotion. There is only one item on avoidance whilst there are five each for items on obsessions and compulsions, although the two items that assess functional interference include avoidance of activities. Thus individuals who are housebound and highly avoidant (e.g., using substances and distracting themselves by watching TV) may score relatively low on obsessions and compulsions as there is marked experiential avoidance of their thoughts about their ugliness and relatively minor degrees of checking and comparing. However, as soon as they start a treatment program or are admitted to hospital and stop avoiding, scores on the obsessions and compulsive items may markedly increase and avoidance scores decrease. Like OCD, compulsions and avoidance may sometimes be on a seesaw, so that when compulsions are high, avoidance may be low, and vice versa. This, though, is not reflected in the weighting of the scale.

It is theoretically possible to modify the scale for use as a self-report measure similar to the self-report YBOCS (Greist et al., 1998), but this has not been validated or the correlation coefficient has not been calculated against the observer-rated version. The YBOCS-BDD takes about 10–15 minutes to administer and thus may be too time-consuming to use in some clinical practices. However, the scale's first three items, which map onto the DSM IV diagnostic criteria for BDD, can be administered in about five minutes and are useful in assessing the client's progress in treatment.

The Body Dysmorphic Disorder Examination
The Body Dysmorphic Disorder Examination (BDDE) is a semi-structured clinical interview designed to diagnose BDD and to measure severity of symptoms of negative body image (Rosen et al., 1995b; Rosen & Reiter, 1996). The items include preoccupation with and negative evaluation of appearance, self-consciousness, and embarrassment, excessive importance given to appearance in self-evaluation, avoidance of activities, body camouflaging, and body-checking. The BDDE has adequate reliability. It correlates with measures of body image, negative self-esteem, and psychological symptoms, and is sensitive to change following treatment. There are two versions, one observer-rated (Rosen & Reiter, 1996) and one self-rated (Rosen & Reiter, 1995). The main disadvantage of the BDDE is that several of the items have a "ceiling effect" and are insensitive to change. For example, the highest score for several behavioral items such as checking are defined as "every or almost every day." Some of our clients may check *hundreds* of times a day and such items will be insensitive to change. The scale was validated in a population who are regarded as less handicapped than those described at other centers and most commonly concerned about their weight and shape.

Conviction of belief

There are two main scales for assessing the strength of conviction over the beliefs in BDD. These can also be helpful for the diagnosis of a delusional disorder and to monitor progress during therapy.

Overvalued Ideas Scale
OVIS (Neziroglu et al., 1999) is a 10-item, clinician-administered scale with good reliability and validity. It is reproduced in Appendix 1. The scale was

developed utilizing 142 obsessive compulsive clients and later studies looking at treatment outcome predictability utilizing 60 BDD clients. OVIS assesses the *severity* of overvalued ideas or conviction of beliefs with regard to their strength, reasonableness, fluctuation over the past week, accuracy, extent to which others share the same beliefs, attribution, insight, and degree of resistance of the belief. It is important to identify clearly the beliefs and values that are to be rated at the beginning of the interview (e.g., "I am unattractive," "my nose is misshapen," "my complexion is full of pimples, so I will not get a date," "my puny body prevents me from getting a good job"). Although most clients usually have more than one belief, the scale asks you to identify the *main* belief. Although beliefs can change in importance, most studies have shown that the belief of utmost importance at any given point usually has the same degree of conviction. In treatment studies, the same main belief is evaluated in order to assess the efficacy of treatment. In some studies two or three beliefs are rated individually.

The main belief is assessed on a scale of 1 to 10 with various probes to assist the therapist with the evaluation of the particular question. Also each item has anchor points to help rate the question more easily. Overvalued ideas have been associated with poorer treatment outcome for both OCD and BDD (Neziroglu et al., 2001), and BDD and hypochondriasis clients have shown more overvalued ideas on OVIS than OCD clients (McKay et al., 1997; Neziroglu et al., 2001). A mean score of seven with a score of eight or above on item 9 (insight) suggests a diagnosis of high overvalued ideation.

Brown Assessment of Beliefs Scale

BABS (Eisen et al., 1998) is a measure of the *strength* of beliefs. It is reproduced in Appendix 1 by permission of the authors. It is a seven-item scale designed not to be content-specific and to assess delusional thinking across a wide range of psychiatric disorders. The scale was developed utilizing 20 clients diagnosed with OCD, 20 diagnosed with BDD, and 10 with mood disorders with psychotic features. It measures degree of conviction, perception of others' views of beliefs, explanation of differing views, the fixity of the belief, attempts to disprove the belief, and insight concerning the belief. In addition to achieving a cut-off of 18 points or more (out of a total of 24), clients are classified as having delusional beliefs only if the first item, conviction, is scored as 4, when a client is completely convinced that the belief is accurate. Item 7 assesses ideas and delusions of reference, but is not included in the total score because it is not characteristic of all disorders that may be characterized by delusional thinking. BABS has shown good reliability and validity, although it is important to clearly define the belief to be rated. When assessing BDD, Phillips (personal communication) recommends asking the individual to identify a global rating of his defect(s) (e.g., "I am ugly and deformed"). She recommends focusing the individual on his beliefs about the defect(s) rather than his overall appearance and to avoid identifying beliefs about specific "defects" (e.g., "My face is so pitted and marked that strangers laugh at me in the street"). This is because the "defect(s)" are often multiple and may change over time, making a subsequent rating of the original belief problematic. It can also be hard to choose which body part to focus on, and focusing on one alone will not incorporate the client's views of the other "defective" body areas. When assessing change over time (e.g., with treatment), it is important always to rate the original belief. BABS is less suited to rating assumptions or core beliefs about the defect(s), which may be identified by using the "downward arrow" technique in CBT. This is because the assumptions and core beliefs are often multiple (e.g., "Because of my defects I'll be alone all my life without a partner"; "I'll be humiliated by others"; "Life is not worth living"; "I'll never be able to work"). It is not therefore clear which belief should be rated and may change over time. In addition, core beliefs often reflect subjective views of oneself which may not easily fit the definition of a false belief (delusion).

You might ask "What words do you use to describe your 'defects'?" If they have difficulty identifying global rating or are too embarrassed, you can suggest a few possibilities without leading the individual on, such as "Some people would say they look 'deformed' or 'disfigured.' What words would you use?" If the words deformed and disfigured are too extreme, you could suggest another, such as unattractive. It is important, however, to identify a belief that most people would consider inaccurate, as this is what BABS measures. For example, it is not helpful to rate a belief such as "I'm not as beautiful as a model." The major difficulties with BABS are identified in the italicized instructions to the rater, so it is important to pay attention to them. One of the main problems with BABS is that the items to be rated in BDD are *evaluations* or global ratings of a person's attractiveness. This is a potential problem as items on BABS are geared towards *beliefs*. Thus in a client with schizophrenia, there is a face validity in rating a belief such as "I have been abducted by aliens." Philosophically, a belief is something thought to be true because of observation or evidence. It can often be subjected to empirical testing or logic to derive facts, which tend to be objective. However, evaluations such as being ugly are a rating of an event or person on a scale of good and bad (or ugly and attractive). In comparison to beliefs, evaluations are not subject to empirical testing and are more subjective. Therefore, in using BABS, the observer has to make a judgement of what he or she thinks most people would rate (rather than the accuracy of the belief).

Measurement of values
Neither BABS nor OVIS has face validity for measuring idealized values. In BDD, the idealized value is conceptualized as the degree of importance

attached to appearance and the degree to which the person identifies himself through his appearance. You may explore values in relative terms by asking your client to allocate a total of 100 points to a series of values according to how important they are to defining his identity. Values might include the importance of one's health, friendships, achievement at work, appearance, and so on. The more points allocated, the more important the value. In therapy, this may lead to a discussion about the disadvantages or consequences of having all one's investments in one stock. Hayes et al. (1999) have developed a Valued Directions Questionnaire to assess a person's valued directions in life (see Appendix 1). This is particularly helpful to understand the values that are important in the absence of BDD and useful for making goals. Thus if one of the valued directions is being a good parent, one of the initial goals in someone who had been neglecting his children because of his symptoms of BDD might be to spend time with his child on a daily basis despite his preoccupation and distress.

Defect Related Beliefs Test

The Defect Related Beliefs Test (DRBT) is based on the Personal Appearance Beliefs Test developed by Butters & Cash (1987) and revised by Geremia & Neziroglu (2001) for BDD (see Appendix 1). It was initially developed to determine the extent to which clients hold dysfunctional beliefs about their overall appearance and is based on cognitive errors described by Beck et al. (1979). Geremia & Neziroglu (2001) added five items to make a total of 10 items on the scale. The instrument now assesses the degree to which clients hold beliefs regarding the importance of physical attractiveness and its ramifications for everyday life.

Quality of life measurements

There is one quality of life measure that is specific to body image; this is the Body Image Quality of Life Scale (BIQL) (Cash & Fleming, 2002). Alternatives to the BIQL include non-specific measures for the impact of the problem such as the Quality of Life Inventory (Frisch, 1994) or Social Disability Scale (Marks, 1986).

The Body Image Quality of Life Scale

The BIQLS scale consists of 19 items and has been validated in healthy controls (Cash & Fleming, 2002). Hrabosky et al. (2009) found that people with BDD had a significantly worse BIQL score (mean -1.81, SD 0.68, N = 56) than those with anorexia nervosa (mean -0.95, SD 1.30, N = 35), bulimia nervosa (mean -1.15, SD 1.07, N = 26) and female healthy controls (mean 0.06, SD 1.16, N = 34) and male healthy controls (mean 0.40, SD 1.21 N = 36). The scale (and several others for measuring body image) is available for a fee direct from the website www.body-images.com/assessments.

Quality of Life Inventory
The QOLI is a measure that assesses fulfillment in 16 areas of life, such as real concerns about money, love, health, work, play, physical surroundings, etc. (Frisch, 1994). It first asks you to rate how important an area is and then to rate it on how satisfied you are with that area. It is a valid and reliable measure used to evaluate outcome with therapy, although it is not specific to body image concerns. However, it is a good instrument that can be used for assessment of quality of life for any disorder.

Social Disability Scale
Marks (1986) developed a widely used scale for quality of life which assesses the degree of handicap in five main domains. The scale is not specific to BDD but four of the domains (interference in occupation, social life, relationship, sexual life) are incorporated and adapted into the Body Image Questionnaire (Appendix 1).

Safety behavior and avoidance checklist
A checklist of common safety-seeking and avoidance behaviors in BDD is provided in the Body Image Questionnaire in Appendix 1. This can lead to an assessment of the *frequency and function* of each safety behavior. Alternatively the safety behavior checklist can be used to define the list of target compulsions for the YBOCS-BDD. The avoidance checklist can be used to develop a hierarchy of feared situations for therapy.

The University of Rhode Island Change Assessment Questionnaire
The University of Rhode Island Change Assessment Questionnaire (URICA) (McConnaughy et al., 1983) is a 32-item questionnaire set up on a Likert scale and based on behavioral criteria for change. It evaluates the client's readiness for involvement in the change process at the start of therapy. Four stages are conceptualized: pre-contemplation, contemplation, action, and maintenance. Eight items measure each of the four stages. They found that in psychotherapy clients progress according to a predictable pattern. Good reliability and validity are established. This scale has been used in assessing change in BDD (Geremia & Neziroglu, 2001) and in OCD (Villano, 1998; Yaryura-Tobias et al., 2001).

Nonspecific measures
Routine assessment includes a general measure for depression and anxiety such as the Beck Depression Inventory (BDI) (Beck et al., 1961) and Beck

Anxiety Inventory (BAI) (Beck et al., 1988). The severity of social phobia can be assessed by the Social Phobia Scale (SPS) (Mattick & Clarke, 1998), which has demonstrated high reliability and good validity. An alternative to the SPS is the Social Avoidance and Distress Scale (SADS) (Watson & Friend, 1969), a 28-item true and false scale which measures the level of affective discomfort in social situations as well as the deliberate behavioral avoidance of social situations. The scale contains 14 items measuring social avoidance and 14 items measuring discomfort. It has good reliability and validity.

Chapter 14

Engagement and formulation

Summary

Engagement is the most important issue in the treatment of BDD to which you will return regularly during therapy. We describe a theoretical understanding of engagement and the practical steps in making a formulation. We particularly focus on how the current solutions are unworkable. Engagement rests on building an alternative model of what the problem is and what is maintaining it. This then allows the model to be tested in therapy through committed action.

Sections

14.1   Introduction

Engagement in CBT is a process with three major components:

a)   A "good enough" therapeutic bond with your client, which means there is sufficient trust to allow the therapy to proceed.

Body Dysmorphic Disorder: A Treatment Manual. David Veale and Fugen Neziroglu
© 2010 John Wiley & Sons, Ltd.

b)   A shared understanding of what the problem is and the factors that maintain it with enough credibility in your explanation and approach you are
offering.
c)   A commitment to change by your client to work towards mutually agreed
goals.

"Commitment to change" is also referred to as "treatment motivation." This
is an ambiguous concept in any form of psychotherapy. Drieschner et al. (2004)
has attempted to define "treatment motivation" or "readiness for therapy."
They define six components that relate to treatment motivation which may be
helpful to explore when clients are unable to commit themselves to change.
These include:

a)   *Level of suffering.* This can result directly from symptoms of BDD, as well
as secondary aspects such as demoralization, shame, or the economic and
social consequences of the problem. This is not usually an issue for clients
with BDD, who usually have high degree of suffering and a poor quality
of life.
b)   *Outcome expectancy.* This is often an important factor for treatment motivation in BDD as clients will still have the same appearance and do not
believe that they can change the way they feel about it. We describe below
changing the agenda towards reducing distress and handicap and to act
as if it was a body image problem (even if they don't yet believe it).
c)   *Problem recognition.* Many BDD clients recognize that they are not
coping, but their solution is to avoid situations or to try to alter their
feature cosmetically. In this regard many clients might either not agree
with the diagnosis of BDD or believe that they have a problem with their
appearance (not the way they feel about it). Alternatively, they may
believe that they have BDD *and* a defect in their appearance (which is of
course incompatible). We focus in this chapter on trying to define the
impracticality of their solutions and being willing to consider an alternative understanding of what the problem is (rather than what it is not).
d)   *Perceived suitability of treatment.* A number of different factors can be
identified that may be regarded by the client as unsuitable, such as the
method and rationale of the therapy, agreement about the goals for
therapy, and the perception of the therapeutic relationship. It helps to be
confident about the outcome of therapy from research and your own
experience in treating BDD. When it is difficult to agree about goals, try
to find goals that you and your client can agree on or break it down into
smaller goals. Your client has a different understanding of what the
problem is but is being invited to test out an alternative understanding.

He is then being asked to act as if it were an emotional problem about his appearance and to act in therapy as if it were an emotional problem (if he doesn't believe it) for at least three months.

e)   *The perceived costs of treatment.* Costs in both private and publicly funded therapy are the time required (especially if it involves time off work) and the costs and inconvenience of traveling a long distance. The most obvious cost in private therapy is the fee (although this does not seem to stop clients taking out loans or spending large sums on a cosmetic procedure). Even more important is the emotional costs and perception of therapy – for example, the client might believe that he will be humiliated if he is in a social situation. In BDD, as in many other psychological disorders, a fear of making things worse is a cost and obstacle to making progress. Frequently normalizing this concern is enough to enable people to try out a process of change. In other cases it can be helpful to review the history and development of the problem if things have been getting slowly worse in any case. Alternatively, the therapist can say that if the individual is unhappy with the results of reducing behaviors related to BDD, it will help him build up his avoidance and safety behaviors again. Worries about the personal cost of therapy are common and it is important to bring these into the open. You can then use discussion of the costs of the individual's current strategy or design a behavioral experiment to move things forward. Other alternatives include home visits or sessions over the telephone.

An example of a behavioral experiment helpful in engaging clients is the "ABA" design. The aim here is to help your client make a clearer link between a particular coping strategy and its effect on distress and preoccupation with his appearance. The key is asking the individual with BDD to significantly *increase* safety behavior such as camouflage (e.g., much longer than usual until they feel "totally satisfied" or "completely comfortable"). It is usually easier for people to increase their coping strategies than it is for them to reduce them and compare the result on preoccupation to a day without their safety behaviors. This can often result in a greater willingness to drop a safety behavior that has been shown to be counterproductive. However, it is particularly important in such situations to ensure that all safety behaviors are dropped because if a client drops a behavior (e.g., stops concealing his chin with his hand), then he may still be excessively self-focused. Note that decreasing safety behaviors may lead to a short-term increase in anxiety or self-disgust. This is, of course, to be expected but the test is whether it leads to a decrease in preoccupation and anxiety in the long term and a realization that safety behaviors never make him totally satisfied and comfortable.

f)　*Perceived external pressure.* External pressure, especially from a close relative or a cosmetic surgeon, may motivate your client to come for an assessment but he cannot be coerced to engage in CBT. He may possibly be "pressured" to take medication under threat of legal sanctions. Pressures such as employers or the legal system do not usually figure in BDD in the way they might in alcohol and substance abuse.

The problem of engagement in CBT is more difficult for disorders with an over-valued idea, where the definition of the problems and goals is not shared by the clinician and it is more difficult to establish a good rapport (e.g., a client with anorexia nervosa whose goal is to lose weight) (Neziroglu & Yaryura-Tobias, 1997; Veale, 2002). Another example is in health anxiety where the client has a different theory about the cause of his symptoms and its treatment (Warwick & Salkovskis, 1990). We draw on a number of approaches in the process of engagement with the use of metaphors and changing the agenda derived from engagement in cognitive models for OCD and health anxiety (Salkovskis et al., 2000) and acceptance and commitment therapy (Hayes et al., 1999). We also, to a certain extent, draw on models of motivational interviewing used in anorexia nervosa (Treasure & Ward, 1997) and substance abuse (Miller & Rollnick, 1991). Motivational interviewing is a way of assessing motivation as well as preparing clients to engage in therapy. Here, motivation is the probability that a person will be ready to change – namely, enter into, continue, and adhere to a specific change strategy. Note that motivation is a state not a trait; therefore, it can change with time. Ambivalence is also a normal, acceptable, understandable aspect of approaching change and is an interpersonal phenomenon.

Issues of engagement are also relevant for pharmacotherapy, although the rationale for treatment will be different. A desire for medication is often seen in clients with a high level of experiential avoidance who prefer a quick solution and are intolerant of emotions. Sometimes you only have one session in which to engage your client sufficiently to ensure he attends the next appointment. The process of engagement therefore starts with your first meeting (email or telephone call) when you have the opportunity to begin building a therapeutic alliance to ensure that your client has sufficient confidence to return. Engagement begins during the assessment because the client will be making his own evaluation of you and your knowledge of body image problems and how much he can reveal. People with BDD are often ashamed about their behavior and unless they are specifically questioned about symptoms of BDD, they may not reveal them. They may have been assessed and treated by other mental health practitioners and been diagnosed as suffering from depression or social anxiety because they have not told their whole story fearing that others will not understand them or they will be viewed as vain or narcissistic because of their preoccupation with their appearance. For many it may be their first experience of discussing their symptoms of BDD in detail. They may be wary of you, especially if they have seen a dermatologist or cosmetic surgeon and have been told that a procedure could make an improvement in their appearance. From the outset in having contact with the individual with BDD keep in mind that engagement is very important to a successful outcome. As is normal practice in CBT, it is helpful for all sessions to be audio-recorded so that clients can listen to their session again, make notes, and at the next session clarify issues they did not understand.

14.2 Location of Assessment

You may need to meet the client outside of your office. Some people with BDD are unable or unwilling to sit in the waiting room; or they may be house-bound or otherwise unable to travel to your office. Be empathic if the client or family informs you that he is having difficulty getting to you. Offer to speak to the client by phone, visit him at home, or, if he can travel to your office, allow him to sit in an unoccupied room away from the waiting room, or perhaps assess him in his car outside your office. We have often conducted such consultations, which have enabled our clients to engage later in therapy. It is preferable to assess a client face to face rather than by telephone, but it is an essential step for some clients until they feel confident enough to see you in your office. Others may cover their face with a scarf or balaclava for some considerable time before they are willing to remove the camouflage. For most BDD clients it may be the first time they have discussed their symptoms. If they have been to other therapists they have often felt misunderstood and their idea of not needing a therapist or psychiatrist has been reinforced.

14.3 Principles of Engagement

For the majority of clients, it is often necessary to return frequently to the issues of engagement throughout therapy. No one strategy will work for all clients. However, there are some broad principles that do apply to everyone with BDD that will help to develop a "good enough" therapeutic alliance to allow you to work on the tasks as a means towards the goals. Some of these factors might seem obvious, but it is easy to be drawn into a discussion about the person's appearance (including what's been done "to" him or "by" him that has affected it), when there is a marked discrepancy between the individual's evaluation and your own and the person you are speaking to is deeply preoccupied with his appearance.

The broad principles of engagement, especially in the initial phase, are these.

Determine the aims of consultation

In section 14.2, we advised you to ensure that you clarify the nature of the referral and whether your client was brought under pressure to see you by a relative or sent for an opinion by a cosmetic surgeon. Not all clients want "therapy" or "treatment." If this is the case, try to establish what the client's expectations are about therapy and outcome (e.g., he may believe it will involve a lot of talking about the past or reassuring him about how he looks). Some clients are too suicidal and depressed or are not ready to change. In these cases you may need to focus on behavioral activation or recommend medication. Some may be seeking medication as a form of emotional avoidance. Alternatively, medication may act as a holding operation whilst trying to engage the client in CBT.

Past experiences

Some clients may have had bad experiences in the past or be suspicious of or angry with all mental health practitioners who have previously told them that they are deluded or that their perceptions are distorted without exploring other explanations for their preoccupation and distress. Clients with more insight will be evaluating whether you appear to be knowledgeable about BDD and can be trusted. Take care not to appear to trivialize your client's symptoms. Raising and normalizing the fact that he had doubts and reservations about treatment can be very helpful. Your client may have had a bad experience with another practitioner and may feel extremely misunderstood. He will be very sensitive to your opinions about the way he feels about his appearance. He does not want to be viewed as vain and be ashamed that focusing on his appearance may be regarded as shallow or narcissistic. Validate the way your client feels, be supportive and encouraging, and recognize his difficulties.

Recognize the role of stigma

Your client has probably had some experience of stigma and shame. Mental disorder is stigmatized by the public; even some health practitioners lack understanding. However, BDD is often at the bottom of the pile for stigmatization. We were horrified to read a glimpse of the attitudes of a doctor who responded to an editorial on BDD in the *British Medical Journal* on the web (Carter, 2001). She wrote:

> "I wonder the value of devoting an editorial to such a condition as body dysmorphic disorder. While it may appear to be a debilitating condition in the 40% of men who responded as being dissatisfied with their appearance, the 1 in 236 one-legged Cambodian mine victims may disagree."

Here the doctor is confusing body "dissatisfaction" with BDD and then proceeds to trivialize it and believes it is unworthy of her attention. More often we have noticed that health professionals lack knowledge about BDD and diagnose the client with depression, low self-esteem, social phobia, or psychosis, or simply tell him that he will grow out of his concerns or that the diagnosis of BDD is a passing fad. Alternatively, they may focus on a supposed "underlying" problem or decide that he is unsuitable for therapy. Even the existence of comorbidity such as borderline personality disorder need not interfere in therapy, although in such instances therapy may take longer.

Such experiences are likely to reinforce the client's low expectations of your consultation. As an antidote to these poor responses it is possible to put a person with BDD more at ease by having a good working knowledge of the emotional, behavioral, and cognitive processes common in BDD. Open up the discussion with remarks like:

> "What some of my clients with BDD who focus on that area of concern worry about is ... [e.g., people being shocked about how I look if they see me more in brighter light]. Do you ever have those kinds of worries?"

When a client begins to develop confidence that you really do have knowledge of his particular kind of problem you can often visibly see him relax and become more open.

The public may be more forgiven for trivializing BDD. A good example was published in a newspaper by a columnist commenting on a report about DIY cosmetic surgery in BDD, when he wrote

> "But why are these people so discontented with their looks, that they are prepared to mutilate themselves? Dr Veale puts their behavior down to mental illness, which he calls body dysmorphic disorder. But surely, it is just an extreme example of the narcissism afflicting thousands of people of both sexes. They all think they have a right to be as good-looking as the glamour babes and hunks they watch on TV."

BDD as "narcissism" is a common misconception. One of the authors had to argue with a psychiatric nurse adviser for an insurance company who thought that a client's symptoms of BDD were those of narcissism and therefore not covered by his health insurance. It is rare for people with BDD to have comorbid narcissistic personality disorder, which will complicate therapy.

Relatives may also trivialize the condition to the client. Your client may have been called vain or told "to pull himself together." It is perhaps no surprise that clients feel misunderstood and it is useful to explore this issue in the first session to help build the therapeutic alliance. Use questions such as:

"Do you feel very misunderstood?"
"Have your problems been trivialized by others in the past?"
"Have you felt ashamed by being preoccupied by your appearance?"

Aim to help your client to feel understood and be compassionate. You may need to correct some of the misunderstandings about the nature of BDD and validate BDD as a recognized problem among health professionals to the client and relatives. This involves communicating to them that BDD is a recognized, serious, and treatable condition.

To help clients reveal more information about areas of concern that they feel ashamed about it can help to give multiple-choice questions. You might also agree to begin working on an area of concern they feel less ashamed of and come back to another area later.

Do not argue about the diagnosis of BDD

Clients often expect a diagnosis at the end of a consultation or shorthand for what the problem is. Sometimes a client will be upset or angry at the diagnosis of BDD. He may have been told or read that BDD means he has an "imagined defect." DSM IV is not helpful in this regard, and it may be more productive to tell him that the diagnosis involves "a preoccupation with the way you feel about your appearance, which has become very distressing or handicapping in your life."

Do not argue with your client about the diagnosis or make the mistake of engaging in a discussion about whether he has an imagined defect or whether his perception is distorted because it is untrue and the situation is more complex. Also such a dialogue will disrupt any therapeutic alliance that you have been building and is unlikely to provide useful information during your assessment. Try to find common ground and be extremely empathic about his distress and handicap. It can be helpful to be explicit that you will not be making ratings about how defective he is or arguing with him about whether his "defect" is real or imagined. He probably has had this conversation many times before. Try to focus on the distress and the effect it has had on his work, the difficulties in studying, loneliness, or in relationships and everyday life. Therapy can then focus on the handicap and desire to change. Stay focused on what *is* (e.g., how many hours a day they are preoccupied or in appearance-related activities) and not what is debatable (e.g., just how bad the flaw is, or what other people *really* think). Clients may acknowledge that there is a discrepancy between the way you (or a relative) feel about their appearance and the way they feel about their appearance, but in general, do not attempt to challenge the evidence for their ugliness or logic of their position, however much the evidence is against a judgement or however illogical their position is. It is extremely tempting but it has no benefit in helping your client to alter his judgement and your client will feel very misunderstood. To progress you only need the individual to be open to the idea of testing a different explanation of his problem and that his current solutions may be his problem. We say that it is not necessary for him to be persuaded to stop believing he is ugly and wholly accept a psychological understanding of BDD, but in order to overcome his preoccupation and distress, he has to experience some distress in testing out the alternative explanation. Seek to understand the person's frame of reference by reflective listening and try to selectively reinforce the client's own motivational statements, expressions of problem recognition even if related to not functioning, and his ability to change. If need be, try to elicit such statements.

Develop discrepancy

Get clients to *recognize* the discrepancy between keeping up their current behaviors and not achieving their valued directions in life. You can ask questions such as "What will your life be like in five years' time if you do not make some changes or at least test out a different understanding of the problem?" Review what the client's life was like before he started having problems with the way he viewed his appearance. Ask him to describe a typical day. *Verbalize the ambivalence* about change and *look forward* by discussing the client's valued directions and the effect of not sticking to them. Use the Valued Directions Questionnaire to develop the values he would like to act on. Ask him what his priorities in life are and whether he thinks he will achieve them. Ask how many of his priorities he would be giving up by continuing to over-value his appearance. Ask your clients to *elaborate* on the difficulties caused by his preoccupation with his appearance.

Do not reassure your clients that they look "all right" or attractive

Apart from some clients who are preoccupied by the size of their genitals or another part of the body that is usually covered by clothing they are likely to have been told by family members or health practitioners that they look "all right" or "OK" or reassured that they are not ugly. No matter what feedback your clients have received they will be certain that the problem is their appearance. It is helpful to be clear that for this reason, from the very outset, you won't be spending much time, if any, on reassuring them about their looks. Furthermore, your clients they may believe that if they could alter their appearance and feel comfortable with it, they could get on with their life.

It is fairly irrelevant to your client whether you think he looks "OK" or think his judgement is based on a felt impression of how he appears to others. Looking "OK" might mean to him that your standards are very low and he therefore does look ugly. He will often have at least one example from the past when he felt teased or humiliated about his appearance. The person is likely to discount what you say (e.g., "You are paid to be nice to me"; "You wouldn't tell someone that he look hideous"; "You can't see the full horror of it because I have my make-up on"). He is already discounting reassurance from his family (e.g., "My parents/partner thinks I look all right because they/she loves me"; "They don't want to hurt me"; "All parents think their children are wonderful"). Your client may also tell you that if he had a friend who was ugly, he would feel sad for them but wouldn't tell them the "truth." Therefore, reassuring him that he looks "all right" is responding to your client's agenda and gets nowhere.

Flexibility is, however, required if it is done once and not repeated as part of reassurance. It is rarely helpful to do a survey with a photograph even if the questions to the respondent are specific and unambiguous and the concerns are mainly about others' evaluation (e.g., "Is this person's forehead out of proportion to the rest of his face?). Most surveys will be easily dismissed or discounted with statements such as those above ("Staff will be nice anyway").

You might note that there is a discrepancy between your observations of how noticeable the feature is compared to that of the client's self-portrait (and perhaps his relatives' opinion). In this regard you may say that you cannot recognize the features that he has drawn. This leads into a description of a cognitive behavioral model of BDD and developing an understanding of how this discrepancy might occur. It must also be part of the process of changing the agenda to focusing on the distress and handicap.

Occasionally, clients with BDD seek reassurance throughout the therapy (similar to some clients with health anxiety or OCD). You may need to help them see that reassurance-seeking is part of the problem rather than the solution. Again, an ABA design (see above) can be helpful with alternating reassurance and no reassurance. Alternatively, you could offer to set aside the remainder of the day reassuring them about their appearance if they can promise that it will stop them from worrying for the next six months. The clients will almost certainly reply that they cannot promise that the reassurance will last for more than a few minutes, and this of course can lead to a fruitful discussion about the value of reassurance-seeking.

Validate the clients' experience

In general, engagement is helped by the credibility of the clinician who has treated other BDD clients and validates their beliefs and does not discount or trivialize them (Linehan, 1993). The clinician should search and reflect on the evidence for their judgement which has led to their conclusions about their defect. The skill is to do all of this collaboratively by means of a Socratic dialogue and to check regularly how an alternative theory might fit with their experience. You can also build credibility by asking questions that indicate that you truly understand the disorder (e.g., "Do you feel your appearance is worse in certain lighting? Do you prefer going out during the night instead of the day?")

Roll with resistance

In general, acknowledge the ambivalence to change and be empathetic. Express empathy, avoid argumentation, and support and develop discrepancy (described above). Sometimes it is better to *roll with the resistance* instead of opposing it (e.g., "Maybe what we are asking you to do is too difficult for you. Maybe you are not ready to change at this time"). You may want to use the Colombo technique. This is used when clients are presenting conflicting information or behaviors (e.g., "On the one hand, you say that you want to date and get a degree and believe that emphasizing attractiveness is shallow, but on the other hand, you spend 90% of your time engaging in appearance-related behaviors").

Finally, emphasize personal choice and control: encourage autonomy by letting the individual make personal choices and have control over his problems. If you tell someone what to do, then he is more likely to be confrontational and oppositional. Even if a person makes what in your view is an unhelpful decision, he is more likely to return to see in the long term.

14.4 Change the Agenda

Your client is focusing on his appearance as the problem and his solution is to camouflage or alter it. Your goal is to build an alternative understanding of what the problem is. Try to change the agenda of focusing on the content (e.g., "I am ugly, my nose is crooked, I'll be alone my life") to the processes involved (self-focused attention, rumination, fusion, avoidance and safety behaviors) in maintaining the distress and handicap. It is not motivational to address resistance; it is better to ignore resistance statements.

The use of metaphors can assist in focusing on the client's solutions as being the problem. Clients with BDD have tried many ways to cope, such as avoiding, camouflaging, or altering their appearance by cosmetic procedures, or trying to sort it out in their head. The "man in the hole" is a helpful metaphor (Hayes et al., 1999) many people with BDD will resonate with.

> "I think the situation is a bit like this. Imagine you're placed in a field wearing a blindfold and you are given a tool bag. You're told that your job is to run around this field blindfolded. Now, unbeknown to you, in this field are a number of widely spaced, fairly deep holes. You don't know that at first – you're naïve. You start running around and sooner or later you fall into a large hole. You feel around with your hands and sure enough you can't climb out and there are no escape routes. So you'd probably look in your tool bag to see what you can use. Now suppose the only tool in your bag is a shovel. So you dutifully you start digging, and pretty soon you are digging faster and faster. But you're still in the hole. So you try big shovelfuls or little ones or throw the dirt further away or not. All this effort and work but oddly enough the hole has just got bigger and bigger.
>
> Does that feel like your experience? Maybe you think what you really need is a gold-plated shovel or a different shoveling technique. Well, someone may sell you a gold-plated shovel or teach you a different way to shovel, but digging is not a way out of the hole.
>
> How might this relate to you?
>
> So, maybe the whole agenda or your solutions are the problem. You can't just dig your way out; that just digs you in."

Shoveling can sometimes be taken literally with skin-pickers. Gold-plated shovels can refer to cosmetic surgery. Putting the earth somewhere else might be a safety-seeking behavior, and so on. Others may express concern with looking dirty when they come of the hole.

The metaphor is generally very flexible depending on the nature of the engagement issue as demonstrated by the following responses:

a)   "Maybe I should just put up with it." Clients who are very depressed or avoidant may view themselves as helpless to do anything and the future as hopeless. You can respond with:

> "I understand you've tried many things. You've tried to tolerate living in a hole. You've tried waiting until you feel comfortable. But that hasn't worked over the past few years and it's no fun living down a hole. So when you suggest that you should just put up with it, what I hear you saying is that you're staying with the same agenda (digging your way out). I'm suggesting something else. I'm suggesting you change the agenda."

This may then lead on to a discussion about a different view of the problem or a different way of coping.

b) "What is the way out?"

"I don't know, but what we do know is that your solutions are not working. If you have an agenda that says dig until you die, what would happen if you were given a way out? Suppose someone puts a ladder down there. If you don't first let go of the shovel as the agenda, you'd just try to dig with the ladder. And ladders are lousy shovels. If you want a shovel, then you've already got a perfect one."

It is also possible to construct a mini-formulation of all the solutions and coping responses that ultimately feed symptoms of BDD (Figure 14.1). There is also a blank version in Appendix 2.

c) The need to let go of the shovel.

"Until you let go of the shovel you can't find out what else might be available. You can't really grab anything else until that shovel is out of your hands. You have to put it back in your bag. You can always shovel again if in, say, six months' time, if you haven't found something else. However, you need to really commit yourself to finding an alternative to shoveling and not go back to it."

d) A leap of faith.

"Notice you can't go anywhere unless you let go of the shovel, so it is a leap of faith. It does mean letting go of something and not knowing whether there is anything else. In this metaphor you are blindfolded after all, and you'll know what else is there only by touch. You can only touch something else when your hands are free. Remember that continuing to shovel also has consequences. Your biggest ally here is your feeling of anxiety. It's only because your shoveling isn't working that you would think of anything as mad as letting go of the only tool you have."

It is important to move on swiftly to introducing the cognitive behavioral model in maintaining preoccupation and distress. This needs to be done using a Socratic dialogue, with an empty model to be completed using the client's own words. Note that a "picture in your mind" can be a "felt impression" of one's appearance.

14.5   Building an Alternative Theory

Engagement rests on building an alternative model of what the problem is and what is maintaining it. Wherever possible one would move on to test out the

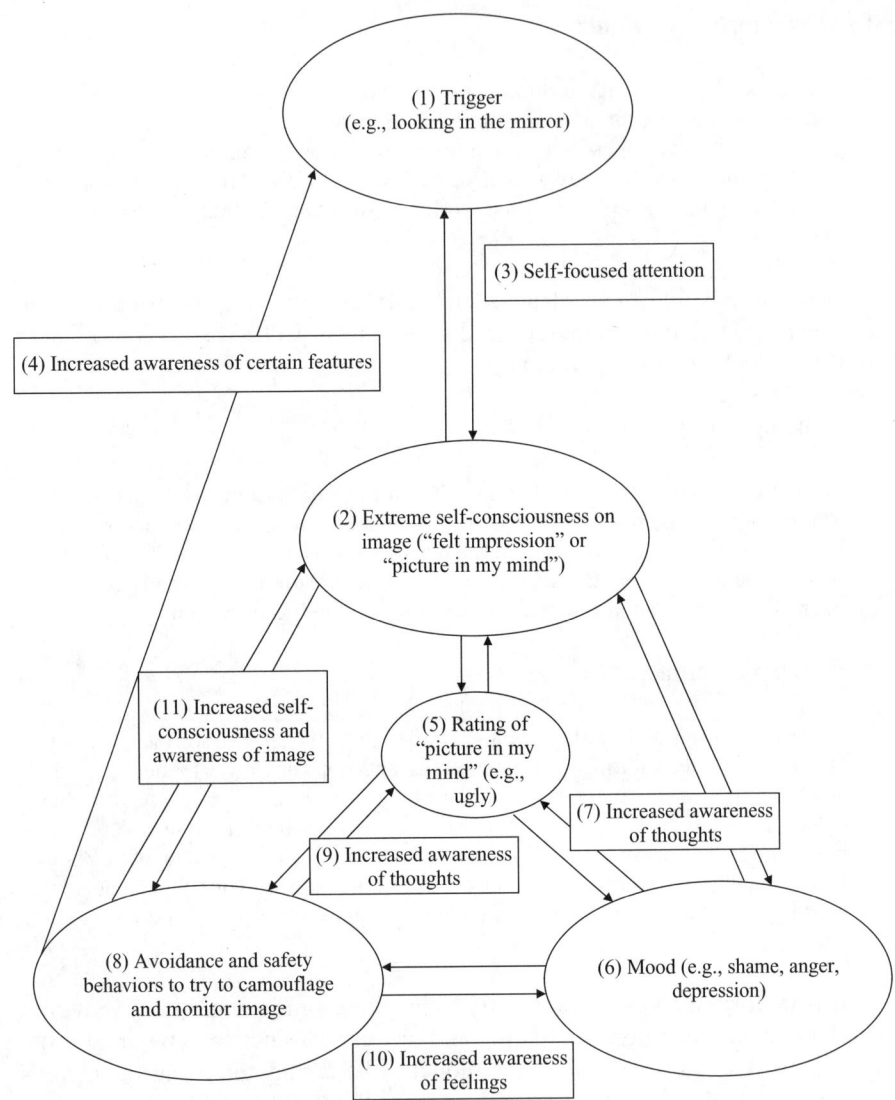

Figure 14.1   Model of BDD

model in a behavioral experiment. This may sometimes be done in a demonstration of selective attention and determining whether the preoccupation and distress decreases.

The following is an example of how one might start to explore an alternative theory for their experience.

> "We know from research that people with BDD may have lost their 'rose-tinted glasses' and have a heightened sense of awareness of their appearance. For example, when healthy people look at themselves in the mirror or in a photo, they have a slightly positive slant and rate their self as more attractive than others would rate them. We also know from research that healthy people tend to focus their attention on those features that are more attractive and focus less on those features that are uglier. Healthy people are also more likely to view themselves as a whole, or like a package job. The opposite tends to happen in BDD as people tend to focus on those parts that are considered ugly and to ignore those features that are more attractive. For example, someone preoccupied by his nose tends to see himself as a walking nose and that's all that he is.
>
> Can you think how this might apply to you?"
>
> The important thing is that someone with BDD has a different way of rating his appearance as he has lost the positive slant used by someone without BDD. Someone with BDD has lost his rose-tinted glasses and has a heightened sense of awareness of his appearance. Second, he tends to focus his attention on those features that are less attractive and to base the rating of himself on those features. For these reasons and others, that's why a cosmetic procedure is unpredictable as it does not alter your heightened sense of awareness of your appearance or give you back a positive slant. Nor does it affect some of the emotional links with ghosts from the past. It's also why a clone of yourself – someone who has identical appearance – can be satisfied with the way he looks, not avoiding anything and functioning normally by doing the things in life that are important to him.
>
> Having a slightly positive slant on your appearance, and focusing more on your attractive features keeps you relatively happy. If you have lost your positive slant and focus your attention on those features that you consider to be ugly, it comes at a cost and causes you to be preoccupied and very distressed.
>
> What have been the main costs to you?
>
> OK, so therapy will partly be about doing less of the things that make you lose your rose-tinted glasses, and being more focused on the whole of you."

With some clients it is helpful to validate their experience and the role of selective attention without "colluding" with them or getting into a discussion about how real a defect is. For example, if a client with very mild acne believes his skin is scarred and open-pored, with his permission we might inspect the area that he is complaining of, sometimes using a magnifying glass, which is similar to the experience of selective attention, and explain the process. You may then "see" the area described as defective and you can then validate the experience of the client albeit with certain caveats.

> "I can see what you are referring to, however only if I look very closely and after you have pointed it out to me today. When I first met you today, I did not notice anything about your nose. So one theory is that I can notice the bump by being up very close up and highlighted, whereas you are very aware of it all the time. This is very understandable as it's a bit like a woman who becomes pregnant who starts to notice other pregnant woman and babies everywhere. It's not that there are more pregnant women and babies but the change in her attention makes her more aware of them. Thus it may feel like holding up a magnifying mirror on certain features."

Other clients with BDD may be concerned that people are staring at them. If this is the case, then others are more likely to notice their safety behaviors and attempts at camouflage.

14.6   Theory "A" or Theory "B"

Your aim is to help change the agenda and solve a different problem. One way of doing this in CBT is to set up two competing theories to be tested out. This method of engagement has been described as a behavioral experiment for hypochondriasis (Clark et al., 1998) and in OCD (Salkovskis & Kirk, 2009) in which a client is presented with two alternative hypotheses to test out. One of the aims of the therapy is to determine which theory best fits the client's experience. We would normally start with open questions and follow with more closed questions that are more specific and optional. These are shown in parenthesis. An example is shown below:

> "I understand that you feel that your appearance is ugly and your solution is to try to change your appearance, to camouflage yourself, or to avoid situations. You've told me that people have tried to reassure you, but you don't believe them. You've also told me that you are very depressed and your life has become increasingly handicapped. You do less, you cannot concentrate enough to study, and you are becoming more socially isolated and at times housebound.
>
> I want to see if we can build a better understanding of what your problem is and how to solve it. It seems to me there are two explanations to test out. The first theory, which I will call Theory 'A,' is the one you have used for the past 10 years, that is, you treated it as a problem of ugliness. As a consequence you have been trying very hard to fix or camouflage your appearance so that you are acceptable to others.
>
> Have you noticed that treating it as Theory 'A' makes the preoccupation and distress about your appearance worse?

I'd like to continue with building an understanding of what might be causing you to rate your features as ugly and being so preoccupied and distressed, which I'm going to call Theory 'B.' I'd like you to think of a specific recent situation when the picture in your mind was very strong and you felt very self-conscious. Can you tell me when that was? (See Figure 14.1.)

You might want to repeat the first exercise for social or public situations and the second one for when they are alone or looking in the mirror. However ensure that the situation chosen is not one that leads to escape or avoidance.

"I'm going to write this event down in the top box (1) and the felt impression (or the picture in your mind) is represented in this box here (2).

When this picture is very strong, what happens to your attention on yourself? (Does your attention feel like you are on the outside looking in at yourself?) This is called being excessively self-focused. I am going to represent the process by these arrows (3).

What may happen is that the picture in your mind becomes your truth of how you look. Sometimes you might see your appearance differently for a brief moment when your attention becomes more aware of certain features in the mirror. Have you had this experience of being excessively aware of certain features? (4) This process also includes the way you have lost your rose-tinted glasses.

When you were very aware of the picture in your mind, what went through your mind? How did you rate yourself? (Did you feel more convinced about how ugly and defective you are?) What did it mean to you when you felt so ugly? (For example, did it mean you would be humiliated? Does it mean you will be alone all you life?) I'm going to put these thoughts in this box (5).

When you were very self-conscious about how you look and judged yourself as very ugly/defective, how did you feel? What's the main emotion you experienced? (6)

(Did you get more anxious? depressed? ashamed?) How did it make you feel physically?

As you notice yourself getting more anxious and depressed, what effect did that have on how ugly you feel and on the picture in your mind? Did it make your feelings of being ugly stronger? (7)

When you were very self-conscious about how you look and were judging yourself as ugly/defective, how did you react? (8) (Did you try to escape from the situation? Did you try to check on whether you look as bad as you think you do? Did you try to camouflage yourself more? Did you try to distract attention away from your feature?

When you did these things did it make it make you feel more ugly? (9)

Did it make you feel more distressed? (10) Did it make you more preoccupied and aware of the picture in your mind? (11)

And when you did these things did it make you want to check more in the mirror?

Are there many things you might do to prevent this cycle from occurring such as trying avoiding certain situations or escaping?

Do you think this model might apply to you?
Do you have any doubts about this?
Do you think this might apply to you?

I'd like to continue building an understanding of what might be causing you to feel ugly and to become so preoccupied and distressed. This is Theory B: you have a felt impression of how your features appear to others, which you find extremely upsetting. You have sought to cope with your excessive focus on your features, which have instead increased your preoccupation and distress. Associations of unpleasant memories (such as teasing or abuse) with a particular feature can complicate the picture further. Distress from past experience can become fused with the picture you now have in your mind. This is known as "body image fusion". What your mind is telling you about your appearance becomes what you see in the mirror.

One of the reasons why your felt impression persists is because it might have started when you had a bad experience such as being teased or humiliated, or it might have been a time in your life when you were becoming more self-conscious. You might have made certain links with what someone said (see Chapter 9, section 9.4). We are going to explore some of these memories in therapy. It is very understandable that the picture in your mind has persisted, perhaps because you feel it might help to keep you safe or to remind you that it could happen again. These pictures are like ghosts from the past, which prevent you from moving on and from having any positive experiences. So one of the reasons that others might judge you differently is because they don't have the same emotional links that you have.

How might this apply to you?

So in summary, the theory to be tested out in therapy is that you have a problem in which you feel ugly because you are excessively self-focused on a picture in your mind which may be linked with various early experiences. This picture in your mind becomes very real to you as to how you look now. By contrast, someone without BDD tend to be focused on a task like talking to a person, rather than looking back at themselves. When they are alone they tend to be focused on a task like reading or on what they can see or hear in the environment."

Those with partial insight may accept the possibility that others do not see them the way they see themselves. Always take the opportunity to explore the way they feel when they have the same intrusion about their appearance but when they were not bothered by it or less than when they usually are. You might say: "What made that different? What did the image mean to you on that occasion? Was it different because of your mood or being less self-focused? Is it different when you have had a drink or are distracted?"

If you can find certain circumstances when the meaning fluctuates with their attention or mood, then you may be able to say: "That's interesting – does that mean your appearance changes and that you don't look ugly on those occasions?" At this point you may be able to draw on your client's experience of fluctuation in the way he feels about his appearance and possible explanations.

Often people may agree with part of your alternative – that is, they believe they are ugly (Theory "A"), as well as having a picture in their mind and being very self-focused (Theory "B"). However, they feel that is too difficult or dangerous to change. Here it important to validate their skepticism but to change the agenda towards coping differently and to ask:

> "Have you ever tried to deal with the problem as if was a picture in your mind with ghosts from the past and being excessively self-focused?"

Few if any clients have done this and so the therapist can ask:

> "Would you be prepared to act *as if* it was Theory 'B' for at least three months and then review your progress? This is a very important commitment because throughout therapy you will have act as if it were true, even if you do not believe it at this stage. You can always go back to digging your way out of your hole and sticking to Theory 'A' if it's not working. Trying to solve it as if it was Theory 'B' would mean dropping your shovel and all the things you do to treat it as a problem with being ugly.
>
> As a result of this discussion, can you describe what would be most helpful way to start to make changes?"

There will be many obstacles to change, such as fears of being humiliated and it is important to validate these worries. They may be as a result of past experiences which have not yet been updated but these will not be ignored in therapy. Note that ruminations are a particular type of safety behavior that have their own micro-formulation in an expanded model. They are discussed in Chapter 18.

Case example

Brian was aged 21 and preoccupied with the shape of his nose. His preoccupation was very distressing and significantly affected his ability to work as well as his social life. He believed that it was misshapen, too big, and did not suit his face. Overall, he felt that his nose was very noticeable and abnormal but others would not admit to observing anything abnormal. When he highlighted his nose to a friend who viewed it very closely, the friend could only see a small bump, while Brian thought it was misshapen. However, his friend was viewing his nose as a whole and did not regard it as his identity.

Brian had had a number of cosmetic procedures earlier in his life, most notably work on his chin, which he said he was happy with, but that it made his nose look worse by contrast. He had approached a number of cosmetic surgeons who did not consider him a good candidate for further surgery. He was spending at least six hours a day preoccupied with his appearance, felt down much of the time, and frequently anxious about his appearance. He worked a few hours from home, having withdrawn from his office, and rarely socialized or took any phone calls.

He experienced a felt impression in his mind of how his nose looked, which he viewed from an observer perspective. Sometimes this led to doubts as to how exactly he did look and to frequent checking of his nose in mirrors that had to have the right lighting. This often led to further doubts. He avoided bright lights, which cast a shadow. He also used reflections in the back of CDs or TV screens to check his appearance. He compared his self to photographs of how he used to look, and compared his nose to the noses of other men of his age. He had avoided developing any relationships. When he met someone, he would tend to keep his head down and avoid eye contact. He would ruminate about his nose during the day about why he was born this way and how he was going to fix it. He believed that if he thought about it hard enough, then maybe he could fix it. He attacked himself as being "ugly, ugly, ugly" as he wanted to make sure that he didn't forget how ugly he was. If he let his guard down and stopped reminding himself of how ugly he was, he was bound to be humiliated.

The formulation below (Figure 14.2) focused on the factors that maintained his preoccupation with his appearance when he walked down a street. It was equally possible to focus on a different trigger, such as looking in the mirror, that would have different set of safety-seeking behaviors (e.g., mirror-checking, comparing with how he used to look) but similar cognitive processes (e.g., self-focused attention on distorted body image and rumination). The aim is to build a good understanding of how the processes maintain a sense of self as an aesthetic object (i.e., the felt impression of how one appears to others).

An alternative formulation is to focus on all the responses to the felt impression and the unintended consequences, all of which feed the preoccupation and distress (Figure 14.3). The aim of the formulation is to build an alternative explanation of the experience and to guide therapy. Thus Figure 14.3 may contain many more petals on the flower, all of which need to be removed in therapy to determine whether there is a decrease in preoccupation and distress.

Lastly, it is important to have a shared developmental formulation. In Brian's case, there were a number of factors in the development of his preoccupation and distress – he was a loner and teased by peers during early adolescence when he was called "chisel" because of his chin. His parents had separated when he was very young. His father did not keep in contact with him and there had been frequent conflict with his stepfather. He had persuaded his parents to pay for his chin to be altered cosmetically. He had not had any sexual relationships. He had grown up believing he was different from others and that he was bound to be rejected in any potential relationship.

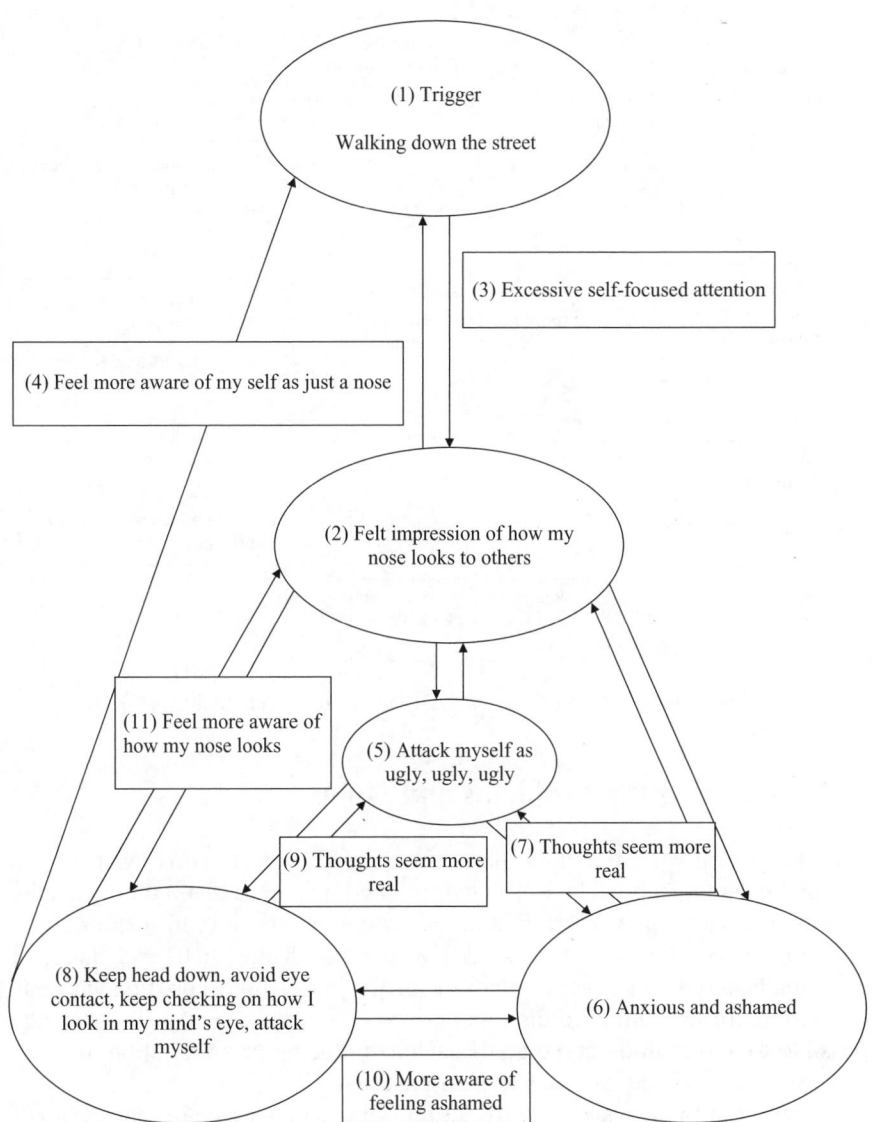

Figure 14.2   Maintenance of BDD in Brian

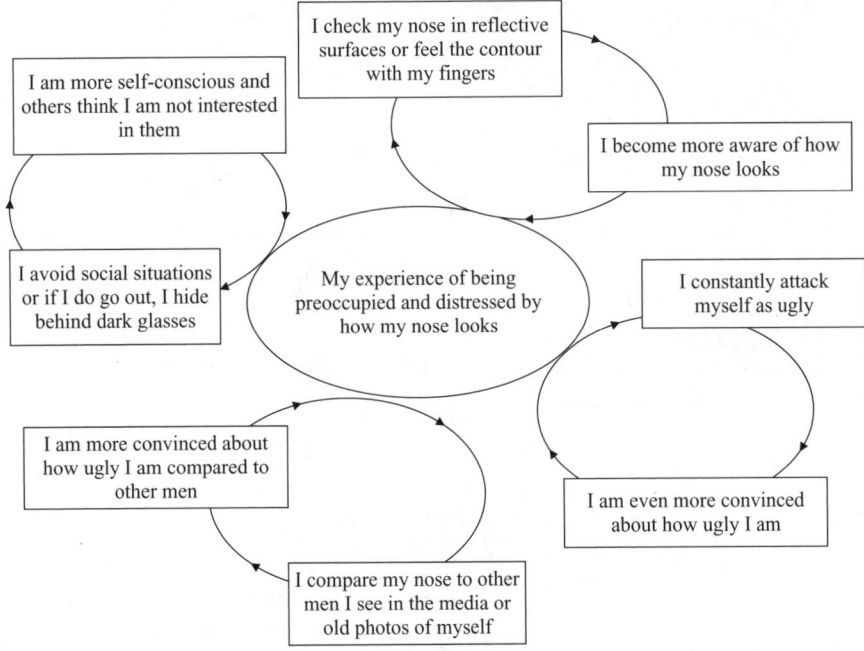

Figure 14.3   Maintenance of BDD in Brian ("Vicious flower")

14.7   Defining the Problems and Goals

Try to focus on what the client has already tried to do to solve his problem and on how handicapped he is. The nature of BDD means that a therapist may disagree with a client's description of the problem in terms of his beliefs about his appearance; this is best avoided. However, both the client and therapist can usually agree on a description of the problem as a preoccupation with one or more features leading to distress and various handicaps. It is then usually possible to agree on outcome goals, such as reducing preoccupation and distress or specific behaviors such as skin-picking.

Ensure that the goals are realistic. Some clients may agree to realistic goals but still plan to change their appearance. If a client is unable to engage, it is best to put the goals to one side and concentrate on engaging the client in the model and later to negotiate the goals. A discussion might ensue on the obstacles to the goal or the process to the goals. His assumption might be that he cannot do anything until he feels comfortable with his appearance or until his body part is altered.

It is important early on to have a discussion on his expectations of therapy. This includes: a) what the client hopes the therapy will consist of; and b) what the client expects therapy to consist of.

What the client hopes and expects from therapy may be different – for example, a client may hope that he will feel a bit better so he can have surgery later. He may also have unrealistic expectations about the frequency or length of sessions or how much time will be required for practice between sessions.

Progress in CBT usually occurs if both the client and therapist can agree on a) a description of the problems and goals and a formulation that is an understanding of how the problem has developed and is maintained; and b) if your client understands your expectations during therapy and is willing to be actively engaged in the therapy. This might mean that your client commits himself not to alter his appearance by cosmetic, surgical, or dermatological procedures and tries to adhere to the homework negotiated in therapy; to act according to a plan rather than how he feels. There would be a discussion of the planned frequency of sessions, the estimated number of sessions required, when the therapy is reviewed, and the expectations of homework. One option is to provide two (or possibly three) sessions a week for the first two to three weeks and then to reduce the frequency to once a week for the next 12–15 weeks. Follow-up sessions might then occur fortnightly and then monthly for three months. Therapy might be discontinued early if it was felt that the person was not ready to change as it may be better for him to return when he is ready. However, for clients who are ready for change, it can be helpful to have daily sessions of 1.5–2 hours' duration during the first couple of weeks (usually one to two months). The frequency of sessions enables clients to engage as well as to test out an alternative understanding consistently and give an opportunity for the therapist to alter their safety-seeking behaviors and processes such as ruminating.

14.8 "Not Ready to Change"

One of the most difficult consultations to manage is when a new client does not want to see you and a concerned relative has dragged him along. He may believe his solution is cosmetic surgery but his parents will not fund it. He is angry about seeing you and minimizes the degree of his handicap with you. His strategy is to impress on you that he is not mentally unwell and may give you as little information as possible. He will usually wear his parents down until they give in to his demands. Regrettably, he often wins and is unlikely to return immediately to see you. In this type of consultation, your therapeutic alliance starts poorly and you do not share the same goals as the client.

Another situation occurs when a client with BDD has been asked to see you by a cosmetic surgeon who has agreed operate unless you advise against it. This is a no-win situation! A decision whether to operate or not is, of course, made by a surgeon, but the client will know that you have responsibility for advising the surgeon. If you diagnose moderate to severe BDD in someone with unrealistic expectations, then you are likely to recommend that surgery is not performed (see Chapter 15). However, a client desperate for surgery may be economical with the truth and they are unlikely to be receptive at this appointment to an alternative treatment. All one can do in the time available is to make a diagnosis, try to engage the client in an alternative understanding of the problem, and inform him of outcome studies of cosmetic surgery in BDD. The information may be interpreted as accepting that an unpredictable outcome can occur in people with BDD clients, but in his opinion, he does not suffer from BDD. The client has usually committed to something he has been mentally planning for many years. The therapeutic bond may be better than in the previous example of the reluctant client, but again the client does not share the same understanding of the problem or goals. We have to accept that some clients are not ready to change and may well go through a long career of unnecessary surgery, beauty therapies, dermatological treatment, or suicide attempts before seeking help from you or another mental health professional. Unless the client is detained as an inpatient under the Mental Health Act in the UK or involuntarily confined in the USA, all you may be able to do is to let your client know that that he has a recognized problem and try to engage him in a understanding of what the problem is and that it is treatable. If he consents, you would try to share your findings with his carers, family doctor, and other health professionals involved, such as dermatologist and cosmetic surgeon.

Your strategy is to ensure that he knows that you are willing to help. In this situation, it may be helpful for the client to meet former clients with BDD or listen to a video of a former client before and after surgery and their regrets. We worry most about those clients who present a long-term suicide risk and in whom it is difficult to justify immediate involuntary treatment. They may refuse to attend again and we believe that a significant proportion of clients may end up committing suicide.

Another case which can be very difficult to engage in the first session is the client who is highly avoidant and ashamed of his problem. It may have taken him many years to pluck up the courage to see you – for example, a man who is worried about the size of his genitals may need a strenuous effort to see you. In all these examples, it is usually better to spend less time on the history and assessment schedules (which it is always possible to return to) and spend more time on engagement and developing a shared understanding of the problem and rationale for your treatment. At the other end of the spectrum, clients may have better insight into the nature of their problem and are so desperate for help that engagement is an easier process but may bring a different set of problems. They may accept the diagnosis of BDD but feel hopeless because they have had surgery and are angry with themselves for making their appearance worse. Furthermore, they may feel they have lost all hope of altering their body part and feel suicidal. Therefore, the first session may focus on suicide risk and engendering hope.

Another problem is if your client is telling himself: "I can only stop avoiding situations or drop my camouflage when I feel *comfortable* or 'right'; when I feel *certain* that I will not be humiliated; or when I feel *confident* or *courageous* enough to test out an alternative." This applies to a wide range of avoidance and safety behaviors, such as mirror-gazing, skin picking, or being house-bound. If your client sticks with these beliefs then he is putting the cart before the horse (Dryden, 1999). In this case, nothing will change until he acts as if Theory "B" was true (not according to how he feels). In the short term, he thus has to act uncomfortably, with uncertainty, uncourageously, unconfidently in order to test out an alternative theory or to determine if the safety behavior has the consequences of increasing or decreasing his preoccupation and distress with his appearance.

Other metaphors can be used for new challenges in which clients will feel uncomfortable and uncertain. Here, the tug of war with a monster metaphor is especially apt (Hayes et al., 1999).

"The situation is like being in a tug of war with a monster. It is big, ugly, and very strong. In between you and the monster is a pit and, as far as you can tell, it is bottomless. If you lose this tug of war, you will fall into this pit and will be destroyed. So you pull harder and harder, but the harder you pull, the harder the monster pulls, and you edge closer and closer to the pit.

The hardest thing to see is that our job here is to not to win the tug of war; our job is to drop the rope."

This is an excellent analogy to use to help your client not to engage in ruminations or safety-seeking behaviors, to detach from the thoughts, and not avoid the emotion. If the client answers "How do I do that?" it's not necessary to answer right now (as this is the whole issue that therapy addresses), but to say, "Well, I don't know exactly how to answer that right now. However the first step is simply to see that you are holding that rope and engaging in a struggle."

Sometimes, however carefully you explain the nature of BDD and the rationale of the model and therapy, your client may still say: "There is no way I am going to be *persuaded* that I can live with my appearance or be *humiliated* by returning to normal society." The key issue is to allow the client to feel understood and to leave the door open so he can return when he may be ready to change. Alternatively, the person may be willing to take medication. This may be the only foot in the door you have to build a therapeutic alliance and increase trust and credibility. Benefits may accrue after medication and it may be easier to engage a client in the therapy. Our clinical experience suggests that it's helpful to engage people in therapy as soon after their cosmetic procedure as possible, to help refocus their attention on non-appearance aspects of life and reduce the chance of the area of concern moving to another location.

14.9   Psycho-education

Clients may be given a general information leaflet about BDD (Appendix 2) and recommended an educational or self-help book about BDD (Phillips, 1996a; Veale et al., 2009), a CD-ROM, or a video about BDD (available through the Bio-Behavioral Institute at www.biobehavioralinstitute.com). Your client might have the opportunity of meeting other BDD clients in your clinic or attend a support group. As support groups exclusive to BDD clients are few and far between, an alternative is an Internet groups. (Details of support groups and national charities around the world are listed in Appendix 3.) Clients are often extremely relieved and surprised to talk to other BDD clients. Support groups help clients to feel understood, although at another level they may not yet identify themselves as having BDD or consider how other people's BDD may relate to them. Note that support groups will sometimes be used to exchange information on surgeons or other non-psychiatric treatments. Be prepared to hear from your client that he can see that others suffer from BDD but he does not. Occasionally, some BDD clients are critical of the appearance of someone else in the group, fortunately outside the group.

Chapter 15

Advice on cosmetic procedures

Summary

This chapter covers the practical aspects of a) assessing a client who has been referred to a mental health practitioner by a cosmetic surgeon or dermatologist; b) advising clients with BDD who are planning a cosmetic procedure; and c) advising public-funded bodies on cosmetic procedures.

Sections

15.1   Introduction

We review the prevalence of BDD in cosmetic and dermatological settings in Chapter 3 and the role of cosmetic procedures in BDD in Chapter 6. It was shown that BDD was relatively common in cosmetic and dermatological settings, with a prevalence of 3–18%. The rate depends on the procedures offered at each clinic, the sex ratio, and the diagnostic threshold and instrument used to measure BDD. However, it is usually not diagnosed and there is one small prospective study on the outcome of cosmetic procedures in people with BDD.

Within a mental health setting, a significant number of clients with BDD will either have undergone one or more procedures or are contemplating a

---

Body Dysmorphic Disorder: A Treatment Manual. David Veale and Fugen Neziroglu
© 2010 John Wiley & Sons, Ltd.

procedure. They may have gone for a consultation with a surgeon or dermatologist; are planning to have a procedure or are searching for the best surgeon; or are spending time dreaming and mentally planning a cosmetic procedure. Clients who have already had a cosmetic procedure may be experiencing subsequent complications: debt, guilt for having caused their feature to worsen, or anger directed at the surgeon for making it worse, or are preoccupied with pursuing a negligence case and complaints to various bodies. The role of a partner or family member may be relevant as they may be dragooned into funding a cosmetic procedure, even when they disagree that it is necessary or helpful ("If it makes her happy, then I'll do it").

15.2   Advice to Cosmetic Surgeons and Dermatologists

This section is addressed to cosmetic surgeons and dermatologists.

It is good practice for cosmetic surgeons and dermatologists to identify patients with BDD in their initial assessment when the patient has a feature that is hardly noticeable or not that abnormal. However, as a surgeon or dermatologist you are not usually trained to do this and are in an invidious position. A patient may not admit that they have seen a mental health practitioner or been given a diagnosis of BDD. A patient may withhold certain symptoms or be economical with the truth. As a patient said to one of us: "If asked, I'll tell him that I have just one area of concern, which is not on my mind that much, that I'm hoping to feel a bit more confident and that the operation won't make much difference to my life." Even if you do identify a patient with BDD and refer him for an assessment, there is no guarantee that the patient will attend. We understand that private cosmetic surgery is competitive and there is likely to be another provider who will perform the procedure requested. It may be more cost-effective in both the public and private sectors to provide screening by questionnaire to assess patients at high risk for dissatisfaction.

As yet, though, there are no prospective studies determining the specific risk factors for dissatisfaction or poor outcome.

Cosmetic surgeons and dermatologists at best can determine if the patient's expectations of a procedure are realistic. In general, patients will have good psychological outcome if patients:

- can clearly describe the feature that concerns them;
- are clear about the desired physical outcome (this can be demonstrated on a photo or face mask);
- have very modest psychosocial expectations and recognize that a procedure is unlikely to reduce the degree of distress and handicap seen in BDD;

■ the cosmetic surgeon can agree with the above and can technically achieve the desired physical outcome.

A surgeon is then in a position to discuss with the patient any limitations there may be for surgically altering his appearance and can outline the consequences and risks of going ahead. If unsure about the desired physical outcome, some surgeons make use of a photographic image that can be electronically modified. Others use a plaster cast and ask the patient to alter the mask or image to the desired outcome.

The advice to any surgeon or dermatologist who believes that a patient has BDD is to tell him that you think he may have such a diagnosis and explain why you would advise referring the patient to a mental health practitioner for a full assessment and further advice. You should clearly state if you do not think that a cosmetic procedure would be helpful even though it may be technically possible. It is unpredictable whether a patient may be satisfied, but the symptoms of BDD are very likely to persist. We discuss below some of the steps you can take, but the key issue is to tell the patient if you do not believe that you (or another surgeon or dermatologist) can help him as there is a significant risk he is likely to be dissatisfied, or if he is satisfied, the cosmetic success may only be partial as it is unlikely to reduce his distress or social handicap as his preoccupation is likely to move to another body area. Acknowledge that the patient may find another surgeon or dermatologist who is willing to perform the procedure but that you would not recommend it. Do not spend time arguing with the patient about whether his "defect" is real or imagined, but say you are concerned that the client may feel worse about his appearance. Try to find common ground and be extremely empathic about his distress. Find out as much as you can about his preoccupation, distress, and the effect on work, his difficulties in studying, loneliness, or relationships. In general, do not refer your patient to another surgeon or dermatologist for a second opinion. It is better to try to develop a relationship with a mental health practitioner you can trust and refer such patients to them. A surgeon will benefit in understanding the motivation and expectations of his patient and improve his ability to select suitable patients in the future – both of which will be useful in the context of litigation. Patients who are unhappy with screening and an exploration of their motivations and expectations are less likely to be satisfied.

We explore in Chapter 6 the evidence that the effect of a cosmetic procedure is unpredictable in BDD and is unlikely to reduce distress and symptoms of BDD. In some situations, it is possible for a surgeon or dermatologist and mental health practitioner to work together, especially where there is scarring from psychogenic excoriation or a patient is undergoing a procedure like a breast reduction, for which she may be satisfied but require further help in overcoming symptoms of BDD.

15.3 Advice to Mental Health Practitioners

Most cosmetic procedures occur in the private sector where liaison between a cosmetic surgeon and mental health practitioner is difficult and the patient may go to a different surgeon. The UK National Care Standards Commission (NCSC) has set a standard for private clinics that "referral to appropriate psychological counselling is available if clinically indicated prior to surgery" (Department of Health, 2000). There are, however, no operational criteria in the National Care Standards as to when appropriate psychological counseling is clinically indicated and for whom. The industry is being increasingly regulated, but there is no evidence base and the NCSC has set a vague standard.

If a client is referred to a mental health practitioner for an assessment prior to a cosmetic procedure, then the first step is to exclude a psychiatric disorder that may contraindicate a procedure. We indicated in Chapter 6 that cosmetic surgery is contraindicated in clients with psychosis, mania, or severe depression, whose judgement about the need for surgery may be impaired or who may have systematized delusions or command hallucinations about cosmetic surgery or the surgeon. This is essentially a decision about *capacity*.

The second group in whom cosmetic surgery is *probably* contraindicated are those with eating disorders, who might be attracted to procedures such as liposuction or abdominoplasty. However, there are no prospective data to guide us. The third group in whom a cosmetic procedure is *probably* contraindicated are clients with BDD. In Chapter 6, we review retrospective data from BDD patients in psychiatric clinics, which suggest that the symptoms of BDD do not tend to improve following a cosmetic procedure or even if the client is satisfied, then the preoccupation may refocus on the same or a different body part. The only other relevant diagnosis to exclude in body image problems might be an eating disorder or body integrity identity disorder (BIID) (see Chapter 1). Note that individuals with BIID feel that one or more limbs (or a part of their body) are not part of their "self" and that amputation will lead to them feeling more able-bodied. It is a preoccupation that does not derive from feeling ugly, defective, or inadequate, but the expectation that they would be so much more comfortable if one or more limbs/digits were amputated. Although such individuals are preoccupied with becoming disabled, they do not generally believe (as in BDD) their limbs to be defective or ugly, nor do they wish cosmetically to alter their limb. Preliminary evidence suggest that clients experienced a better quality of life once the effort involved in seeking amputation or removal of foot or finger is removed.

Apart from diagnosing a mental disorder, the role of a mental health practitioner is to assess the client's psychosocial expectations about a procedure. When these are made explicit, then the likelihood of satisfaction should increase. An assessment can help a client clarify his motivation for the procedure and reach a reasoned and thoughtful decision about whether to proceed.

Some of the issues in the assessment are highlighted below which are in a self-report form in the Body Image questionnaire in Appendix 1.

1. *Can you describe the features for which you are seeking a cosmetic procedure?*

A drawing may assist in this. Some clients use bizarre descriptions of their feature that will immediately alert a problem.

2. *How long have you been planning the procedure?*
3. *How noticeable do you feel your feature is to other people if you do not camouflage yourself (e.g., with clothes, padding and/or makeup) and the feature has not been pointed out to them?*
4. *How abnormal do you think the feature is?*

A significant discrepancy between how noticeable and how abnormal you think it is supports one of the criteria for the diagnosis of BDD.

5. *On whose initiative is surgery being sought?*
6. *Is the procedure supported by family or friends?*

There is some evidence that dissatisfaction is more likely to occur in those who have been motivated by a family member or friend (i.e., externally motivated) or who have been strongly discouraged by a family member or friend.

7. *What expectations do you have for changes in your social life, work, or relationships?*

Dissatisfaction is likely to occur in those who have unrealistic expectations for change (e.g., their social life and their ability to develop a relationship would vastly improve).

8. *What cosmetic procedures have you had in the past? Did the procedure lead to improvements in self-consciousness and distress? Were you satisfied by the procedure?*

Previous dissatisfaction is more likely to be associated with increasing dissatisfaction.

Whatever your opinion is on the benefit of a procedure, make sure it is well documented and that your advice to the surgeon is clear. In any report, surgeons do not want pages of background history. What they do want is a clear recommendation on whether or not to operate. Dermatologists may still be willing to provide further treatment (which is not as drastic as surgery), but this can make it more difficult for clients to commit themselves fully to CBT. However, it is usually best to remain flexible on this if it is issue.

15.4   Engaging Clients with BDD Planning a Cosmetic Procedure

If a client with BDD who is being treated by you tells you that that he is planning a cosmetic procedure, it is sensible for you to try to liaise with his surgeon or dermatologist. However, your client may not be willing to divulge the name of his surgeon, knowing that the surgeon may not then operate. Fortunately, most BDD clients who state they want surgery at assessment or during therapy do not go ahead with it. The main reasons for not proceeding with surgery are insufficient money or fear that the feature may be made worse. Alternatively, we may not know the outcome of those who drop out of therapy as there is a selection bias in favor of those who remain in therapy.

There is no specific time to discuss the effect of a cosmetic procedure although it is preferable to establish your client's plans before any therapy commences. In general, it is advisable for clients to delay until any cosmetic procedure has been completed since there is a risk that they will not otherwise be engaged in therapy. Alternatively, you may focus your intervention on the unworkability of a cosmetic procedure and developing an alternative formulation.

You can inform your client that a diagnosis of BDD makes the outcome of cosmetic procedure unpredictable for both satisfaction with the procedure and overall symptoms of BDD. In some cases a cosmetic procedure can lead to satisfaction with the altered appearance, especially when the desired outcome is unambiguous (e.g., mammaplasty – reduction or augmentation) and the main focus of the BDD is on a different feature. However, where there are multiple concerns and a procedure is done on one area of preoccupation, it may transfer to a different area of the body and the individual remains with the same symptoms of BDD. Most remain dissatisfied. At worst, a cosmetic procedure may go wrong and symptoms of BDD may intensify.

It is very difficult to predict which cases will result in satisfaction or alleviation of BDD symptoms other than to say that the chance of satisfaction is greater the milder the symptoms and the less the client's expectations of significant changes in BDD symptoms or the psychosocial situation. Some procedures such as breast augmentation may be associated with a good outcome as the surgeon and client agree on the desired outcome, including trying different sized augmentations within the client's bra. However, such clients usually have other bodily concerns and the symptoms of BDD persist.

It is important for you to be empathetic to the client's desire to resolve their negative body image through a cosmetic procedure. Try to sound authoritative and understanding, but also acknowledge the uncertainties in a cosmetic procedure in BDD. If you state that there is no need for a cosmetic procedure, then your client is likely to become argumentative or withdraw from treatment. Use motivational interviewing and the strategies in the Chapter 14 to try to change the agenda. In the man in a hole metaphor, cosmetic surgery is depicted as a gold shovel. Ruminating and dreaming about a gold shovel is further avoidance of dealing with the problem psychologically and is another safety-seeking behavior that maintains the preoccupation. To summarize, we make it clear that we are not opposed to cosmetic procedures *per se*, but the outcome is unpredictable in clients with BDD. The evidence for most clients without BDD is that cosmetic procedures are associated with very small psychosocial benefits. However, BDD clients are often expecting marked improvements in psychosocial outcomes (e.g., that they will now be able to develop a relationship, be able to concentrate enough to study or work).

Cost–benefit analysis

Some clients preoccupied by a cosmetic procedure as a solution may be helped by a cost–benefit analysis. This involves helping your client to complete a list of costs against the benefits of a cosmetic procedure in both the short and long term, to himself and others. He should then repeat the exercise on costs and benefits of the CBT or medication being offered. Depending on the circumstances, the disadvantages may include:

- the financial cost;
- the surgery may go wrong and make the problem worse;
- the expected psychosocial outcome will not be achieved;
- the area of concern may move to another body part;
- the fact that someone is willing to operate does not mean it is an acknowledgement of the defect (cosmetic surgery is an industry where some clinics are always willing to operate);
- the results of a cosmetic procedure in other BDD clients are unpredictable. Other clients either report dissatisfaction or the preoccupation frequently moves to a different area of the body so that symptoms of BDD remain the same.

The possible disadvantages are not usually sufficient for most BDD clients and it is more important to focus on an alternative understanding of what the problem is and what is maintaining it. Agree that a cosmetic procedure may alter appearance but not body image or the way the client feels about his appearance or the picture in his mind.

One option is to suggest your client delays the surgery until he has completed CBT or medication and has recovered from BDD. The disadvantage of this strategy is that your client may not be fully committed to therapy and continue to dream about surgery. In general, always try to focus clients on psychological understanding of what the problem is rather than what it is not, and try to steer the agenda towards the preoccupation and distress (see Chapter 14).

If clients agree to stop seeking a cosmetic procedure, the next goal is attitudinal change when clients often engage in "mental cosmetic surgery." In other words, individuals with BDD may try to alter their appearance mentally either in front of a mirror or by ruminating. Although this is a lot cheaper than "real" cosmetic surgery, it is a major obstacle in therapy for overcoming BDD as it is difficult to test out alternative hypotheses and engage in therapy whilst the client is mentally planning a cosmetic procedure.

It is sometimes impossible to engage clients in therapy until they have had surgery. In such situations, we usually discontinue therapy and try to contact clients a few months after surgery to enquire about the progress and remind them of our willingness to help. Unless you can wholly trust a surgeon not to operate without consulting you, we would advise you not to refer clients for an opinion. In our experience, if a client then has surgery with which he is dissatisfied, the anger will also be directed at you for referring him to a particular surgeon and any therapeutic alliance you had will be disrupted and the client will be less likely to return for therapy. If he opts to go for surgery on his own, encourage him to return to you after surgery. Most BDD clients who dream of a cosmetic procedure do not go ahead with it, but we have no good follow-up data on this.

15.5   Advice on Public Health Funding of a Cosmetic Procedure

Purchasers view publicly funded cosmetic procedures as a low priority in people with disfigurement. Cosmetic procedures are not covered by any health care organization in the USA. In Europe too, public health care has generally excluded cosmetic procedures for all clients other than in exceptional circumstances. You may therefore be asked to assess a client with a disfigurement to determine if there are exceptional circumstances for public funding. Some health care purchasers require a psychiatric or psychological assessment of all clients prior to cosmetic surgery although there is no evaluation of the cost and benefits of routine evaluations.

In conditions of disfigurement, there is no relationship between the degree of disfigurement and the distress flowing from it; on the contrary, minor physical disfigurement may be associated with great distress and handicap (Robinson, 1997). This is a difficult concept for health purchasers to understand and a mental health practitioner may be burdened with the invidious task of helping to assist a purchaser to set priorities to determine which clients should be publicly funded. Cook et al. (2003) examined the clinical guidelines from 32 health authorities in the UK. Guidelines mostly concerned arbitrary sets of cosmetic procedures and lacked any evidence base. Most guidelines permit surgery "exceptionally" for psychological reasons. They found that the guidelines did not appreciably alter surgeons' decisions. Surgeons' decision criteria included:

1. the cost of the procedure (e.g., moles were routinely excised as it was easier for the surgeon to operate than to explain why surgery could not be offered);
2. whether the client sought restoration or improvement of appearance (an ugly scar might be operated on because it was restoration to normality);
3. the degree of abnormality;
4. the degree to which the client is seen to *deserve* the treatment (e.g., a woman who has made the effort to lose a considerable amount of weight but is left with an overhanging skin "apron" might be granted a tummy tuck while one who is seen to be requesting a "quick fix" would not);
5. the impact on the future quality of life (e.g., a young girl unable to form a relationship might be operated on while an older woman in a stable relationship is refused).

Some surgeons have described feeling pressured to offer surgery by clients' emotional and insistent presentations and believe that some clients contrived their presentation in an attempt to elicit the desired surgical decision. However, in the current financial environment in the UK, referrals for a cosmetic procedure are usually screened out and family doctors will usually have to appeal to the body responsible for purchasing care. The purchaser may then request an assessment by a mental health practitioner to assist them in their decision.

Typically, a report will conclude that you are of the opinion that there are no psychological contraindications for a procedure. You might state the person is not suffering from BDD and has capacity to make a judgement about the risks and benefits and be able to give consent. He may not be coping because of his disfigurement and have mixed anxiety and depressive symptoms. You may well believe that there would be some psychosocial benefit and modest improvement in the quality of his life and relationships. However, how will you decide that the client is an exceptional case for public funding, especially when there are no alternatives? It is usually very difficult to distinguish between the client you have assessed and the many other clients in terms of the degree of psychological distress or handicap and the benefit that might occur. Exceptional cases might be someone with congenital hypoplasia in breast development, an altered appearance from a medical treatment (e.g., lipodystrophy from a drug regime), or consistent unwanted intrusions from others commenting on their appearance. In one author's' experience (DV), it is an impossible task and one's own values are likely to impact on this judgement. Agreed national guidelines and a better evidence base may assist purchasers in the long term. It may also be better that such procedures are means-tested as many of the clients turned down for public funding may borrow or find money to pay for the procedures.

Chapter 16

Imagery rescripting

Summary

In BDD, the self is viewed as an aesthetic object, which is manifested by mental imagery or a "felt" impression of how a person appears to others from an observer perspective. Fusion between past aversive experiences and a "felt impression" of the self is thought to be an important factor in maintaining the evaluations about being ugly and all the avoidant and safety-seeking behaviors associated with it. This chapter describes imagery rescripting of aversive memories associated with the self. We recommend using imagery rescripting at an early stage of therapy, especially when your client experiences intrusive images of his appearance and there is a developmental formulation that links the image with past aversive experiences.

Sections

16.1   Introduction
16.2   Assessment
16.3   Imagery rescripting
16.4   Historical role-play

16.1   Introduction

A core component of the model of BDD is the self as an aesthetic object, which represents mental imagery or a "felt" impression of how a person appears to others from an observer perspective. We describe in Chapter 4 the evidence for imagery in BDD (Osman et al., 2004) and in Chapter 10 how images take the form of different modalities. Central to the model is the way

Body Dysmorphic Disorder: A Treatment Manual. David Veale and Fugen Neziroglu
© 2010 John Wiley & Sons, Ltd.

imagery acts as a trigger to drive the subsequent evaluation of ugliness and response (ruminations and safety-seeking behaviors). Furthermore, people often identify their imagery as closely linked to a particular meaning and aversive early experiences. Typical themes include being teased and bullied at school; self-consciousness about appearance changes or acne during adolescence; medical procedures; accidents; or occasionally sexual trauma. Not everyone will identify with having a "picture in their mind" of how they look, but will usually experience a "felt impression" of themselves or a memory of how they look in the mirror. Imagery is not just visual but is often multisensory and includes bodily feelings. A minority of clients report only thoughts or feelings about being ugly. However, this does not preclude exploring some of their early memories with imagery when they first started to feel ugly or humiliated. The relevant experiences though may be earlier than when they started to experience thoughts about being ugly, which becomes a *post hoc* rationalization.

An important cognitive process that maintains symptoms in BDD is cognitive fusion or relational framing. The process of cognitive fusion relates to the ways in which memories and associations from the past become fused with imagery and verbal representations in the present (see discussion in Chapter 9). Where there is marked avoidance and anxiety about intrusive imagery, then it is especially important to experience these images and identify the meaning at the time of the adverse event(s) being described.

Imagery appears to have a direct link in representing emotionally charged material (Kosslyn et al., 1985; Vrana et al., 1986; Holmes & Mathews, 2005). Imagery in the form of flashbacks tends to be prominent in post-traumatic stress disorder (PTSD). Jaycox et al. (1998) found that imaginal exposure allowed a person to attach context within a safe environment and the opportunity to discriminate between traumatic and non-traumatic events. Ehlers & Clark (2000) noted that evoking imagery of past trauma allows memory fragments to be elaborated and given a context within an autobiographical base and wider knowledge of current experience. Articulating traumatic memory provides an opportunity to reflect on unhelpful appraisals. Lastly, a time code is attached so that imagery is no longer a current threat and the feelings and thought can start to be defused from the imagery.

Wild et al. (2008) assessed rescripting aversive memories in a series of 11 clients with social phobia, who attended two sessions, one week apart. The first was a control session in which their images and memories were discussed but not modified. The second was an experimental session in which the rescripting imagery procedure was used to contextualize and update the memories. No change was observed after the control session. The experimental session led to significant improvement in negative beliefs, image and memory distress and vividness, fear of negative evaluation, and anxiety in feared social situations. The results suggest that rescripting unpleasant memories linked to negative self-images may be a useful adjunct in the treatment of social phobia. Imagery with rescripting techniques that focus on modifying aversive memories have also been used in CBT for borderline personality disorder (Giesen-Bloo et al., 2006) and for PTSD arising from childhood sexual abuse (Smucker & Niederee, 1995). However, the impact of imagery rescripting in other disorders has not been assessed as a separate procedure as in social phobia. The first component of imagery rescripting is to align to exposure in the imagination and the person is asked to visualize the image within its full context, including all sensory modalities attached to the image. In OCD and health anxiety this has been found to be useful (Neziroglu et al., 1999).

The optimal procedure within imagery rescripting and how this should be matched to the client is not yet known. Thus one approach might emphasize just experiencing intrusive image and memory as a form of exposure in imagination and emotional processing. This might be more important where there is marked experiential avoidance. Another approach is to emphasize detached mindfulness and developing a different relationship with the image or memory so that the self is no longer fused with past memories. Others emphasize using cognitive restructuring and the broader experience of the adult self to alter the meaning of past memories within the rescripting. Another approach is to develop a caring, compassionate approach by the adult self or others towards the child self. This may be more relevant when the adult self has developed an extremely critical evaluative component. You will need to use your clinical skills to determine which components to emphasize in imagery rescripting. Further background information on working with images and aversive memories in CBT can be found in Hackmann (2005) and in Holmes et al. (2007).

We are currently evaluating the role of imagery rescripting for people with BDD in single case series designs. Generally, we try to introduce it early in therapy as part of the developmental formulation. The following sections describe how it is possible to rescript imagery and reduce preoccupation and distress. As it is impossible to alter the past, the goal in imagery rescripting in BDD is a) to develop a different relationship with the image – to view past experiences as a bad memory rather than an event that is being repeated or has great importance now; b) question the accuracy of the encapsulated meaning of an event; and c) develop a compassionate and caring approach to the self. This is done by updating the image so that it is emotionally processed and given a context rather than fused with the present so that the individual intervenes in the memory as an adult with new information that he knows now and with compassionate imagery. Clinical experience suggests that rescripting may not have an immediate impact. Sometimes there are number of aversive memories to choose from (all of them may need addressing). Even if a person does not report intrusive imagery or a felt impression of his feature, we may still try to use imagery rescripting for any early experiences that are associated with the onset of the problem.

Note that imagery in this chapter refers to involuntary and usually distressing intrusive imagery. Clients may also use imagery as a safety-seeking behavior to check on how they appear to others (a mental check rather than checking in the mirror). However, both have the same function and unintended consequences of increasing preoccupation and distress. We cover mental checks in Chapter 18.

16.2   Assessment

The interview below for assessing imagery and rescripting imagery in BDD is adapted from Osman et al. (2004) and a training manual for social phobia (Wild et al., personal communication). The therapist might say:

"I'd like to learn more about what goes through your mind when you are particularly distressed about your appearance. People think in different ways and when people are distressed a mixture of thoughts and fleeting pictures of how they look often pop into their mind. I'm interested in any images of your appearance in your mind that you may have. Images could be in the form of a picture in your mind or felt impression of how you appear. It could be a sensation on the body (e.g., feeling very heavy or tight) or inside the body (e.g., tiredness), and may even involve smells. I would like you to think about a recent time when you have felt really distressed about your appearance when you were not looking in a mirror or a reflective surface.

Have you ever experienced a picture in your mind's eye or a felt impression of how you look when you were distressed about your appearance?
If *yes*:
What word shall we use for them?
Did you find that any of your pictures or felt impressions were recurrent and always involved in the same aspect of your appearance?
Is it mainly a pictures in your mind or were there other feelings – for example, a sensation of touch or pressure or a movement within the image?
Are they intrusive in that they just pop into your mind? (Or do you ever bring the picture to your mind to mentally check on what you look like?)

If *no*:
Sometimes even if people do not get an actual picture, they still form a felt impression of the way they appear to others or how they think others might see them. Do you remember ever getting that kind of felt impression when you were distressed about your appearance?
How often does the picture/felt impression occur? Is it distressing for you?
When was the last time you had a picture/felt impression when thinking about your feature? Could you re-create this picture/felt impression in your mind now, making it as vivid as possible?

If it is easier for you to bring the picture/felt impression to mind with your eyes shut, that's OK (you might want to take your glasses off, and relax with your legs uncrossed).

Can you describe what you see in the picture/felt impression?

Is what you see in the picture/felt impression, the same as what you see in a mirror?

Thinking about the picture/felt impression, are you mainly viewing your feature looking out through your eyes, observing the details of what is going on around you, or are you mainly looking back at yourself?

Do you use the picture to check how you are looking when there is no mirror around?

Is there more than one picture or felt impression?"

Summarize the nature of the image, asking "is that right?" and make a written summary. Then use a downward arrow technique to identify assumptions and beliefs about the imagery.

"Let's assume for the moment that the image/felt impression you had of yourself is correct.

What's the most distressing aspect about this image/felt impression?

If that were true, what would be so distressing about it?

What would that mean about you?

How strongly do you believe that on a scale of 0 –100%?

If it were true, what would it mean about your relationship to other people?

(If it were true, what would it mean about the world generally?)

Do these assumptions reflect your current views?

As you dwell on the image, how vivid (real) does the image feel right now on a scale 0–100 (where 0 is not at all vivid and 100 is extremely vivid)?

How much would you rate your distress regarding this image on a scale of 0–100 (where 0 is not at all distressing and 100 is extremely distressing)?"

Summarize the feeling and encapsulated meaning to your client. The next step is to make an emotional bridge between the image and past experiences. To evoke the image, ask the client to close his eyes and in the first-person present tense to recount all the sensory detail, emotions, and thoughts when describing experiences linked to the image. The memories should, if possible, be recounted in field perspective and in chronological order, as in a frame-by-frame account of a video. (This is described in more detail below.)

"When in your life do you first remember feeling like this?

Is there a particular memory associated with this?

Where were you?

How old were you?

What was happening in your life at that time?
How did you feel about yourself at that time?
Is there a particular memory from that time that seems to be closely linked to the image/felt impression?
If so, do you think you could evoke it in your mind now and describe it to me?
Can you see anything in the memory?
Are there any other sensations is the memory (e.g., do you notice any sensations or feelings within your body? Do you notice any sensations of smell? Are you touching anything in the memory? Are you performing any actions within the memory?)
What does it mean about you? (Rate belief between 0 and 100.)
How similar is the memory compared with the spontaneous image/impression?"

If your client denies the existence of any intrusive imagery or felt impression, then he may still have aversive memories that may be linked to his body image by sharing the same meaning (e.g., being humiliated and alone in the world). We would try to ask open questions about whether he can remember any early experiences that might in any way be linked with how he feels about his appearance or related to them (e.g., being humiliated or teased). Note that occasionally the memory may not be an aversive experience but may be linked to a pleasant feeling (e.g., seeing someone who is very attractive).

Information about how one appears to others is obtained from one's image or felt impression. It is helpful to reinforce the idea that the image has usually been formed long ago. In this regard the meaning *may* have been helpful or accurate at the time, but has never been updated.

"The image may be like a ghost from the past, which has become fused with past experiences. Therefore, when you look in the mirror or think about your appearance, you might be triggering memories from the past that are very unpleasant and have not yet been updated. This in turn influences the way you feel about your features in the present. The memory of that event is something that happened. However the picture in your mind and the associated memory are something that you may be afraid will happen again or is important to you now."

The therapist should validate the imagery as important and be explicit about not being ashamed about the meaning he has derived and validate his way of coping.

"If you've strongly believed the felt impression in your mind as how you appear to others, it's not really surprising that you've wanted to try to fix it in various ways, to try to avoid situations and have constantly tried to work out how to solve it. I'd like to see therefore if you can update these memories so they lose some of their meaning and emotional links and become just a bad memory rather than something that is just accepted as a fact."

When the current meaning of the memory is determined, guided discovery can be used to determine if there are alternative interpretations of the adverse event and to explore what the implications are for the present. For example, if a client has been bullied and interpreted the event as meaning that they were different, ugly, and alone in the world, he would be encouraged to come up with an adult view of the event. For example, are there reasons why children bully other children? What might this mean about the children who did the bullying? Was the child really different and alone in the world or did he *feel* that way? Is there a difference between what the child felt and what the adult has been told by many people over many years?

The child meaning of the event can be contrasted with the evidence as an adult in two columns. Some clients will struggle with this when historical role-play (see next section) may be more helpful. It is also possible to use detached mindfulness and not to engage with imagery (see Chapter 18). The goal with all imagery is to view past adverse events as something that has occurred as a child without any implications for the experience as an adult.

16.3 Imagery Rescripting

Imagery rescripting is a procedure derived from Arntz & Weertman (1999) and Smucker & Dancu (1999) for trauma (originally it was part of Gestalt). Imagery rescripting as an intervention can be used not just for distressing memories identified when self-imagery is first experienced, but memories that are identified as important in the development of the view of the self. It is particularly suited to experiences that are trauma-based or experiences that are very aversive (e.g., being bullied, humiliated, teased, or rejected). However, it can also be adapted to experiences in the absence of others, associated with the onset of the picture in the mind (e.g., looking in the mirror and seeing oneself as ugly) to learn more about the experience and the meaning that is attached and whether it can be updated. The procedure consists of three stages.

Reliving the experience

The first stage involves reliving the memory from the age when the client first experienced the image. This may overlap with the principles of exposure in imagination. The therapist would say:

"I'd like you to sit comfortably and keep your eyes closed. I'd like you to now imagine being in the event and describe it from the beginning like a frame-by-frame account of a video. However I'd like you to describe it in the first-person present tense as if it was happening now and looking out from your own eyes. Try to start with describing how old you are and describing where you are. For example, 'I am aged 10 and I am standing in the playground.' Then describe what you can see, what you can hear, and what you feel in as much detail as you can. I'd also like you to say if there were any links to your appearance and what the situation meant to you. Lastly, we need to understand what the child needs."

Ensure that there are no "hot spots" that are being avoided and, if necessary, ask the client to describe in more detail those aspects that are more anxiety-provoking. Check if there were any mirrors or reflective surfaces at the time or whether there were comments about the person's appearance that have led to a specific meaning. The key issue is for the therapist to understand the meaning (if this has not already been elicited) and what the child needs or would like to happen so that the meaning of the event can be updated in the next phase. Thus a child self may say he wants to know what is happening or for someone to protect him from another child or adult who is being abusive. The client is then allowed to open his eyes and the experience is summarized by the therapist. Ensure that you can summarize the meaning of the situation to the child or young person and what the child has said he would like to happen.

Once you have determined a meaning of the event to the child self you should use a Socratic dialogue to determine if there is an alternative meaning when viewed from an adult perspective. Validate the experience for the child of, for example, feeling rejected or humiliated, but try to determine if this is really the case from an adult perspective. This may have been done prior to the rescripting, but should be completed before the next phase.

Repeating the memory from an adult self perspective

The second stage involves repeating the memory from the perspective of an adult self who will be compassionate and understanding towards the child. You will already have discussed an alternative meaning of the event from the adult perspective. This can then be used by the adult self when revisiting the child self as well as trying to provide the child with what he needs.

Depending on the context, a child self may prefer to be taken to a safe place. Others will prefer the adult self to remonstrate with the abuser or bully. Some people (especially those with severe personality disorder) may find it difficult to allow their self to be compassionate or caring towards their younger self. If they lack confidence, they may prefer to bring an older relative or friend or an authority figure to protect them, rescue them, and be caring towards the younger self. Others may use a mythical character, like a guardian angel. You might say:

> "I'd like now to repeat the experience, but from the viewpoint of you as an adult. From what your child self said and felt, can you think how you might like to help your younger self?
>
> Would your child self like you or an adult to rescue the child or to say something to the person who was bullying/harming you? Do you need the help of anyone else to assist you?
>
> From what you know as an adult, what will you be saying to your child self?"

Always start the rescripting by naming the part of the self (e.g., "I am now my child self/adult self/dissociated self") or the role the person has adopted (e.g., "I am now my younger brother/sister/doctor") and then describes the context. This may then switch to the perspective of another person in the scene, or the client may prefer to open their eyes, come out of the scene, and start it in a different role.

It may be worth checking with the adult self as to what their younger self looks like before the aversive experience. In the debriefing, this can be explored as, in the authors' experience, when the adult self evaluates the younger self, they are not as critical as they are of themselves as an adult. This may assist in updating their body image when they are reflecting on the experience with the therapist.

Sometimes it can be helpful to take the perspective of another person in the rescripting. The adult self may be very critical of the actions of the child self (e.g., "She should have escaped from the situation or sought help"). In this case, the adult self should go very close to the child self and allow the adult to "see" the emotional pain of the child so that they can become more empathic.

Rescripting the memory

The third stage involves rescripting the memory. The person is asked to relive the memory from the perspective of their younger self but with their adult self arriving on the scene to rescue them or remonstrate with their bully or abuser.

They would be asked to consider what else might they need to happen in order to feel better, and the image then incorporated into this material too. The younger self may request extra nurturing and compassion at this point.

> "What would you like to tell your older self?
> Is there something else you would them like to do or do more of?"

Three case examples are described in which there are direct or indirect links between earlier life experiences and current imagery. Sometimes the memory relates directly to an experience associated with their appearance. A striking example relates to sexual assault or rape when the woman has looked at herself in a mirror during or after a rape or comments were made about her appearance during an assault, as in Case A.

Case A

A 27-year-old single woman was preoccupied with asymmetry in her breast size, complaining that her right breast was larger than the left. She had a breast reduction from bra size 36F to 36C with the motivation of reducing shoulder pain. This was successful, but soon after the operation she became extremely dissatisfied with the result as she felt her breasts were asymmetrical and that her right breast was still larger than the left. She desired further surgery for the right nipple to be lowered and to raise the level of the lower part of the breast. The surgeon had refused as although the right was very slightly larger, it was well within the normal range of symmetry.

It was so distressing for her that it interfered with her ability to work. She was socially withdrawn and inactive. She felt that the asymmetry was markedly noticeable (even when clothed) and highly abnormal. She avoided wearing a swimming costume or wearing tight tee-shirts or certain blouses and dresses. She tried to avoid looking at herself in the mirror. She was not in a relationship and did not want a partner. She often harmed her right breast with a razor in an attempt to force a surgeon to do the procedure properly. She would compare her breast to others in magazines or to other people she met. When in social situations she tended to slouch or lean forward to try to camouflage herself. She generally tried to hide her breasts with baggy clothing, and occasionally measured the asymmetry herself.

What emerged during therapy was that she had been sexually assaulted at the age of 13 by a youth. He had commented about her right breast being bigger, which she thought at the time was untrue. In the assault he had also touched her right breast. She escaped from the assault but never told her parents or peers about the incident. They discussed why the boy might have said something that was untrue and that she was not to blame. From the perspective of an adult, she was able to view the boy as someone who was trying it on and trying to put her down by saying something that was untrue. However, it was acknowledged that it now felt as if it was true.

In the rescripting phase, Ms A found it helpful to return to the scene as an adult just before the assault so the boy was confronted then left the situation. She learnt to be compassionate and caring towards her younger self and reassured her that she was not abnormal and that there was nothing to be ashamed of. They discussed why the boy might have said something that was untrue and that she was not to blame.

In third phase, the child self described the arrival of the adult before the abuser had attacked and now felt more in control as the adult self was able to confront the boy. She felt comforted and could feel safe as she walked home with the adult self.

Case B

Sometimes the early memories may be a more general issue, such as being bullied about something (e.g., appearing gay and effeminate) and this has now transferred to a different aspect of a client's appearance. This was the case with Mr B, a 32-year-old gay man, who could remember being bullied as an adolescent by his peers who guessed that he was gay. At the time he felt different and abnormal.

His preoccupation now was with his skin and its loss of tone, which he believed made him look prematurely old and therefore abnormal. He thought that others were disgusted by his skin and anticipated that any man he was attracted to would reject him. In the formulation the history of being bullied for being gay contributed to his beliefs that he looked different and abnormal. His adult self was able to take a different perspective.

During imagery rescripting, he rescued his younger self from the bullies and was able to reassure his younger self that this was a brief time in his life. Furthermore he was not alone.

Case C

Ms A is a 23-year-old woman whose main problem is BDD but who also has borderline personality with a tendency to dissociate, marked mood swings, and impulsive self-harm behaviors. Her preoccupation is with her face, which she feels is like putty and not human. Her felt impression is of it caved in on one side with many scars and holes. She believes she is ugly and has mainly coped by avoidance by being housebound or only occasionally coming out heavily made up or at night. Exposure without make-up leads her to dissociate and impulsive behaviors. She avoids mirrors, but endlessly compares her image with others and ruminates. She links her felt impression with a memory at the age of six when she was in a road traffic accident when she first dissociated (or had a near-death experience) and thought she was going to die. During the first phase describing her child self, she remembered her face and arms being covered in blood although she seems to have had only soft tissue injuries in which her face was swollen. It was possible to repeat the imagery from the perspective of her dissociated self in which she described herself as like a ghost watching her actual self from outside the car. She described it as very peaceful.

The meaning to her was that she should be buried as she could not see her actual self move or speak.

The aim of the rescripting phase was to stop her dissociating and to return to her body. To do this her dissociated self wanted to know that the child was human and still alive by getting her to move and speak. In the rescripting phase she brought with her a casualty doctor who was going to wipe away the blood from her face and arms and stop any further bleeding on the child. The adult self persuaded her to say something to her. She also brought a psychiatrist who spoke with the dissociated self and reassured her that she could go back into the body and see that the child was moving and talking. She was still worried about the swelling on the face. The therapist suggested she might like to bring a nurse who specializes in massage therapy who very gently massaged the swelling on the face.

Rescripting imagery should be practiced as a homework task (Table 16.1) and the meaning explored again in later sessions. Sometimes other perspectives may be required or it may be developed over time depending on whether new information is obtained.

Table 16.1:   Imagery practice

Date/Time	Situation	Imagery Used	Comments

16.4   Historical Role-play

We described how prior to rescripting it is possible to use guided discovery to determine if there are alternative interpretations of the early event and to explore what the implications are for the present. Some clients struggle with guided discovery to determine an alternative meaning and it may be more helpful to do a historical role-play to update the meaning from an adult perspective. This occurs in three phases.

1) Original interaction

Reliving original interaction involves the therapist proposing to the client that he play the "younger self" from the memory elicited, with the therapist playing "other" (e.g., a peer or parent involved in the aversive experience). It is recommended not using the chairs on which the client and therapist are normally seated to prevent subsequent confusion between roles. The therapist also asks if she played the other person well enough. If not, the client gives further directions and the interaction is played again. After the role-play, the emotions and thoughts elicited by the interaction are discussed and the central meaning clarified. The therapist might ask:

> "What's the worst aspect about this interaction?
> Which is the strongest emotion you experience in this situation?
> What does it mean about you?
> What does it mean about your "other"?
> What would it mean about the world?"

2) Reverse role-play

Reliving the original interaction in which the client experiences the perspective of "other" and therapist is "younger self." The client is instructed to try to identify as much as possible with the other person's situation and to experience the situation from the "other" perspective. Again, after the role reversal, emotions and thoughts about the interaction are explored.

> "Which is the strongest emotion you now experience as the other person who did the bullying?
> What does it mean about you?
> What does it mean about your younger self?
> What would it mean about the world?"

You should take a special interest in any new cues or perspective on the intentions of the other person. The therapist and the client (now using his insight from an adult) then try to formulate an alternative interpretation, which the client can test in the next phase. It is important to emphasize that any new ideas and behaviors could not be expected of the child in the given situation.

3) Rescripting interaction

Rescripting interaction in which client (younger self) behaves in new ways (client plays "younger self" and therapist plays "other"). Because the younger self's behavior is completely new, the therapist has to improvise the reaction of the "other" in a way that convinces the client and also respects the child's new behavior. If the therapist does not respond realistically, then the client can give further instructions and the role-play repeated. Depending on the context (e.g., sexual abuse as a child), this last stage may not be possible and it may be more helpful to move on to imagery rescripting in which an adult rescues the younger self.

Chapter 17

Modifying attentional biases

Summary

An important factor that maintains symptoms of BDD is excessive, self-focused attention in which a person's attention is predominantly on intrusive thoughts, images, and emotions that influence the self and behavior in the present. We describe in this chapter procedures that can be used to a) switch attention externally within situations that are anxiety-provoking ("situational attention refocusing" or "task concentration training"), b) increase the flexibility in switching attention to an external focus ("attentional training"), c) develop an alternative appraisal of intrusions, and d) explore the motivation for self-focused attention and how it is used as a safety-seeking behavior to prevent feared consequences.

Sections

Body Dysmorphic Disorder: A Treatment Manual. David Veale and Fugen Neziroglu
© 2010 John Wiley & Sons, Ltd.

17.1   Introduction

There are two types of attentional bias in BDD (or indeed any mental disorder). When there is a low level of threat, attention may be biased to being very narrowly focused with increased depth and scanning for threat. This is referred to as hyper-vigilance. Examples are a person looking at a picture of a model in a magazine and scanning it for a feature with which to compare his own, or looking in mirror and focusing on a specific feature and being excessively vigilant for any changes that have occurred.

When an individual perceives a moderate to high level of threat (e.g., in social situations and in front of a mirror), he may concentrate on avoiding attracting people's attention and his image becomes fused with what he sees in the mirror. This pattern of behavior leads to a heightened self-consciousness where the self is processed as an aesthetic object; this maintains the symptoms of BDD. When there is a very high level of threat, he is more likely to seek an escape route in order to leave the situation. Another example of self-focused attention is when an individual is checking his "internal mirror" and how he appears to others or ruminating about past events or reasons for being ugly. When severe, an individual may dissociate.

Attentional procedures have been successfully used in people with social phobia, who are excessively self-focused and process the self as a social object in anxiety-provoking situations (Clark & Wells, 1995). Individuals with BDD are inclined to adopt a similar process in social situations or when there is any external representation of the self (e.g., their reflection in a mirror). When individuals are self-focused, information about the self is generated internally from their intrusive thoughts and images, which are associated with past experiences. Thus strategies designed to shift attention externally help to reverse this and allow an individual to disconfirm beliefs, be less anxious, and interfere with safety-seeking behaviors that require self-monitoring. This strategy is referred to as "situational attentional refocusing" (Wells, 1990) and "interrogating the environment" (Clark et al., 2003). These procedures should be introduced to all clients by session 2 or 3 to ensure that plenty of practice can be done for gains to be made by the end of therapy. Shifting attention to external information when they are anxious allows individuals to modify their negative beliefs about their self and can enhance the outcome of CBT in other disorders (Wells & Papageorgiou, 1998; Bögels, 2006). It also assists "defusing" learnt associations and developing a view of one's intrusions as "just thoughts" or "just a picture in one's mind." Thus all clients with BDD learn the principles of situational refocusing and practice it regularly. For clients in whom there is marked avoidance of social and public activities, a decision should be made to use situational refocusing in the context of task concentration training (section 17.6). Here the person practices situational refocusing in a graded manner.

If during practice sessions your client has difficulty in switching attention, it may be helpful to explore the motivation for self-focused attention and what the effect of self-focused attention is on others. This is discussed in section 17.5. Individuals may believe that self-focused attention from an observer perspective allows them to monitor how they look in threatening situations. Conducting a functional analysis on the strategy can allow people to focus on the unintended consequences of their actions on others.

In those who continue to have difficulty in switching attention, we recommend adding attentional training technique (ATT) (Wells, 1990). This should start by session 4 or 5. This a method of helping clients to improve the *ability* to switch their attention from the self to their external environment, so increasing the flexibility of their focus and enabling them to respond more appropriately to what is going on. ATT consists of three categories of auditory attentional exercises, involving selective attention, attention-switching, and divided attention. It lasts about 10–15 minutes a day. It has been evaluated in four single-case series evaluations and two randomized controlled trials (RCTs) as a treatment for panic disorder (Wells, 1990), social phobia (Wells et al., 1997), recurrent major depression (Papageorgiou & Wells, 2000; Siegle et al., 2007), and health anxiety (Papageorgiou & Wells, 1998; Cavanagh and Franklin, 2000). The aims of ATT are to reduce perseverative thinking, increase flexibility over processing, reduce threat monitoring and self-focused attention, and increase attention to disconfirmatory information. The data on ATT are preliminary, but it is linked to a theoretical model (Wells, 2000) and we are currently evaluating its use in BDD.

17.2 Monitoring the Focus of Attention

The first step is to build an attentional profile of biases in both threatening and less threatening situations. The threats may be both internal stimuli (e.g., intrusive thoughts or images) and external (e.g., people, situations, activities). A profile of attentional biases is drawn up for self-focused attention and hypervigilance in the contexts in which these occur and how these maintain preoccupation and distress. Clients are taught to monitor and become aware of their attentional biases and apply a more helpful strategy for reducing preoccupation and distress.

Self-focused attention

Individuals are encouraged to regularly monitor how self-focused they are at any given moment (see Table 17.1). Self-focused attention occurs especially in BDD when individuals are checking their "internal mirror" and how they appear to others and ruminating about past events or reasons for being ugly (see Chapter 18). Wells (1990) suggests monitoring the focus of attention on a scale of −3 to +3, where −3 represents being entirely self-focused on one's thoughts, feelings, the picture in one's mind, and felt impression, +3 means being entirely externally focused on a task or the environment, and 0 indicates that a person's attention is divided equally between self and external focus. Task-focused attention means that attention is directed towards whatever behavior is required in the context (e.g., having a conversation), including attention on the other (relevant) person(s) in that situation. Environment-focused attention concerns those aspects of the environment that are uncon-nected with performance of the task (e.g., trees blowing in the wind). Most people with BDD tend to rate themselves as being generally focused on their imagery or felt impression of how they look at −3 or −2 when in front of a mirror and in social situations rather than externally focused. Focusing on the task or environment has some similarities to mindfulness, but attention is directed outwards. It is important to be mindful of what one is doing at any given moment, even when performing simple activities such as walking. You may demonstrate, for example, mindful walking or sitting by teaching focusing on the movements involved in these activities.

Start to build up a list of situations or activities where the individual is excessively self-focused in a context of threat and anxiety. It may be possible to identify a pattern to increase awareness of when it is more likely to occur so that a person can be better prepared for such situations. *An explicit goal of therapy is to convert the pattern of self-focused attention to that of a person who is predominantly externally focused in the context of threat.* Ensure your client regularly monitors his degree of self-focused attention while applying princi-ples of situational refocusing in his everyday life and monitor this at each session. Where clients are especially avoidant we would recommend applying situational refocusing in a graded manner. This is done formally in task con-centration training.

Hyper-vigilance

Hyper-vigilance occurs when scanning for threats in a context that increases preoccupation and distress. A common experience for someone with BDD that involves hyper-vigilance is when it leads to comparing a feature they believe to be ugly with that of another person. To monitor hyper-vigilance use a percentage scale where 0% represents an extremely narrow focus of atten-tion and 100% means they are taking in all the sounds, textures, or sights around them.

Start to build a list of situations or events where the person is excessively narrowly focused in a context of scanning for threat. Hyper-vigilance can include internal events with a narrow focus of attention on an image, which as a consequence may appear more distorted. *An explicit goal of therapy is to convert the pattern of narrow focus of attention to that of a person who is more holistic and can take in a broader range of information.*

Flexibility in switching attention

How easily can your client switch from an internal to an external focus of attention in the context of threat and anxiety? At one extreme someone with severe BDD and delusional disorder may find it extremely difficult to relinquish his internal focus and concentrate on external factors. At the other extreme, a person without a mental disorder can switch relatively easily from an internal to an external focus. It may be measured on a 0–100% scale where 0% indicates being totally unable to shift focus to external experience when anxious to 100% which indicates being totally able to shift focus of attention. As yet there are no known neuropsychological measures of the ability to switch attention from an internal to an external focus, although there are self-report measures of flexibility in switching attention from self to an external focus. *An explicit goal of therapy is to increase the flexibility of switching attention to the external environment in the context of threat.* This is described under attentional training.

17.3 Situational Refocusing

The first step is to explain the rationale for reducing self-focused attention by demonstrating the effect on preoccupation and distress of BDD. This was first described by Clark et al. (2003) in treating social phobia.

To increase self-focused attention, first ask the client to rate his degree of self-focused attention on the scale of –3 to +3 (see page 266), his level of anxiety or distress on a scale of 0–100%, and his degree of preoccupation on a scale of 0–100%.

You can then demonstrate first increasing then decreasing self-focused attention (with appropriate consent). Examples of demonstrating *increasing* self-focused attention include a) bringing one or two colleagues into the consulting room with instructions to stare at the client, b) getting the client to look in a mirror, and c) encouraging the client to ruminate. In these situations the client should be instructed to focus his attention on how he is coming across and how he feels. Then ask the client to complete a task that is designed to *decrease* self-focused attention. If necessary, he may need to be seated with his back to you talking for a few minutes about an unrelated subject, such as a recent holiday or a keen interest. Then ask him to re-rate the degrees of his self-focused attention, anxiety, and preoccupation.

Table 17.1:   Record of attention switching

Rating of attention: −3 represents being entirely self-focused on your thoughts and feelings or the impression you have of yourself, and +3 means being entirely externally focused on a task (e.g., listening to someone) or the environment (e.g., what you can see or hear). 0 indicates that your attention is divided equally between being self-focused and externally focused.

Date	Situation	How self-focused I was (−3 to +3)	Degree of preoccupation with feature(s) (0–100%)	Level of distress (0–100%)

Assuming that the ratings have decreased (even if only slightly) during the second exercise, you can move on to discuss the role of self-focused attention in maintaining preoccupation and distress.

The next step is to encourage your client, as homework, to monitor the degree of self-focused attention in different contexts and various situations. In subsequent sessions and homework, the degree of self-focused attention would be regularly monitored. This can be recorded on Table 17.1. The rationale for targeting attentional bias is described in Table 17.2 and may be discussed and then given to the patient.

Table 17.2:   Instructions for attentional switching

If you have been pregnant, or have wanted to become pregnant, you may have noticed that suddenly the world seemed to be flooded with pregnant women and babies. Or how about if you have just bought a new car? Have you found that you kept noticing the same make on the road? It's not that there are more babies being born, or more cars of the same model being bought; it's just that our attention is seeking out the subjects that interest us: it is biased towards those subjects and you become more aware of them. What is on our minds will influence what we notice; it's just part of how the human brain works.

How about someone who is anxious about spiders or insects? Have you ever observed that they see them where and when you hadn't noticed anything? When people are anxious about something they tend to be more vigilant for examples of it. This is, of course, one of the helpful aspects of anxiety should we be in a genuinely threatening situation. For example, it's helpful to be watchful if we are at risk from being attacked by a wild animal – our attention becomes very narrow in observing where the animal is and what its next move is going to be.

How might this apply to you and your awareness of features in others' appearance? Are you very aware of certain features in others which you feel ugly in yourself?

In body image problems, this attention bias towards monitoring how you look is one of the factors that keeps the condition going. Being self-focused means being on the outside looking in at yourself as an observer and very aware of your thoughts and the impression of how you appear to others. This means you are not giving attention to how people are behaving towards you. This in turn leads to further doubts and worries. Overcoming a body image problem will mean broadening your attention to take everything in, not just focusing on your features and refocusing your attention away from your inner world.

If you are frequently comparing yourself against others, you should try to focus your attention externally and become more aware of other, non-threatening aspects of the environment. If you are talking to someone, focus all your attention on what they are saying and doing. When you have finished, concentrate not on your self or doing a post-mortem but try to focus on all the sounds, textures, or sights around you. Don't buy into what your mind is saying. Don't answer back to your mind, just focus on your experience and concentrate on what people are actually saying and doing around you. Even though your mind may keep going back to your own self-image, keep refocusing externally. Remember that thoughts can be observed and let go. One does not have to pay attention to every thought or give it importance.

Another situation where self-focused attention occurs is in front of a mirror. We know from research that people with body image problems are more likely to focus on their felt impression and on certain features that are viewed as defective compared to people without a body image problem. Furthermore, when individuals *without* a body image problem look at themselves in a mirror they tend to focus more on features that they consider attractive. We shall discuss later about how to use mirrors in a healthy way.

Table 17.2: *Continued*

In the right situation, it can be productive for your attention to be focused inwards – for example, when you are trying to solve a particular problem or come up with a new theory of relativity. (However, we have never yet met anyone who has had a "Eureka!" moment when they are preoccupied with their appearance.) Spending a lot of time going over problems in your mind serves only to stimulate stress on your mind and body. Refocusing your attention on the outside world gives your brain a rest and allows you to take in what the world has to offer. Equally, if you are looking at yourself in a mirror you will be more aware of how you feel than of how others are seeing you. Other people may be very self-focused when they are ruminating and trying to figure things out or find reasons. Most people find that being self-focused causes them to dwell more on the past, and feel more distressed about their appearance. Learning to refocus your attention externally will allow you to act on your experience rather than on what your mind is telling you. This means being less on the "outside looking in" at yourself and more on the "inside looking out" at the world.

The form can be used to keep a record of your practise of attention switching in different situations. When you have particular difficulty switching attention be sure to discuss it with your therapist.

17.4   Functional Analysis of Self-focused Attention

A strategy to use when people have difficulty in switching attention is to conduct a functional analysis and determine the intended, immediate, and unintended consequences of being self-focused. The apparent benefits can be gently undermined by questions that focus on the unintended consequences of the strategy (Figure 17.1).

17.5   Motivation for Self-focused Attention

When individuals have difficulty switching attention externally, it may be helpful to explore further the motivation (or positive beliefs) for being self-focused. This may have been discovered in the functional analysis by determining the intended consequences. For example, clients might use the picture of themselves as an "internal mirror" that can be easily carried around with them. Thus a person with BDD may check his appearance internally so he knows exactly what he looks like at all times (especially when there is no external mirror available). The motivation can be written in the form of an assumption (e.g., If I am self-focused, I can prevent others humiliating me) (see Figure 17.2). You can then undermine the assumption by Socratic questioning.

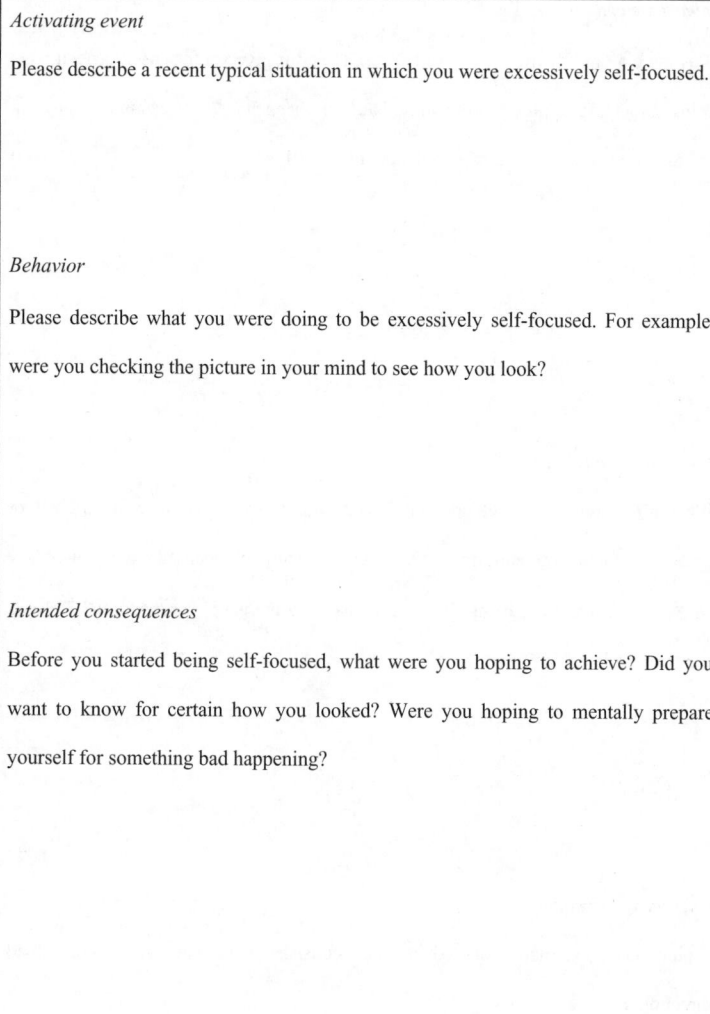

Activating event

Please describe a recent typical situation in which you were excessively self-focused.

Behavior

Please describe what you were doing to be excessively self-focused. For example, were you checking the picture in your mind to see how you look?

Intended consequences

Before you started being self-focused, what were you hoping to achieve? Did you want to know for certain how you looked? Were you hoping to mentally prepare yourself for something bad happening?

continued

Figure 17.1 Functional analysis of self-focused attention

Immediate consequences

Was there a pay-off from being self-focused? Did it give you a sense that you were doing something to prevent something bad from happening? For example, were you trying to prevent people being humiliating or critical?

Unintended consequences

What effect did being self-focused have? Did it make you more distressed or preoccupied with your appearance? Is the cost of being self-focused too expensive?

What effect did being self-focused have on the people around you? Did you appear to be less friendly or warm?

Alternative directions

Would being externally focused be more consistent with your goals and valued directions?

Figure 17.1　*Continued*

What is your motivation for being self-focused? Do you feel that being self-focused can help you? For example, do you feel it might prepare yourself for being humiliated or something bad happening?

1.

2.

3.

- *Does this assumption help you in your goals and valued directions in life?*

- *Would you recommend to others checking in an internal mirror or being self-focused? If not, why not?*

- *Is it possible that the picture in your mind is different from how others might see you? What might have influenced your felt impression of your self over time?*

- *What doubts do you have about being externally focused and concentrating on what you see, hear and smell?*

- *Can you make an alternative assumption about being self-focused?*

Figure 17.2   Assumptions about being self-focused

17.6   Task Concentration Training

Another attention training procedure (similar to situational refocusing), which has been used successfully in social phobia, is task concentration training (TCT) (Bögels, 2006). It has also been described in cases of fear of blushing (Mulkens et al., 1999; 2001) and BDD (Mulkens, 2007). Like situational refocusing, the aim is to help direct a client's attention away from the self and towards the task at hand and the environment. *It is probably best used when clients are highly avoidant so that the attention refocusing can be incorporated into a program of graded exposure or behavioral experiments.*

TCT consists of three phases: a) acquiring insight in the role of attention and the effects of heightened self-focused attention; b) focusing attention outward in non-threatening situations; and c) focusing attention outward in threatening situations.

The rationale of TCT is explained to a client thus:

> "An important factor in overcoming your preoccupation and distress is to increase your outward attention. When you are very self-focused, you will feel more anxious and it will cause problems in concentration and difficulties in relating to others. By learning to direct your attention outward (to both task and environment) you will be able to break the cycle and reduce your preoccupation and distress."

The first step is to monitor the degree of attention in different contexts in a diary. This would record:

a)   situations that trigger distress and preoccupation;

b)   the degree of anxiety or distress;

c)   the percentage of concentration that was directed towards each of the three elements: the self, the task, and the environment, at that moment. These ratings must add up to 100%.

Table 17.3 should be used to monitor: a) situations that trigger distress and preoccupation; b) the percentage of concentration directed towards each of the self, the task, and the environment at that moment (these ratings must add up to 100%); c) the degree of preoccupation on your feature(s)(on a scale of 0–100%); and d) the degree of anxiety or distress on a scale of 0–100%.

For example, the situation may be sitting alone in front of a mirror, or attending a social event. Task-focused attention is the degree of attention focused on the behavior that is required for that situation (e.g., having a conversation), including attention to the other (relevant) person(s) in that situation. Environment-focused attention concerns those aspects of the environment that are not necessary to perform the task (e.g., background hum of a computer or noticing a picture on a wall). Someone *without* an emotional problem might estimate about 70% of their attention to be focused on task (e.g., having

Table 17.3: Task concentration training record

Date	Situation	Attention to self (0–100%)	Attention to task (0–100%)	Attention to environment (0–100%)	Preoccupation (0-100%)	Distress (0–100%)

a conversation), about 10% on environmental sounds, and 20% on the self. This is likely to be reversed in someone with an emotional problem so that 70% of their attention is directed at the self, about 10% at the environment, and about 20% at a task.

By tracking their attentional focus, clients are encouraged to monitor the way they process information. This enables them to obtain insight into the way they divide their attention in situations that evoke fear of negative evaluation or negative self-evaluation. Later in therapy, these diaries can be used for homework assignments. Concentration exercises, which are built up hierarchically, are practiced during the sessions.

First listening exercise

The therapist and client sit with their backs to each other so that no eye contact can take place and the therapist tells the client a neutral, two-minute story (e.g., about his holiday). The client is instructed to concentrate on the story (task), try to remember the whole story, and summarize it afterwards. The client estimates the percentage of attention that was directed towards the self, towards the task, and towards the environment. The client also estimates the percentage of the story he was able to summarize and so does the therapist. Typically, clients have little problem successfully listening to and summarizing the story.

Second listening exercise

The therapist and client now turn round, so that eye contact takes place. The therapist tells another two-minute story. As in the first listening exercise, the client has to concentrate on the story and summarize it afterwards. The client estimates the percentage of attention directed towards the self, task, and environment and therapist and client both estimate the percentage of the story the client is able to summarize. Typically, clients become self-focused because of the eye contact with the therapist and, as a result, remember less of the story than in the first exercise. This result is linked to the rationale for TCT.

Third listening exercise

The therapist tells another two-minute story. The client must distract himself while listening by thinking twice about something that evokes his fear of negative evaluation and then try to concentrate again on the story. Alternatively, the client twice touches the part of the body they worry about, or looks twice at their reflection in a mirror, which is placed next to the therapist. As in the first listening exercise, client estimates the percentage of attention directed towards the self, task, and environment and both therapist and client estimate the percentage of the story the client is able to summarize. Typically, clients become more self-focused while thinking about their problem and, as a result, have gaps in their summary of the story at the moments where they were thinking about it. This result is linked to the rationale for TCT.

Fourth listening exercise

The therapist tells another two-minute story, which involves thoughts of negative evaluation of their self (e.g., meeting somebody who has a large nose if this is the main feature of concern). The person is instructed as in the first exercise.

All four exercises need to be repeated until at least 51% of the attention is focused on the task. The effect of the more complex elements in exercises 2 and 3 is that most clients first become more self-focused, but are able to refocus on the task after some practice. Also, the rehearsal of the complex exercises helps them to increase resistance to distraction by elements associated with their evaluation concerns.

Speaking exercises

The speaking exercises are practiced in the same way as the listening exercises. The client tells the therapist a two-minute story, while concentrating on the task (speaking and observing whether the therapist is listening and understands what he is telling). The therapist listens. The speaking exercises are built up in the same hierarchical way.

TCT in non-threatening situations

The client is instructed to concentrate on the task in non-threatening, everyday situations. An example is walking through a quiet park. The client should pay attention to all aspects of the park – visual, auditory, olfactory, tactile – as well as to his own body sensations while walking, one at a time. Another example is to listen to music, first to each instrument separately, then to all instruments at the same time. This exercise is intended to teach the client first to focus on one aspect (deliberate focus of attention), then to switch to another aspect (flexible attention), and finally to integrate all aspects (integrated attention). These exercises are generally given for homework.

TCT in threatening situations

The therapist draws up a list of approximately 10 situations in which the client believes he experiences negative self-evaluation. These situations are arranged in ascending order, with the first item being the least fearful. The goal is to employ task concentration in each situation and quickly re-focus attention to the task after being distracted as a result of fear of negative evaluation or negative self-evaluation. The exercises are built up hierarchically, since in extremely fearful situations the fear absorbs most of the client's attention and, as a result, directing the attention to the task is more complex.

If possible, situations should first be practiced in a session using role-play (including stand-ins) and then *in vivo*. The steps in practicing TCT in threatening situations are:

a) monitor where the client's attention is usually focused in this situation;
b) determine the task;
c) determine where attention is focused.

The situation is then practiced with focus on the task.

The exercise is evaluated using the percentage of task focus, and repeated with more attention on the task if the task focus is less than 51%, by asking the client to focus more on what he can see, hear, etc. These tasks can be carried out as homework and recorded in a diary. Difficulties that may have arisen should be discussed during the next session.

17.7   Detached Mindfulness

Clients may be trying to avoid, suppress, or distract themselves from intrusive thoughts and images. Learning how to focus on the threat that they are trying to avoid with detached mindfulness can assist in the process of defusion (Wells, 2005). Detached mindfulness is similar to exposure, but now the emphasis is on a) identifying both the internal and external stimuli being avoided; b) targeting the attentional bias when exposure occurs; and c) practicing detached mindfulness during exposure. Some clients confuse detached mindfulness with having a blank or empty mind, or try to use the strategy to achieve such a goal or to distract themselves (Wells, 2005). In these cases, it is important to help them to distinguish between suppression and detached mindfulness so that they do not misunderstand or misuse the strategy. A suppression/counter-suppression experiment can be used. It consists of a brief period of suppression contrasted with a subsequent counter-suppression period. Wells (2005) describes this as follows:

> "If you try to prevent certain thoughts or images coming into your mind or if you avoid paying attention to particular words, you will be unable to learn that your thoughts are not a threat and you will continue to feel fearful. By paying attention to those things you would prefer to avoid, you can come to accept them as simply thoughts or pictures passing through your mind. Therefore trying not to have particular thoughts or pictures in your mind is buying into them as you are actively trying to push them away. The effect is likely to be the opposite of what you intend and you can end up with more or stronger thoughts and images rather than fewer or weaker ones. You can try this for yourself if you try not to think a particular thought. Let's try that now.
>
> For the next three minutes I would like you to avoid thinking about pink rabbits. Don't allow yourself to have any thoughts or pictures in your mind connected with pink rabbits. Off you go … What did you notice? Let's now try being mindful of those thoughts and pictures and see what happens. For the next three minutes let your mind roam freely and if you have thoughts of pink rabbits, I want you to watch them in a passive way as part of an overall landscape of thoughts. Try that now.
>
> Can you try to use the same approach on the thoughts and images you are trying to avoid. Try very hard to experience your unwanted thoughts or images without reacting to them in any way. Just notice them in a passive way as part of an overall landscape of thoughts and pictures."

A useful analogy of detached mindfulness is that of traffic in the road:

> "An analogy for watching your thoughts and feelings is to imagine them as cars passing on a road. When you are preoccupied by how you look, you might focus on particular 'cars' that tell you that you are ugly. You might cope by either trying to stop the cars or by pushing them to one side (if you're not in danger of being run over, that is). Alternatively, you may try to flag a car down, get into the driving seat and try to park it (that is, analyzing the idea and sorting it out until you feel 'right'). Of course, there is often no place to park and as soon as you have parked one car another one comes along.
>
> Distancing oneself from one's thoughts means being on the pavement and playing in the park. It means acknowledging the cars and the traffic but just noticing them and then walking along the pavement and focusing your attention on other parts of the environment (such as talking to the person beside you and noticing other people passing you and the sights and smells of the flowers on the verge). You can still play in the park and do what is important for you despite the thoughts. In other words, such thoughts have no more meaning than passing traffic – they are 'just' thoughts and are part of the rich tapestry of human existence. You can't get rid of them, just as if you are in a city there is always some slight traffic noise in the background and you learn to live with it. Just notice these thoughts and feelings and acknowledge their presence."

17.8 Attentional Training

Attentional training is designed to *increase flexibility in one's ability to switch attention* to an external focus when desirable. It was devised by Wells (1990; 2000; 2009) as a means of becoming more flexible in switching attention from the self to the external environment. It has been shown to be of some benefit in depression and health anxiety for reducing self-focused attention in the long term. Because the effects may take a few months to have full benefit, ATT is introduced in the first few sessions with an expectation for homework practice on a daily basis thereafter. For clients who are more significantly depressed, the attention training should also be done in the session to assist adherence. Guidance notes on practicing ATT can be downloaded from the www.mct-institute.com.

It is described to clients with the following rationale:

> An important factor keeping your preoccupation and distress with your appearance is the way your attention becomes locked onto the picture in your mind and your thoughts about your appearance; this can be difficult to control. One technique that can reduce this tendency is called attentional training. It's a form of mental training, like going to a psychological gym to get your attention muscles

in shape. In this technique you practice focusing attention outwardly onto sounds in a special way, as instructed. It is not a technique to distract yourself when you are distressed or when you are ruminating – it needs to be practiced when you are alert and not especially distressed. The aim is to allow you to practice using your attention in a different way. You may well have negative thoughts or feelings during the exercise – that is perfectly normal – and if you do you should merely treat them as additional noise and return to focusing your attention as instructed. The aim is not to blank out your mind but to practice flexibly using your attention and awareness in a particular way.

The exercises should be practiced twice a day when you are alone and not distracted. If you can practice them twice a day over the next three months, the training can help you to interrupt the cycle of being self-focused so that you eventually become more aware of the external environment. The exercises can appear difficult at first but it is worth persevering. Build up by doing a small step at a time.

The exercise consists of collecting between six and eight sounds that can be heard at the same time (this can include a mixture of pre-recorded sounds provided on a CD). Examples could be: the hum of a computer, the noise of a water filter in an aquarium, a dripping tap, a radio at a low volume, a hi-fi, a vacuum cleaner elsewhere in the building, and the noise of traffic. Label each sound – for example, sound 1: the hum of the computer. Try to ensure that one or two sounds do not drown out the others and that all are continuous. Sit in a comfortable chair, relax, and focus your gaze on a spot on the wall. You should keep your eyes open throughout the procedure. You may experience distracting thoughts, feelings or images that just pop into your mind during the exercise. This doesn't matter – the aim is to practice focusing attention in a particular way. Also don't blank any thoughts out or try to suppress them while you are doing the exercise.

To begin with, focus on the sound of my voice (S1). Pay close attention to that sound. No other sound matters. Try to give all of your attention to the sound of my voice. Ignore all of the other sounds around you. You may hear them, but try to give all of your attention to the sound of my voice. Focus only on the sound of my voice. No other sound matters. Focus on this one sound.

Now turn your attention to the sound I am making as I tap on the desk (S2). Pay close attention to that sound, for no other sound matters [pause]. Try to give all of your attention to the tapping sound [pause]. Closely monitor the tapping sound [pause]. If your attention begins to stray or is captured by another sound, refocus on the tapping sound [pause]. No other sound matters. Focus on this one sound.

Now focus on the sound of (S3) (e.g., the ticking of a wind-up timer) [pause]. Pay close attention to that sound, for no other sound matters [pause]. Try to give all of your attention to the sound of the timer [pause]. Closely monitor the sound the timer makes [pause]. If your attention begins to stray or is captured by another sound, refocus on the timer [pause]. No other sound matters. Give this one sound all of your attention [pause]. Continue to monitor this sound and if you are distracted, return your attention to this sound as soon as you can [pause].

Now focus your attention on sounds that you might hear outside of this room, but nearby. Focus on the space outside and behind you (S4). Pay close attention to that space and try to detect sounds that might occur there [if there are specific sounds, the therapist draws attention to them]. Even if there are no other sounds, keep your attention on that space. Try to give all of your attention to it [pause]. Closely monitor for sounds there [pause]. If your attention begins to stray or is captured by a sound elsewhere, refocus on that place. No other sound matters. Give all of your attention to that place and what you might hear there. Continue to monitor and if you are distracted return your attention to it [pause].

The instructions above are repeated for additional sounds (S5–S7) and/or spaces (e.g., on the left, on the right, in the far distance).

Now that you have identified and practiced focusing on individual sounds and locations I am going to ask you to quickly shift your attention between them as I call them out [pause]. First, focus on the tapping sound (S2), no other sound matters [pause]. Switch your attention and focus on what you might hear behind you in the near distance (S4) [pause]. Pay close attention to (S4), no other sound matters. Now turn your attention to (S7), no other sound matters [pause]. Turn your attention again, this time to the sound of the timer (S3) [pause] Now switch and focus on the tapping sound (S2) [pause]. Now focus on (S6) [pause], now on (S5) [pause], (S4) ... (S2) ... (S3) ..., etc.

Finally, I want you to expand your attention. Make it as broad and as deep as possible. Try to absorb all of the sounds and all of the locations that you have identified at the same time. Try to focus on and be aware of all of the sounds both inside and outside of this room at the same time [pause]. Covertly count the number of sounds that you can hear at the same time [pause]. Try to hear everything simultaneously. Count the number of sounds you can hear this way.

This concludes the exercise. How many sounds were you able to hear at the same time?

The exercise needs to be practiced twice a day for about 15 minutes on each occasion. If possible try to introduce new sounds on each occasion so you don't get used to them. As time goes by, you should try to add more sounds to, say, nine sounds. You can also vary it by putting some of the sounds in different locations. I appreciate that this is a difficult task. Like physical training, effort is required and the exercise needs to be practiced repeatedly or your attention muscles won't get bigger."

Practicing ATT on a daily or twice daily basis may be a problem. It is recommended that for more depressed clients you incorporate ATT for 15 minutes within a therapy session with one of the sounds being the therapist's voice or the tapping of a pen on a table. Several sounds can be introduced in the immediate consulting room, with additional sounds identified outside the room in the near and far distance. The technique has also been used with a range of sounds introduced in the consulting room at different spatial locations (left, right, front, rear) in relation to the participant. Recording sounds on a CD or MP3 player has the benefit of introducing sounds which are more interesting and varied. However, one may lose the spatial location if it is not recorded and played back with surround sound. Whether the sounds are recorded or *in vivo*, they should be fairly continuous and change over time to prevent repetition. Ensure that your client has a place to practice where you can introduce or identify a range of different sounds (at least three, but the more the better). Ensure that the client will also incorporate:

a)　sounds that may occur outside in the near distance;
b)　sounds that may occur in the far distance;
c)　sounds that may occur on the left;
d)　sounds that may occur on the right.

Adherence can be encouraged by asking the client to keep a practice diary and to note whether there were any difficulties. This should be checked at the beginning of each session. A form for monitoring homework is shown in Appendix 2. The instruction for ATT emphasizes that the aim of the procedure is not to suppress thoughts or images, but to practice focusing attention as instructed. If internal events such as thoughts or sensations do intrude, then the client is asked not to react to them but to refocus attention as instructed.

17.9　Alternatives to Attentional Training

There are alternative attentional procedures, which have been described for social phobia, but as a procedure they are less well researched than attentional training. In Clark et al. (2003), clients with social phobia are also encouraged to increase the flexibility of switching attention in non-anxiety provoking situation. They are instructed as below.

> "Although self-focused attention is unhelpful, it has probably become a habit. As with all habits, practice will be needed to help you turn off self-focused attention and shift your attention to what is happening in the social situation. Two types of practice are likely to help. First, focusing on the world around you, rather than on yourself, in non-social situations. Second, doing the same in social situations.
> 　Because self-focus is particularly automatic when you are anxious in social situations, some people find it easier to start by practicing an external focus in less threatening, non-social situations. We suggest that you practice in non-social

situations, for at least 10 to 15 minutes each day. However, it is unlikely that you will be able to be fully externally focused during this time. Your attention may well repeatedly come back onto yourself. Don't worry about this. Simply focus externally again.

The world around us is full of different sounds, colors, objects, textures, and events. During your practice sessions, we would like you to become more aware of what is happening around you. As you do so, you will probably find that you become less aware of yourself. Each practice session should have three components."

Becoming aware of different sounds/sights

Practicing inside

- Listen to a music CD or the radio: in turn pay attention to the different instruments that are playing (guitar, drums, piano, violin, clarinet, etc).
- Alternatively, sit quietly and pay attention to the sounds in the room and any sounds you can hear outside.
- Now pay attention to what objects are around and the colors you can see. Where is there light and where is there shade? Pay attention to what it would feel like to touch the objects around you. What textures would they be? Would they be hard or soft?

Practicing outside

- Go for a walk: pay attention to the sounds around you. What sounds can you hear nearby? What sounds can you hear in the distance? Can you hear cars, people, birds, etc?
- Now pay attention to what buildings, plants, traffic, and people are around. What colors and shading can you see? Pay attention to these. What are the different textures around you?

Switching your attention between the different sounds/sights

In the second step you need to switch your attention between the different sounds and sights. You can try this equally well indoors and outdoors.

- Choose several different sounds.
- Start by focusing on one of the sounds, noticing all that you can about it and letting it fill your awareness.
- Don't worry if your attention shifts to something else, just gently bring it back to the first sound.

- After following the first sound for a little while (maybe a minute), shift your attention to another sound and become absorbed in following that.
- Do the same for a third sound.
- Now move on to colors, objects, or textures.

Pulling everything together

- Once you have spent time focusing on a number of different sounds and/ or sights, try to become aware of all of them at once and for a few minutes let them all fill your attention.
- Let yourself get lost in the outside world.
- Don't worry if your attention drifts back to yourself. Simply notice this and gently shift your attention back to the outside world.

Clients are asked to record their practice in a table giving date, situation (including whether inside or outside), what they focused their attention on, how long they practiced for, and any other comments).

17.10   Conclusion

Learning to switch attention away from an excessive self-focus is theoretically an important task in BDD although we do not yet have evidence from a dismantling procedure. Future research will determine how important a component of therapy it is and for whom. It is worth emphasizing to clients that correcting attentional bias is a difficult skill and requires regular practice in situations that are anxiety-provoking (situational refocusing or task concentration training) and in non-anxiety-provoking situations to increase flexibility in the ability to switch attention (attentional training). The procedures should be introduced early in therapy to ensure that the gains can be made by the end of therapy. Developing a different relationship with one's intrusive thoughts is a concept that is used throughout therapy so that one's view of one's thoughts and images as being reality is undermined.

Chapter 18

Modifying cognitive processes in BDD

Summary

Individuals with BDD use effortful cognitive strategies such as ruminating, mental planning, worrying, comparing, or self-attacking in an effort to control or avoid aversive thoughts and images about their appearance. These processes can be regarded as forms of safety-seeking behaviors, which are usually motivated by preventing humiliation and rejection. This chapter focuses on developing a micro-formulation to determine the motivation for such processes and using a functional analysis to determine the factors that maintain them. Various alternatives to such ruminating and other effortful cognitive processes are described and include "detached mindfulness" and acting on one's valued directions.

Sections

Body Dysmorphic Disorder: A Treatment Manual. David Veale and Fugen Neziroglu
© 2010 John Wiley & Sons, Ltd.

18.1 Introduction

Chapter 4 described how individuals with BDD use effortful cognitive strategies such as ruminating in response to aversive thoughts and images. These processes are broadly categorized as:

a) Ruminating (usually described as "brooding" or "just thinking" to patients), which typically refers to past-oriented events and is more often associated with depressed mood, inactivity, and avoidance of situations or activities. There is endless analysis of the wrong problem or trying to find a reason (e.g., "Why am I so ugly?" or "If only I hadn't had the surgery"). The emotion is often one of intense frustration and despair. Other common themes may be feeling hurt or angry at the actions of an individual who has humiliated them, feeling lonely and hopeless, and an inability to escape from their thoughts. Ruminating is usually an automatic process, which is associated with being self-focused, feeling more depressed, inactive, and socially withdrawn. It tends to be global, analytical, abstract, and evaluative and focuses on the implications of past events or their current situation. The process of ruminating is therefore one type of response to an intrusive thought or image that enters one's mind.

b) Worry is similar to ruminating but typically refers to future events and anxiety ("What if" questions about events that could happen, e.g., "What if someone stares at me and makes a comment about my appearance?"). Thus worry is another *response* to an intrusive thought or image. This might then lead to further effortful strategies, such as mental planning, checking in the mirror, or avoidance of situations that are anxiety provoking.

c) Mental planning refers to the individual making mental plans for how the "defect" can be fixed or better camouflaged. It might have the function of instilling hope and lead to a search for solutions on the Internet or other sources. Thus mental planning is a response to an intrusive thought, an image, or other responses such as ruminating.

d) Comparing takes the form of comparing "defective" feature(s) against that of another person (usually of the same sex and similar age), a picture in the media, or an old photograph of themselves. Comparing is usually another response to a range of triggers, such as seeing someone in the media or *in vivo* as a form of threat monitoring. The consequences may be further ruminating, worry, or mental planning. Comparing is fairly common (more so in women than men without body image problems) but occurs more frequently in people with body image problems. There is nearly always an upward comparison to people who have the same feature that is considered more attractive. Related to comparing are mental checks of how one looks (in an internal mirror), which may then be compared to a previous image or an ideal image.

e) Self-reassurance is uncommon in BDD but can occur in clients with features more like obsessive compulsive disorder (OCD). Here a client has intrusive thoughts and doubts about a defect that, at one level, they "know" is absurd. They may respond to the thought with "Don't be ridiculous" or "It's only a worry." The self-reassurance then becomes a factor in maintaining the intrusion as it increases the doubt and preoccupation.

f) Self-attacking takes the form of a "hostile self" trying to attack the "actual self." An example is "You ugly piece of s—, you deserve to look like an alien." This usually leads to various submissive and avoidance behaviors. Self-attacking is thus another response to intrusive thoughts or images.

There may also be experiential avoidance, such as distraction or thought suppression, which has the effect of increasing preoccupation and distress. In BDD, perseverative thinking tends to be characterized by ruminating, especially when the individuals are more depressed. They are likely to be frequently comparing their features with the same sex and mentally planning how they are going to fix it.

Worry occurs in more anxiety-based BDD, especially in anticipation of exposure to threatening situations. Self-attacking occurs in more personality disordered or depressed individuals with BDD. Patients are often unaware of when they are ruminating and when it is becoming a habitual pattern of thinking. By contrast, patients are more aware of when they are worrying and often complain of worry as a presenting symptom. In keeping with other cognitive behavioral models of ruminating, the immediate consequences may be to avoid aversive thoughts and images of one's appearance. However, the unintended consequences of ruminating are to increase preoccupation with one's appearance and distress. They are then more likely to avoid situations and reduce activity or approach behaviors. This is equally true of worry and self-attacking, although comparing may be a different motivation in threat-monitoring. The content of the automatic thoughts or core beliefs in BDD are held rigidly and there appears little value in questioning them empirically or logically (discussed in Chapter 20). It is, however, possible to understand the meaning of their experiences with imagery that is more powerful than verbal techniques (Chapter 19).

The following formulation and models for perseverative thinking are adapted from Martell et al. (2001), Watkins et al. (2007) and Wells (2005; 2009). Each of these approaches overlaps in that none of them focuses on the content of rumination nor are they an attempt to challenge "core beliefs" or assumptions about evaluations of the self. The emphasis is on a functional analysis of the cognitive processes of ruminating and strategies to increase activity and to refocus attention externally.

Martell et al. (2001) emphasize that ruminating is a form of avoidance and teach patients to recognize when they are ruminating and to use a goal-directed activity. Watkins et al. (2007) have developed "rumination-focused CBT" for depression; it includes alternative goal-directed activity. They also focus on: a) identifying abstract and evaluative "Why"-type questions and, when relevant, turn them into problem-solving (e.g., "How"-type questions which are specific, concrete, non-judgmental, and in keeping with one's goals); b) absorption exercises from memory of experiences when they are caught up in a task; c) compassionate mind training and use of imagery. The focus in Wells (2009) is to identify the meta-cognitions (positive and negative beliefs about ruminating) and to use attentional refocusing and "detached mindfulness" for intrusions. Each of these approaches has different emphases and it is not yet known which approach is superior for which type of problem. The clinician has the flexibility to construct an idiosyncratic formulation of ruminating and to integrate the different approaches. We discuss below how these strategies can be applied to BDD. The key in working with cognitive processes is to avoid discussing content, which includes trying to question automatic thoughts, core beliefs, assumptions, and rules.

18.2   Formulation

The first step is to understand the consequences and motivation of rumination (worry, comparing, self-attacking) and therefore what is maintaining the process. Patient should be socialized to a model of perseverative thinking by constructing an idiosyncratic mini-formulation from tracing out a recent episode. Help your patient to identify the main style of perseverative thinking (ruminating, worrying, comparing, self-attacking) and then use it as part of a functional analysis. Note that meta-cognitions are the same as intended consequences in a functional analysis.

Ask your patient to describe a typical episode of thinking. Each of the questions below relates to either a specific process (represented by a box in Figure 18.1) or content (represented by a circle in Figure 18.1). Note, however, that the patient may not give the answers for each component in the order that is asked for. The aim is to explore the motivation or beliefs about the benefits of ruminating (or any other effortful process) (Wells, 2009). Wells (2005) would explore first the negative beliefs and then the positive beliefs about a process such as ruminating. An example of a negative belief would that "ruminating is uncontrollable – I can't stop myself" or "worrying will make me more stressed and make me have even more lines on my face." An example of a positive belief is "worry helps me to mentally prepare for when I am humiliated." These are termed "meta-cognitions". There is some overlap between understanding the meta-cognitions and identifying the intended consequences in a functional analysis. Thus in a functional analysis the intended consequences of worry is that a person may believe that worry helps to them feel better prepared.

The task is to explore the goals of rumination and whether rumination has achieved those goals. Patients with BDD might report that they ruminate or worry because:

- I need to be sure how I look.
- If I can work out why I am so ugly, I may be able to fix it.
- I do it so I don't forget how ugly I am.
- I can prepare myself for the worst.
- I can figure out where I went wrong so I won't make the same mistake again.
- If I don't, it will let people who have hurt me off the hook.
- It means I don't have to think about the bad things that are happening now.
- It prevents me from having to face my problems, I can just think about them.

Examples of beliefs about mental planning:

- I feel I am doing something about the problem.

An empty mini-formulation for beliefs about ruminating (or any other perseverative process) which can be photocopied is shown in Figure 18.1.

Homework might require identification of further examples once the patient is socialized into the formulation for which various forms are provided. It is particularly important to try to separate intrusive thoughts and images, which are involuntary, from the response (e.g., comparing, ruminating, self-attacking), which is more voluntary even if it is like a habit. Intrusions cannot be controlled, but the response can only when the client can identify the process and the consequences.

The process of ruminating can be described as follows:

People often have intrusive thoughts or images about the way they look that just pop into their mind. However, analyzing or brooding is different and describes the way you react to the way you feel you look. It describes the way someone thinks for long periods of time, and going over something in your mind time and time again. Alternatively, people may be worrying a lot about all the

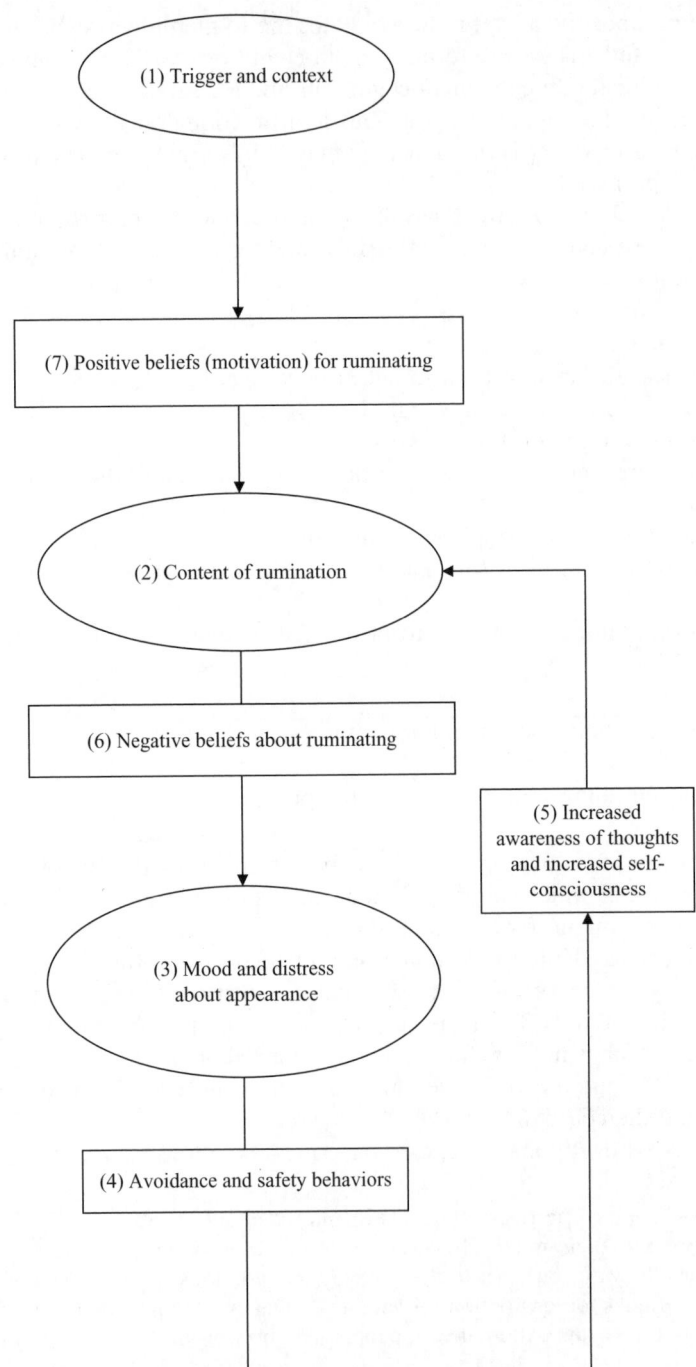

Figure 18.1   Beliefs about rumination

bad things that could happen in the future or are constantly attacking themselves. This type of thinking is not usually productive as it involves thinking excessively about past events or about questions that have no answers. It might involve trying to find reasons for the situation you are in or worrying about what might happen. People often analyze because they are attempting to solve problems by trying to figure things out or a problem that can't be solved. Does that seem like what you do?

How much time do you spend thinking this way?

I'd like to find out more about what keeps this going and feeds your preoccupation and distress with your appearance. Can you think of a recent typical episode when you were thinking a lot about your appearance?

When was this episode?

1) *The trigger or the context for the rumination*
What was the trigger for thinking a lot?
Was it an intrusive thought or picture in your mind of your self, feeling or memory?
(Were you trying to compare your feature with others?)
(What was going through your mind at the time?)
What were you doing at the time?

2) *The content of the rumination*
What were you telling yourself? Was it a "Why" or "If only I had …"-type question? Were you trying to find a reason? Did you try to think about why you look the way you do, or why you had the surgery etc?
Do you try to think if only you didn't look so ugly or other fantasies?
Do you try to solve it in your head?
Do you try to reassure yourself?
(Identify the thinking style and a term that you can both use for the process. We have used "ruminating" in the example below but others prefer "brooding," "analyzing," or "thinking a lot.")

3) *The unintended emotional consequences*
How did you feel when you were ruminating?
Did you feel angry and frustrated with yourself?

4) *The unintended behavioral consequences*
What did you then do?
Did you avoid something?
Did you become more withdrawn or inactive?
Did you try to distract yourself or control the intrusions for example by trying to suppress them?

5)   *The unintended consequences on symptoms of BDD*
Did you become more aware and preoccupied with thoughts about your
   appearance?
Did you feel uglier?
Did you feel more self-conscious?
How self-focused were you on a scale from −3, which is totally focused on
   what you were thinking or feeling, to +3, which is totally focused on the
   environment or tasks.

6)   *The negative beliefs about ruminating*
If thinking a lot made you feel worse, could you simply stop doing it?
When you were worrying a lot, what did you fear might happen?

7)   *The intended consequences (or positive beliefs) about ruminating*
If thinking a lot about your appearance helps, why do you still have a problem?
Do you sometimes think that thinking a lot could help you?
Do you feel as if you need to prepare yourself for being humiliated or rejected
   or something bad happening?
Do you feel as if you need to find out what made you "ugly," so that you can
   then do something about it?

(The numbers refer to the boxes in Figure 18.1.)
   It may also be helpful to explore the termination criteria to stop ruminating:

What makes you stop yourself brooding?

Some patients may have problematic criteria such as when they feel "sure"
or "comfortable" similar to patients with OCD, where the "right feeling" or
"feelings of certainty" have been achieved. These are, of course, problematic
and lead a person to have long periods of rumination.
   You might then summarize the model by saying,

> "It seems from what you have told me that when you think and analyze things,
> there are disadvantages. It makes you more preoccupied and distressed with your
> appearance and it leads you to avoid/check more. This then seems to prevent
> you from following what is important in your life and you feel more depressed.
> Is this right?
>   What we need to do is to focus on the beliefs and actions that are maintaining
> the rumination. These relate to your motivation for ruminating, when you decide
> you can stop, and the way you try to cope by avoiding situations or become more
> self-focused that all increase your awareness of your thoughts and brooding in
> a vicious circle."

This can be repeated for each process such as comparing, worrying, self-attacking, and mental planning. In patients who are not convinced that ruminating is detrimental, one might conduct a behavioral experiment that compares the consequences of ruminating with detached mindfulness (see below). This might be done on alternate hours or half-days depending on for how long a client can switch attention. You might also use the "man in the hole" metaphor (see Chapter 14). For ruminating, the man might be asking himself where he should put the earth he has dug out.

18.3   Self-monitoring

Having identified the different components that are maintaining rumination, the patient may need to increase his awareness of when he is ruminating, comparing, worrying, mental planning, or self-attacking as it is usually automatic. Self-monitoring can increase awareness of automatic processes and can be assisted by a frequency chart.

An example of a frequency chart is shown in Table 18.1. It has separate rows for each type of process: ruminating, mental planning, comparing, worrying, self-attacking. If a process is very frequent, then one can use a tally counter.

The explicit goal is for clients to distinguish between their response to their intrusive thoughts and images, and to identify their cognitive process and label it as such. Being aware of an unhelpful thinking style is the first step to stopping it. It is also often helpful to elicit more information about the nature of the process and the contexts in which it occurs so that the client becomes aware of a pattern and the situations in which he is at greater risk of ruminating and so take preventative action.

18.4   Functional Analysis of Ruminating

The next step is for clients to learn how to conduct their own functional analysis on the process of ruminating. The same analysis may need to be repeated with other processes (worrying, comparing, mental planning) if they are problematic. (Self-attacking is discussed in the section 18.5.) The explicit goal is to stop engaging in all such effortful mental activities that do not contribute to any of one's goals or valued directions and to test out an alternative strategy to determine the effect on preoccupation and distress.

The Analysis of Thinking Style is reproduced in Appendix 2. It can be used within a session and as part of a homework exercise to collect other examples of thinking styles. The same approach can be used to analyze safety behaviors such as mirror-checking as the intended consequences for the activity may well overlap.

Table 18.1   Self-monitoring chart for thinking styles

Complete and tick any column that is relevant or write in the total number of times you clicked on your tally counter for each process.

	Mon	Tues	Wed	Thurs	Fri	Sat	Sun
I thought a lot about or tried to find reasons for:							
I worried about:							
I was mentally planning:							
I compared my _____ with the feature on others							
I attacked myself about:							

Analysis of Thinking Style

Activating event
Describe a recent typical situation in which you were thinking a lot (e.g., brooding, worrying, comparing). Did it start with an intrusive thought, image, or memory? What were you doing at the time?

Behavior
What did you tell yourself? Was it a "Why" or "If only ..." or "What if ..." question? Were you trying to find a reason for the way you look? Were you mentally planning or investigating a solution for what you believe to be an appearance problem? Can you label your thinking style as an example of brooding, worrying, or some combination of the above? Did you then become more withdrawn?

Intended consequences
Before you started this episode, what were you hoping would happen? Did you think that trying to reason things out could help you? Were you hoping to prepare yourself mentally for something bad happening? Were you hoping to find out what made you "ugly" so that you can then do something about it?

Immediate consequences
Was there any immediate pay-off from your thinking a lot? Did you avoid anything that was uncomfortable? Did it stop any intrusive images about how you look? Did you think it gave you some hope or certainty for the future?

Unintended consequences
What effect did thinking a lot have on the way you feel?

What effect did it have on how self-focused you became on a scale of −3 (totally focused on what you were thinking) to +3 (totally focused on the environment or task)?

What effect did thinking a lot have on the time you can devote to what is important in your life?

What effect does your thinking style have on the people around you?

Did you do anything in excess as a consequence (e.g., drinking more, using drugs, binge eating, checking more in the mirror?)

Overall how helpful was your thinking style?

Alternative directions
What alternatives could you use that are consistent with your goals and valued directions instead of thinking a lot? Could you test this out at the next opportunity to see what effect it has on your distress and preoccupation?

Is there a pattern to the situations that are typically linked to thinking a lot that you could change? For example, can you do anything to prevent such situations from occurring? Do you need to buy that celebrity magazine? Can you put old photographs back in album, etc.?

18.5   Challenging Beliefs about Ruminating

In meta-cognitive therapy, the therapist first looks for evidence that is inconsistent with the beliefs about ruminating (e.g., that it is uncontrollable). Patients are taught to become more aware of when they are ruminating and an alternative, such as "detached mindfulness." This is a type of inner awareness, but in the absence of effortful processing of the self (Wells, 2009). Wells defines detached mindfulness as consisting of:

a)   meta-awareness (consciousness of thoughts);
b)   cognitive de-centering (comprehension of thoughts as events not facts);

c)   attentional detachment (attention is flexible and not anchored to any single event);

d)   low conceptual processing (low levels of analytical and meaning-based appraisals, i.e., an inner dialogue);

e)   low goal-directed coping (goals to remove or avoid threat are not paramount).

In practice, it means disengaging from all further analysis and ruminations whilst being aware of one's intrusive thoughts and feelings. It consists of just noticing and experiencing intrusive thoughts and feelings without rating them or attempting to avoid or control them. It means increasing one's attention on goal-directed behaviors (e.g., listening to someone) or the environment (e.g., sounds, sights, and smells) and separation of self from thought or image. It is also described in ACT as "distancing" from the thoughts or images and no longer "buying into" them (Hayes et al., 1999). The therapist might use various metaphors depending on the context:

> "In the right situation, it can be productive for your attention to be focused inwards, for example when you are trying to solve a specific, concrete problem or come up with a new theory. However, spending time thinking about your appearance or working out exactly how you look or how to fix your impression of yourself seems to be making you more preoccupied and distressed. Most people find that being self-focused causes them to dwell more on the past, and feel more distressed with their appearance, which in turn makes them feel uglier and do less. The alternative is to practice something called 'detached mindfulness' and to refocus more of your attention externally into activities that are important for you.
>
> Think of yourself as a bus driver with lots of passengers. Each of the passengers is trying to tell you how to drive. One is telling you to make a sharp right turn, another shouts, 'No, turn left,' and others shout 'Don't listen to them, just go straight ahead.' Everyone is screaming and at first you start listening, but when you listen to them you are really unable to drive. Each passenger is a thought. You do not need to listen to the passengers (your thoughts). You can be in control and not pay any attention to them and just pay attention to the street signs and other things in the environment. You are in the driver's seat and you don't need to listen to anyone. You just have to follow the route you have chosen for your bus."

Alternatively:

> "Try to think of your thoughts, images, and urges as cars in the traffic. If one engages with the thoughts, then one might stand in the road and try to divert them. Alternatively, you might try to sort out your thoughts by trying to get into a car and parking it. When you are distressed about your appearance, you might focus on particular 'cars' that tell you that you are ugly and that you will be alone all your life. However even when you have managed to divert or park one car

there are always more cars to be dealt with. Detached mindfulness means noticing the thoughts but not attempting to stop them or trying to sort them out. Take
notice of the thoughts but imagine them as soldiers marching in front of you,
one by one. If images of soldiers are not acceptable, you can think of each
thought as a leaf floating down a river.

People may hold positive motivations about worrying (for example, 'I must
worry in order to think through all the possible things that could go wrong')
while recognizing the negative consequences ('If I worry, then I will go crazy
and I won't be able to think straight'). Not surprisingly, this induces a further
state of anxiety and depression. Feeling anxious and depressed will pull you into
brooding and being self-focused."

Positive beliefs about a thinking style can usually be challenged on pragmatic
grounds and by focusing the patient on the consequences of their ruminating
or worrying. One might ask:

"How helpful is this belief if it leads you to feel more distressed and
   preoccupied?
Is thinking a lot something you would recommend to others with intrusive
   thoughts about the way they look? If not, why not?
Is this something that perhaps you learnt was helpful in the past but perhaps is
   no longer helpful?
What alternative to ruminating could you do that is consistent with your goals
   and valued directions?
What could help you stay in the moment rather than drifting into your mind?"

The type of questions to ask about beliefs about a thinking style might be:

"Does this assumption about your thinking style help you in your goals?
Can this rule about your thinking style be made more flexible?
Does your assumption help you to follow the directions in life that you want?
Is the cost of your thinking style too expensive?
While you hold this assumption about your thinking style, do you become more
   preoccupied and act in ways that are unhelpful?
For how long will you carry on with your solution?"

Trying to solve the wrong problem

Another issue that takes up a lot of mental time in BDD is of worrying and
trying to solve the wrong problems. A therapist might introduce it like this:

"Problem-solving is a good skill to have in resolving a current problem, but have
you noticed it is unhelpful if the focus is trying to prevent a possible bad event
in the future? Can you think of an example?"

Another example:

> "If your car has broken down and you have to get to a job interview, you could worry about 'What if I don't get the job?' (and make yourself more anxious). You can problem-solve only if you can turn worry into a 'How?' question – for example, 'How am I going to get to the center of town on time? I could ring for a taxi, but that will be a bit expensive. I could get a train, but I might now miss the one that would get me there in time. Getting this job is important, so I'll take a taxi.' The important point is to solve existing problems only or ones that you can do something about. Sometimes you can practice for an event, but this is usually fairly limited. For example, if you have an interview coming up, then you might ask a friend to do a role-play and practice being interviewed.
>
> People with body image problems often spend a lot of time making mental plans on how they will prevent something bad from happening. They feel they cannot do anything until they know how it can be fixed or camouflaged. ('If I can get my nose fixed, then I can do things I want to do in life' or 'If I can get the right skin product, then it may fix my skin').
>
> Is this something you do?
>
> Mental planning might have the function of instilling hope, but it usually leads to an endless search for solutions that never help (or make things worse) or do not reduce the preoccupation or distress. Have you noticed trying to solve it as an appearance problem increases your preoccupation and distress with your appearance?
>
> Trying too hard to prevent something bad from happening needs to be seen in the context of past experiences that have not been updated. If you act as if it was an emotional problem, it has a completely different solution. This involves focusing on what you are avoiding in life and what you want your life to stand for despite how you feel. So try to turn 'worry' into a 'How' question that focuses on how you can do the activities that are important to you despite what your mind is telling you."

18.6 Alternatives to Ruminating

The general principles are not to challenge or engage with the *content* of the rumination using empiricism or logic. Nor is it usually necessary to identify or challenge the core beliefs derived from the ruminating. The focus of intervention is on identifying when ruminating occurs and using pragmatism (e.g., the helpfulness of ruminating) and acting in a manner in keeping with the person's valued directions. Activities should be done with no avoidance of aversive thoughts and emotion and, wherever possible, as behavioral experiments to determine whether ruminating (or another process) is helpful.

Problem-solving

Watkins et al. (2007) identify any global, abstract, and evaluative questions (e.g., "Why?" and "If only ..."-type questions) and turn them into "How"-type questions which are specific, concrete, non-judgemental, and relate to an activity which is in keeping with goals and valued directions (e.g., How can I be a good friend?). It is important to ensure that the "How" questions can be turned into specific behaviors that are in keeping with the goals of therapy and the patients' valued directions rather than how they are going to find a good cosmetic surgeon or fix their appearance.

Labeling thoughts

A strategy for intrusive thoughts and not engaging with them is to label the thought by saying it out loud (perhaps in a cartoon character voice) and writing it down, for example:

> "I am *having a thought* that my nose is too crooked.
> I am *having a memory* of being bullied as a child.
> I am *having the feeling* of being anxious.
> I am *making a rating* of myself that I am ugly."

As an alternative, some people find it more helpful to distance themselves from such thoughts by labeling them as a product of their mind:

> "My mind is telling me I am ugly."

All these strategies can help to distance and defuse the thoughts from the "self."

Absorption exercise

Watkins et al. (2007) describe the use of visualization exercises as an alternative to ruminating. Patients are asked to re-create from memory a time when they were caught up in a task such as canoeing, skiing, painting (e.g., "being in the zone"). They are asked to focus on their image, posture, sensory experiences, bodily sensations, motivation, action feelings, and facial expression at the time.

Activity

Patients can be helped to identify what they are avoiding when they ruminate (or compare or attack themselves). This might involve experiencing aversive thoughts or images and feelings of being ugly or defective. It may "work" whilst ruminating but in the long term it maintains preoccupation and distress. Instead of ruminating, patients are taught to act on an activity that is in keeping with their goals and valued directions in life despite aversive thoughts and images (identified in the initial assessment). There are usually many different cognitive and behavioral activities that are being avoided (see Chapter 22). Patients should be focused not just on what they do but on the way they do it. Goal-directed activities (e.g., being a good partner) should be done with full attention and, if necessary, using detached mindfulness to intrusive thoughts.

Wells (2005) has described various exercises for promoting detached mindfulness of intrusive thoughts and images, which can be adapted for use in BDD. Thus in one exercise patients are asked to sit quietly and let their mind wander without controlling or responding to it and then report back to the therapist what happened. If a patient struggles with detached mindfulness, this may be linked to beliefs about the consequences of not responding to intrusive thoughts (e.g., a belief that he might go mad) and this would be explored in more detail.

When patients conduct such an activity, it is important to validate their experience and congratulate them on having a lot more courage than they give themselves credit for (rather than proving that their predictions were wrong) (Gilbert, 2007).

Activity scheduling

Activity scheduling and stimulus control (with reminders on cue cards) can be used for situations and times when a person is more likely to ruminate. This needs an understanding of the context in which the ruminating occurs and therefore trying to prevent these cues being activated. You might ask:

> "Is there a pattern to the situations that are typically linked to ruminating (or mental planning, etc.) that you could change? For example, can you do anything to prevent such situations from occurring?
>
> Can you plan the day using an activity schedule that follows your valued directions? What can you do to stop yourself from being alone at certain times?"

18.7   Comparing and Mental Checking

Beliefs about comparing usually involve knowing where one stands in relation to others as a form of threat-monitoring. This usually leads to safety-seeking behaviors, such as keeping one's head down and trying to camouflage one's "defect" to avoid conflict.

Examples of beliefs about comparing:
- I know where I stand in relation to others.
- I can be ready if I am humiliated.
- I can try to emulate those people.

Related to comparing are mental checks; these involve checking how one appears to others from an observer perspective. This is like having a mirror in one's head. The current image may then be compared to a past image, an ideal image, or trigger, or checked in an actual mirror. An example of a belief that motivates mental checks is:

"I have to know exactly how I look all the time in case I am humiliated."

Comparing and mental-checking can be approached in the same way as ruminating by self-monitoring, doing a functional analysis of the response, and understanding the beliefs that motivate the behavior.

18.8   Self-reassurance

Self-reassurance is uncommon in BDD but can occur in clients with symptoms similar to OCD. Here a client has intrusive thoughts and doubts about a defect that at one level he "knows" are absurd.

He may be responding to the thought by trying to reassure himself (e.g., "It's just a small spot. I'm being over the top" or "I'm just imagining it"). The self-reassurance then becomes a factor in maintaining the intrusion as it increases the doubt and preoccupation. In this instance the belief that motivated self-reassurance was:

"If I tell it to myself enough, then maybe it will sink in."

Use the same approach as for rumination in understanding the motivation for self-reassurance and functional analysis of the response.

18.9   Self-attacking

When ruminations are more severe, they become self-attacking or punishing, especially in those who have a comorbid borderline personality disorder. It is helpful to acknowledge that the self can be made up of different parts or motives, which may be in conflict (e.g., "One part of you may want to eat ice-cream and another part of you tells you that would be stupid when you want to lose weight").

Where self-attacking is prominent, therapists should do a mini-formulation (as above for rumination) and a functional analysis (see Figure 18.2) to understand the motivation of the inner bully (or positive beliefs) and the factors that maintain the self-attacking.

People critical of themselves (e.g., telling themselves that they are ugly, weak, or pathetic) might also have reasons for allowing themselves to be bullied by their mind. It is often helpful to ask yourself: "What is my greatest fear if I give up criticizing and bullying myself?" Criticism can also act as a warning ("If I don't tell you how ugly you are and you don't improve yourself, then nobody will love you"). Sometimes self-criticism can be triggered from a memory or be linked to one's identity. This sort of reasoning is probably an important factor in maintaining long-standing beliefs about ugliness and depression. You might like to consider the costs and benefits of keeping up self-attacking and how they are being maintained.

The motivation for self-attacking can be self-improvement, the assumption being that if the person does not bully himself, he will lose motivation to improve himself.

Other examples of beliefs behind self-criticism:

"If I don't put myself down, then I'll be arrogant."
"If I don't get in first with criticism, someone else will."
"If I don't criticize myself, I'll get fat."

In more personality disordered individuals, the motivation of self-attacking is for punishment. For example the belief may be:

"I attack myself in order to get the humiliation I deserve."

There are many different exercises that can be used to increase compassion for the self, which is a whole book in itself (Gilbert, 2007; 2009). We summarize next some of the key issues.

Once the person can identify and verbalize their self-attacking, it is helpful to label it as such (e.g., as one's "inner bully") and to understand the context in which it occurs and its function. This may be done using a two-chair technique by observing the nature of the attack and submissive response. Ask your patient to use two chairs for the interaction between their "hostile self" (inner bully) and "submissive self." The two chairs chosen are preferably different from one used by the therapist, in case it leads to confusion of roles. The therapist might say:

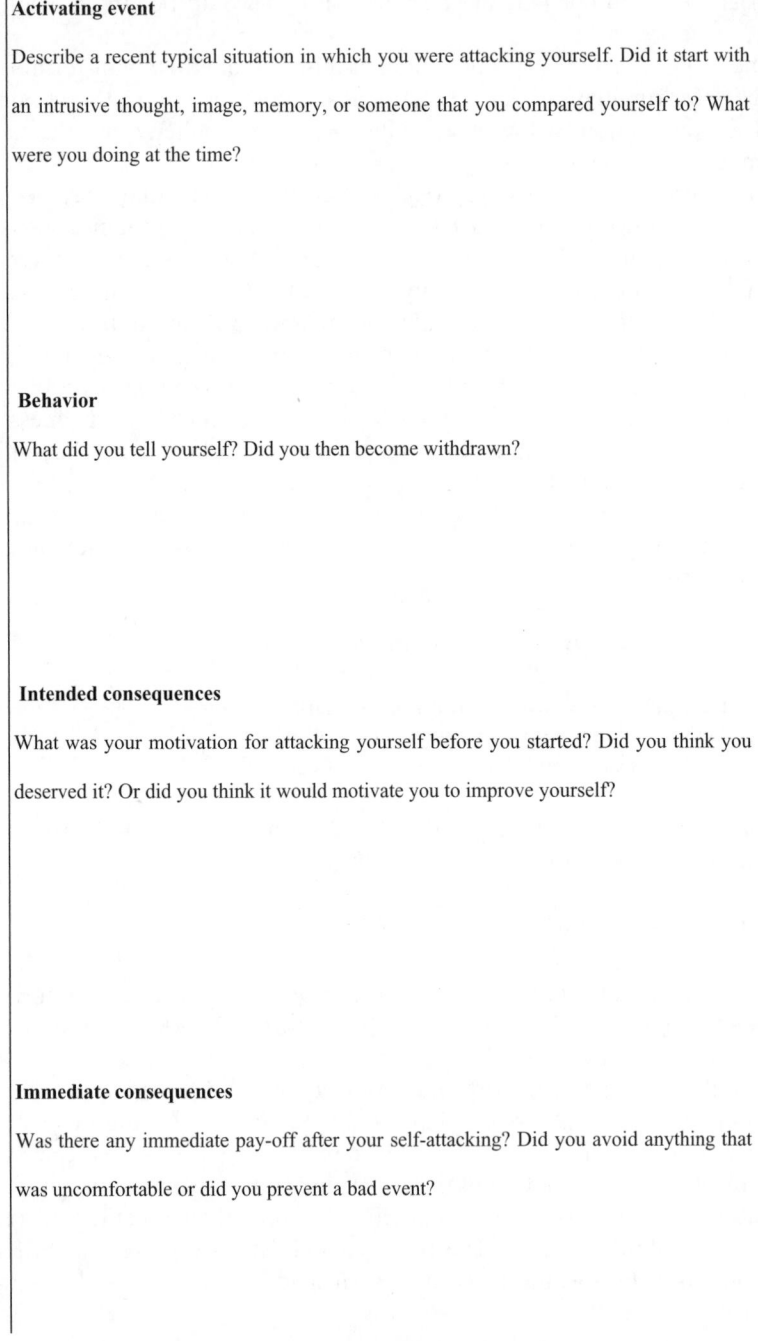

Activating event

Describe a recent typical situation in which you were attacking yourself. Did it start with an intrusive thought, image, memory, or someone that you compared yourself to? What were you doing at the time?

 Behavior

What did you tell yourself? Did you then become withdrawn?

 Intended consequences

What was your motivation for attacking yourself before you started? Did you think you deserved it? Or did you think it would motivate you to improve yourself?

Immediate consequences

Was there any immediate pay-off after your self-attacking? Did you avoid anything that was uncomfortable or did you prevent a bad event?

Figure 18.2 Analysis of Self-attacking

Unintended consequences

What effect did the self-attacking have on the way you feel, your preoccupation and distress?

What effect did it have on how self-focused you became on a scale of −3 (totally focused on what you were thinking) to +3 (totally focused on the environment or tasks)?

What effect did your self-attacking have on the time you can devote to what is important in your life?

What effect does your self-attacking have on the people around you?

Figure 18.2 *Continued*

Did you do anything in excess as a consequence (e.g., drink more, use drugs, binge eat, purge)?

Overall, how helpful was your self-attacking?

Alternative directions

What alternatives could you do that are consistent with your goals and valued directions instead of self-attacking? Could you test this at the next opportunity to see what effect it has on your distress and preoccupation?

Is there a pattern to the situations that are typically linked to self-attacking that you could change? For example, can you do anything to prevent such situations from occurring? Do you need to buy that celebrity magazine? Can you put old photographs back in an album, etc?

Figure 18.2   *Continued*

Summary: Costs of self-attacking

Does self-attacking make your preoccupation and mood worse?

Does it help you achieve the goals you have set yourself?

Does it help you stick to your valued directions in life?

Is self-attacking something you would teach a friend or relative in a similar position? If not, why not?

Once you have identified the costs and benefits of self-attacking, you could talk through these ideas with your therapist to see whether self-attacking helps or whether there is an alternative to your strategy. You might want to consider whether there is an alternative, compassionate approach that might help you to achieve the goals you want in life. Compassion means putting yourself in another person's shoes and being able to understand their emotional experience and to be moved by it. It means being non-judgemental and sensitive to the distress and needs of your mind. So, it is very understandable for your mind to want to try to protect you and prevent you, for example, from being arrogant or being rejected. However, there are alternative ways of achieving the same goal.

Figure 18.2   *Continued*

"I wonder if we could watch a conversation between your inner bully and your other self and then reflect on how it makes you feel. Could your inner bully first sit in this chair and for you to say out loud what it is saying to the other part of you that is in the chair opposite? Can you think of a recent situation when your inner bully was very strong and you were upset? What was the situation?"

After the patient has demonstrated a recent episode of self-attacking, the therapist might say:

"Thank you. That was very helpful for me to understand the nature of your inner bully. Would you now swap chairs. Can you tell your bully how you feel when you are being attacked and bullied?"

After this, the two parts of the self may be invited to have a conversation and to discover more about the bully's motivation. Most people feel submissive and helpless when they are bullied because they cannot defend themselves as they usually agree with their inner bully. The bully can often be regarded as a response to a threat and worries about being rejected or humiliated. Clients are gently led to an alternative of compassion towards one's inner bully. These exercises include: a) detached mindfulness and standing back from one's inner critic; b) questioning whether one's inner critic is genuinely concerned with the person's well-being or best interests; c) sending a compassionate letter to the self acknowledging the conflict in feelings; d) using compassionate imagery; e) standing up to a self-critic; and f) acting in approach behaviors in an opposite direction using the principles of dialectical behavior therapy.

In borderline personality disorder, there is often a relentless stream of self-attacking and comparing oneself to others, for example:

"You are so ugly compared to her. You just love wallowing in your misery, don't you? I'll give you something to really worry about it. You need a good boot up the backside."

Here the motivation is hatred and the belief that they deserve to be punished (Gilbert, 2007). Not surprisingly, self-attacking and ruminating make the person become submissive and can make him feel very small, more depressed, and even uglier. The therapist should try to move the patient towards self-compassion.

Chapter 19

Avoidance, compulsive, and safety-seeking behaviors

Summary

When clients are engaged in understanding how avoidance and safety-seeking behaviors might be maintaining their symptoms of BDD, they are introduced to behavioral experiments and graded exposure without safety-seeking behaviors to situations that have been avoided. Additional strategies are described for mirror retraining and video and photo feedback.

Sections

19.1 Introduction

There are a number of different types of avoidance in BDD, all of which serve to maintain preoccupation, distress, and handicap. Sometimes avoidance takes the form of engaging in safety behaviors or compulsions. Both are considered

Body Dysmorphic Disorder: A Treatment Manual. David Veale and Fugen Neziroglu
© 2010 John Wiley & Sons, Ltd.

as avoidance because the goal of both is to avoid aversive images, thoughts, and feelings.

Avoidance behavior can include: a) intrusive thoughts, memories, and images about the feature(s) considered defective (experiential avoidance); b) looking at the features that are regarded as defective (either directly or in any reflective surface) or using them (which might trigger aversive imagery, thoughts, or emotions described above); and c) interpersonal, social, or public situations which are avoided because of the fear of negative evaluation about the feature(s). These in turn may be graded according to how anxiety-provoking each situation or activity is.

In addition, people with BDD use various safety-seeking behaviors within situations, which are designed to prevent the risk of a feared catastrophe (e.g., that the person will be humiliated or rejected). This may involve excessive monitoring of threat and various behaviors to alter or camouflage one's appearance. However, there are a number of unintended consequences of avoidance and safety-seeking behaviors: a) they prevent disconfirmation of beliefs or expectations; b) they increase self-consciousness, preoccupation, and distress; and c) they may make a person appear cold and aloof in social situations. The rationale of the role of safety-seeking behaviors should be explored in a Socratic dialogue. If there has been adequate defusion from past aversive experiences or the use of imagery rescripting, then clients will find the approach easier.

19.2   Assessment of Avoidance and Safety-seeking Behaviors

A checklist of avoidance, safety-seeking behaviors, and compulsions is provided in the Body Image Questionnaire (Appendix 1). Situations avoided include: leaving home; attending a family or other social gathering; going to school or college; going to work; a medical examination; dating or revealing the feature(s) to the partner in intimacy; being outdoors; bright lighting; crowded situations with little personal space; shopping malls; having a haircut; shopping for clothes; going swimming. There is usually a common theme of the feared consequences that links with an association with an earlier aversive experience. If imagery rescripting has been successful, then exposure and behavioral experiments will be easier.

Predicting how anxiety-provoking each of the situations might be allows the person to develop a hierarchy of feared situations and later determine if the anxiety is as predicted or if the feared consequences actually occurred. Some of the situations will need to be broken into smaller steps – for someone who is housebound, the first step may be to draw back the curtains or go into the garden. Thus a series of goals can be agreed, starting with situations predicted to have moderate levels of anxiety. The feared consequence may be expressed by clients in the form of what others are thinking (rather than how they might act). This is discussed in more detail in section 19.5.

19.3   Graded Exposure

Graded exposure to diminish anxiety is a well-established principle for anxiety disorders. We discuss below how graded exposure can be framed as a behavioral experiment to test out predictions or hypotheses that a client has in certain situations as a way of enhancing exposure. At this stage, we do not know the mediating process for exposure. The goal in BDD is to overcome all avoidance strategies and to do so without resort to safety-seeking behaviors. To be maximally effective, exposure tasks usually aims to be:

a)   Done in a graded manner. Adherence to a graded hierarchy is more effective than "flooding." Early tasks should aim to be moderately anxiety-provoking (i.e., challenging, but not overwhelming).

b)   Relevant to the person's lifestyle so they can be repeated and reinforced easily as often as possible. As a minimum the target should be daily.

c)   Done without alcohol, substances, or prescribed medication (e.g., benzodiazepines) before or during the task.

d)   Done without any cognitive avoidance or safety-seeking behaviors, with attention focused externally and without making any evaluation of an image in a reflective surface. (Further guidance on reducing the frequency of safety behaviors and mirror-checking is given below.)

e)   Sufficiently prolonged for any emotion to subside. This will largely depend on being consistent in not being self-focused and paying full attention to the experience in the moment.

f)   Done with a constant stimulus, rather than frequent escaping and returning to the situation.

g)   Done *in vivo*. This is generally more effective than in the imagination, but the latter can be useful as a preparation for *in vivo* tasks.

h)   Done with the client taking responsibility for his own program.

i)   Done without ways of trying to control or escape the experience of anxiety.

Many clients avoid aversive imagery, thoughts, and emotions ("experiential avoidance") and this should be monitored. They should be told that avoidance prevents their memories from being updated and maintains their distress. They should be encouraged to experience any aversive thoughts, images, or feelings and reassured that these will fade over time. By experiencing the feelings they can also test out their predictions. Covert ruminating may interfere with exposure when clients are constantly trying to problem-solve their perceived defect or mentally planning the steps they need to take. Exposure is therefore best done with the principles of acceptance and detached mindfulness (Wells, 2005). Thus clients are asked to "notice" or "be aware of" any aversive images, thoughts, or feelings that might occur during exposure, but just to experience them without making any evaluation or trying to control them.

Therapists should explore with clients strategies that will prevent them from engaging in the compulsions and carry out response prevention with the exposure (E&RP). Clients who are most successful are those who experience anxiety during exposure and habituate within or between sessions. Clients can sometimes experience within-session habituation but not between-session habituation. To get optimal benefit it is important to experience between-session habituation. This is sometimes a matter of repeatedly putting oneself in anxiety-provoking situations as well as ensuring there are no safety-seeking behaviors. Alternatively, a client may go back to ruminating between sessions or conducting a post-mortem after an anxiety-provoking situation. This usually consists of mental reviews of what the client said or did, whether someone could see his defect, and what he thinks a person was thinking. A functional analysis of the post-mortem process can be conducted, with the aim of reaching a conclusion that post-mortems (like ruminations) are unhelpful and increase preoccupation and distress. Like ruminations, the process can be monitored to increase awareness. The goal is for no extended post-mortems after exposure tasks. It has also been suggested that within- and between-session habituation may be governed by two mechanisms. Short-term habituation may involve the autonomic nervous system; whereas long-term habituation may involve cognitive processes (Groves & Lynch, 1972). Assessment of habituation has been obtained from both self-reports (reports of SUD levels) as well as from physiological measurements. Clients who react physiologically with high arousal habituate more slowly than those who demonstrate lower levels of arousal. Clients who have comorbid depression also habituate more slowly than those who are not depressed.

Exposure-based therapies operate on the process of extinction via habituation. Habituation occurs when there is continual bombardment of sensory neurons that ultimately fatigue. Clients then report they no longer feel as anxious; thus habituation is the extinction of fear. Groves & Lynch (1972) reported that habituation occurs at the cellular level in the area of the brainstem reticular formation, particularly in the mesencephalon. In BDD, in addition to anxiety, there may be feelings of self-disgust as reported by Neziroglu et al. (in press). Disgust habituates more slowly than anxiety.

There is emerging evidence that exposure tasks may be more efficient if done as a behavioral experiment in which individuals are invited to make predictions about the planned task and to test out their theory in the context of the model for BDD. You might want to ask:

> "What would you predict will happen if Theory A (that you have an appearance problem) were true?
> What would you predict if Theory B (that you have an emotional problem in which you are extremely preoccupied by your appearance) were true?
> What predictions are you making about the risk of a bad event occurring (e.g., that you will be humiliated or how distressed you will be)?
> What safety seeking behaviors might occur that are important to resist?"

The predictions are then compared after the experiment against their actual experience. An example of the form used for behavioral experiments is shown in Figure 19.1. In other situations the prediction may be that the anxiety will persist for several hours. Here it is necessary to monitor their anxiety level (Standard Unit of Distress Scale, SUDS) on a scale of 0–100 in order to make a prediction of what the maximum SUDS will be and how long it will continue.

It is important for clients to keep a record of what they did, including situations when they do not succeed, in order to elicit more information. Where possible, one might start with therapist-aided exposure/experiments depending on the problem. Here the normal session may need to last two hours or more. One might accompany a client for a walk in a shopping mall, prompting him to keep externally focused and to model appropriate behavior. With all tasks, the therapist needs to be empathic and to remind the client of the model and the need to be focused on the situation rather than on how he feels or what he thinks he looks like.

The ultimate exposure tasks would involve not just dropping safety behaviors but highlighting or exaggerating the "defect" by using certain make-up or clothes in anxiety-provoking situations, especially if these are linked with some specific predictions. Thus a client preoccupied with spots or redness of the skin may be encouraged to exaggerate these with make-up. The therapist is encouraged to join in on such exercises in public situations. Although these experiments are powerful demonstrations, clients often avoid them. The aim is not only to test out various predictions clients make, such as people humiliating them, but also to allow for extinction over time.

19.4 Dropping Safety-Seeking Behaviors and Behavioral Experiments

Safety-seeking behaviors are actions that aim to prevent a catastrophe in a feared situation and reduce harm (Salkovskis, 1985).

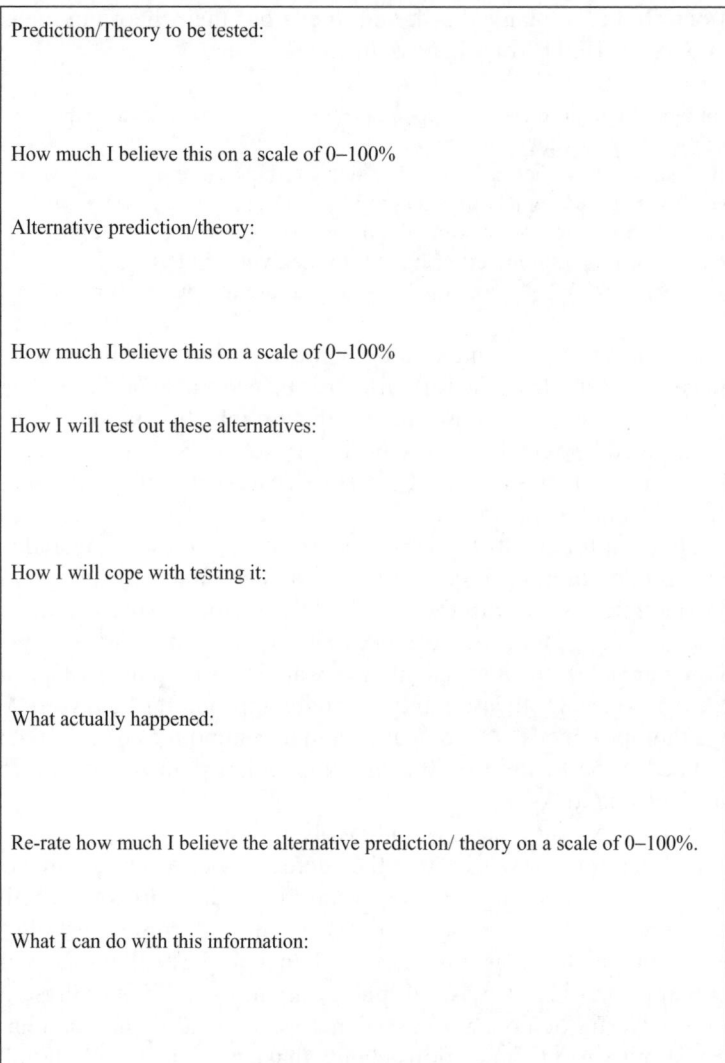

Prediction/Theory to be tested:

How much I believe this on a scale of 0–100%

Alternative prediction/theory:

How much I believe this on a scale of 0–100%

How I will test out these alternatives:

How I will cope with testing it:

What actually happened:

Re-rate how much I believe the alternative prediction/ theory on a scale of 0–100%.

What I can do with this information:

Figure 19.1   Behavioral experiment record

Safety-seeking behaviors are different from compulsions in that the former refer to behaviors that are performed to *avoid* aversive experiences, whereas compulsions are behaviors performed to *undo* an aversive experience. Thus safety behaviors are preventative (i.e., they appear to prevent negative outcomes), whereas compulsions are restorative of homeostasis by taking away the negative outcome (e.g., feeling anxious). Safety-seeking behaviors may be within anxiety-provoking situations, such as avoiding eye contact and keeping one's head down to prevent a feared catastrophe or an aversive experience, or not within anxiety-provoking situations to prepare for aversive experiences.

We discuss the myriad of safety-seeking and compulsive behaviors in Chapter 4. A comprehensive list of safety-seeking behaviors and compulsions which are used when alone (e.g., mirror-checking, feeling a feature with fingers, checking on a camera phone, wearing a cap to hide the hairline, using concealers to cover blemishes, wearing a lot of make-up to get "smooth" skin, cosmetic surgery) and when in public or social situations (e.g., excessive make-up, keeping the head down, making poor eye contact, camouflaging a feature with hair or hands; changing posture to hide a feature, wearing bulky clothes to hide large arms) needs to be compiled. Typical compulsions include mirror-checking (when it has a restorative action), questioning others, excessive washing to clean pores of dirt or sweat after a walk, and skin picking.

Once a client is engaged in therapy, there needs to be an agreement on the goals the client will aim at when alone and also in social situations. This should include approach behaviors without safety-seeking behaviors and preventing compulsions (the latter is known as response prevention).

The rationale for dropping safety-seeking behaviors is best provided in a Socratic dialogue. The goal is for clients to learn from behavioral experiments that safety-seeking behaviors maintain symptoms of preoccupation and distress with their feature(s) and prevent them from discovering that some of their fears may be unrealistic. Only by gradually approaching situations without safety-seeking behaviors are they able to discover that the consequences either do not occur or they are not as bad as they predicted.

Clients often make predictions that are not observable or objective (e.g., "They still think I am ugly and are laughing at me"). This is the thinking style of mind-reading and, wherever possible, try to ensure that the predictions are based on objective information (e.g., how people behave towards them and not what people are thinking or how they are coming across) and non-judgemental evaluations (e.g., "How long will I be anxious for and how anxious will I get?" rather than "How ugly I am"). It is often more helpful to tie the prediction in with "Theory A" or "Theory B" (Chapter 14) and whether the person became more preoccupied and distressed by using a safety-seeking behavior. For example, "Does the evidence best fit with Theory B" (i.e., "I have a problem with being preoccupied with a rating about being ugly and of trying too hard to prevent myself from being humiliated which has in turn increased my preoccupation and distress")?

A common behavioral experiment is to use alternating behaviors, where the client compares the effect of increasing the safety-seeking behavior (e.g., checking more than usual) and dropping the safety behavior for a sufficient period to collect data on the effect of the desired variable (e.g., the degree of preoccupation, distress, and self-consciousness). It is also important to have done the preparatory work in that clients understand the difference between self-focused attention and external-focused attention (section 17.8) and are able to switch attention from being self-focused in anxiety-provoking situations. Clients are encouraged to experiment with dropping their safety behaviors and focusing on what they can see or hear rather than on how they think they look or imagine what others are thinking. They should keep a written record of what they experience which can be reviewed during therapy.

A behavioral experiment

A 34-year-old woman who was preoccupied with lines on the skin on her arms used a thick moisturizer daily to reduce the wrinkles. She was unable to stop using the moisturizer because she believed that the lines would get worse if she did and people would find her very unattractive. Excessively moisturizing her arms was her safety-seeking behavior. We encouraged her to use the moisturizer less and less. In the interim we asked her to wear short-sleeved blouses so her arms could be exposed. We went with her to department stores and deliberately exposed her arms to salespeople. She tried on various bracelets and would ask the salespeople to take a look and comment on how it looked. She became very anxious in these situations but she learnt that people did not comment on her wrinkles, nor did they behave as if they were repulsed by her arms or avoid her and go on to other customers. In fact, most salespeople were very friendly and helpful.

An alternative approach is to apply moisturizer to one half of the body for a set period which can then be compared against the half of the body which has had no moisturizer. An experiment can be devised whereby a series of people can be asked whether they can tell which arm has been moisturized.

Exposure and response prevention

Sally was a 25-year-old who would constantly ask her boyfriend if her nose was crooked. He had always told her that she was beautiful and had nothing to worry about. However, she continued to feel insecure and would spend hours checking the mirror and trying to fix her nose by playing with it. Sally understood the formulation but found it very difficult to resist the urge to question her boyfriend, even though she agreed that it was unhelpful and fed her preoccupation. The formulation was discussed with the boyfriend and how responding to Sally maintained her preoccupation. He agreed he would no longer answer her questions but pay her plenty of attention when she was not seeking reassurance. It was agreed with Sally that if she asked more than three times he would tell her that her nose was very crooked and so unattractive that he would not want to be seen with her. He was encouraged to respond with comments like: "Didn't you notice how people walked out when you came in?" and other comical-sounding statements. Sally was also encouraged that every time she had the urge to check in the mirror she should try to walk away and do a pre-planned activity, such as making a phone call, doing some star jumps, or going for a walk. When her hand went to her face to correct the crookedness she was asked to sit on her hands, wear jingling bracelets to make herself aware that her hand was going to her nose, and use the principles of habit reversal (see Chapter 21).

19.5   Mirror Retraining

Individuals with BDD commonly use mirrors or reflective surfaces (so they know exactly how they look) as a safety-seeking behavior (to prevent bad events) and as a compulsion to "undo" bad events (Veale & Riley, 2001). Some may avoid "unsafe" mirrors. Avoiding mirrors altogether is an unrealistic goal and will cause problems in the long term. The goal is to be able to use mirrors briefly for functional reasons.

The first step is to monitor the frequency of mirror-gazing and identify the motivation for mirror-checking. The most common beliefs are:

- "I hope I don't look as bad as I think I look."
- "I have to know what I look like and I can't until I look in the mirror."
- "I look in the mirror to see how I feel."
- "I have to be certain of how I appear in public."
- "I have to make myself look my best."
- "I believe that if I stare long enough, I might see a different image."
- "If I resist looking in the mirror, I will feel worse."
- "I need to see what I don't like about myself."
- "If I don't look, I might forget about how ugly I am."

These beliefs can usually be examined in a functional analysis – challenged on pragmatic grounds and by re-examining the formulation (e.g., How long does the hope last for? What happens after that? For how long do you feel certain you know what you look like?)

Alternatively, they may be directly tested in a behavioral experiment – for example, compare two different time-frames of checking once a day with 20 times a day and whether this leads a person to forget how ugly they are.

Clients are therefore encouraged to develop the following goals with mirrors:

a) To use mirrors at a slight distance or ones that are large enough to reflect most of their body.

b) To deliberately focus attention on their reflection in the mirror rather than an internal impression of how they feel.

c) To use a mirror only for an agreed function (e.g., shaving, putting on make-up) for a limited period of time.

d) To use different mirrors and lights rather than sticking to one they "trust."

e) To scan their body and focus attention on the whole of the face or body rather than a specific "defect" or in any detail. As there is some evidence that healthy people focus attention on their features considered to be most attractive, this is an alternative strategy if preferred by the client.

f) To be non-evaluative about their appearance and to use detached mindfulness when there are intrusive thoughts about being ugly or defective.

g) Not to use mirrors that magnify their reflection.

h) Not to use ambiguous reflections (e.g., windows, the backs of CDs, cutlery, dusty or cracked mirrors).

i) Not to use a mirror when they feel the urge to check, but to delay the response and do other activities until the urge has subsided.

The frequency of mirror-checking can be monitored for a single day (e.g., time, situation) in a table. Some clients have an extremely high frequency (several hundred times a day) of mirror-checking. In this case a tally counter can be used to monitor frequency.

For some, it is more important to monitor the duration of mirror-gazing as this can last several hours. Here the termination criteria may be problematic, similar to the internal criteria used in terminating a ritual in obsessive compulsive disorder (Richards & Salkovskis 1995; Salkovskis 1999). Thus clients may cease mirror-gazing only when they feel "comfortable" or "just right." People without BDD might finish grooming or combing their hair when they can "see" that they look good enough. A discussion would then ensue on the helpfulness of the criteria that they have adopted and how the duration of mirror-checking is likely to persist whilst they use the same criteria. Salkovskis (personal communication) gives an example of an obsessional client who would check his door until it felt just right. This could last anything from five minutes to three hours. Salkovskis suggests asking whether clients use the same criteria when taking a right turn when driving. This can be adapted for mirror-gazing by asking questions such as:

- Why wouldn't you use the same criteria?
- What would the effect of not using the same criteria be?
- How do these situations compare to looking in the mirror?

A client is introduced to the idea that by seeking a particular feeling in a mirror, he may become even more uncertain and it may further increase his preoccupation and distress and ratings of ugliness. We ask clients to try to alternate between using a "just right" feeling and "just doing it" without using internal criteria. This strategy can be used as a behavioral experiment to test out their predictions and to alternate between the two.

The ultimate goal is for the client to stop when he feels "not right" or "uncomfortable" and to "just do it" and to finish with only objective criteria. If a client can reduce the amount of make-up or grooming, this will tend to reduce significantly the amount of time spent in front of a mirror (when clients tend to check that their camouflage is adequate). However, this is often not possible at an early stage in therapy. It is also worth remembering that when women reduce the amount of excessive camouflage on their face, they may well receive comments from others that they look different. This requires some preparation, as the comments about looking different may be interpreted as being "ugly."

19.6 Mirror feedback

Mirror feedback is sometimes necessary for individuals who avoid all or certain mirrors. It can be done as graded exposure with varying degrees of light or the amount of body exposed. If the problem is with the whole body, then a swimming costume can be worn with a therapist present. Clients are taught the difference between making an evaluation (i.e., rating good/bad or attractive/disgusting), which is subjective, and an observation that a blind person can understand. Clients are therefore instructed to describe their appearance objectively (e.g., their complexion, height, build, the color of their eyes), without any evaluation or rating. They should scan their body and not focus attention on specific "defects" or go into any detail. They should not make any evaluations and should look at the reflection in the mirror as if it were a stranger's.

19.7 Video feedback

Whilst clients frequently use mirrors or take their own photos using a camera phone, they either avoid being videoed or have not had the opportunity to have video feedback. Video feedback has been described as a component for the treatment of social phobia (Rapee & Hayman, 1996) and anorexia nervosa (Farrell et al., 2005) and can be used in BDD in the right context. Video feedback is best used when clients can make a specific prediction beforehand of how they look (e.g., the degree of redness of their skin) and there is an objective measure to compare it against. It is not helpful if the prediction is an evaluation of their appearance in general (e.g., "My face will just look ugly") or when they have been using video as a means of checking their appearance. Sometimes seeing movement in their face helps to disconfirm a static picture in their mind.

The following instructions for video feedback are adapted from Clark et al. (2003):

a) The conspicuousness of the appearance should if possible be operationalized and made as objective as possible. For example, the degree of redness can be calibrated against a color chart with varying degrees of redness. Other predictions can be made by running a "mental video" first, by drawing what they imagine, or writing an essay beforehand as if they are describing what they see to a blind person, and comparing their predictions against what they actually see on the video. If writing an essay, they should give objective descriptions (e.g., blue eyes, six feet tall) rather than evaluations (e.g., disgusting, horrible).

b) Care should be taken to ensure that the person does not watch the video with self-focused attention. Thus they are instructed to watch the video *as if* watching a stranger and only make observations on what they *see and hear* and not what they feel or rating how ugly they look.

c) When watching the video, they are asked to rate the degree to which they correspond to their predictions and the two ratings are then compared.

Video feedback can also be used when a specific prediction is made on the effect of dropping of a safety-seeking behavior, by demonstrating that they are more observable than the feared consequences (Harvey et al., 2000). In this case it is best to have all parties in the social interaction on the video (not just the client) but to make sure that any safety behaviors can be seen. In this case, the client makes a prediction before the video is taken of how anxious he will appear or the degree to which he will reveal the feared consequence under two conditions: a) when using safety-seeking behavior; and b) without using the safety-seeking behavior. After the video is taken he watches it and re-rates the degree to which he looked anxious or revealed the feared consequence under the two conditions.

One would then explore what he learnt from the video:

"Were the things that you were afraid of as noticeable as you thought they would be?

What does the video tell you about using the picture in your mind to judge how you come across?

What did the video teach you about using a safety-seeking behavior?

What did the video teach you about self-focused attention?"

19.8 Photo feedback

Photo feedback can be used in the same way as video feedback. Again, it works best if there are specific predictions of an observation (not an evaluation) that can be tested against an objective viewpoint. Thus it may be possible to superimpose an outline of a drawing onto an actual photo of the feature in photo-editing software. Thus a person who feels he has a disproportionately large forehead or chin, which he has drawn, may have it superimposed on a photo of his actual face. Like video feedback, care should be taken to ensure that the person does not look at the photo with self-focused attention. Thus he is instructed to look at the photo as if he is looking at a stranger and only make observations on what he sees (not what he feels) and not to rate how ugly he looks.

There are alternatives approaches when using photographs – for example, measuring the size of a feature and comparing it to that of the therapist, and making predictions. Whatever method is chosen, it is important that it does not become an exercise whereby the therapist "proves" the client has a distorted body image. It should be seen as an exercise to open up a discussion about his felt impression and whether it is helpful to use it as a guide for current behavior.

Before and after looking at the photo, clients are asked to rate the degree to which their prediction is consistent with Theory A or Theory B. One might ask questions such as:

"What does this exercise tell you about using the picture in your mind to guide your behavior?

What does it tell us about any difference between your felt impression and how others might see you?"

Photo feedback may also be helpful if it provides disconfirming evidence from others. For example, a man preoccupied by the size of his head made a prediction that the circumference was one and half times the average. We measured the circumference around the forehead of about 10 men, photographed them, and printed off the photos. We then compared these with the circumference of the patient's head. This showed that he was within the average range and helped establish Theory B – that his problem was feeling as if his head was disproportionately large.

19.9   Face and Body Mask Feedback

Another behavioral experiment is to make a face or body mask over the features that are considered defective using a dental alginate mould. This probably works best when a client complains about a specific structural problem such as a belief that one side of the face is caved in or the nose is crooked. You can also use plaster of Paris to make a mold, but we recommend dental alginate as it makes a more accurate mold and sets faster than plaster, in 3–4 minutes. To make a face mask, apply petroleum jelly (e.g., Vaseline) liberally over the eyebrows and any other facial hair. Your client should wear old clothes and a plastic apron and a disposable shower cap.

Mix the dental alginate with a spatula. You will need about 500 g for a face. Ask your client to lie down and put a drinking straw (about 7 cm in length) in each nostril. Start applying the dental alginate around the top of face. Take special care when applying it around the nose and eyes. If the straws fall out, ask your client to reinsert them. Apply the alginate or plaster liberally over the whole face and cover up any patches that look thin. While it is setting the person needs to keep his face perfectly still and to use an agreed hand signal if he wishes to communicate.

To remove the mask, ask your client to move his face muscles while gently pulling the mask from his face. One can either use the inside of the mold for feedback or put fine plaster of Paris into the mold to make a mask. If a mold or mask is used for feedback you can use the same principles as described for photo or video feedback. Specifically, the client should look at it as if he is examining a stranger. Ask him initially to feel the mask with his fingers with his eyes closed (to test the prediction about symmetry or the crookedness of the nose) and then examine it visually. You can explore whether the results best fit Theory A (the problem is a defect in one's appearance) or Theory B (the problem is emotional – his mind is providing him with information that is inconsistent with what he sees on the mask). Be careful not to use the results to "prove" that he is wrong.

19.10   Obstacles

A common obstacle is the belief: "I can only stop avoiding situations or drop my safety-seeking behaviors when I feel comfortable or right"; or when "I know for certain that the consequences I fear will not happen"; or when "I feel confident enough to test out my fears." This applies to a wide range of avoidance and safety-seeking behaviors (and not just in BDD). If your client sticks with these beliefs, he is putting the cart before the horse (Dryden, 1999). There may be high-level emotional intolerance and a struggle to stop controlling events. Progress will be based on his willingness to accept and embrace aversive emotions and to drop the "spade" with a "leap of faith" (see Chapter 14). This means in the short term doing tasks uncomfortably, with uncertainty, unconfidently, in order to obtain the long-term gains. Another metaphor that can be used is "the tug of war with a monster" (Hayes et al., 1999; see Chapter 14 above) to understand how he is engaging in a struggle and that it will be easier when he drops his unworkable solutions. Some clients may have a good *intellectual* understanding of the problem, but are not yet ready to change *behaviorally* to test out their predictions. In these cases, one may have to think of smaller steps and check their understanding of the problems and goals. For some clients, there may be social problems or other priorities (albeit often related to their BDD) so that it may be preferable to leave the door open for them to return when they are more ready to change.

Chapter 20

Modifying appraisals

Summary

Previous chapters have described modifying effortful cognitive processes and behaviors. This chapter discusses trying to modify the cognitive content or appraisals. We discuss the target of the appraisals and, if this is done, the timing and type of challenge. Lastly, we discuss the use of reverse role-play and assertive defense of the self.

Sections

20.1 Introduction
20.2 Distancing
20.3 Identifying common thinking styles
20.4 Identifying assumptions and core beliefs
20.5 Idealized values
20.6 Reverse role-play
20.7 Assertive defense of the self

20.1 Introduction

Strategies aimed at modifying appraisals are well established in CBT for emotional disorders (Hawton et al., 1992). Here we include negative automatic thoughts, assumptions, rules, and core beliefs. However, the issue in modifying appraisals in BDD is deciding on the target for modification and whether it is necessary or helpful to try to modify the content of the beliefs about appearance. One would not, for example, help someone with OCD look for evidence

Body Dysmorphic Disorder: A Treatment Manual. David Veale and Fugen Neziroglu
© 2010 John Wiley & Sons, Ltd.

of whether an intrusive doubt about being a pedophile is true or not. In the same vein, it is generally unhelpful to question the content of the person's *evaluations* in BDD using empiricism or logic (e.g., "What's the evidence that your nose is crooked and ugly?"), or to set up a behavioral experiment of a survey to test out whether such a *belief* is true or not (e.g., a survey of people's opinions about whether the feature is ugly). Such strategies may be helpful in normal appearance concerns, but most people with BDD will dismiss anything that others have said (e.g., "You have to say that. You're paid to"; or "People say that because they don't want to hurt me"; or "They didn't see me in the right light"). Alternatively, if there is a reduction in the strength of the conviction or belief, it does not last. There are exceptions – for example, it can be helpful to question the beliefs of an individual who does not have any awareness that other people do not perceive a flaw in the same way and/or that others do not think he is ugly. A behavioral experiment (e.g., taking a survey of how others rate a perceived defect) may be helpful in increasing insight and thereby decreasing the likelihood of interpreting others as laughing, staring at, or criticizing his appearance. It may then increase the likelihood of generating alternative explanations of others' apparent rejecting behavior.

20.2 Distancing

In order to reduce attention placed on and time spent thinking about appearance, the rule for you as a therapist, the client, his family and friends is not to engage with any thoughts and feelings about appearance or a feature, but to focus on the process of the helpfulness of engaging with such thoughts. We therefore discuss first the role of distancing and identifying thinking styles.

Distancing is a strategy that involves labeling any intrusive thought or image by suggesting that your client say it out loud or write it down (e.g., "I am having a thought that I am ugly"; "I am having a picture of what my mind thinks I look like"). Some people find it helpful to speak their thoughts out loud in the voice of a cartoon character. The aim is to distance the individual from his thoughts and defuse them from his "self." This acknowledges the existence of such thoughts, labeling them for what they are, and acting in a valued direction despite their presence.

20.3 Identifying Common Thinking Styles

Some people find it easier to distance themselves from their thoughts once they understand common thinking styles (see Table 20.1) in BDD and can

Table 20.1: Thinking styles in BDD

Catastrophizing
Jumping to the worst possible conclusion – for example, "someone will notice my scarring and I will be humiliated."

All-or-nothing (black-or-white) thinking
Thinking in extreme, all-or-nothing terms – for example, "I am either very attractive or very ugly."

Over-generalizing
Drawing generalized conclusions – for example, involving the words "always" or "never"– from a specific event – for example, "because my ex rejected me I know I'll never find a partner."

Fortune-telling
Making negative predictions about the future – for example, "I know I'll never get over this"; "I will be unhappy unless my appearance changes"; "If someone saw me without my make-up, they'd be really surprised at how bad I look."

Mind reading
Jumping to conclusions about what other people are thinking about you – for example, "That person is looking at me, I can tell they are noticing my bad skin and thinking I'm disgusting."

Mental filtering
Focusing on the negative and overlooking the positive – for example, paying too much attention in your mind to the one person who was not friendly to you and overlooking the fact that everyone else was very warm towards you; or tending to overlook the positive aspects of yourself and what you have going for you.

Disqualifying the positive
Discounting positive information or twisting a positive into a negative – for example, thinking "That person was only nice to me because they thought I was repulsive and felt sorry for me. They'll probably have a good laugh about me with their friends later."

Labeling
Globally putting yourself down, in an extreme and self-attacking way – for example, "I'm a worthless, hideous alien."

Emotional reasoning
Listening too much to your negative gut feeling instead of looking at the objective facts, e.g., "I know I'm hideous and will end up alone because I feel it deep inside."

Personalizing
Taking an event or someone's behavior too personally or blaming yourself – for example, thinking "That person pushed in front of me when I was trying to get on the train because they think my appearance makes me inferior."

Demands
Rigid "should,""must,""ought," or "have to" rules about your appearance – for example, "I must know just how I look so that I can do whatever I can about it"; "I should always try to look as good as possible"; "I must know that I won't regret dropping my safety behaviors by feeling humiliated that I look worse and have exposed myself to other people."

Low frustration tolerance
Telling yourself that something is "too difficult,""unbearable," or that "I can't stand it," when, though it is hard to bear, it is bearable.

label them as such. As in cognitive therapy for other emotional disorders, this helps people distance their self from their mind and view their thinking as unhelpful (and therefore not really worth listening to) rather than as a fact. For example, if the person has the thought "I'm disgusting," he can then identify the process as a thinking style – "Oh yes, a very good example of labeling." Strategies of distancing and labeling the thinking style do not attempt to alter the content of the intrusive thoughts or images but just to stand back and observe the process. An explicit goal is to develop a different view of one's intrusions to that of "just thoughts" or "just pictures in one's mind," rather than a depiction of reality. One way to communicate this idea is to agree on a metaphor for selectively ignoring information such as:

- a spam filter for e-mails;
- throwing out junk mail unopened;
- ignoring "too good to be true" telesales pitches;
- learning to ignore propaganda on a radio program;
- personifying BDD as a bully or demon, and the thoughts as attempts to hurt or influence.

Another strategy is to help a person see that his thoughts about his appearance are a form of mental bias. A metaphor for this is steering. Ask what he would do if he was driving a car down a straight road, with the steering wheel held straight and he notices that the car is veering to the left. The answer, of course, is that he would steer slightly to the right. This can then lead to a discussion about what the sufferer tends to over-assume (e.g., people are staring at me) and what he then needs to assume (steer) towards to keep his thinking straight (e.g., people aren't really paying much attention to me) even though it is counterintuitive.

20.4   Identifying Assumptions and Core Beliefs

Assumptions and core beliefs about being defective in BDD are discussed in Chapter 4. An example of an assumption is "If I am defective and ugly, I will be alone all my life." An example of a rule in BDD is "I have to look perfect." An example of a core belief is "I am worthless." However, is it necessary to question these assumption and core beliefs in CBT for BDD? In general, we think it is important to keep focused on reducing preoccupation and impairment. Intellectual debate on the importance of appearance or an assumption about being alone all one's life has the danger of increasing preoccupation, since attention is being focused on appearance and yet more time is spent thinking about it and there may be no shift in the strength of conviction. Thus our advice on trying to change appraisals should primarily focus on the beliefs about intrusive thoughts and imagery and the cognitive processes rather than their content. However, we have no empirical evidence, for there are no single-case experimental designs in BDD that compare modifying cognitive processes against content or whether this depends on the severity of the disorder.

Modifying assumptions or core beliefs would not be in keeping with theoretical models from which modifying cognitive and attentional processes are drawn (Martell et al., 2001; Wells, 2009) and the evidence in severe depression. Thus our approach has been to make the therapy more parsimonious and to ignore the credibility of the assumptions, rules, and core beliefs. A question to ask at assessment is: "Would you still hold this (belief, rule or assumption) about your appearance if you believed you looked positively different from your image or felt impression of being ugly?" Most clients report that if they looked different, they would not hold such assumptions. Thus, if the distorted view of the self can be altered by the strategies described in the previous chapters, then the dysfunctional assumptions and rules will fade away.

When might we help question the content of a core belief or assumption about appearance in BDD? In our current lack of knowledge we think it's important to be flexible. Thus, if a client has successfully reduced his effortful cognitive processes (e.g., ruminating, self-focused attention), has done any relevant imagery rescripting, reduced his safety-seeking and avoidance behaviors, and developed alternative and compassionate beliefs about his intrusions, and yet still has dysfunctional assumptions about his appearance, then these are a focus for change. For example, if the beliefs appear to be part of a premorbid personality (i.e., before the onset of BDD), then it suggests vulnerability to BDD (and to relapse in the future). If the assumptions or rules are conceptualized as important in the development of BDD, then it may be helpful to question the beliefs or assumptions on *pragmatic* grounds. Questions might include:

- How helpful for your mental health is it to hold on to this assumption/rule?
- Whilst you continue to hold this assumption/rule, in what direction is it likely to lead you? Is this in keeping with your values and what you want your life to stand for?
- Does following this rule make you more or less vulnerable to relapse and becoming preoccupied and distressed by your appearance in the future?
- Does following this assumption/rule help you adapt to different circumstances in the future?
- Is this a philosophy you would teach your children? If not, why not?

It may also be helpful to do a cost–benefit analysis on the assumption or rule and its alternative (see Appendix 2). This might focus on the costs and benefits to the self and others in both the short term and long term of the old rule/assumption and the new rule/assumption.

Wherever possible, derive testable predictions from targeted assumptions/rules and carry out behavioral experiments. For example, if the target belief is "I'm worthless, I have nothing to offer," then the idea can be tested by developing a testable prediction stemming from that belief (e.g., "If I see my friends, I'll have nothing to say"), then considering an alternative (e.g., "If I talk about the things I'm interested in rather than appearance-related things, then there might be some scope for conversation"). A suitable experiment can be devised, the results noted, and the validity of the belief can then be considered in light of these findings. It's important to remember that your aim is not just to reduce the strength of conviction in an unhelpful belief or assumption, but to increase strength of belief in a more helpful alternative and to help your client act as if it is true (even if he doesn't yet believe it).

20.5   Idealized Values

We assess later in therapy whether an individual still holds an idealized value about the importance of his appearance and the degree to which his feature defines him (see Chapter 13). If a client no longer believes his felt impression to be true yet still believes that his appearance is extremely important and defines his self, then it may be helpful to question the value on pragmatic grounds (as above). In this respect perfectionism and identifying one's self through one's appearance are usually defensive strategies to prevent feared consequences.

The following big "I" and little "i" technique (Figure 20.1) is described by Lazarus (1977) and Dryden (1998) for over-identification of the self with perceived defect(s). Thus individuals with BDD preoccupied by their nose see themselves as a "walking nose" – and that's all they are. The message is that the self is too complex to be identified with just one aspect of one's appearance. At the most, one's features are only one little "i" or one aspect of a person, which even if he rates it negatively cannot be the whole of the self. The therapist might say:

> "You've identified how you regard your feature as defining your identity. Someone else might view their feature(s) as only one aspect of himself, rather than defining him as a person. (For example, you are more than your nose!) Consider the 'big I, little i' illustration. This is one way of showing that each and every one of us is made up of a huge number of parts and that appearance is

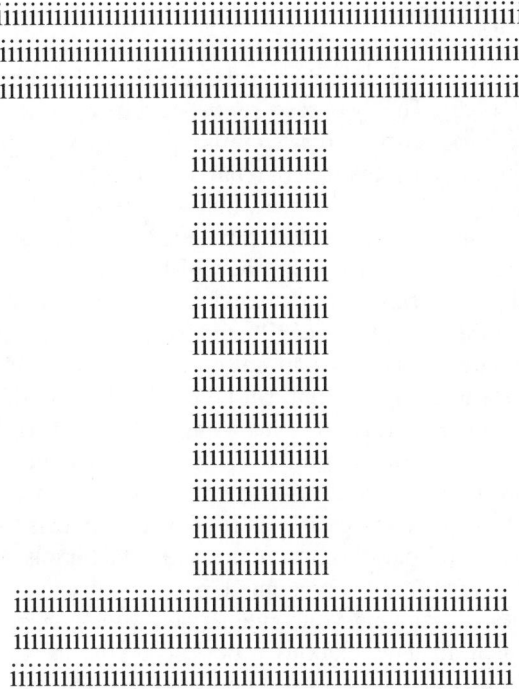

Figure 20.1   Big I, little i

only a part (or even a few parts) of who you are. Thus one little 'i' might be the fact that you used to learn to play the saxophone; a second little 'i' was when you won the 100 meter race when you were 10. Another little 'i' might be your nose, and so on. Human beings are far too complex to be defined by one aspect of their self. Would you define someone else by one aspect of themselves?"

The big "I", little "i" technique can also be used with Post-its to stick on the person:

"Take a pack of large flip chart or sticky notes and a large wall or a door (or another person if they're prepared to help). Write on a note a characteristic that you, as a whole person, possess and stick it on the wall, door, or a volunteer. Keep doing this, trying to think of all aspects of yourself, until you run out of characteristics (or notes). This can be a very memorable illustration of how multifaceted you are."

20.6   Reverse Role-play

Reverse role-play has been described in BDD (Newell & Shrubb 1994; Cromarty & Marks 1995). The two case reports used a reverse role-play in a courtroom as if a barrister was cross-examining a witness. In this scenario the therapist plays the client (in the role of a barrister) and what he believes about his "defect." The client plays a witness being cross-examined and responds with evidence to support the alternative beliefs (even though the client does not believe the alternative). Thus the therapist's role is to present evidence (however ridiculous) that the client's belief is true. Preparation is required in homework before the role-play is conducted. If this approach is used, we recommend using it later in therapy and not on the content or evaluation about appearance (unless it is a belief that can be externally tested, as described in the case reports in the literature). Thus it might be used for beliefs about a cognitive process or an assumption (e.g., "I put it to you that appearance defines you as an individual and if you're not attractive in your appearance, then your life is totally meaningless"). If reverse role-play is used too early in therapy and without preparation, or where self-attacking is prominent, then clients are more likely to be overwhelmed, become very upset, and unable to respond. Imagine role-playing your client's self-attacking beliefs as a bully (e.g., "You are such an ugly, hideous little bitch. You are a worthless piece of —. You should be ashamed for even being born"). This type of role-play is best done by the client playing both parts of the self within the context of compassionate mind training with a focus on understanding the motivation and developing a different relationship with his bully (see Chapter 18).

20.7   Assertive Defense of the Self

Related to the strategy above is a reverse role-play in which clients practice coping with their feared consequences (e.g., being criticized, rejected, or humiliated by a significant other) (Padesky, 1997). Preparation is required to help develop a series of assertive responses and ways of coping. The role-plays are then repeated and extended to criticism between a therapist and client whilst the latter assertively defends himself. Each role-play is debriefed and the therapist and client discuss how his response may have changed to one of irritation rather than shame. The next phase is to practice it *in vivo*. Since this is not something that can occur to order, the client can still imagine that someone is thinking that others are being critical and mentally practicing the assertive response. This can be used in BDD in which a client role-plays responding to humiliation or rejection because of his appearance. Again, this is usually best done later in therapy. This approach is often used for people with disfigurements who may receive unhelpful comments about their appearance from strangers. We are not yet sure whether this strategy might be viewed in BDD as an acknowledgement by you that the client really does have a defect for which he needs to prepare themselves. The rationale needs to be carefully presented so that it is not misinterpreted.

Each of the strategies described above needs further investigation in single case experimental designs so clinicians are able to generalize in terms of what strategy may be helpful in which person at what stage in therapy.

Chapter 21

Habit reversal for psychogenic excoriation

Summary

Chapter 5 provides an overview of psychogenic excoriation and a review of the evidence for the efficacy of pharmacotherapy and cognitive behavior therapy (CBT). This chapter focuses on assessment and the application of CBT in psychogenic excoriation. The assessment includes a functional analysis of psychogenic excoriation before implementing targeted strategies. Much of this chapter draws on the approach described for trichotillomania and repetitive or habit disorders (Azrin & Nunn, 1973; Azrin et al., 1980; Ottens, 1981; Gluhoski, 1995; Mansueto et al., 1999; Rothbaum, 1992).

Sections

21.1 History
21.2 Assessment scales
21.3 Functional analysis
21.4 Self-monitoring
21.5 Identifying and choosing treatment strategies

21.1 History

At the initial assessment, the therapist should take a detailed history and then conduct a functional analysis of the behavior. Suitable questions to ask about the development include:

a)   age of onset of first picking;
b)   age picking first became a problem;

c)   pattern since picking became a problem (e.g., episodic, continuous, static, or deterioration);
d)   associations with onset (e.g., acne);
e)   location on the body for picking and whether this has varied over time;
f)   target of picking (e.g., pimples, scabs, mosquito bites, scars, healthy skin) and whether this has varied over time;
g)   methods used to pick (e.g., fingers or fingernails; scratching; squeezing; razors; picking; digging or lancing with pins; tweezers);
h)   typical times of the day that picking occurs and how long each episode lasts;
i)   permanent physical damage, ulcers or scarring caused;
j)   surgery or consultations with dermatologist and current treatments;
k)   any directly related diagnosis (e.g., BDD, OCD, or borderline personality disorder);
l)   other associated habit disorders (e.g., body rocking, nail biting, thumb sucking, knuckle cracking, cheek chewing, head banging, teeth flicking, lip biting);
m)   the degree to which the person is aware of the cues and behavior during a typical episode. Awareness refers to the ability to recognize the urge or other cues prior to picking, not once the picking has occurred. The excoriation may be categorized as automatic, focused, or a mixture of the two depending on the context. Automatic behaviors are done with little awareness during some other activity and are more like a tic. Focused behaviors are deliberate and preceded by an urge or some degree of planning. It is done in place of any other activity and has more ritualistic features.

21.2   Assessment Scales

There is currently one published rating scale on handicap which is specific to psychogenic excoriation. Keuthen et al. (2001a) have developed a Skin Picking Impact Scale (SPIS), a self-report instrument used to assess the psychosocial consequences of repetitive skin excoriation. In order to develop this scale, an initial 28-item scale was administered to 31 individuals with severe self-injurious skin excoriation and 78 individuals with non-self-injurious skin excoriation. This resulted in a 10-item scale with good internal consistency. The operational criteria for self-injurious behavior were based on client self-report and required both repetitive skin excoriations resulting in significant tissue damage and marked distress or impairment in daily functioning secondary to excoriation. In addition to the SPIS, participants completed the Beck Depression Inventory (BDI) (Beck et al., 1961) and the Beck Anxiety Inventory (BAI) (Beck et al., 1988). SPIS scores for those with psychogenic excoriation were significantly higher than for those with non-psychogenic excoriation.

SPIS scores for those with psychogenic excoriation correlated with duration of daily excoriation, satisfaction during excoriation, and shame subsequent to excoriation, as well as the BDI and BAI scores. Sensitivity and specificity analyses indicate that a scale cut-off score of 7 optimally discriminates individuals with psychogenic excoriation from those with non-psychogenic excoriation. The Skin Picking Scale (Keuthen, et al., 2001b) can also be used as an outcome scale to assess frequency of skin picking urges, time engaged in skin picking, distress, avoidance and handicap associated with picking.

There are additional outcome scales that are relevant for BDD – for example, the Yale-Brown Obsessive Compulsive Scale modified for BDD (see Chapter 13). This may be useful to assess time, distress, handicap associated with picking, the effort used to resist picking, and degree of control over picking.

21.3　Functional Analysis

Conduct a contextual functional analysis of the problem behavior to identify antecedents, behaviors, and consequences. The antecedents are those conditioned stimuli (via classical conditioning) that cue the urge to pick. The behavior may become reinforced via operant conditioning by removing aversive states or by the memory of achieving a desired goal (e.g., smooth skin), thus maintaining the behavior. This understanding will then allow the therapist and client to choose collaboratively an intervention that is more likely to be effective. The client then reports on the helpfulness of the intervention and collects further observations by self-monitoring, and the cycle of functional analysis thus repeats itself. The functional analysis begins with an assessment of the antecedents, a detailed description of the behavior, and the consequences. A version of this analysis can be found in Appendix 1.

Antecedents

Two types of antecedents can be identified: a) cues that trigger the urge to pick; and b) discriminative stimuli that facilitate or inhibit the excoriation.

Cues that trigger the urge to pick may be external (i.e., generated outside the person) or internal (i.e., generated inside the person). External cues include:

a)　Settings (e.g., being alone in the bathroom, putting on make-up, driving, studying, being bullied or teased, before a big event).
b)　Implements (e.g., the presence of a mirror and tweezers).

Internal cues include:

a)　Affective states. Any emotional state can be a trigger for excoriation but the most common are boredom, loneliness, hurt, emptiness, disgust, depression, anger, and anxiety.

b) Visual stimuli (e.g., looking in a mirror and seeing a scab or imperfections or not looking "right").
c) Tactile sensations (e.g., feeling an area that is uneven on one's skin with one's fingers).
d) Physical sensations at the site of skin (e.g., experiencing an itch, irritation, burning under one's skin or pain).
e) Cognitions. Record the content of any intrusive thoughts, rumination, or image prior to excoriation (e.g., "My skin is dirty and disgusting and has pus under it"; "I don't deserve to be rejected, it's unfair"). The intensity of some of the antecedents (e.g., pain, itch, hurt, boredom) can be rated on a simple severity scale and repeated immediately after the picking to determine the reinforcing nature of the consequences.

Discriminative stimuli

The next step is to identify the discriminative stimuli that facilitate or inhibit excoriation. Like cues, facilitators or inhibitors may be internal or external. Facilitators may overlap slightly with cues or chains of events that lead to excoriation and it is best to focus on inhibitors.

External discriminative stimuli include:

a) The absence or presence of other people is more likely to inhibit excoriation.
b) The absence or presence or implements (such as mirrors or tweezers) that are likely to inhibit or usually facilitate excoriation

Internal discriminative stimuli include urges, postures, or cognitions. Certain postures such as holding one hand near one's face may facilitate excoriation. Beliefs that make picking more likely include "I'll pick just this one area" or "I deserve this pick." Emotional states such as a background of increased anxiety may facilitate excoriation.

Behavior

This section requires a detailed description of the actual behavior so that the behavior and the antecedents may be chained. Three stages may be identified in excoriation:

a) Preparatory stage – for example, going to a specific place, securing implements, choosing a site on the body, or conducting a visual or tactile search, for a target area. Cleansing the skin excessively with a variety of soaps or cleansers may also precede it.

b) In the second stage the skin is picked, squeezed, pressed, gouged, lanced, burnt, removed, or possibly examined.

c) The final stage usually involves getting rid of the picked skin and camouflaging the skin with cover-up sticks or make-up.

Consequences

The consequences that either maintain or terminate excoriation should then be identified. Both positive and aversive consequences are possible. The former usually occur immediately, only to be followed by the aversive consequences.

a) Immediate positive consequences – the individual might experience satisfaction at, for example, getting rid of dirt; removing a scab or blackhead; or escape or distraction from negative thoughts or affective states such as boredom. These may be sufficient to terminate the excoriation and fulfill the immediate urge.

b) Unintended aversive consequences might then be involved in terminating excoriation. They include emotional states such as shame, which may act as a trigger to cease excoriation or as cues for further excoriation. Excoriation might also result in bleeding, pain, or discomfort. Alternatively, excoriation may cease because of an interruption by a relative, a scheduled activity, or awareness of the degree of damage that has been caused.

Example of case history of psychogenic excoriation

Mary is a 27-year-old woman with a 14-year history of excoriation. During her teens she began excoriating when she had mild acne which she felt made her unattractive. At presentation she feels ugly because of the damage caused by her excoriation. Below is a functional analysis of her problem.

Antecedents
Cues before the behavior occurs:

a) Setting. Three settings were identified for the picking: in front of a mirror in the bathroom; in the car; and whilst using the computer. Mary would see her image in the bathroom mirror in the morning when putting on make-up, or at night when washing her face and brushing her teeth, or when she came out of the shower or bath. There were other occasions when she would notice her complexion in the mirror but they were not as bothersome as the ones mentioned above. The car mirror was something of a problem, but she would often just feel her face and begin picking even if she was not looking in the mirror. Another setting was when using the computer in the evenings.

b)   Implements. Although she usually picked with her fingernails there were occasions when she used tweezers or a pin.

Internal triggers included:

a)   Emotional states. Any negative emotional state could trigger the picking behavior, however, it was often when she was anxious, worried, bored, or was loathing herself, disgusted with her appearance, feeling hurt or frustrated.

b)   Visual stimuli. A blemish would often serve as a trigger, especially if she noticed it in bright or harsh lighting.

c)   Tactile sensations. Although Mary tried to keep her hands away from her face, she was not successful a lot of the time. She would feel her face for bumps, scabs, blemishes, and pimples and would start picking as soon as she felt one. All of these imperfections made her feel unattractive and thus elicited the picking behavior. There were times when she would pick areas that had not yet healed.

d)   Physical sensations at the site of skin. Picking was cued whenever she felt her skin was greasy or throbbing. She reported that when she was young she used to try to camouflage the spots on her forehead by wearing a hat to school. The hat would make her feel hot and itchy and that would just lead to further rubbing, scratching, and picking of her skin. At the time of the initial assessment she was wearing a hat half the time.

e)   Thoughts. Several thoughts were identified before excorciation. They were as follows: "I must get the pus out, otherwise my skin will be blotchy and ugly"; "My skin must be smooth with small pores"; "Smooth skin, without blemishes makes a person attractive and desirable"; "Everyone notices your face first and if your skin is ugly, you are ugly." Sometimes the thoughts would take over and she would continue to pick, totally out of control, mesmerized, almost in a trance, scratching and squeezing for hours. Even if she stopped for a little while the thoughts would come back and she would start all over again.

f)   Degree of awareness. Mary's awareness fluctuated depending on what activities she was engaging in and the presence or absence of various stimuli. Usually her picking started when she engaged in checking her face and felt a bump. If the pus came out quickly she knew that she was in for a long session in a mesmerized state. She described it as like a shark that smells blood and she feels out of control. She became more aware of her long picking sessions and how she got lost in them when her external world drew her attention to it. For example, she recalled being on a plane or changing room a few times when it was obvious to her that she had left a big red mark on her face and she had been lost in the behavior. Suddenly she had to face people with a bigger scar or imperfection than the one she had started with. However, there are days when her picking behavior is premeditated and she knows she is going to do it. Usually she does it very consciously, typically once or twice a day, and she does a little once over and will squeeze harmlessly at a blackhead or two but gently without damaging her face. Because it is planned and done at a time when she is level-headed usually this is fine – done when she is applying make-up or washing her face. Sometimes it is highly planned and premeditated, for example, when she has felt or seen a big pus-filled spot forming, which immediately makes her feel she has to urgently squeeze it. She will feel very edgy and anxious until she can do so. This will often lead to frenzied picking once she finds a mirror and privacy.

Stimuli that make the behavior easier or harder
Certain situations make it unlikely that Mary will pick. She will only engage in superficial picking in front of family members, sometimes in front of her boyfriend or a very close friend, but this is quite rare. If, mistakenly, she takes it too far, she retreats to her home and hides away from "judgemental eyes." She is very uncomfortable and self-conscious putting make-up on (cover-up) in front of people and finds it very intrusive if a boyfriend, family members, or friends watch her. The absence of tweezers would probably help for the occasions that she might use them, but these are rare. The absence of mirrors and bright lighting helps her to pick less (but does not guarantee it). Another external stimulus is the weather. If it is hot and humid and she is sweaty, her skin gets spottier and so does her urge to squeeze it. In her head her skin in greasy, pus is forming, and her skin is getting out of control. All the above are external stimuli that inhibit or elicit picking behavior. Internal stimuli that control the picking behavior are her posture, beliefs at the time, emotional state, and certain behaviors (e.g., when Mary aimlessly puts her fingers over her skin she is more likely to pick).

If scars are forming she may be able to wait a while for them to heal without picking but if they don't heal fast enough she will resort to picking at the scabs. If she has an appointment she will have more of an urge to pick to get at what she perceives is pus underneath. After a while if she is not able to get satisfaction from taking the pus out she will lose control and pick for a very long time. She feels mesmerized scratching and squeezing for hours until she bleeds and her flesh is raw. She may occasionally use tweezers hoping to squeeze the pus out when she knows it will not happen. She tells herself that the pus may have been pushed inwards, or it is just swelling up in preparation for a spot appearing, but hasn't formed yet. Her desire to squeeze out pus becomes stronger, so she will scan her whole face and squeeze at blackheads and the tiniest imperfection to relieve herself and squeeze out what she can. The worse her face is damaged, the angrier, more scared, and out of control she gets and continues doing it, sometimes for hours. This is all with the knowledge and fear that she is going to have to deal with the consequences in the morning and for the next week. She will not want to face her boyfriend whom she lives with, she will not go to college, shops, gym, or any social event until she has healed. Even at the time of squeezing she is terrified of the scars it may leave.

If it has been an insignificant picking session that hasn't caused much damage she will usually just splash her face with cold water and cover up the spots with make-up and go to bed (so that when her boyfriend gets up in the morning and sees her sleeping he will not be able to see her spots in the darkness). But if she has caused a lot of damage to her face she will usually have a bath and wash her face, usually not with products as it would be too painful, but in water. Then she will apply make-up for hours, in between holding tissue or cloth to her wounds to soak up the fluid, and stop the fluid flowing so that she can apply the make-up powder.

Beliefs

As she is picking she thinks about how her face is ugly with the pus coming through, how her friends have smooth skins and do not have to go through what she goes through, how much she hates her body, her face, how she would be much better off if she had perfect, small pore skin. She thinks that her boyfriend is probably repulsed by her but he is a nice guy and doesn't want to her hurt her feelings. She wants to break up with him but believes no one else would ever want to be with her.

Consequences

There are some positive consequences of picking which maintain the behavior. She derives immediate satisfaction if she has squeezed out a lot of pus, especially if it is a "problem spot." She obtains special satisfaction from squeezing spots that feel very deep and throbbing, originating from a place deep under her skin. (She also experiences special distress when unable to expel this kind of spot.) She has some satisfaction with squeezing surface whiteheads, but not as much. Squeezing blackheads is mildly satisfying as she feels that she is cleaning her face and expelling dirt. Sometimes if the squeezing is straightforward and not messy, and hasn't left any significant damage or red marks, she feels extremely proud that she has managed to clean her face without losing control and hurting herself.

The unintended consequences of the picking behavior are usually a feeling of disgust, shame, embarrassment, depression, social isolation, and inability to engage in college or other activities. Ultimately, what usually stops Mary from picking or squeezing is the inability to continue to squeeze because her face is a mess – bloody and red with numerous areas where she has scratched off several layers of skin and squeezed it very hard. In these cases it is not shame or realization of the damage which stops her. It is simply impossible to squeeze anything else out.

21.4   Self-monitoring

The best evidence for decreasing skin excoriation is habit reversal. The first step in habit reversal is self-monitoring. The rationale for self-monitoring is that an individual a) can increase his awareness of the behavior so that he is better able to resist the urge; b) can, with the therapist, identify different chains of small events that eventually lead to excoriation, this allows the individual to anticipate and identify high-risk situations, and therefore resist excoriation; and c) can monitor whether the intervention is helpful. After the initial assessment, ask your client to keep a frequency chart for at least one or two weeks (see Appendix 2). At this stage, self-monitoring is used for the purpose of assessment and increasing awareness of the sensations on the skin. This may be enhanced by wearing a plaster or false nails on the fingers, for example. This alters the sensations when the fingers touch the skin. If the form is kept accurately, it will give a more valid account of his behavior than that gained during interview. The chart may need to be adapted depending on the information required and the client's time and motivation. There is often a trade-off between choosing to monitor every possible variable and having a more accurate but shorter form. If the picking is extremely frequent, a tally counter or a tick chart may initially be needed for whenever the behavior occurs.

The chart may be used later for increasing awareness of the cues for excoriation and to determine whether an intervention is helpful or not in reducing the frequency of excoriation. The form may later be revised to focus on fewer variables such as the frequency of excoriation. Alternatively, if your client finds that being more anxious is an important trigger to pick, the chart may be adapted to include a column for a relevant variable (e.g., the associated thoughts that are activated).

Wearing gloves may enhance resisting the urge to pick, as well as artificial (acrylic) nails applied over the real nails, or cutting the fingernails short. These strategies may also enhance self-monitoring and awareness training as they alter the sensations on the skin.

It is worth spending time training your client on how to use the form and always ask to see it at the beginning of each session. The history and self-monitoring chart will allow you to determine together the most common cues where he is likely to pick in each modality. Monitoring might cover:

a) times of the day and how long each episode lasts;
b) location – settings or activities before the picking began;
c) strength of urge to pick;
d) degree of awareness;
e) emotion before the picking began;
f) thoughts or images before the picking began;
g) tactile sensations before the picking began;
h) physical sensations at the site of skin before the picking began;
i) area or areas of the body picked;
j) effect of picking on thoughts, feelings, and sensations;
k) effort to resist and what he did to resist.

A form derived form these variables is reproduced in Appendix 2.

Information from the frequency chart can be used to make an episode graph (e.g., the number of times picked against each day). A chain can then be constructed for typical episodes. The rationale is that once a chain (or series of chains) is recognized, it is possible to predict when and where future episodes will occur and it is easier for the individual to make changes to his routine (changing the antecedents) and reduce the frequency of picking or prevent it from occurring by changing the context or chain of events. For example, one component of the chain may be feeling the skin for imperfections which invariably leads to picking. This then becomes an event to monitor to increase awareness of the behavior and then resist when it occurs.

21.5 Identifying and Choosing Treatment Strategies

Having established self-monitoring and conducted a functional analysis, you and your client will be able to consider the most appropriate interventions and when to use them. We shall assume that your client is "ready" to change and there is a mutually agreed goal of stopping excoriation (or at least reducing its frequency) rather than your client just wanting to stop feeling ashamed or socially anxious about his excoriation. Note, however, that shame about excoriation may interfere in engagement with therapy. If your client is not "ready" to change, then you may need to return to the Chapter 14 on engagement and reducing stigma. The emphasis here will be on motivational interviewing and a focus on the disadvantages of excoriation or reasons not to excoriate.

Dermatological opinion should be sought if the skin is inflamed and damaged. Topical anti-inflammatory creams (e.g., hydrocortisone) or Eurax cream (hydrocortisone and crotamiton) can help to decrease the itching. Dry skin should be moisturized regularly (e.g., with Eucerin).

Different strategies have been described for psychogenic excoriation but there are no controlled trials or component analyses to determine the most effective ones. We think a long-term strategy is important as many clients have a lifetime habit to alter. In the absence of any controlled trials on psychogenic excoriation the therapist and client will have to choose the most appropriate strategy acceptable to the client's presentation. This will be based on the formulation and comorbidity (e.g., presence of BDD). The most common strategies are self-monitoring followed by habit reversal and stimulus control strategies.

Habit reversal

Habit reversal (or competing response training) is a core strategy which consists of a number of steps:

a) Identifying a competing response that is incompatible with excoriation (e.g., clenching the fist; knitting; squeezing a Koosh ball; extending the arm behind the body; sitting on the hand). Azrin & Nunn (1973) suggested that a competing response should be incompatible with the habit; maintained for a minute or more without appearing unusual to others; not interfere with normal activities; and raise awareness that the habit is not occurring. Try to identify the muscle groups that are involved in the behavior (i.e., picking, scratching, or holding tweezers) and then train the individual to tighten the opposite muscle groups.

b) Practicing the competing response, which should be held for at least one minute until the urge to pick subsides. It should be commenced as soon as the person is aware of the urge to pick. If the individual starts to pick, he should be instructed to use the competing response to interrupt the excoriation or use it after excoriation has terminated. If the urge persists, then the competing response should be repeated. The person may be asked to practice the competing response in their imagination ("symbolic rehearsal") and do it *in vivo* several times a day when there is no urge to pick so that eventually it becomes automatic and part of his normal routine.

Habit reversal practice should be monitored by the client to record whether he used the competing response before, during, or after an episode of excoriation or when there was no urge to pick (see Appendix 2). It is worth emphasizing that the success of the technique cannot at first be measured in terms of a reduction in the frequency of excoriation but as to whether they are using the competing response (even if it is after picking). This is important, as clients will often give up before reaching their goal. In addition, some may find it helpful to delay the response: the individual should select 10 activities to conduct before they pick, such as exercising, making a phone call, logging onto the Internet.

Stimulus control

These include strategies that alter the antecedents or environment to block the habit or decrease the opportunity to pick and minimize the time spent in high-risk areas. The individual is asked to try to disrupt the chain of events in his or her daily routines that lead to excoriation. This might mean altering the settings in which a person picks to disrupt the opportunity and reduce the time spent in high-risk areas. For example, he could:

- Remove or temporarily cover mirrors (especially magnifying mirrors) or bright lights.
- Wear dark or tinted glasses when around mirrors.
- Remove any glasses or contact lenses before looking in a mirror.
- Give the equipment used for picking to a significant other or throw it away.
- Switch grooming and applying make-up to times of the day when there is less risk.
- Stay out of certain high-risk rooms (e.g., bathroom) or find an alternative.
- Tell significant other(s) about the picking and allow them to point out when they pick.
- Reduce time spent alone and use a different routine.
- Use plasters and petroleum jelly or antibiotic ointment on scabs and skin to aid healing.
- Minimize time spent alone and go to bed at the same time as one's partner.
- Not touch the skin unless as an agreed activity.
- Wear bandages on the fingers used for excoriation.
- Wear white cotton dermatological gloves in bed or other high-risk areas.
- Keep nails trimmed and smooth.

- Wear jangling bracelets to become aware if one's hand is going to pick.
- Put heavy moisturizing cream to make it difficult to pick (as the fingers slide).

Acceptance and mindfulness

Acknowledgement and acceptance of the intrusive thoughts, emotion, and urges without engaging with them are described in Chapter 18 (Hayes et al., 1999). If shame acts as a cue, try to separate the behavior from the identity of the individual (excoriation is just one aspect of his self) and use compassionate mind training (see Chapter 18).

Covert sensitization

This involves pairing the thought or urge to pick with an image of consequences of excoriation that is relevant to the individual (e.g., a partner interrupting the person picking). This approach should not be used with someone who has very low self-esteem as it may lead to an increase in shame.

Affective strategies

Relaxation
Various strategies can be used for relaxation and help reduce arousal, such as meditation, exercise, taking a warm bath, progressive muscular relaxation, or diaphragmatic breathing. It is usually helpful for individuals to practice relaxing and breathing with the diaphragm when the urge occurs before applying the competing response (see below). O'Connor (2005) has developed a treatment manual for tic disorders with a particular emphasis on tension reduction.

Exposure (and response prevention)
Imaginary and *in vivo* exposure to the stimulus for excoriation and behavioral experiments may be relevant when there is marked avoidance and social anxiety. One can enhance the "defects" on the skin using make-up to make the skin look uneven, or create blemishes, red marks or spots, blackheads and imperfections during the session. A behavioral experiment can then be conducted to test the theory that others do not respond to them any differently and, even if they do, the client can cope. If the exposure is too difficult, you might do this exercise either in imagination or recorded on audiotape.

Cue exposure can be graded to the chain of events where excoriation normally occurs. This would begin in low-risk situations for short periods of time (up to five minutes), gradually increasing the time and location resulting in high-risk situations.

Additional sensory strategies

a) Distraction (this include strategies to be done when the urge occurs):
   - Having a bath or shower (possibly cold).
   - Applying an ice pack, especially if there are itching or burning sensations.
   - Massaging the skin or applying a facial mask.
b) Substitution (this is aimed at providing, replacing, or increasing stimulation in the fingers. These strategies seem to be less relevant in skin excoriation compared to trichotillomania):
   - Knitting, crocheting, embroidery, sewing.
   - Playing a musical instrument or taking lessons.
   - Stroking or massaging a pet.
   - Playing with Silly Putty or hand-sized sacks (Koosh balls).
   - Popping the bubbles on bubble-wrap.
   - Playing with worry beads.
   - Playing video games that require the use of both hands on a controller.
   - Nibbling food (e.g., sunflower seeds) in high-risk situations.
   - Taking a steam bath (e.g., to provide a feeling that impurities are being removed from the face).
c) Extinction (prolonged sensory exposure on fingers using any of the above methods).

Additional environmental strategies

These include strategies that disrupt the chain of events in daily routines that lead to excoriation. Contingency management describes altering the consequences to decrease the likelihood of excoriation. This consists of rewards and response costs ("penalties"). Rewards and penalties are best provided immediately after success of fully resisting an urge to pick and should be individually tailored. A response cost should generally be used as a last resort and imposed with caution as you don't want to shame your client. Examples of response costs are:

a) Enlarging a photo of the area of excoriation taken at its worst and when it looks at its best and kept by the most common locations for excoriation.
b) Using a cue card – writing down on a card the consequences of excoriation which is readily available to read in locations where the person is likely to pick.
c) Post "high-risk area" signs at the bathroom door and other areas associated with excoriation.

d) Doing 10 press-ups or sit-ups (or a cost that is relevant to the individual) with every pick.

e) As an *extremely* last resort in clients who are not responding to other strategies, you might suggest that your client agrees a maximum number of picks during a week and, if this is exceeded, for him to write a cheque for an agreed amount to send to his most hated organization at the end of week.

The strategies employed should be reviewed weekly with the self-monitoring chart to determine if the frequency has altered. Standard relapse prevention involves trying to identify situations or activities which are riskier. The individual can then prepare for setbacks by having a plan to implement immediately they occur. Emphasis is placed on developing other activities in life and following one's valued direction in life.

Chapter 22

Behavioral activation for depression in BDD

Summary

Depression is the most frequent comorbid diagnosis in BDD. It needs to be treated concurrently with BDD to optimize progress, since a low mood will increase the frequency and intensity of appearance-related negative thoughts and memories. If left untreated, depression can interfere in treatment motivation and the ability to adhere to homework for overcoming BDD. Anti-depressant medication (specifically SSRIs or clomipramine) may help. Standard cognitive therapy (CT) is an effective psychological treatment for depression. However CT may focus on challenging thoughts and core beliefs (e.g., beliefs about being ugly and being alone all one's life) and this is usually unhelpful in BDD. Moreover, a recent component analysis of CT for depression suggests that challenging automatic thoughts or schemata are unnecessary and that activity scheduling is just as effective and a more appropriate treatment (Cuijpers et al., 2007). Activity scheduling has been further developed into a formal therapy: behavioral activation (BA). One large controlled trial found that BA is as effective as an anti-depressant and more effective than CBT in severe depression (Dimidjian et al., 2006). In our experience, BA can be readily incorporated into the treatment of BDD, since it also emphasizes doing what one is avoiding, engaging with the outside world, and reducing ruminations. This chapter therefore gives a brief introduction to BA. The reader is encouraged to consult the treatment manual (Martell et al., 2001), and textbooks (Veale & Willson, 2007; Kanter et al., 2009).

Sections

Body Dysmorphic Disorder: A Treatment Manual. David Veale and Fugen Neziroglu
© 2010 John Wiley & Sons, Ltd.

22.1   Background

Depression is the most common comorbid condition in BDD and is commonly secondary to BDD where:

a) The client describes BDD as his biggest problem.
b) The symptoms of depression developed after the onset of the BDD.
c) The person predicts that the symptoms of depression will improve if the BDD is effectively treated.
d) Symptoms of BDD drive depression in the formulation (e.g., avoidance makes daily life much less pleasurable and he misses out on positive experiences in life).

Very occasionally clients have a bipolar disorder or recurrent depression in which BDD is a symptom of their depression; when the depression is treated their BDD improves. In Chapter 13, we recommended you used the "magic wand" question to try to ascertain whether symptoms of depression are secondary to their symptoms of BDD.

Symptoms of depression are closely linked with BDD. Rumination ("brooding" or "mulling things over in one's mind") is both a key feature in depression and fuels preoccupation in BDD. It helps to consider that depressive rumination is usually focused on the past, whereas anxious worry is typically focused on the future. For example, a person preoccupied with his nose may feel depressed when he looks back and thinks "If only I hadn't had that second nose job" and anxious when he thinks "What if I let people see me in bright light." The important thing here from the perspective of BDD maintenance is that both thinking processes fuel preoccupation because they mean more time is spent thinking about the perceived flaw in his appearance.

Over three decades ago, Ferster (1973) developed a model of depression based on learning theory: it stated that when people become depressed, many of their activities function as avoidance and escape from aversive conditions (from thoughts and feelings or from external situations). Depression therefore occurs when a person develops a narrow repertoire of behaving passively and efficiently avoids aversive stimuli. As a consequence, someone with depression engages less frequently in pleasant or satisfying activities and obtains less positive reinforcement than individuals without depression. Lewinsohn et al. (1976) developed the first behavioral treatment of depression, in which clients increased the number of pleasant activities and positive interactions with their social environment. Several promising trials were conducted but these were forgotten with the emergence of cognitive therapy (CT) in the 1980s. Although CT incorporated activity scheduling, an important dismantling study was conducted by Jacobson et al. (1996). They randomized depressed clients to three groups (N = 150): a) activity scheduling; b) activity scheduling plus cognitive challenges on automatic thoughts; and c) activity scheduling plus cognitive challenges to automatic thoughts and core beliefs and assumptions. They found no statistically or clinically significant differences between the groups and concluded that the cognitive component was redundant. These results remained after a two-year follow-up (Gortner et al., 1998). Cuijpers et al. (2007) have more recently conducted a meta-analysis of activity scheduling involving 16 studies and 780 subjects. They found no difference in the effect size between activity scheduling and CT in the treatment of depression in adults. Activity scheduling has also been used with success in dementia patients after training their caregivers (Teri et al., 1997) as well as in depressed inpatients (Hopko et al., 2003). Longmore & Worrell (2007) have reviewed the literature on the necessity to challenge the content of thoughts. They found little evidence that trying to challenge cognitive content significantly increased the effectiveness of therapy and little empirical support for the role of cognitive change as causal in the symptomatic improvements achieved in CT. The review did not, however, include some of the more recent studies in anxiety disorders, which have found CT to enhance graded exposure and response prevention.

Behavioral activation (BA) is a development of activity scheduling by Martell et al. (2001). BA has now been compared in a large RCT against standard CBT, against an anti-depressant (paroxetine), and against a placebo for depression in outpatients (N = 241) (Dimidjian et al., 2006). There was a maximum of 24 50-minute sessions over 16 weeks. There were measures of depression, therapist adherence and competence, response, and remission. BA focuses on a) activities that are being avoided as a guide for activity scheduling, and b) functional analysis on avoidance behaviors and cognitive processes such as rumination. BA was found to be comparable to paroxetine and more efficacious than CBT among more severely depressed participants. Compared to paroxetine, BA brought a greater percentage of patients to remission and retained a greater percentage in treatment. BA, therefore, has important implications for stepped care from the delivery of low-intensity treatments in mild to moderate depression in the community up to more intensive treatments in severely depressed day-patients and inpatients. The advantage of BA over traditional CBT for depression is that it is generally easier to train staff in BA; and it may have greater efficacy in severe depression. The advantage of BA over an anti-depressant is that it may be more acceptable and cost-effective in the long term.

BA may be unpopular with some clients and therapists because it lacks the complexity of other psychotherapies (e.g., challenging the core beliefs and schemata in CT or discovering unconscious conflicts). For some, BA is associated with rewards and punishments or a therapist who is cold and unresponsive. Others may think it is relevant only for straightforward cases. The principles may be relatively simple but it is still hard for clients to do. Like any psychotherapy, BA needs to be delivered in the context of a good therapeutic relationship in which a client feels understood and has a good rationale. However, complex problems often require a therapist to carry out simple principles well, rather than undertaking ever more complex ones.

It's not very surprising in BDD that there is high level of comorbidity with major depressive episode, dysthymia, or at least severe demoralization. BDD clients have significant avoidance behavior and have many deficits in their life. They have lost opportunities in their occupation or education, are single or separated, have discord in relationships, or have few close friends. There are frequent interpersonal conflicts with others who do not understand or agree with their perception of the problem. They are frequently ruminating on these issues and on their ugliness and defect. BA fits well in the treatment of depression and BDD although we do not have the data from a randomized controlled trial yet to support this. The main aim is to help clients to use approach behaviors rather than avoidance and to become active in spite of how they appear to others or lack motivation. BA overlaps with acceptance and commitment therapy (ACT) in that the individuals are encouraged to engage in behaviors they value and make a commitment to experience aversive emotions.

22.2   Theory and Rationale

A detailed rationale and treatment protocol of BA can be found in Martell et al. (2001) and in textbooks (e.g., Kanter et al., 2009). Clients should be provided with a clear rationale for BA, which is grounded in learning theory and contextual functionalism. BA is not about scheduling pleasant or satisfying events (as in the first stage of CT). It does not focus on an internal cause of depression, such as a person's thoughts or internal conflicts. The focus is on the whole event and variables that may influence the occurrence of unhelpful responses (these include both overt behavior and cognitive processes). Contextualism takes a pragmatic approach, being interested in what predicts and maintains an unhelpful response by various reinforcers and allows clients to reach their goals.

The therapist gives clients a positive explanation for their symptoms and seeks feedback to illustrate how their solutions are the problem, which are maintaining their distress and handicap. Thus a client might be told that his depression is highly understandable given the context in which he finds himself (e.g., feeling very isolated and frequent conflicts in a relationship). Furthermore, the experience of depression is regarded as a consequence of avoiding or escaping from aversive thoughts or feelings. It is emphasized that this is an entirely understandable and natural response. Clients are taught how to conduct functional analyses on their ways of responding, including inactivity and ruminating (e.g., trying to find reasons for the past or attempting to solve unsolvable problems.) The effect of such coping is that a person becomes withdrawn and avoids both his normal activities and social interaction. This

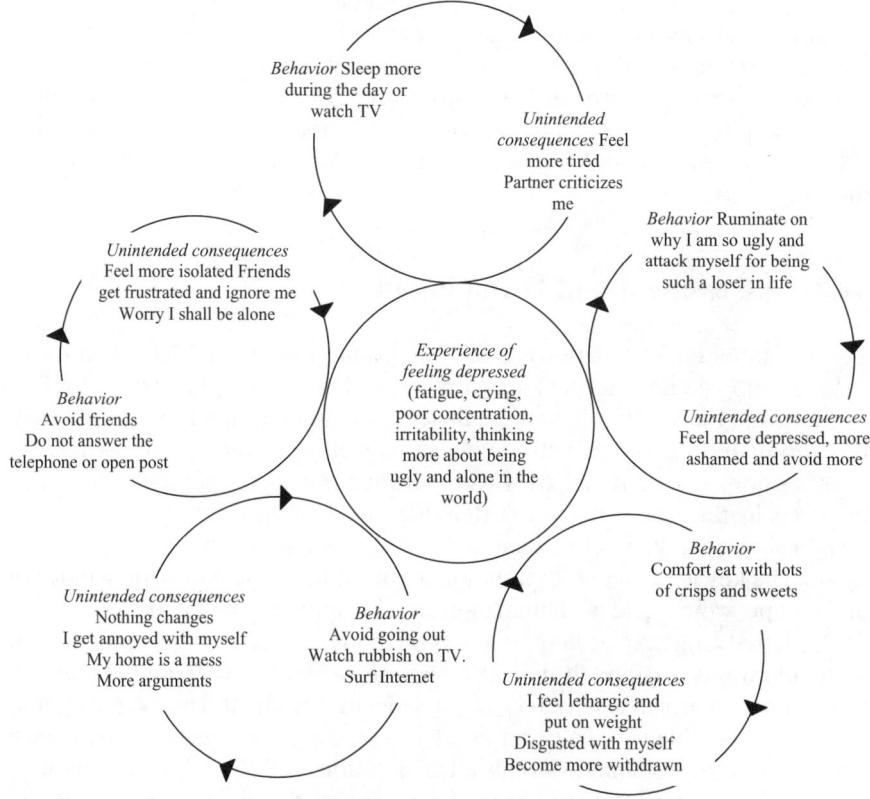

Figure 22.1 Formulation for depression

in turn leads him to become more depressed, to ruminate more, and to miss out on experiences in life that normally bring satisfaction or pleasure. Furthermore, the way a person acts has an effect on others and the environment which may then aggravate the depression. This is highlighted in Figure 22.1 with a formulation of a man who was virtually housebound and was avoiding making any decisions. Here depression is regarded as a consequence of avoiding or escaping from aversive thoughts or images about being ugly, about being a failure, or feelings of shame. Avoidance led to low levels of positive reinforcement and a narrowing of his normal repertoires.

Figure 22.1 highlights the various secondary coping strategies that were maintaining the experience of being depressed. This is shown diagrammatically as a vicious flower with a series of circles (petals) that describe the response to feeling ashamed and the unintended consequences. These include the effect on his partner and on friends who were either critical of his way of coping or had given up on him and lost contact. Secondary coping behaviors are targeted in BA on all types of depression, especially when a person is unaware of any precipitating factor, or in chronic depression when there is no obvious onset. BA aims to break off each of these "petals" and help the person to use approach behaviors rather than avoidance and become active in spite of negative feelings or lack of motivation (Veale & Willson, 2007). Experiential avoidance is viewed as understandable but unhelpful in the long term.

22.3   Assessment and Formulation

A developmental formulation is made but the emphasis is on the social context, such as being alone, interpersonal conflict, and loss of employment or ability to study, and the way in which these factors have led the client to cope. Clearly, this formulation overlaps with a conceptualization of the person's BDD. In each session, the therapist tries to determine which contextual factors are involved in the way a person is thinking and feeling and how that person responds to whatever factors seem to be assisting in maintaining his depressed mood. The key issue in the formulation is determining the nature of avoidance and escape, which guides planning alternative approach behaviors.

An activity log may be kept to assess the pattern of responding and the link with alterations in mood. It may also be used to assess the breadth or restriction of activity, which can then be discussed with the client. The Cognitive and Behavioral Avoidance Scale can assist in assessing the degree of avoidance across different domains (Ottenbreit & Dobson, 2004), and again this may need to be interpreted in the light of a person's appearance concerns. Being socially withdrawn and not answering the telephone are obvious examples of avoidance of social activity. However, avoidance may also occur in non-social

Table 22.1: Example of a contextual functional analysis in a client who has BDD and comorbid depression

---

A) Antecedents (or context of an event): In what situations in the past have you thought that you were ugly and feel alone?

B) Behavior in response (includes cognitive processes): What do you do next when you think you are ugly and feel alone? Does your way of responding include a pattern of avoiding (e.g., staying home, not answering the phone, lying down and ruminating)? Or does it involve doing an excessive behavior (e.g., drinking or spending all day surfing the Internet)?

C) Immediate consequences: What immediate effect does this activity have? Does it make you feel comfortable? Does it mean you can stop thinking about being something more painful?
Unintended consequences: What unintended effects does this activity have? Does it make you feel more hopeless, tired or depressed? What effect does this activity have on others? Do others get annoyed and critical?

D) Valued directions: What alternatives can you choose to do that are in keeping with your goals and valued directions?

E) Effect of following valued direction: What effect did following your goal or valued direction have?

---

situations (e.g., not doing any challenging tasks such as filling out forms, being inactive, or spending excessive time in bed). There is also cognitive avoidance (e.g., not thinking about problems in relationships with a partner; not making decisions about the future; not taking opportunities; not being serious about work or education). There are also many activities when done in excess that *function* as avoidance of an aversive state (e.g., watching rubbish on television, playing computer games, gambling, comfort eating, excessive exercise). To this list might be added use of alcohol and other substances that function as emotional avoidance. Any of these activities may be subject to a contextual functional analysis (see Table 22.1) and clients are trained in how to conduct their own analysis of their way of coping in any situation to determine if it is unhelpful and what is being avoided. Clients are shown that they do have a choice; even if they choose to use avoidance, they should monitor its effect on their mood. They can then conduct a behavioral experiment to compare the effect of avoiding and ruminating with approach behaviors (e.g., on alternate days) and record the effect on their mood and distress.

22.4 Goals and Values

All clients should have clearly defined goals in the short, medium and long term, which are related to their avoidance and can be incorporated into activity scheduling and regularly monitored. Sometimes there will be competing goals, which will be met only some of the time. Goals should include a return to work and social activity as soon as possible. For those who have been out of work for a long time, this may be graded from working short hours in a voluntary capacity or retraining. An influence of ACT (Hayes et al., 1999) is to identify clients' valued directions and what they want their life to stand for. The content of their activity schedule can then be focused not only on what they are avoiding, but also on what is important to them (these often overlap). The Valued Living Questionnaire has various prompts for different types of values, or "areas," for clients to write down a brief statement. Clients should be warned not to follow values they think they should have because others will approve of them. Values are not goals – they are more like a compass – and must be lived out by committed action. Thus getting married is a goal, but with values, you never reach your destination as there is always something more you can do to be a good partner. If a valued direction in life is to be a good parent, then the first goal for depressed clients might be spending an hour with their children, playing, reading, or talking.

22.5   Structure

Like CBT, a typical session is structured with one or two items on the agenda; to review the homework; to progress towards the goals; and to request feedback on the session. Homework is more likely to be carried out if a client is actively engaged in setting it and if there are set times or places when and where it will be carried out. The sessions are collaborative and the client is expected to be active and to try to generate solutions. Like CBT, BA is not didactic but takes the form of a Socratic dialogue. Sessions are best video- or audiotaped for the client to listen to again and for therapist supervision.

The context of the relationship with the therapist is also important. Functional analytic psychotherapy is an extension of BA. It brings learning theory into the therapeutic relationship and shows how it may enhance change towards goals (Kohlenberg et al., 2004). It draws the client's attention to what he is thinking, feeling, and *doing* in the moment with the therapist or the therapeutic relationship. The therapist would identify relevant behaviors within the session that are examples of the client's problems, which the therapist's behavior is contingent to decreasing. An example is a client who may be passive and avoiding discussing difficult issues in therapy. The therapist may then prompt and reinforce naturally assertive and approach behaviors that are consistent with the goals. The effect of the therapist's behavior on the client is observed and the reinforcement adjusted as necessary. Natural reinforcers by the therapist could include disclosing personal reactions and showing care and empathy in the moment (Kanter et al., 2009).

22.6   Activity Scheduling

The core of BA is to gradually approach the activities or problems that are avoided and to add instances of the client's valued directions into a planned timetable. Clients are encouraged to start with their short-term goals and act as if they have a series of appointments with themselves. A major mistake is for clients to focus on all the things they think they should be doing. The aim is to introduce small changes building up the level of activity gradually towards their long-term goals. The aim is not to fill the day with activity for activity's sake. The activities chosen need to relate to what they have been avoiding and help them to act in their valued directions in life. However, it is not all hard work and clients are encouraged to reward themselves with some activities that are soothing and pleasurable. Clients should monitor the effect of their scheduled activities (and deviations from their plan) and evaluate the effect on their mood and whether this was in keeping with their goals and valued directions in life. Clients are encouraged to monitor, and the therapist should assess, areas the clients are avoiding, or activities that are being overused to avoid problematic or painful thoughts and feelings. The therapist might use role-play to practice some activities during a session or to assist with problem-solving.

The most common obstacles to BA are avoiding situations. These arise when a person's mind tells him that he needs to engage in a particular activity that he finds difficult or uncomfortable only when he becomes motivated or feels like it. The solution is always to act according to the person's plan – not according to how he feels. Clients are told that the longer they wait, the greater the chance they will become even less motivated; the solution is to start doing a task in an unmotivated way. "Just doing it" leads to differences in the way a person thinks and feels, which increases motivation and changes the way others view the client.

22.7   The Role of Cognition in BA

In BA, therapists do not tend to become engaged in the content of thinking but use functional analysis to focus on the context and process of their response. Thus if a client believes he is ugly, the therapist would conduct a functional analysis of the context in which it occurs and what he does in response (see Table 22.1).

Cognitive *processes* such as rumination, fusion, and self-attacking are forms of responses in BA. Rumination is characterized by the client trying to answer questions that cannot be answered or looking for reasons for why he is depressed or fantasizing ("If only I'd found a way to make him different") or self-pity ("What have I done to deserve to be treated this way?"). Other clients with chronic depression and low self-esteem may attack themselves verbally (e.g., "You fat, useless piece of —") or frequently compare themselves to others. All these activities serve to avoid aversive conditions like silence or provide escape from thinking about interpersonal problems or feelings. The therapist encourages the client to be aware of the context (the antecedents) in which ruminating or self-attacking occurs and the consequences of engaging in the process of ruminating, comparing, or self-attacking. The consequences usually involve some form of avoidance and non-goal-directed activity. Clients are helped to turn "Why" or "If only'-type questions into "How"-type questions that relate to reaching their goals and which can be incorporated into activity schedules and "doing," despite what one's mind might be saying.

The process of cognitive fusion relates to the ways in which thoughts, images, and memories from the past become fused with current experience and information about the world is obtained from one's internal reality. Clients are taught to become more aware of their surroundings and to see events for what they are, rather than what their mind is telling them. This process is akin to detached mindfulness and involves separating the thought of an event from the experience of an event. Clients are taught to distance themselves from thoughts and no longer to engage with or "buy into" them. A metaphor for thoughts and urges is of traffic on the road. If one engages with the thoughts or images then one might stand in the road and try to divert the cars (and get run over) or try to get into a car and find a parking space for it. However, even when a person has managed to divert or to park one car there are always more to be dealt with. The goal is to acknowledge the thoughts but not to attempt to stop, control, or answer them. The aim is to accept fully aversive thoughts and to walk along the side of the road – for example, in a conversation with a friend or playing in the park – and to engage with life despite the traffic, which one can simply ignore.

22.8   Suicide

A key concern with more severely depressed BDD sufferer is suicide. Chapter 1 highlights how individuals with BDD have a relatively high rate of suicide compared with clients with OCD. In our experience clients who blame themselves for the flaw in their appearance may be particularly at risk. One young man took his life because believed he had damaged his nose by pressing it repeatedly with his hand. He believed that he could never forgive himself and that he had completely ruined his life and – because nobody could agree that there was a problem with his nose – no one could help him. Another at-risk group are people who have high expectations from surgery and after it fails, feel hopeless as they believe there is no other solution. For example, a woman with BDD was dissatisfied with the result of her cosmetic surgery. She felt her eyes looked worse and spent a lot of time ruminating on "If only I'd seen the cosmetic surgeon my friend had recommended." She felt that she had wasted her only chance of happiness and had burdened herself with significant debt only to be disappointed with the surgery she thought would transform her life. As a consequence she became depressed, hopeless, and made plans to kill herself. Suicide is regarded in BA as the ultimate form of escape and avoidance of aversive thoughts and emotions. It goes without saying that risk assessments should be made regularly and, when suicide intent is strong, priority must be given to increase a sense of hope and ensure safety. The emphasis is on providing an alternative explanation for the experience of BDD and testing it out.

22.9   Anti-depressant Medication

Anti-depressant medication may assist in treating depression in the context of BDD. Pharmacotherapy of depression comorbid with BDD is likely to have a similar response to OCD. Potent or selective serotonin reuptake inhibitors (SSRIs) are more effective than noradrenergic reuptake inhibitors (NRIs) in treating depression in OCD (Hoehn-Saric et al., 2000). If two or more SSRIs are ineffective, then augmenting the SSRI with an NRI may be helpful for depressive symptoms (Mancini et al., 2002). Medication for BDD is discussed in more detail in Chapter 23.

Chapter 23

Pharmacotherapy

Summary

For adults or adolescents with BDD (including those with an additional diagnosis of a delusional disorder), a selective serotonin reuptake inhibitor (SSRI) should be offered as the initial pharmacological treatment. The highest tolerated dose should be prescribed unless a lower dose is effective. The duration should be for a minimum of 12 weeks. If there is no response to one SSRI, then an alternative SSRI may be offered. If there is no or only a partial response to at least two SSRIs, then clomipramine can be offered. If there is no response or only a partial response to an SSRI or clomipramine, then an augmentation strategy may be offered. These include clomipramine combined with an SSRI (especially citalopram or escitalopram), and buspirone combined with an SRI. Pimozide or other anti-psychotics should not be used as monotherapy or as an augmentation strategy in BDD with or without delusional disorder. Anti-psychotics in a low dose might theoretically be of benefit in certain symptoms – for example, when a patient is significantly agitated or if there is psychogenic excoriation. D-cycloserine has shown some efficacy in enhancing CBT for OCD, social anxiety, and other anxiety disorders (Wilhelm et al., 2008) and might justifiably used in treatment of refractory BDD.

Sections

Body Dysmorphic Disorder: A Treatment Manual. David Veale and Fugen Neziroglu
© 2010 John Wiley & Sons, Ltd.

23.1 Adults with BDD

The following guidelines are drawn from the evidence described in Chapter 12, and follows the NICE guidelines on Obsessive Compulsive Disorder (OCD) and Body Dysmorphic Disorder (BDD) (National Collaborating Centre on Mental Health, 2004) and expert opinion (Phillips, 2002). It is recognized that the guidelines are not underpinned by a strong evidence base. There are only three RCTs on which to base the recommendations, and there may be concerns about the generalizability of patient samples. No medications are licensed for BDD and the following guidelines are therefore the best available evidence.

Adults with BDD may be offered an SSRI as an initial pharmacological treatment in moderate to severe BDD. Note that an SSRI is also the initial pharmacological treatment for BDD with an additional diagnosis of a delusional disorder. An SSRI is preferred to clomipramine as it is usually better tolerated and is safer in an overdose. SSRIs are also recommended for the pharmacological treatment of other anxiety disorders and depression or bulimia and it is therefore not specific to BDD. For most adults with BDD, any SSRI can be used, but a clinician might want initially to choose fluoxetine since this has an evidence base from one RCT and it is the most cost-effective. However, from the evidence of open label trials, SSRIs are likely to be equally effective as a class and any SSRI could be offered. A different SSRI is indicated if there has been a previous response to that SSRI, patient preference for another SSRI, or sensitivity to fluoxetine.

23.2 Children and Adolescents with BDD

Fluoxetine is the recommended SSRI for a child or adolescent with BDD (based on the evidence in adults and because fluoxetine appears to be the safest SSRI for adolescents with depression). There is one RCT on fluoxetine in adolescents in progress in the USA that may enlighten these recommendations. At present any SSRI prescribed for children and adolescents should be monitored closely by a psychiatrist because of the lack of information on its long-term use in adolescents.

Table 23.1: Serotonin reuptake inhibitors used in BDD

Chemical name	Usual starting dose	Target dose	Liquid Preparation
Citalopram	20 mg	50 mg	Yes
Clomipramine	50 mg	225 mg	Yes
Escitalopram	10 mg	30 mg	Yes
Fluoxetine	20 mg	60 mg	Yes
Fluvoxamine	50 mg	200 mg	No
Paroxetine	20 mg	40 mg	Yes
Sertraline	50 mg	200 mg	No

23.3 Dose

No evidence exists on the optimal dose of an SSRI in BDD but expert opinion is that SSRIs in BDD may have a dose–response relationship similar to OCD. Therefore, the highest tolerated dose (at least up to the maximum recommended for OCD) should be offered unless a lower dose is effective (see Table 23.1). Expert opinion is that high doses of an SSRI are often needed to treat BDD effectively and the most common reason for failure of an SSRI is that too low a dose was prescribed. The dose can usually be increased to the maximum recommended once a week (or two weeks for fluoxetine) and wait for at least three weeks before increasing. However, if the patient does respond at a higher dose, you may not then know whether there is a response at a lower dose.

23.4 Duration

No evidence exists on the optimal duration of a trial of an SSRI but expert opinion suggests that a minimum of 12–16 weeks and at least three weeks at the maximum tolerated dose should be used to determine efficacy. Patients should be cautioned that any response may only occur gradually and that the most common reason for a poor response is not being on a high enough dose for long enough.

23.5 Failure of Response to an SSRI

Most of the following is based on expert opinion as there are no RCTs to guide treatment after failure of response to an SSRI (Phillips, 2002). If there is no or poor response to one SSRI, then one should try switching to an alternative SSRI as any one may be more effective in a given individual. The SSRI should again be given at the highest tolerated dose (unless a lower dose is effective) for a further 12–16 weeks. Alternatively, some individuals who have made only a partial response to an SSRI and who are tolerating an SSRI may benefit from a dose that exceeds the maximum recommended by the manufacturer (e.g., citalopram or paroxetine 80–100 mg or 100 mg of fluoxetine). There is a theoretical risk of serotonergic syndrome at a higher dose and patients should be monitored.

If there is no or only a partial response to *at least* two and preferably three SSRIs, clomipramine can be offered for the maximum tolerated dose (unless a lower dose is effective) for a minimum of 12 weeks. Oral clomipramine should not normally be increased above 250 mg because of increasing anticholinergic side-effects and the risk of seizure. Caution should be taken for slow metabolizers or those who may overdose, and an ECG is required. At higher doses, serum levels of clomipramine should be monitored to determine the optimum safest dose. If an individual is unable to tolerate oral clomipramine, intravenous clomipramine pulse loading may be offered (this option is rarely used because of the need for ECG monitoring and it is not readily available).

Tricylics (other than clomipramine) and non-SSRI anti-depressants should not normally be used for BDD without comorbidity. However, when there is significant depression and failure to treat with an SSRI alone, one may justifiably try a tricyclic or an SNRI (venlafaxine, duloxetine) or bupropion. There are no data to guide treatment when there is comorbidity.

23.6   Discontinuation and Maintenance Phase

SSRIs and clomipramine are probably associated with a high rate of relapse on discontinuation (similar to the treatment of OCD). If an SSRI or clomipramine has been of benefit, then it should be continued at the same dose for at least 1–3 years to reduce the risk of relapse. These figures are based on expert opinion as long-term follow-up studies have not been completed. The duration should be adjusted according to the individual response, patient preference, and whether he has also received CBT. For example, in an individual with severe symptoms who has responded to an SSRI, and has previously relapsed on discontinuation and not received CBT, the maintenance phase on an SSRI may be for many years. Patients should be given standard advice on withdrawal of an SSRI and the possible symptoms. This is usually to reduce the dose slowly over several months and to choose a time when symptoms are stable and there are no other significant stresses in the patient's life.

23.7 Failure to Respond to Two or More SRIs

If there is no response or only a partial response to an SSRI or clomipramine, then there are a number of augmentation strategies. There is no guidance on the choice of sequence of augmentation or whether augmentation should occur after one or more SSRIs and clomipramine.

a) Clomipramine may be augmented with citalopram or escitalopram. Other SSRIs may interact with clomipramine and are less predictable because they increase the serum level of clomipramine. The maximum tolerated dose of an SSRI and clomipramine should be tried for up to 12 weeks. If another SSRI is used, then serum clomipramine levels should be carefully monitored. It is unknown whether this combination is superior to increasing the dose of one of the drugs used alone.

b) Buspirone 30–60 mg daily (and in some patients up to 90 mg daily if tolerated) may be used to augment the response to an SSRI or clomipramine.

c) Other anti-depressants can be added to an SSRI, especially where depression is prominent. These include mianserin, mirtazapine, venlafaxine, and buprorion, but there are no controlled trials in this area. Note that mirtazapine may be associated with weight gain, which is not usually desired in a patient with a body image problem.

d) Inositol (vitamin B complex) has been used in OCD either alone or as an augmenting agent. Dosages in the study were gradually built up to 18 mg a day. It may also be used as an augmenting agent. The dose might start with 2 mg twice a day, and go as high as 6 mg three times a day in adults.

e) Omega 3 fatty acids. Of relevance to individuals with comorbid depression is the role of highly unsaturated fatty acids (HUFAs) as two-thirds of the brain is made from HUFAs. There are two main types of HUFAs – omega 3 and omega 6 fatty acids. Omega 3 fatty acids are a nutritional supplement, which appear to have some benefit in some controlled trials of depression. Research on omega 3 fatty acids is at an early stage. It might help people with more severe forms of depression associated with an elevated cortisol response. The optimal dose in depression is not known and there are no known trials in BDD with or without comorbid depression.

There is some preliminary evidence that medications that reduce Glutamate hyperactively (for example, riluzole, memantine) may be efficacious in treatment resistant OCD, skin picking, depression and eatning disorders (Pittenger et al., 2006) such agents may therefore be worth considering in treatment refractory BDD.

23.8   Anti-psychotics in BDD

There is no evidence for the efficacy of pimozide in BDD. There is a lack of controlled trials for other anti-psychotic drugs in BDD either as a monotherapy or augmentation strategy with a SRI. In Phillip's (1996) retrospective chart review, there was no evidence for the benefit of anti-psychotics alone.

If a patient is significantly agitated, then an atypical anti-psychotic drug in a low dose or a benzodiazepine may be added in the short term to an SRI. Note that some of the atypical anti-psychotics (especially olanzapine) may be associated with reduced libido and weight gain and the person's body image may deteriorate. It remains open whether patients with comorbid tics or psychogenic excoriation benefit from the addition of a neuroleptic or whether an atypical (e.g., risperidone, olanzapine) may be more effective than pimozide or other, older anti-psychotic drugs. In general, anti-psychotics, especially in higher doses, pose a long-term risk of emotional numbness, excessive sedation, and weight gain.

23.9   Pharmacotherapy for Psychogenic Excoriation

The evidence for pharmacotherapy for psychogenic excoriation in BDD is described in Chapter 12. Not only is there paucity of RCTs, but the evidence is difficult to interpret because of the heterogeneity of psychogenic excoriation with different underlying diagnoses, the difficulties in diagnosing BDD and various subtypes (compulsive, impulsive, and mixed), and making a diagnosis historically (as disfigurement has occurred as a consequence of the excoriation). The clinical guidelines for the compulsive type of psychogenic excoriation are similar to BDD in general. The treatment algorithm commencing with a SSRI is as above. When there are more impulsive or tic-like features in psychogenic excoriation, then there is some rationale for the patient being offered augmentation with a lose dose of an anti-psychotic or alternatives such as an alpha-adrenoceptor blocker (e.g., clonidine or lofexidine) since these strategies are effective in individuals with tics. Another strategy may be the use of naltrexone or inositol. It is to be hoped that future RCTs with psychogenic excoriation will have more homogeneous populations with the same diagnosis of BDD or sub-type (compulsive, impulsive, or mixed).

23.10   CBT or Pharmacotherapy?

The following guidance is based only on expert opinion as there are no RCTs that compare CBT with an SSRI or a combination of the two. A meta-analysis of all case series and RCT of CBT and medication is discussed in Chapter 9. This favors CBT, but the methodology has significant limitations.

There is frequent comorbidity of depression and OCD in BDD, which may also influence outcome. There is evidence from OCD that a combination of CBT and an SSRI may do slightly better in some individuals. Expert opinions in BDD are influenced by their own biases, cultural variations, availability of CBT, and the experience of the practitioner. However in general, the most important choice is patient preference and the availability of CBT. The NICE guidelines on OCD and BDD are discussed in Chapter 11. Individuals with severe BDD or with delusional disorder are normally advised to have a combination of CBT and SSRI, depending on patient preference, especially because of the high rate of relapse on discontinuation of SSRI. Some individuals may not engage in CBT but are willing to take medication as it involves less effort and is often better when avoidance is extremely severe so that they are not ready to participate in any behavioral experiments or tolerate any discomfort. Although D-cycloserine as an enhancer of CBT has not been tried in BDD, it has shown promise in other anxiety disorders and in OCD (Wilhelm et al., 2008). It may therefore be justified in treatment refractory BDD. If it is helpful, it is more likely to be of benefit in those with marked symptoms of anxiety with specific cues.

Appendix 1

Diagnostic interviews and assessment scales

1. Body Dysmorphic Disorder Diagnostic Interview
This is a structured diagnostic interview for body dysmorphic disorder based on DSM IV. It can be used if, after open questioning, the patient has indicated that he has concerns or worries about his appearance.

2. Body Image Questionnaire (also known as Cosmetic Procedure Screening Questionnaire)
The Body Image questionnaire is used clinically to assess people presenting with BDD. There are sections that are used for assessing a) avoidance behavior, b) safety-seeking behaviors, c) expectations for a cosmetic or dermatological procedure. The questionnaire is currently undergoing validation. It is free to use, and can be downloaded from http://www.iop.kcl.ac.uk/cadatquestionnaire.

3. Brown Assessment of Beliefs (BABS)
The BABS is designed to assist in the diagnosis of a delusional disorder and to measure the strength of conviction in a belief. A discussion on the use of the BABS in BDD is found in Chapter 13. The BABS is reproduced with the permission of Jane Eisen.

Eisen, J. L, Phillips, K.A., Beer, D. et al. (1998). The Brown Assessment of Beliefs Scale: reliability and validity. *American Journal of Psychiatry, 155*(1), 102–108.

4. Yale-Brown Obsessive Compulsive Scale modified for BDD (YBOCS-BDD)
The YBOCS-BDD was developed by Phillips et al. to measure the severity of symptoms in BDD (see Chapter 13). This is the adult version, revised in 1997.

Body Dysmorphic Disorder: A Treatment Manual. David Veale and Fugen Neziroglu
© 2010 John Wiley & Sons, Ltd.

Phillips, K. A., Hollander E., Rasmussen, S. A. et al. (1997). A severity rating scale for body dysmorphic disorder: development, reliability, and validity of a modified version of the Yale-Brown Obsessive Compulsive Scale. *Psychopharmacology Bulletin, 33*, 17–22.

5. Overvalued Ideas Scale (OVIS)
The OVIS is a 10-item clinician-administered scale to assess the degree of conviction in an overvalued idea.

Neziroglu, F., McKay, D., Yaryura-Tobias, J. A. & Stevens, K. P. (1999). The Overvalued Ideas Scale: development, reliability, and validity in obsessive compulsive disorder. *Behaviour Research and Therapy, 37*(881), 902.

6. Valued Directions Questionnaire
The Valued Directions Questionnaire is adapted from Hayes et al. (2002) and is used in the assessment of valued directions.

Hayes, S. C., Strosahl, K. & Wilson, K. G. (1999). *Acceptance and Commitment Therapy: An Experiential Approach to Behavior Change*. New York: Guilford Press.

7. Functional analysis of psychogenic excoriation
This is a semi-structured interview and functional analysis for psychogenic excoriation. It can be used in anyone who reports he is picking his skin or spots. It is free to use, but the source should be acknowledged.

8. Skin Picking Impact Scale
Keuthen et al. (2001) developed the Skin Picking Impact Scale (SPIS), a self-report instrument used to assess the psychosocial consequences of repetitive skin excoriation.

9. The Defect Related Beliefs Test (DRBT)
Based on the Personal Appearance Billings Test developed by Butters & Cash (1987) and revised by Geremia & Neziroglu (2001) for BDD.

Body Dysmorphic Disorder Diagnostic Interview

For this interview questions in parentheses are used to clarify an answer. If you make a diagnosis of BDD, then continue with a screening for an additional diagnosis of delusional disorder on the Brown Assessment of Beliefs. A diagnosis of BDD can be made if item (2) is rated for no noticeable defect or a minor physical anomaly AND Item (3) is rated as at least an hour a day AND at least one item from (4) to (8) is rated as significant AND another mental disorder such as an eating disorder does not better explain symptoms (for which you may need to use an additional diagnostic interview). If the feature is rated as moderate or severe disfigurement in item (2) and quite noticeable, then consider diagnosis of an adjustment disorder or another Axis I disorder that better accounts for the distress associated with the feature.

I'd like to like to ask a few questions about the way you feel about your appearance over the past month.

1. Features disliked
Can you tell me what features you dislike most?
(Can you describe what you dislike most about each feature?)
(Do you feel your feature(s) is (are) defective or ugly?)

2. Observe how noticeable is the "defectiveness" of the feature
How noticeable is the main feature described by the patient (if they do *not* camouflage themselves, e.g., with clothes and/or make-up)? How noticeable is the feature (if it is not highlighted) or how does the feature(s) compare to others? (A diagnosis of BDD requires an imagined defect or a minor physical anomaly that is only slightly noticeable or has a feature that is comparable to others.)

3. Time spent thinking about feature
Do you currently think a lot about the features you dislike?
If yes*: On a **typical** day, how many hour(s) do you spend thinking about your feature(s)? Please add up all the time that your features are at the forefront of your mind and make the best estimate.*

4. Distress
Does thinking about your feature(s) cause you a lot of distress?
(Describe and rate the degree of distress or anxiety related to thinking about the feature(s), not general anxiety or depression associated with other problems.)

5.   Occupational handicap

Has the distress about your feature(s) interfered with your ability to work, study, or your role as a homemaker?
(How much time off work or college have you had because of this problem?)
(Have you been late for work or college?)

6.   Social handicap

Does disliking your feature prevent you from doing anything in your social life?
(Do you try to avoid situations that involve people because of your appearance?)

7.   Handicap in relationships

If no partner: *Has disliking your feature(s) had an effect on dating or interfered with your ability to form an intimate relationship?*
If regular partner: *Has disliking your feature(s) had an effect on the relationship with your partner?*
(E.g., Are there many arguments or problems with jealousy?)

8.   Handicap in family life

Does the distress about your feature(s) interfere in other relationships with your family or the people you live with?
(E.g., Have the lives of your family been affected by your preoccupation?)

Body Image Questionnaire

Name _____   **Date** _____

This questionnaire is part of a routine assessment. All information will be kept strictly confidential. Thank you.

Question 1 Notes

Please study this example before completing question 1. In a moment, we will ask you to describe the feature(s) of your body which you dislike or would like to improve.

This is an example of a woman whose main worry was her nose and who was concerned to a lesser extent by her skin and bottom. She is currently seeking a procedure to her nose.

1) Features Causing Concern

Please describe the feature(s) of your body you dislike or would like to improve and tick the box if you are seeking a cosmetic or dermatological procedure for the feature either now or in the future. Please tick the appropriate box.

1st Feature

Nose is too crooked with a bump

Procedure sought　☑ Now　☐ Future

☐ Not desire any procedure

2nd Feature

Blemishes and acne scars on face

Procedure sought

☐ Now　☑ Future

☐ Not desire any procedure

3rd Feature

Bottom is too big

☐ Now　☐ Future

☑ Not desire any procedure

We will then ask you to draw a pie chart and estimate the percentage of concern allocated to each feature. The person above completed her pie chart like this.

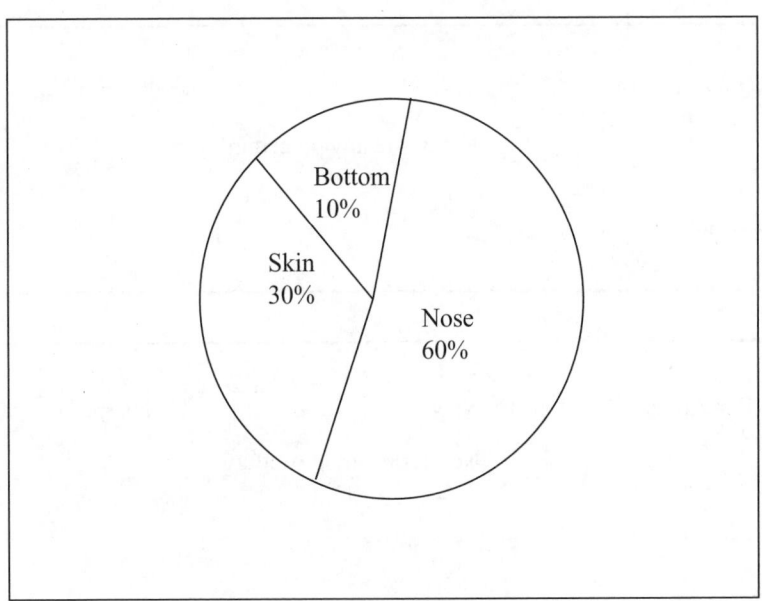

1) Features Causing Concern

Please describe the feature(s) of your body which you dislike or would like to improve and tick the box if you are seeking a cosmetic or dermatological procedure for that feature either now or in the future.

Please tick the appropriate box.

1st Feature (that is the feature you are most concerned about)

_____

_____

Procedure sought   ☐ Now   ☐ Future

                      ☐ Not desire any procedure

2nd Feature

Procedure sought   ☐ Now   ☐   Future

                   ☐ Not desire any procedure

3rd Feature

Procedure sought   ☐ Now   ☐   Future

                   ☐ Not desire any procedure

4th Feature

Procedure sought   ☐ Now   ☐   Future

                   ☐ Not desire any procedure

5th Feature

Procedure sought   ☐ Now   ☐   Future

                   ☐ Not desire any procedure

Now please draw a pie chart and estimate the percentage of concern allocated to each feature. Please ensure that your percentages add up to 100%!

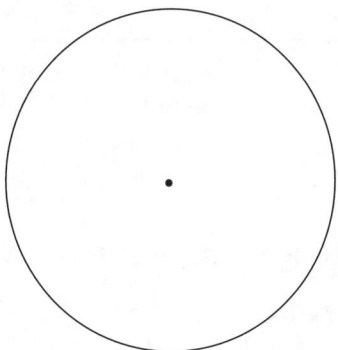

From now on, we will refer to these concerns as your 'feature(s).'

2)   On an *average day*, how many minutes or hour(s) do you currently spend thinking about your feature(s)? Please add up all the time that your features are at the forefront of your mind and make the best estimate.

_____ minutes or _____ hour(s) a day

Please read the next set of questions below carefully and *circle* the number which best describes the way that you feel about your feature(s).

Please read the labels carefully to ensure you are circling the number that reflects how you feel because some of the answers are worded in a reverse order.

3)   How often do you *deliberately* check your feature(s)? *Not accidentally catch sight of it*. Please include looking at your feature in a mirror or other reflective surfaces like a shop window or looking at it directly or feeling it with your fingers.

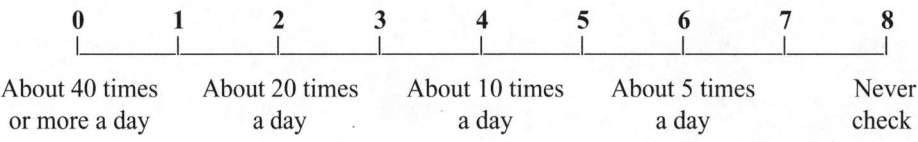

0	1	2	3	4	5	6	7	8
About 40 times or more a day		About 20 times a day		About 10 times a day		About 5 times a day		Never check

4) How much do you feel your feature(s) are *currently* ugly, unattractive or "not right"?

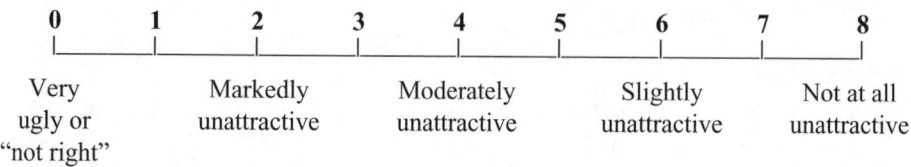

| 0 | 1 | 2 | 3 | 4 | 5 | 6 | 7 | 8 |

Very ugly or "not right" — Markedly unattractive — Moderately unattractive — Slightly unattractive — Not at all unattractive

5) How much does your feature(s) *currently* cause you distress?

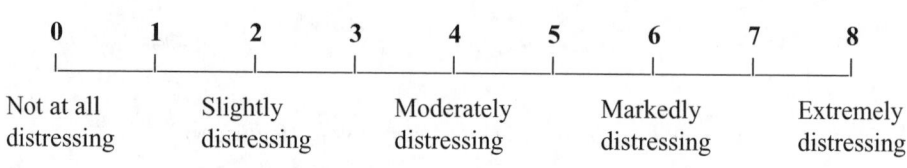

| 0 | 1 | 2 | 3 | 4 | 5 | 6 | 7 | 8 |

Not at all distressing — Slightly distressing — Moderately distressing — Markedly distressing — Extremely distressing

6) How often does your feature(s) *currently* lead you to avoid situations or activities?

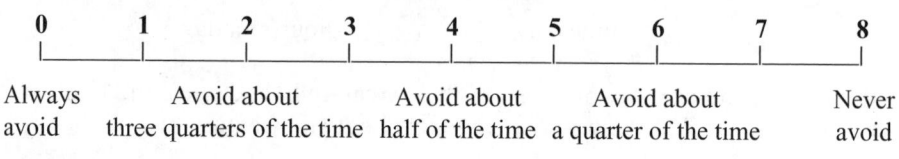

| 0 | 1 | 2 | 3 | 4 | 5 | 6 | 7 | 8 |

Always avoid — Avoid about three quarters of the time — Avoid about half of the time — Avoid about a quarter of the time — Never avoid

If so, what do you avoid?

_____

_____

7)   How much does your feature(s) *currently* preoccupy you? That is, you think about it a lot and it is hard to stop thinking about it?

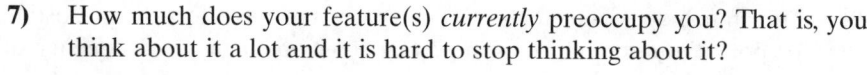

| 0 | 1 | 2 | 3 | 4 | 5 | 6 | 7 | 8 |

Not at all   Slightly   Moderately   Very   Extremely
preoccupied   preoccupied   preoccupied   preoccupied   preoccupied

If you rated you preoccupation with your feature(s) as 4 or above, for how long has it preoccupied you?"

Months _____ or Years _____

8)   **If you have a partner,** how much does your feature(s) *currently* have an effect on your relationship with an existing partner? (e.g. affectionate feelings, number of arguments, enjoying activities together) **If you do not have a partner,** how much does your feature(s) currently have an effect on dating or developing a relationship?

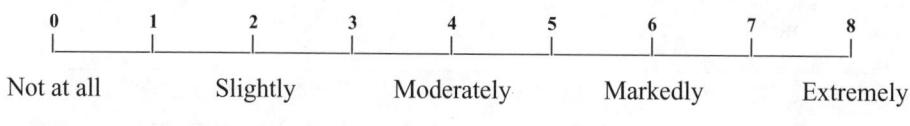

| 0 | 1 | 2 | 3 | 4 | 5 | 6 | 7 | 8 |

Not at all   Slightly   Moderately   Markedly   Extremely

If so, how does it affect your relationship your ability to date or develop a relationship?

_____

_____

9) How much does your feature(s) currently have an effect on an existing or potential sexual relationship? (e.g., enjoyment of sex, frequency of sexual activity)

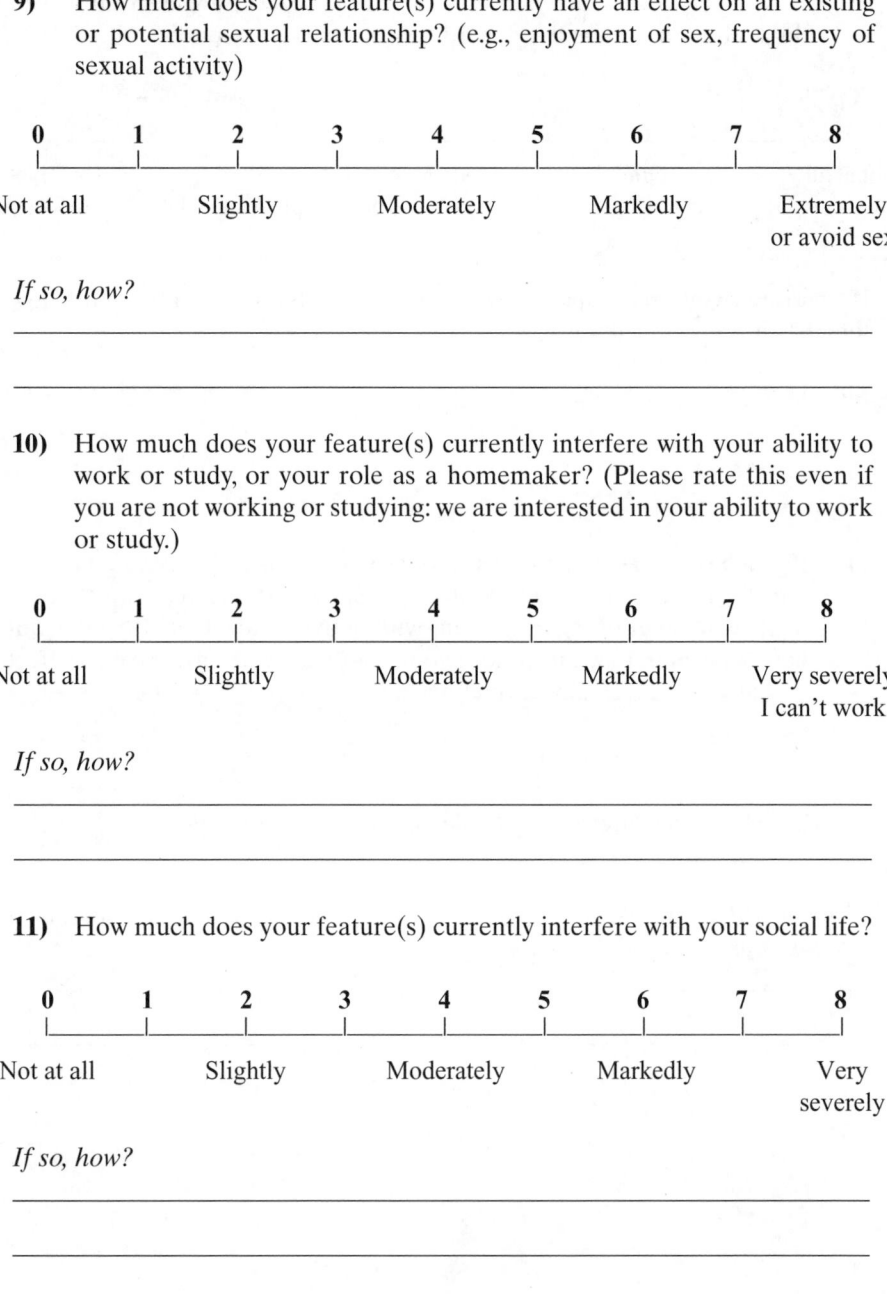

```
  0        1        2        3        4        5        6        7        8
  |_____|_____|_____|_____|_____|_____|_____|_____|
```
Not at all   Slightly   Moderately   Markedly   Extremely
                                                                          or avoid sex

If so, how?

_____

_____

10) How much does your feature(s) currently interfere with your ability to work or study, or your role as a homemaker? (Please rate this even if you are not working or studying: we are interested in your ability to work or study.)

```
  0        1        2        3        4        5        6        7        8
  |_____|_____|_____|_____|_____|_____|_____|_____|
```
Not at all   Slightly   Moderately   Markedly   Very severely
                                                                          I can't work

If so, how?

_____

_____

11) How much does your feature(s) currently interfere with your social life?

```
  0        1        2        3        4        5        6        7        8
  |_____|_____|_____|_____|_____|_____|_____|_____|
```
Not at all   Slightly   Moderately   Markedly   Very
                                                                          severely

If so, how?

_____

_____

12) How noticeable do you feel your feature is to other people (if you do *not* camouflageyourself, e.g., with clothes, padding and/or make-up) and the feature has not been pointed out to them? Please rate this question for your 1st feature (ie. the feature you are most concerned with)

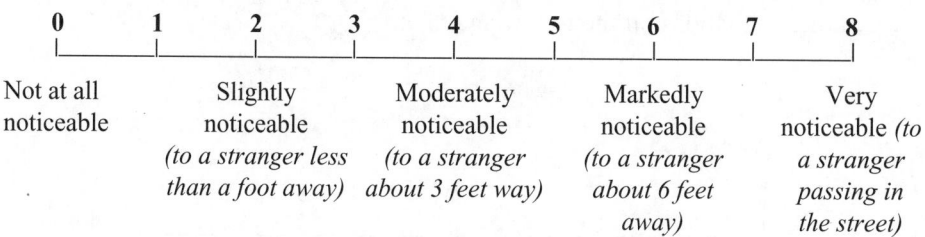

| 0 | 1 | 2 | 3 | 4 | 5 | 6 | 7 | 8 |

Not at all noticeable

Slightly noticeable *(to a stranger less than a foot away)*

Moderately noticeable *(to a stranger about 3 feet way)*

Markedly noticeable *(to a stranger about 6 feet away)*

Very noticeable *(to a stranger passing in the street)*

13) How does your 1st feature compare to others of the same age, sex, and ethnic group?

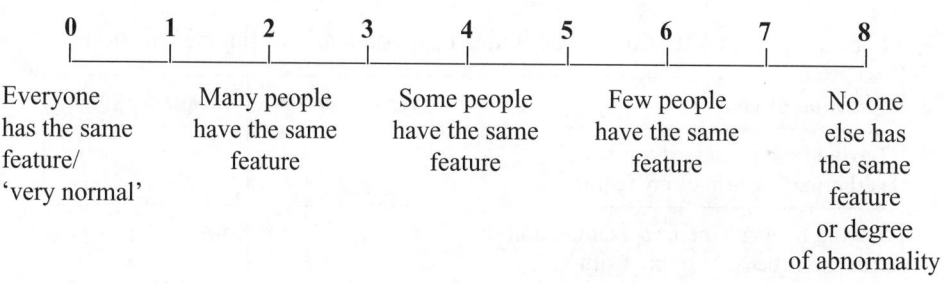

| 0 | 1 | 2 | 3 | 4 | 5 | 6 | 7 | 8 |

Everyone has the same feature/ 'very normal'

Many people have the same feature

Some people have the same feature

Few people have the same feature

No one else has the same feature or degree of abnormality

14) How much do you feel your appearance is the most important aspect of who you are?

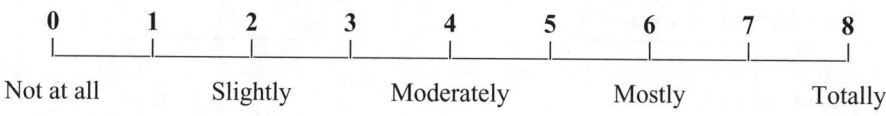

| 0 | 1 | 2 | 3 | 4 | 5 | 6 | 7 | 8 |

Not at all

Slightly

Moderately

Mostly

Totally

15) What do you avoid because of the way you feel about your feature(s)? Please read the situations below and in the second column rate the degree of anxiety that you anticipate in each of the situation on a scale between 0 and 100 where 0 is no anxiety at all and 100 is total panic. In the third column, rate the degree to which you currently avoid each of these situations on the following scale:

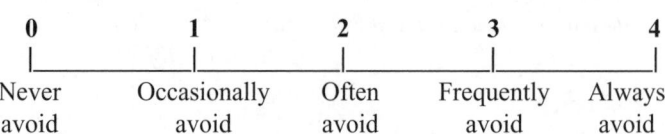

0	1	2	3	4
Never avoid	Occasionally avoid	Often avoid	Frequently avoid	Always avoid

Please add other situations or activities that you avoid at the end of the list.

Situation or activity	Anxiety (0–100)	Frequency (0–4)
I avoid going to a party or social gathering because of my features		
I avoid having a medical examination or treatment because of my features		
I avoid going to public changing rooms because of my features		
I avoid exercising in a gym or playing a sport because of my features		
I avoid wearing a swimming costume on a beach because of my features		
I avoid being physically close to someone because of my features		
I avoid making love or intimacy because of my features (or only under certain conditions, e.g., lights off or wearing your make up).		

Situation or activity	Anxiety (0–100)	Frequency (0–4)
I avoid certain types of clothes because of my features (please specify)		
I avoid certain types of lighting because of my features (please specify)		
I avoid looking at pictures in magazines or on television because of my features		
I avoid having a photo or video taken by someone else because of my features		
I avoid looking at old photographs because of my features (Please specify if you have destroyed them)		
I avoid having my hair cut at all		
I avoid having my hair cut at a hairdresser		
I avoid looking at my features in mirrors or reflective surfaces		
OTHERS (please specify)		

16)   Please read the list of activities below that you might do because of the way you feel about your feature(s). In the second column rate the degree to which you use each of the behaviors on the following scale:

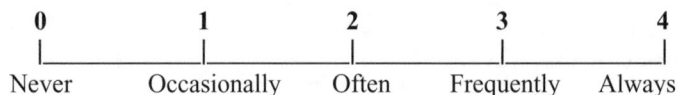

0	1	2	3	4
Never	Occasionally	Often	Frequently	Always

Behavior	Frequency
I check my feature(s) in mirrors	
I use a particular light to check my feature(s) in a mirror. Please specify:	
I check my feature(s) in other reflective surfaces (e.g. cutlery, windows, CDs). Please specify:	
I check my feature(s) directly by looking at it without a mirror	
I check my feature(s) by taking photographs of myself	
I check my feature(s) by feeling it with my finger(s)	
I compare my feature(s) to others in magazines or on television and film	
I compare my feature(s) to other people I meet	
I compare my feature(s) with old pictures of myself	
I pinch the fat on my skin	
I wear something to distract attention from my feature (e.g. jewelry, a tattoo). Please specify:	
I change my posture to avoid my feature being seen at a certain angle. Please specify:	
I hide my feature(s) with something (e.g., my hand, a baseball cap, hat, scarf, baggy clothing, newspaper). Please specify:	
I use padding in my clothes to camouflage or increase the size of a feature. Please specify:	
I try to convince others about how unattractive my feature is	
I ask others to confirm the existence of the defect in my features	

Behavior	Frequency
I seek reassurance about whether my feature has got worse	
I seek reassurance about whether my feature is camouflaged (e.g., by make-up)	
I keep changing my clothes before I go out	
I get my partner or family member to "help" me in camouflaging or checking my appearance. Please specify:	
I keep measuring my feature(s)	
HAIR: I wear a wig because of my features	
I grow or arrange my hair to hide certain features. Please specify:	
I comb or groom (smooth/straighten) or adjust my hair more than most people	
I shave, cut, or pluck hair more than most people. Please specify:	
I use medication to promote hair growth on my head	
SKIN: I clean my skin more than most people	
I wear more make-up than most people to hide my feature(s)	
I use a cover-up stick for spots or blemishes	
I use facial peels, scrubs, or saunas for my skin	
I bleach my skin	
I use a sun bed to darken my skin	
I pick my skin or squeeze spots more than most people	
SHAPE OR WEIGHT: I exercise to alter my shape or weight	
I body-build with weights	
I use steroids	
I weigh myself more than necessary	
I restrict my food to improve my shape or reduce my weight	

Behavior	Frequency
I sit with my toes on the floor to avoid my thighs spreading	
I eat more food to increase my weight	
I use diet pills, laxatives, or diuretics. Please specify:	
OTHERS (please specify)	

17   Self-portrait

Please draw a portrait from the picture in your mind or impression that you have of your face or body (depending on the features that distress you). You can choose whatever medium you wish. Don't worry if you are not artistic!

The Body Image Questionnaire. In Veale, D. & Neziroglu, F. (2009) *Body Dysmorphic Disorder: A Treatment Manual.* Chichester: Wiley.

Brown Assessment of Beliefs Scale (BABS)

Introduction

The BABS© scale has been developed to rate the degree of conviction and insight patients have concerning their beliefs. These beliefs include delusions as well as the beliefs that may underlie obsessional thinking and phobias. Obsessions and delusions have traditionally been viewed as dichotomous phenomena, with obsessions being defined as intrusive egodystonic thoughts about which the patient maintains insight. On the other hand, delusions have been defined as false beliefs held firmly by the patient without insight into the irrationality of the content of the belief. However, obsessions and delusions might be better conceptualized as existing on a continuum of insight that ranges from good insight to poor insight (overvalued ideation) to no insight (delusional thinking). Such a continuum of insight may be present in a variety of psychiatric disorders, such as obsessive compulsive disorder, body dysmorphic disorder, anorexia nervosa, and hypochondriasis, as well as in disorders traditionally considered psychotic, such as schizophrenia and delusional disorder.

The BABS© is based on this premise – that insight (i.e., degree of delusionality) exists on a continuum. It is also based on the premise that insight itself consists of a number of dimensions. Thus, the BABS© rates a number of dimensions that underlie delusional and non-delusional beliefs. These dimensions are: *conviction, perception of others' views of beliefs, explanation of differing views, fixity of ideas, attempt to disprove beliefs, insight,* and *ideas/delusions of reference.*

Administration

Ratings

The BABS© consists of seven items: the first six items are added to obtain the total BABS© score. An additional item (ideas of reference) is not included in the total score. Each item corresponds to one of the dimensions listed above. Each item is rated from 0 to 4 (from least to most severe). The instrument is semi-structured. The interviewer should assess the items in the listed order and should read the questions provided. However, additional questions may be asked to clarify patient responses. The italicized statements in parentheses that follow some of the questions are instructions to the interviewer that may assist in obtaining valid ratings.

In general, the items are rated based on the patient's report; however, the final answer selected for each item depends on the interviewer's clinical judgement. If the patient volunteers information at any time during the interview, that information should be considered. Ratings should be based primarily on reports and observations gained during the interview. Additional information supplied by other sources may be used to determine ratings if it is felt to be useful and valid. If the rater judges that the information being provided is grossly inaccurate, then the reliability of the patient or informant is in doubt and should be noted accordingly on the interview.

Rate each item according to the patient's experience *during the past week* up to and including the time of the interview. Scores should reflect the *average* (mean) occurrence of each item for the entire week. If insight has changed notably and rapidly during the past week (as may occur in psychotic mood disorders, for example), the patient's current state should be rated. The rater should note this departure from the standard BABS© convention.

If the patient has *more than one belief related to the same disorder* (e.g., two different OCD obsessions), these beliefs should be rated as a *composite*. However, if the patient has *beliefs connected to two distinct disorders*, e.g., beliefs of body distortion (body dysmorphic disorder) and obsessions about contamination (OCD), these beliefs should be rated *separately*.

Identifying the Belief(s)

This instrument can be used to assess beliefs in a variety of diagnoses. For example:

Diagnosis	*Belief*
Obsessive compulsive disorder	I will get contaminated from touching doorknobs.
Body Dysmorphic Disorder	My nose is grotesquely deformed.
Anorexia nervosa	I am fat.
Mania	I am the president of the United States.
Depression with psychotic features	My insides are rotting.
Schizophrenia and other psychotic disorders	A war is being waged within my body and the military has removed my heart.

If the patient expresses his concern as a fear or worry, it is important that the interviewer *determine and rate the nature of the underlying belief* and associated consequence other than anxiety. For example, if the patient describes a fear of touching doorknobs, the interviewer should determine what the underlying belief or consequence is – for example, that touching doorknobs will lead to illness. Question 1 would then read: "How convinced are you of your idea – that touching doorknobs will make you ill?" Some examples of beliefs that underlie fears or worries are listed below:

Fear or worry	*Underlying belief (preferred)*
I'm afraid of environmental contaminants.	If I step on a chemically treated lawn, I'll get cancer.
I worry I'll harm my grandchildren.	I can't touch my grandchildren because if I do, I'll sexually molest them.
I'm afraid the CIA will get me.	If I don't barricade myself in my house, the CIA will poison me.
I'm afraid of snakes.	If I go into my backyard, I will be bitten by a snake and die.

Even though the underlying belief is what should be assessed, the rater should use the most clinically appropriate term for the belief being assessed– e.g., idea, belief, thought, worry, fear, or concern.

The more specifically the belief is stated, the more likely the rating is to be valid. The interviewer should help the patient *state his belief as specifically as possible.* Some examples of less specific and more specific beliefs (the latter being preferable) are listed below.

Vague belief	*Specific belief (preferred)*
To prevent illness, I must take special precautions with my food.	To prevent illness, I must throw away any food touched by anyone else.
I have special powers.	I'm the most powerful person in the universe and the ruler of Jupiter and Mars.
I'm ugly.	I have big red spots on my face, which make me very ugly.
I'm a bad person.	I'm responsible for the California earthquake.

If the patient uses an *action* (such as a compulsion in OCD, or dietary restriction in anorexia nervosa) to prevent a feared consequence from happening, then *the action should be incorporated into the question about the belief.* For example, if the patient is afraid of getting AIDS, the interviewer should determine what measures the patient takes to avoid or prevent possible exposure to AIDS and should incorporate these measures into the question. The interviewer should ask, "How convinced are you that you will get AIDS if you don't spend three hours a day washing?" not "How convinced are you that you will get AIDS?" Some examples of beliefs that incorporate actions are listed below on the right-hand side:

Belief without action	*Belief incorporating an action (preferred)*
I'll get fat.	I'll get fat if I eat more than 20 Cheerios a day.
I'll harm others if I'm not careful.	I need to check the newspapers to make sure I'm not a hit-and-run driver.
I'll fail my test.	If I don't put all of my papers in a certain position, I'll fail my test.

The rater should also *assess what the patient thinks is actually true*, not what might be true. For example, if the patient states that he is 100% convinced that he *might* get cancer from stepping on a lawn, the interviewer should attempt to determine how convinced the patient is that he *will* get cancer from stepping on a lawn and should rate the latter response.

Other potential difficulties ascertaining the core belief include:

Potential Mistakes	*Solution*
1. The core belief is too narrow. For example, "My nose is crooked."	Obtain a more fundamental belief, such as, "I look like the Elephant Man" because this belief encompasses all the patient's beliefs about his or her appearance and is more clearly false (see below).
2. The core belief is not clearly false. For example, "I have to stay in the hospital until I'm cured."	Obtain a belief that is clearly false, e.g., "I will be picked up by trolls in a spaceship."
3. The core belief shifts during the interview.	Be sure to rate the same belief throughout the interview.

To administer the scale, the rater and the patient need to agree on which beliefs/ideas/obsessions are being evaluated. Prior use of other instruments (such as the Structured Clinical Interview for DSM IV to identify diagnoses, or the YBOCS symptom checklist to identify obsessions) can be helpful in identifying such beliefs/ideas/obsessions. In addition, a list of ideas/beliefs/obsessions to be rated can be generated by asking:

Are there certain ideas or beliefs you have that are of significant concern to you?
Which one would you rate as being of most concern?

_____ [Principal belief]

Do you have other ideas (thoughts/beliefs) that you are preoccupied with?

_____

Can you answer the following questions about the ideas/beliefs that you've been most concerned about during the past week?
As was noted previously, the interviewer should assist the patient in: 1) stating his or her beliefs as *specifically* as possible, and 2) identifying any *actions* associated with the belief so they can be incorporated into questions about the belief.

In general, the patient's *specific belief can be incorporated into the question*. For example, question 1 could be read as, "How convinced are you of your belief that you're practically bald? Are you certain your belief is accurate?"; question 2 could be read as, "What do you think other people think of your belief that you're practically bald? How certain are you that most people think your belief makes sense?"

On repeated testing, the belief should be reviewed, and, if necessary, revised before doing the ratings.

Instructions for specific items:

Item 1:	Conviction	Description: The purpose of this item is to determine the patient's degree of conviction about his belief(s).
Item 2:	Perception of others' views of beliefs	Description: The purpose of this item is to evaluate the patient's ability to accurately assess how others view his concerns.

Scoring considerations: Patients may answer with what other people have told them. However, the point of this item is to ascertain what the patient thinks others REALLY think. Interviewer should clarify, if necessary, that the patient answers this question assuming that others are giving their honest opinion. An additional probe to clarify this might be, "What do you think others would say if they had to be honest?" Another pitfall with this item is not rating what MOST people think. This question should not be answered according to what a few people think or what selected people think, e.g., friends and family.

Item 3:	Explanation of differing views	Description: The purpose of this item is to have the patient explain differences in his response to items 1 and 2, i.e., why other people have a different view of the belief than the patient does.

Scoring considerations: The interviewer should not ask this item if responses on item 1 and 2 are in agreement. If responses on item 1 and 2 are in agreement, item 3 should be given the same response, e.g., if item 1 and 2 are scored as a 2, then item 3 should be scored as a 2.

Item 4:   Fixity of ideas

Description: The purpose of this item is to evaluate how fixed or unshakable the patient's conviction about the belief is.

Scoring considerations: The interviewer should determine whether the patient can be convinced that his ideas are false **during** the interview. An additional probe might be, "As we sit here now, could I convince you that your appearance is not grotesque?" If necessary, supply a non-confrontational example. Patients may answer according to whether they would LIKE to be convinced that their belief is false. Rate on the basis of whether the patient could be convinced, not whether he wishes he could be convinced. Try to differentiate, if necessary, the patient's compliance and desire to please the interviewer from his true ability to be convinced.

Item 5:   Attempt to disprove ideas

Description: This item assesses how actively and frequently the patient attempts to disprove or reject his ideas as being untrue or wrong. It does not simply rate the patient's efforts to push the thoughts away.

Item 6:   Insight

Description: The purpose of this item is to determine the patient's ability to assign a psychiatric or psychological cause for the belief.

Scoring considerations: Interviewer should determine what the patient actually believes, not what he has been told is true.

Item rated but not included in the total BABS© score:

ADDITIONAL ITEM:

Item 7: Ideas/delusions of reference

Description: This item assesses whether the patient has referential thinking about the environment based on the content of the belief(s).

Scoring considerations: This question pertains only to the belief(s) being assessed by the interviewer – not if the patient thinks he is noticed for a reason unrelated to the beliefs being assessed.

Examples:
1. Do you think people take special notice of you or make fun of you because of your appearance?
2. Do you think people take special notice of you because you seem like someone who might harm their children?
3. Do you think people take special notice of you because you're an angel? [PAUSE] What about receiving special messages from the environment because you're an angel?

Scoring

All items should be rated. The total score is the sum of items 1 through 6. Item 7 should be rated but not included in the total score.

Name_____   Diagnosis_____

Date_____   Treatment_____

Belief (describe principal belief(s) during the past week):

_____

For each item, circle the number identifying the response that best characterizes the patient **over the past week**. The patient's specific belief can be incorporated into the question – for example, "How convinced are you of this belief that touching doorknobs will make you ill?" Optional questions are indicated in parentheses; instructions to the interviewer are italicized.

1. Conviction
How convinced are you of these ideas/beliefs? Are you certain your ideas/beliefs are accurate? (What do you base your certainty on?)

0. Completely convinced beliefs are false (0% certainty).
1. Beliefs are probably not true, or substantial doubt exists.
2. Beliefs may or may not be true, or unable to decide whether beliefs are true or not.
3. Fairly convinced that beliefs are true but an element of doubt exists.
4. Completely convinced about the reality of held beliefs (100% certainty).

2. Perception of others' views of beliefs
What do you think other people (would) think of your beliefs? [PAUSE] How certain are you that <u>most</u> people think your beliefs make sense?

*(Interviewer should clarify, if necessary, that the patient answers this question assuming that others are giving their **honest** opinion.)*

(Interviewer should make sure that the patient answers according to what MOST people think not some people or selected people.)

0. Completely certain that most people think these beliefs are unrealistic.
1. Fairly certain that most people think these beliefs are unrealistic.
2. Others may or may not think beliefs are unrealistic, or uncertain about others' views concerning these beliefs.
3. Fairly certain that most people think these beliefs are realistic.
4. Completely certain that most people think these beliefs are realistic.

3. Explanation of differing views

You said that (*fill in response to item 1*), but that (*fill in response to item 2*). [PAUSE] How do you explain the difference between what you think and what others think about the accuracy of your beliefs? (Who's more likely to be right?)

(Interviewer should not ask this item if responses on item 1 and 2 are the same. In that case, give the same score as items 1 and 2.)

0. Completely certain that beliefs are unrealistic or absurd (e.g., "my mind is playing tricks on me.")
1. Fairly certain that beliefs are unrealistic or absurd.
2. Uncertain about why others don't agree – beliefs may or may not be true.
3. Fairly certain that beliefs are true; view of others is less accurate.
4. Completely certain that beliefs are true; view of others is not accurate.

4. Fixity of ideas

If I were to question (or challenge) the accuracy of your beliefs, what would your reaction be? [PAUSE] Could I convince you that you are wrong? [PAUSE] Would you consider the possibility?

(If necessary, supply a non-confrontational example.)

(Rate on the basis of whether the patient could be convinced, not whether he wishes he could be convinced.)

0. Eager to consider the possibility that beliefs may be false; demonstrates no reluctance to entertain this possibility.
1. Easily willing to consider the possibility that beliefs may be false; reluctance to do so is minimal.
2. Somewhat willing to consider the possibility that beliefs may be false, but moderate resistance is present.
3. Clearly reluctant to consider the possibility that beliefs may be false; reluctance is significant.
4. Absolutely refuses to consider the possibility that beliefs may be false – i.e., beliefs are fixed.

5. Attempt to disprove ideas

Over the past week, how often have you tried to convince yourself that your beliefs are wrong?

(Interviewer should rate attempts patient makes to talk himself out of the belief, not attempts to push the thoughts/ideas out of his mind or think about something else.)

0. Always involved in trying to disprove beliefs, or not necessary to disprove because beliefs are not true.
1. Usually tries to disprove beliefs.
2. Sometimes tries to disprove beliefs.
3. Occasionally attempts to disprove beliefs.
4. Makes no attempt to disprove beliefs.

6. Insight

What do you think has caused you to have these beliefs? [PAUSE] Do they have a psychiatric (or psychological) cause, or are they actually true?

(Interviewer should determine what the patient actually believes, not what s/he has been told or hopes is true. Psychological etiology should be considered equivalent to psychiatric illness.)

(Recognition that the thoughts are excessive – i.e., taking up too much time – or causing problems for the patient should not be considered equivalent to psychiatric/psychological etiology. Instead, rate patient's awareness that the source/cause of the beliefs is psychiatric/psychological.)

0. Beliefs definitely have a psychiatric/psychological cause.
1. Beliefs probably have a psychiatric/psychological cause.
2. Beliefs possibly have a psychiatric/psychological cause.
3. Beliefs probably do not have a psychiatric/psychological cause.
4. Beliefs definitely do not have a psychiatric/psychological cause.

TOTAL BABS© SCORE __ = SUM OF QUESTIONS 1 THROUGH 6

ADDITIONAL ITEM:

7. Ideas/delusions of reference
Does it ever seem that people are
talking about you or taking special
notice of you because of *(fill in
belief)*?

OPTIONAL:
What about receiving special
messages from your environment
because of *(fill in belief)*? (How
certain are you of this?)

*(This question pertains only to the
belief(s) being assessed by the BABS
interviewer–not if patient thinks he is
noticed for a reason unrelated to the
beliefs being assessed.
Interviewer should NOT base answer
on observable actions or compulsions;
instead, rate core belief.)*

(Do not include in total score)

0. No, others definitely do not take
    special notice of me.
1. Others probably do not take special
    notice of me.
2. Others may or may not take special
    notice of me.
3. Others probably do take special
    notice of me.
4. Others definitely do take special
    notice of me.

BABS© KEYSHEET ®

Patient Initials:_____Date of Interview:____/_____/_____

Rater:_____Diagnosis:_____

Treatment:_____

Principal Belief:_____

1. CONVICTION   _____

2. PERCEPTION OF OTHERS' VIEWS   _____

3. EXPLANATION OF DIFFERING VIEWS   _____

4. FIXITY OF IDEAS   _____

5. ATTEMPT TO DISPROVE BELIEFS   _____

6. INSIGHT   _____

TOTAL BABS© SCORE (total of items 1-6)   _____

ADDITIONAL ITEM:

7. IDEAS/DELUSIONS OF REFERENCE   _____

RATE YOUR OVERALL IMPRESSION OF THE PATIENT'S DEGREE OF INSIGHT:

0.   Excellent Insight; fully rational
1.   Good Insight
2.   Fair Insight
3.   Poor Insight
4.   Lacks Insight; delusional

Yale-Brown Obsessive Compulsive Scale modified for BDD (YBOCS-BDD)©

Purpose: This rating scale is designed to rate the severity and type of symptoms in patients with body dysmorphic disorder (BDD). BDD is defined as a preoccupation with an imagined or slight defect in appearance – for example, "thinning" hair, a "large" nose, or a "scarred" face. The scale is derived from the Yale-Brown Obsessive Compulsive Scale (YBOCS). Like the YBOCS, the first five items rate BDD-related *preoccupations*, and the second five items rate BDD-related *behaviors*. The YBOCS-BDD also rates *insight* (item 11) and *avoidance* (item 12).

Format: This rating scale is intended for use as a semi-structured interview. The interviewer should assess the items in the listed order and read the questions provided. However, the interviewer is free to ask additional questions for purposes of clarification. In general, the ratings should depend on the patient's report; however, the final rating is based on the interviewer's clinical judgement.

- Brackets [ ] indicate material that should be read. Brackets are also used to indicate a pause.
- Parentheses ( ) indicate optional material that may be read.
- Italicized items are instructions to the interviewer.

Sources of Information: If the patient volunteers information at any time during the interview, that information should be considered. Ratings should be based primarily on reports and observations gained during the interview. Additional information supplied by others (e.g., spouse or parent) may be included in a determination of the ratings only if it is judged that 1) such information is essential to adequately assess symptom severity, *and* 2) consistent, week-to-week reporting can be ensured by having the same informant(s) present for each rating session. If you judge that the information being provided is grossly inaccurate, then the reliability of the patient or informant is in doubt and should be noted accordingly on the interview.

Ratings: Rate each item *during the past week* up to and including the time of the interview. Scores should reflect the average (mean) occurrence of each item for the entire week. For questions 1 through 5 (which rate BDD-related preoccupations), rate the *total* (composite) effect of *all* body parts of concern. For items 6 through 10 (which rate BDD-related behaviors), also rate the *total* (composite) effect of *all* behaviors. For items 9 and 10 (resistance and control items), if the patient's responses differ for different behaviors, select the response that represents an average score for the different behaviors. For item 12, do *not* rate avoidance of compulsive behaviors such as looking at mirrors; instead, rate the extent to which the patient avoids activities that contribute to adequate functioning – e.g., avoidance of social interactions or work-related activities.

Diagnosing BDD: Before proceeding with questions 1–5, you must first determine that the patient has BDD and identify the body parts with which he is excessively concerned. The diagnosis is made if the person is preoccupied with an imagined defect in appearance; if a slight physical anomaly is present, the person's concern must be markedly excessive. Any body part can be the focus of concern, and patients are commonly preoccupied with more than one body part. In addition, the preoccupation must have caused clinically significant distress or impairment in social, occupational, or other important areas of functioning. Finally, to receive a diagnosis of BDD the preoccupation cannot be better accounted for by another mental disorder (for example, the person's concern cannot be limited to body shape and size if he has anorexia nervosa). It is important that only those concerns related to ugliness or a sense of physical defectiveness be rated. For example, if a patient dislikes his self-inflicted wounds because they remind him that he is mentally ill, do not rate this concern with the YBOCS-BDD.

To determine whether the person has BDD, and to identify the body parts of concern, the following questions should be asked:

Are you very worried about your appearance in any way?
IF YES: What is your concern? Do you think (body part) is especially unattractive? What about the appearance of your face, skin, hair, nose, or the shape/size/other aspect of any other part of your body?
Does this concern preoccupy you? That is, you think about it a lot, and wish you could worry about it less? Do others say you're more concerned about (body part) than you should be?
What effect does this preoccupation have on your life? Does it cause you a lot of distress? Does your concern have any effect on your family or friends?

List body parts of concern here:

_____

_____

Identifying BDD behaviors: Associated behaviors, which are inquired about with questions 6–10, must also be identified before proceeding with the interview. They can be identified by asking the patient whether he engages in any behaviors in association with his concern about the "defect." The following behaviors, which are common in BDD, should be specifically asked about *(check all that apply):*

____Checking the "defect" in mirrors or other reflecting surfaces (or checking it directly if visible without the use of a mirror)

____Seeking reassurance from others about the appearance of the body part

____Asking others to look at or verify the existence of the "deformity"

____Requests for surgery, dermatologic treatment, or other treatment

____Comparison of the body part with the same body part of others

____Touching the body part

____Grooming behaviors (e.g., hair combing, hair styling, or shaving)

____Skin picking

____Applying make-up

____Camouflaging (e.g., with make-up or with hats or other clothing)

____Rearranging clothing to hide the "defect"

____Other; describe:_____

On repeated testing, you should review and, if necessary, revise the list of "defects" and associated behaviors before doing the ratings. It is useful to be aware of past symptoms because they may reappear during subsequent testing.

SUB ID:_____   DATE:_____
FOLLOW-UP:_____   RATER:_____

For each item circle the number identifying the response which best
characterizes the patient during the *past week*.

---

1. *TIME OCCUPIED* **BY THOUGHTS ABOUT BODY DEFECT** How much of your time is occupied by THOUGHTS about a defect or flaw in your appearance [list body parts of concern]?	0 = None 1 = Mild (less than 1 hr/day) 2 = Moderate (1-3 hrs/day) 3 = Severe (greater than 3 and up to 8 hrs/day) 4 = Extreme (greater than 8 hrs/day)

---

2. *INTERFERENCE* **DUE TO THOUGHTS ABOUT BODY DEFECT** How much do your THOUGHTS about your body defect(s) interfere with your social or work (role) functioning? (Is there anything you aren't doing or can't do because of them?) Y/N Spending time with friends Y/N Dating Y/N Attending social functions Y/N Doing things with family in and outside of home Y/N Going to school/work each day Y/N Being on time for or missing school/work Y/N Focusing at school/work Y/N Productivity at school/work Y/N Doing homework or maintaining grades Y/N Daily activities	0 = None 1 = Mild, slight interference with social, occupational, or role activities, but overall performance not impaired. 2 = Moderate, definite interference with social, occupational, or role performance, but still manageable. 3 = Severe, causes substantial impairment social, occupational, or role performance. 4 = Extreme, incapacitating.

For each item circle the number identifying the response which best characterizes the patient during the *past week*.

---

3. *DISTRESS* **ASSOCIATED WITH THOUGHTS ABOUT BODY DEFECT**
How much distress do your THOUGHTS about your body defect(s) cause you?

Rate "disturbing" feelings or anxiety that seem to be triggered by these thoughts, not general anxiety or anxiety associated with other symptoms.

0 = None
1 = Mild, not too disturbing.
2 = Moderate, disturbing.
3 = Severe, very disturbing.
4 = Extreme, disabling distress.

---

4. *RESISTANCE* **AGAINST THOUGHTS OF BODY DEFECT**
How much of an effort do you make to resist these THOUGHTS? *[Pause]*
How often do you try to disregard them or turn your attention away from these thoughts as they enter your mind?

Only rate effort made to resist, NOT success or failure in actually controlling the thoughts. How much patient resists the thoughts may or may not correlate with ability to control them.

0 = Makes an effort to always resist, or symptoms so minimal doesn't need to actively resist.
1 = Tries to resist most of time.
2 = Makes some effort to resist.
3 = Yields to all such thoughts without attempting to control them but yields with some reluctance.
4 = Completely and willingly yields to all such thoughts.

---

5. *DEGREE OF CONTROL* **OVER THOUGHTS ABOUT BODY DEFECT**
How much control do you have over your THOUGHTS about your body defect(s)?
How successful are you in stopping or diverting these thoughts?

0 = Complete control, or no need for control because thoughts are so minimal.
1 = Much control, usually able to stop or divert these thoughts with some effort and concentration.
2 = Moderate control, sometimes able to stop or divert these thoughts.
3 = Little control, rarely successful in stopping thoughts, can only divert attention with difficulty.
4 = No control, experienced as completely involuntary, rarely able to even momentarily divert attention.

6. *TIME SPENT* IN ACTIVITIES RELATED TO BODY DEFECT

The next several questions are about the activities/behaviors you do in relation to your body defects.

Read list of activities below to determine which ones the patient engages in.

How much time do you spend in ACTIVITIES related to your concern over your appearance [read activities patient engages in]?

> *Read list of activities (check all that apply)*
> ___Checking mirrors/other surfaces
> ___Grooming activities
> ___Applying make-up
> ___Excessive exercise (time beyond 1 hour a day)
> ___Changing/selecting clothes
> ___Scrutinizing others' appearance (comparing)
> ___Questioning others about/discussing your appearance
> ___Picking at skin
> ___Touching
> ___Other _____

0 = None
1 = Mild (spends less than 1 hr/day)
2 = Moderate (1–3 hrs/day)
3 = Severe (spends more than 3 and up to 8 hours/day)
4 = Extreme (spends more than 8 hrs/day in these activities)

For each item circle the number identifying the response which best characterizes the patient during the *past week*.

7. *INTERFERENCE* DUE TO ACTIVITIES RELATED TO BODY DEFECT

How much do these ACTIVITIES interfere with your social or work(role) functioning? (Is there anything you don't do because of them?)

0 = None
1 = Mild, slight interference with social, occupational, or role activities, but overall performance not impaired
2 = Moderate, definite interference with social, occupational, or role but still, manageable
3 = Severe, causes substantial impairment in social, occupational, or role performance.
4 = Extreme, incapacitating.

8. *DISTRESS* ASSOCIATED WITH ACTIVITIES RELATED TO BODY DEFECT

How would you feel if you were prevented from performing these ACTIVITIES?
How anxious would you become?

Rate degree of distress/frustration patient would experience if performance of the activities were suddenly interrupted.

0 = None
1 = Mild, only slightly anxious if behavior prevented.
2 = Moderate, reports that anxiety would mount but remain manageable if behavior is prevented.
3 = Severe, prominent and very disturbing increase in anxiety if behavior is interrupted.
4 = Extreme, incapacitating anxiety from any intervention aimed at modifying activity.

9. *RESISTANCE* AGAINST COMPULSIONS

How much of an effort do you make to resist these ACTIVITIES?

Only rate effort made to resist, NOT success or failure in actually controlling the activities.
How much the patient resists these behaviors may or may not correlate with his ability to control them.

0 = Makes an effort to always resist, or symptoms so minimal doesn't need to actively resist.
1 = Tries to resist most of the time.
2 = Makes some effort to resist.
3 = Yields to almost all of these behaviors without attempting to control them, but does so with some reluctance.
4 = Completely and willingly yields to all behaviors related to body defect.

10. *DEGREE OF CONTROL* OVER COMPULSIVE BEHAVIOR

How strong is the drive to perform these behaviors?
How much control do you have over them?

0 = Complete control, or control is unnecessary because symptoms are mild.
1 = Much control, experiences pressure to perform the behavior, but usually able to exercise voluntary control over it.
2 = Moderate control, strong pressure to perform behavior, can control it only with difficulty.
3 = Little control, very strong drive to perform behavior, must be carried to completion, can delay only with difficulty.
4 = No control, drive to perform behavior experienced as completely involuntary and overpowering, rarely able to even momentarily delay activity.

For each item circle the number identifying the response which best characterizes the patient during the *past week*.

---

11. *INSIGHT*

This question should not be asked to the patient. Instead, complete the BABS, and then return to this question afterwards and score it based on the responses to the BABS questions.

Is it possible that your defect might be less noticeable or less unattractive than you think it is? *[Pause]*

How convinced are you that [fill in body part] is as unattractive as you think it is? *[Pause]*

Can anyone convince you that it doesn't look so bad?

0 = Excellent insight, fully rational.
1 = Good insight. Readily acknowledges absurdity of thoughts (but doesn't seem completely convinced that there isn't something besides anxiety to be concerned about).
2 = Fair insight. Reluctantly admits that thoughts seem unreasonable but wavers.
3 = Poor insight. Maintains that thoughts are not unreasonable.
4 = Lacks insight, delusional. Definitely convinced that concerns are reasonable, unresponsive to contrary evidence.

---

12. *AVOIDANCE*

Have you been avoiding doing anything, going any place, or being with anyone because of your thoughts or behaviors related to your body defects?

If YES, then ask: What do you avoid?

Rate degree to which patient deliberately tries to avoid things such as social interactions or work-related activities. Do not include avoidance of mirrors or avoidance of compulsive behaviors.

0 = No deliberate avoidance.
1 = Mild, minimal avoidance.
2 = Moderate, some avoidance clearly present.
3 = Severe, much avoidance; avoidance prominent.
4 = Extreme, very extensive avoidance; patient avoids almost all activities.

Brackets [ ] indicate material that should be read. Brackets are also used to indicate a pause.
Parentheses ( ) indicate optional material that may be read.
Italicized items are instructions to the interviewer.

Overvalued Ideas Scale

Complete the following questions about obsessions and/ or compulsions which the patient reports as being applicable on the average in the **PAST WEEK, INCLUDING TODAY.**

List the *main* belief which the patient has had in the last week. It should be the one that is associated with the greatest distress or impairment in social and occupational functioning to the patient as assessed by the rater (e.g., I will get AIDS if I do not wash properly after visiting the hospital; my house may burn down if I do not check the stove before leaving the house; I may lose important information if I throw out items that I collect; I am unattractive; my nose is misshapen; my complexion is full of pimples, etc.). The ratings should reflect the patient's beliefs (e.g., how reasonable does the patient perceive the belief, how effective does the patient believe the compulsions are in preventing the feared consequences, etc.). *Only list a belief related to obsessive compulsive disorder. Rate all items according to your evaluation of the patient's belief. You may use the three questions provided below each category to assess various aspects of the belief (e.g., strength, reasonableness).*

Describe the main belief below:

_____

_____

_____

_____

As you rate the patient on each of the items incorporate the patient's specific belief, e.g. How strong is your belief that you will get AIDS if you visit the hospital?

1) STRENGTH OF BELIEF
In the past week, including today;

How strongly do you believe that ___ is true?
How certain/convinced are you this belief is true?
Can your belief be 'shaken' if it is challenged by you or someone else?

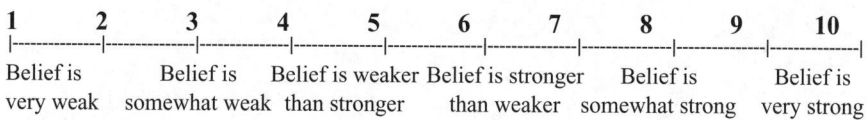

1	2	3	4	5	6	7	8	9	10
Belief is very weak		Belief is somewhat weak	Belief is weaker than stronger		Belief is stronger than weaker		Belief is somewhat strong		Belief is very strong

(Very weak to very strong refer to the possibility of the belief being true, i.e. very weak – minimally possible; very strong – extremely possible.)

Rating Item 1:_____

2)   REASONABLENESS OF BELIEF
In the past week, including today;

How reasonable is your belief?
Is your belief justified or rational?
Is the belief logical or seem reasonable?

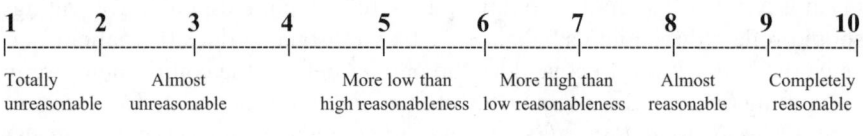

Rating Item 2:_____

3)   LOWEST STRENGTH OF BELIEF IN PAST WEEK

In the last week, what would you say was the lowest rating of strength for your belief?
How weak did your belief become in the last weak?
Were there times in the past week that you doubted your belief, even for a fleeting moment, whether____ was true? If so, tell me more about it?

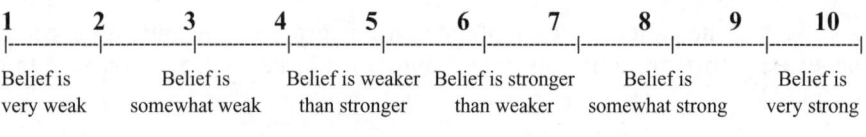

Rating Item 3:_____

4)   HIGHEST STRENGTH OF BELIEF IN PAST WEEK

In the last week, what was your highest rating of strength for your belief?
How strong did your belief become in the last week?
How certain/convinced were you about your belief in the past week?

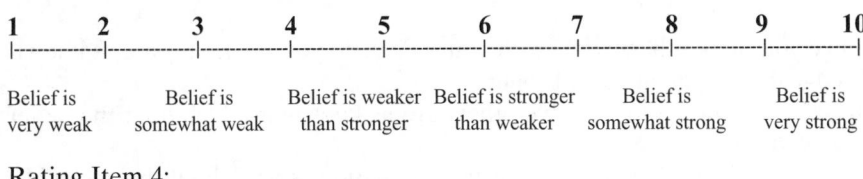

1	2	3	4	5	6	7	8	9	10

Belief is   Belief is   Belief is weaker Belief is stronger   Belief is   Belief is
very weak   somewhat weak   than stronger   than weaker   somewhat strong   very strong

Rating Item 4:_____

5)   ACCURACY OF BELIEF
In the past week, including today;

How accurate is your belief?
How correct is your belief?
To what degree is your belief erroneous?

1	2	3	4	5	6	7	8	9	10

Totally   Almost   More low than More high than   Almost   Completely
inaccurate inaccurate   high accuracy low accuracy   accurate   accurate

Rating Item 5:_____

6)   EXTENT OF ADHERENCE BY OTHERS

How likely is it that others in the general population (in the community, state,
    country, etc.) have the same beliefs?
How strongly do these others agree with your belief?
To what extent do these others share your belief?

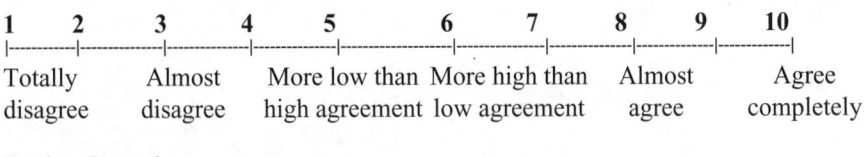

1	2	3	4	5	6	7	8	9	10

Totally   Almost   More low than More high than   Almost   Agree
disagree   disagree   high agreement low agreement   agree   completely

Rating Item 6:_____

7)   ATTRIBUTION OF DIFFERING VIEWS BY OTHERS

Do others share the same belief as you? Yes____ No____
If the patient answers Yes go to 7a, if the patient answers No go to 7b.

7a)   VIEWS OTHERS AS POSSESSING SAME BELIEF

Since you think others agree with your belief, do you think they are as knowl-
    edgeable as you about this belief?
To what extent do you believe others are as knowledgeable about the belief
    as you are?
Do you believe others have as much information as you about this belief?

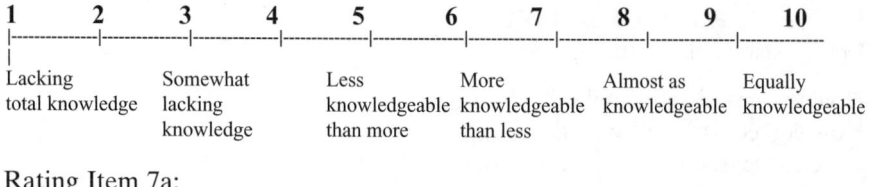

Rating Item 7a:_____

7b)   VIEWS OTHERS AS HOLDING DIFFERING BELIEF

Since you think others disagree with you, do you think they are less knowl-
    edgeable than you about this belief?
To what extent do you believe others are less knowledgeable about the belief
    than you are?
Do you believe others have less information than you about this belief?

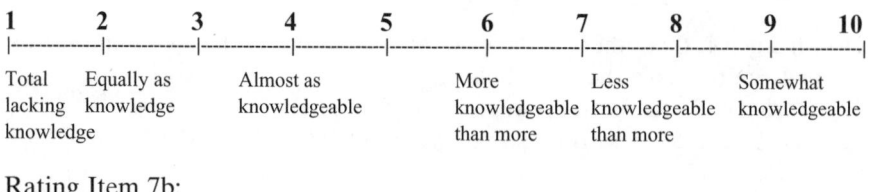

Rating Item 7b:_____

8) EFFECTIVENESS OF COMPULSIONS

In the past week, including today:

How effective are the compulsions/ritualistic behaviors in preventing negative
 consequences other than anxiety?
Are your compulsions of any value in stopping the feared outcome?
Is it possible that your compulsions may not help prevent the negative
 outcomes?

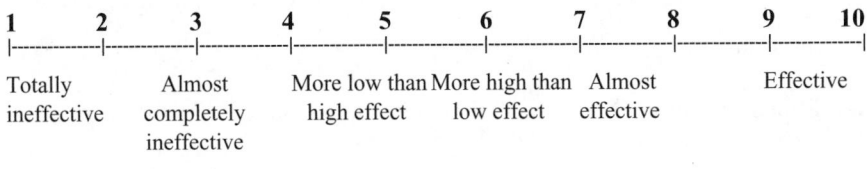

1	2	3	4	5	6	7	8	9	10
Totally ineffective	Almost completely ineffective		More low than high effect	More high than low effect	Almost effective			Effective	

Rating Item 8:_____

9) INSIGHT

To what extent do you think that your disorder has caused you to have this
 belief?
How probable is it that your beliefs are due to psychological or psychiatric
 reasons?
Do you think that your belief is due to a disorder?

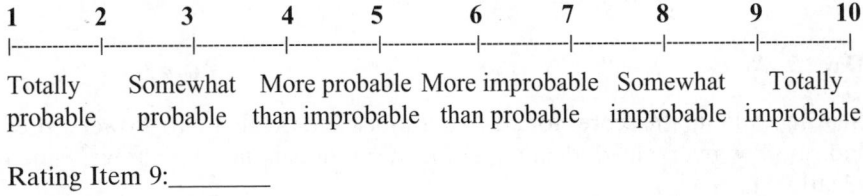

1	2	3	4	5	6	7	8	9	10
Totally probable	Somewhat probable	More probable than improbable	More improbable than probable		Somewhat improbable		Totally improbable		

Rating Item 9:_____

10) STRENGTH OF RESISTANCE

How much energy do you put into rejecting your belief?
How strongly do you try to change your belief?
Do you attempt to resist your belief?

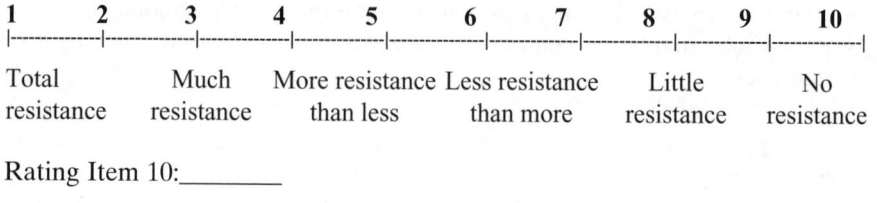

| 1 | 2 | 3 | 4 | 5 | 6 | 7 | 8 | 9 | 10 |

Total resistance | Much resistance | More resistance than less | Less resistance than more | Little resistance | No resistance

Rating Item 10:_____

Additional question (not to be included in the scoring)

11) DURATION OF BELIEF

a) During the time that you have had this belief did it ever fluctuate?

If so, within what period of time?

Check one of the following:

____   ____   ____   ____

Day   Week   Month   Year

b) In retrospect, how long have you held this particular belief?

Check one of the following:

____   ____   ____   ____

Day   Week   Month   Year

Scoring: Add up the scores for all 10 questions and divide by 10. Lower scores indicate low overvalued ideation and higher scores indicate high overvalued ideation.

Valued Directions Questionnaire

Understanding your values

In this questionnaire, there are various prompts for each area for you to write down a brief statement. You don't have to fill in a values statement for every area, just leave it blank if you think it is inappropriate. After writing down your statement for each area, you may want to clarify them with a friend or therapist. *Be careful not to write down values that you think you **should** have because others will approve it.* Only write down what you know to be true to yourself. It is probably a valued direction if you have acted on it consistently before you experienced your problem. Some individuals who have had an emotional problem for many years may struggle with this exercise but persevere because the exercise is very important.

Note that values are not goals – values are more like a compass – and must be lived out by committed action. Goals are part of the process of committing yourself to action. With values, you never reach your destination as there is always something more you can do to be a good partner or parent or whatever direction you have chosen. This does not mean you will not fail at times – it means that if and when you fail, you can learn from it, take responsibility and restart the commitment to the action. It might take some time to discover all of your values, so alongside the questionnaire, here are some ideas to help you:

- Imagine what aspects of life you would be engaging in if you had never felt depressed.
- Brainstorm all the activities/interests you can think of and consider which *might* be close to your valued directions.
- Remind yourself of what you used to value or aspire to when you were younger. Have any simply been "squashed" by your mood?
- Consider whether fear of what other people will think, or fear of failing might be holding you from pursuing.
- Consider a role model or hero and the values he or she holds.
- Have a chat with a trusted friend (or therapist) who knows you well and see what he or she would guess your values to be.
- Be prepared to experiment and "try on for size" living consistently with a given valued direction to see how it "fits."

Area	Valued direction
1. Intimacy (What is important to you in how you act in an intimate relationship? What sort of partner do you want to be? If you are not involved in a relationship at present, how would you like to act in a relationship?)	
2. Family relationships (What is important to you in how you want to act as a brother/sister; son/daughter; father/ mother or parent-in-law? If you are not in contact with some of them, would you like to be and how would you act in such a relationship?)	
3. Social relationships (What is important to you in the way you act in the friendships you have? How would you like your friends to remember you? If you have no friends, would you like to have some and what role would you like in a friendship?)	
4. Work (What is important to you in your work? What sort of employee do you want to be? How important to you is what you achieve in your career? What sort of business do you want to run?)	
5. Education and training (What is important to you in your education or training? What sort of student do you want to be? If you are not in education, would you like to be?)	
6. Recreation (What is important to you in what you do to follow any interests, sports or hobbies? If you are not following any interests, what would you ideally like to be pursuing?)	
7. Spirituality (If you are spiritual, what is important to you in the way you want to follow a spiritual path? If you are not, would you like to be and what do you ideally want?)	
8. Voluntary work (What would you like to do for the larger community? For example, voluntary or charity work or political activity?)	
9. Health/physical well-being (What is important to you in how you act for your physical health?)	
10. Mental health (What is important to you generally in how you look after your mental health?)	
11. Any other values that are not listed above	

Functional Analysis for Psychogenic Excoriation

1. *History*
When did your skin picking first begin?
When did it become a problem?
Is it something you want to stop?
Did you have any skin problems (e.g., acne) when you first started picking your skin? Have you seen a dermatologist? (When? What was the diagnosis and treatment? Did you tell him or her about your picking?)
Do you experience or have you ever experienced any other habitual behavior (e.g., nail biting; thumb sucking; knuckle cracking; cheek chewing; head banging; teeth flicking; lip biting)?

2. *Antecedents:*
Determine the cues for picking
2.1 *Are there any specific triggers for your picking?*
2.2 *Is there a particular setting in which you pick? (e.g., at your bathroom mirror, putting on make-up, driving, studying)*
2.3 *Do you use any particular implements (e.g., using a mirror and tweezers)*
2.4 *Is the way you feel a trigger to pick? (e.g., feeling bored, lonely, hurt, guilty or anxious)*
2.5 *Is seeing something on your skin in the mirror a trigger to pick? (e.g., seeing a scab, or acne spot, scars, vascular markings, freckles, moles, imperfections, lack of symmetry)*
2.6 *Is feeling something on your skin with your finger a trigger to pick? (e.g., a bump on your skin; when the area does not feel right)*
2.7 *Is a physical sensation on your skin a trigger to pick? (e.g., an itch, irritation, burning; something under your skin)*
2.8 *Is there anything that goes through your mind that will act as a trigger to pick (e.g., "my skin is dirty and disgusting and has pus under it").*
2.9 *How aware are you of the triggers for picking? Is it something that is automatic, that you plan or is it a mixture of the two? (e.g., is some of the picking more automatic and others more planned)*

2. *Discriminative stimuli*. As with cues, facilitators or inhibitors may be internal or external.
2.10 *Do the presence of other people around you make it easier or harder to pick?*
2.11 *Do you use implements, such as mirrors or tweezers that may inhibit or facilitate picking? (Are there any urges or postures such as your hand near your facial skin?)*

2.12 Do you have any beliefs that make picking more likely? (e.g. "I'll pick just this one area" or "I deserve this pick")

3.   Behavior
Can you describe in detail what you actually do when you pick your skin?
3.1) Preparatory stage – *Do you go to a specific place?*
What sites do you choose to pick most often?(e.g., pimples; scabs; scabs; freckles; scars; mosquito bites; healthy skin)
Do you then secure your implements?

3.2) Actual picking
Where on your body do you pick?
Do you choose a site on the body?

Do you conduct a visual or tactile search, for a target area?
Is it preceded by cleaning the skin excessively with soaps or cleansers?
Is the skin then picked, squeezed, or pressed, removed or examined?
What do you use to pick your skin with? (fingernails; razors; pins; bruise skin; tweezers; any specific instruments)
When in the day do you pick?

3.3) Final stage
Does the final stage involve getting rid of the skin and camouflaging the skin with cover-up sticks or using make-up?

4.   Consequences
4.1) Intended consequences
What specific outcome are you trying to achieve?
What do you tell yourself that you want to achieve?

4.2) Immediate consequences (These may be sufficient to terminate the picking and fulfilled the individual need.)
Do you get a feeling of satisfaction, e.g., at getting rid of dirt; removing a scab or blackhead?
Do you escape or distract yourself from uncomfortable thoughts or feelings such as boredom?

4.3) Unintended or aversive consequences that might be involved in terminating picking include emotional states such as shame which may either act as trigger to cease picking or it might be a cue for further picking. Picking might also result in bleeding, pain or discomfort. Alternatively picking may cease because of an interruption – e.g., a scheduled activity, or awareness of the degree of damage that has been caused.

What level of physical damage typically results from an episode of skin picking?
None
Mild skin damage (i.e. redness, irritation)
Moderate skin damage (i.e. visible cuts or wounds on the skin, bleeding)
Severe skin damage (i.e. open wounds that require medical attention)
Have any physical complications resulted from your skin picking behavior?
Does it lead you to alter your behavior in other ways (e.g., become housebound)?
Have you ever required surgery for injuries sustained from your skin picking?
What do you feel is your overall purpose for picking?

Skin Picking Impact Scale (Keuthen et al., 2001)

Name: _____   Date: _____

INSTRUCTIONS: Make a check mark next to any statements which you have found to be true for you. For true statements, please indicate degree of severity (0–5) over the PRECEDING WEEK.

		None		Mild		Severe	
1.	I don't look people in the eye because of my skin picking.	0	1	2	3	4	5
2.	I think my social life would be better if I didn't pick my skin.	0	1	2	3	4	5
3.	I hate the way I look because of my skin picking.	0	1	2	3	4	5
4.	It takes me longer to go out because of my skin picking.	0	1	2	3	4	5
5.	I feel embarrassed because of my skin picking.	0	1	2	3	4	5
6.	There are some things I can't do because of my skin picking.	0	1	2	3	4	5
7.	I feel unattractive because of my skin picking.	0	1	2	3	4	5
8.	It takes me longer than others to get ready in the morning because of my skin picking.	0	1	2	3	4	5
9.	I don't like people looking at me because of my skin picking.	0	1	2	3	4	5
10.	My relationships have suffered because of my skin picking.	0	1	2	3	4	5

Defect-Related Beliefs Test

Instructions: Please read the following statements and rate each according to the scale provided.

1. If there are people around me who are more attractive than me overall, then I don't feel attractive.

   < 1 --------------2-------------- 3-------------- 4 --------------5 >
   Strongly disagree   Strongly agree

2. If I notice someone whose (body part of concern) is better looking than mine, then I think mine is unattractive/ugly.

   < 1 --------------2-------------- 3-------------- 4 --------------5 >
   Strongly disagree   Strongly agree

3. If I *feel* that my (body part of concern) is unattractive/ugly, it means that it *looks* unattractive/ugly.

   < 1 --------------2-------------- 3-------------- 4 --------------5 >
   Strongly disagree   Strongly agree

4. If my (body part of concern) is not beautiful, then it must be ugly.

   < 1 --------------2-------------- 3-------------- 4 --------------5 >
   Strongly disagree   Strongly agree

5. If there is one thing wrong with a body part of mine, then I feel that part is ugly.

   < 1 --------------2-------------- 3-------------- 4 --------------5 >
   Strongly disagree   Strongly agree

6. If there is one flaw in my *overall* appearance, then I feel unattractive.

   < 1 --------------2-------------- 3-------------- 4 --------------5 >
   Strongly disagree   Strongly agree

7. How I feel about myself as a person is usually related to how I feel about the way I look.

< 1 --------------2 -------------- 3-------------- 4 --------------5 >

Strongly disagree   Strongly agree

8. If I looked better, my *whole life* would be better.

< 1 --------------2 -------------- 3-------------- 4 --------------5 >

Strongly disagree   Strongly agree

9. Happiness comes from looking good.

< 1 --------------2 -------------- 3-------------- 4 --------------5 >

Strongly disagree   Strongly agree

10. Physical perfection is both possible and desirable.

< 1 --------------2 -------------- 3-------------- 4 --------------5 >

Strongly disagree   Strongly agree

Appendix 2

Leaflets and forms used during therapy

BDD information leaflet

This is a general information leaflet about BDD written for the lay person. It is free to copy.

Cost–benefit analysis

A cost–benefit analysis can be used in helping a person focus on the advantages and disadvantages of a behavior or valued directions.

Skin picking monitoring

These forms can be used to monitor the frequency and pattern of skin picking and of the competing response.

Body Dysmorphic Disorder: A Treatment Manual. David Veale and Fugen Neziroglu
© 2010 John Wiley & Sons, Ltd.

BDD Information Leaflet

What is body dysmorphic disorder (BDD)?

Body dysmorphic disorder (BDD) is a condition that involves an extreme preoccupation with one or more features that are not noticeable or abnormal to others. People with BDD usually feel they are ugly, that they are "not right," and are very self-conscious. They usually have compulsive behaviors such as mirror-checking that are difficult to resist. They may resort to needless cosmetic and dermatological procedures, which they are often either dissatisfied with or that have little impact on their preoccupation and distress. People with BDD also tend to be very secretive and reluctant to seek help because they are afraid that others will think them vain or narcissistic. (Of course, they are *not* vain at all, as their goal is to fit in rather than to stand out and they usually hate their appearance.)

The older term for BDD, "dysmorphophobia," is sometimes still used. The media sometimes refer to BDD as "Imagined Ugliness Syndrome." This isn't particularly helpful, as the ugliness is very real to the individual concerned. A few people with BDD acknowledge that they may be blowing things up out of proportion. At the other extreme, others are firmly convinced of the reality of their supposed abnormality. Whatever the person's degree of insight into their condition, someone with BDD usually knows that others believe their appearance to be "normal" and will have been told so many times.

How much does BDD interfere in people's lives?

The degree of disability caused by BDD varies from slight to very severe. Many people with BDD are either single or divorced, which suggests that they find it difficult to form relationships. It can make regular employment and family life impossible. Those who are in regular employment or who have family responsibilities would almost certainly find life more productive and satisfying if they did not have the symptoms of BDD. Their partners may also become involved and suffer greatly.

How common is BDD?

About 1–1.5% of the world's population may have BDD, and it may be more frequent in some cultures where appearance is more valued. The exact figure is not known. It is recognized to be a hidden disorder, as many people with BDD are too ashamed to reveal their problem.

Does it affect both sexes?

Both sexes are equally affected by BDD. People with BDD are most commonly concerned with their skin, followed by concerns about their nose, hair, eyes, chin, lips, or overall body build. People with BDD may complain of a lack of symmetry, or feel that something is too big or too small, or that it is out of proportion to the rest of the body. Any part of the body may be involved in BDD, including the breasts or genitals. Although women are more likely to have hair concerns (e.g., that hair is the wrong color, or it lacks body, or there is excessive body hair), men are significantly more concerned with hair thinning or baldness.

The sex differences also occur with body size and shape. Women are more likely to be preoccupied by their breasts, hips, weight, and legs, usually believing that they are too large or fat. In contrast, men tend to be preoccupied with their body build, which has also been described as muscle dysmorphia (described below). Another significant sex difference is that men are more likely to report hair thinning and preoccupation with their genitals (usually a concern that their penis is too small), or be concerned about breast development, which they see as too feminine. Women may also feel that their genitalia or labia are too large and seek cosmetic surgery to reduce their size.

Muscle dysmorphia is a variation of BDD in which a man is usually worried about being too small or too skinny or not muscular enough. Despite such concerns, many such men are unusually muscular and large. Many of them spend hours lifting weights and pay great attention to nutrition. Others may abuse steroids. In our experience, such individuals are less likely to seek help than other people with BDD and may be less disabled by the condition.

When does BDD start?

BDD usually begins in adolescence, a time when people are generally most sensitive about their appearance. However, many people wait for years before seeking help. They may repeatedly consult dermatologists or cosmetic surgeons but often get little satisfaction from these treatments. When they do finally seek help from mental health professionals, they often ask about other symptoms such as depression, social anxiety, or obsessive compulsive disorder (OCD) and do not reveal their real concerns. However, people with BDD are often also depressed with a high rate of attempting suicide.

What treatments are available for BDD?

The National Institute of Health and Clinical Excellence (NICE), which is highly regarded throughout the world, has produced treatment guidelines for

BDD, based on published research into BDD. At present, unfortunately, there is very little research into BDD compared to, say, depression. Furthermore, the published research is only a snapshot of current evidence, which will be updated as new evidence becomes available. The treatment guidelines on OCD and BDD can be downloaded from the NICE website (www.nice. org.uk/guidance/CG31). We have summarized the NICE recommendations for the treatment of BDD below.

The guidelines are based on scientific "evidence" – that is, studies in which people with BDD are randomly selected to receive one or more different treatments or to remain on a waiting list. One group might be given a placebo or dummy treatment so that researchers can see to what extent the attention of a doctor or therapist and the passage of time affects the outcome. At the end of the study the researchers then re-test participants to see which treatments are more effective.

In all the guidelines, there is particular emphasis on patient choice and on the patient's experience with previous treatment. However, treatment options partly depend on the availability of therapists and local resources. If you are seeing a doctor or therapist, he or she will advise you as to what is best for you given the resources available. It isn't always obvious which treatment is most effective for a particular person. Sometimes you may have to try two or three different approaches before you find one that is effective for you. The core message is that there is evidence that BDD *is treatable and you can get back to a normal life.*

Cognitive behavior therapy (CBT) for BDD

CBT was initially described by Aaron T. Beck, who revolutionized the psychological treatment of depression in the early 1970s. CBT has been adapted for BDD and has been shown to be effective for adults in a few small studies. CBT is therefore recommended for treating BDD. More research is needed to compare CBT with other psychological treatments and to assess its effectiveness for adolescents. At present, there is no evidence that counseling, psychodynamic therapy, or hypnosis is effective for BDD. This does not mean that such therapies are ineffective but that they have not yet been investigated. It also means that people with BDD should first be offered CBT from a competent practitioner, as it has been shown to be effective.

Medication for BDD

Anti-depressant medication (a serotonergic reuptake inhibitor) is not recommended for mild symptoms of BDD. However, if a patient's doctor believes that the BDD symptoms are likely to get worse (or if the symptoms have lasted for a long time), medication may still be recommended. Anti-depressant medi-cation is also recommended as an option in treating moderate to severe symptoms of BDD. Suitable medications include fluoxetine, sertraline, citalopram, paroxetine, fluvoxamine, and clomipramine. In general, it is thought best to increase the dose to the maximum tolerated.

Combining medication with CBT

In general, it is not recommended using medication alone because there is usually a higher rate of relapse when a person stops taking it. Results are probably better than medication alone when the medication is combined with CBT especially in more severe cases. However, given that there may be different types of BDD, a few people may do well on medication alone and get back to a normal life with just that. The difficulty lies in identifying such individuals. Equally, there are some people who want medication (especially tranquillizers) to avoid having painful feelings. The two approaches may seem incompatible, but we have no evidence that one interferes with the other. If anything, people with more severe problems are likely to do better on a combination of medication and CBT. However a lot more research needs to be done in BDD to provide more definite answers.

David Veale and Fugen Neziroglu

Further reading

Veale, D., Willson, R. & Clark, A. (2009). *Overcoming Body Image Problems (including Body Dysmorphic Disorder)*. London: Martin Robinson.

Cost-Benefit Analysis Form

Option 1 _____

SHORT-TERM COST	SHORT-TERM BENEFIT
To Myself	To Myself
To Others	To Others
LONG-TERM COST	LONG-TERM COST
To Myself	To Myself
To Others	To Others

Option 2 _____

SHORT-TERM COST	SHORT-TERM BENEFIT
To Myself	To Myself
To Others	To Others
LONG-TERM COST	LONG-TERM COST
To Myself	To Myself
To Others	To Others

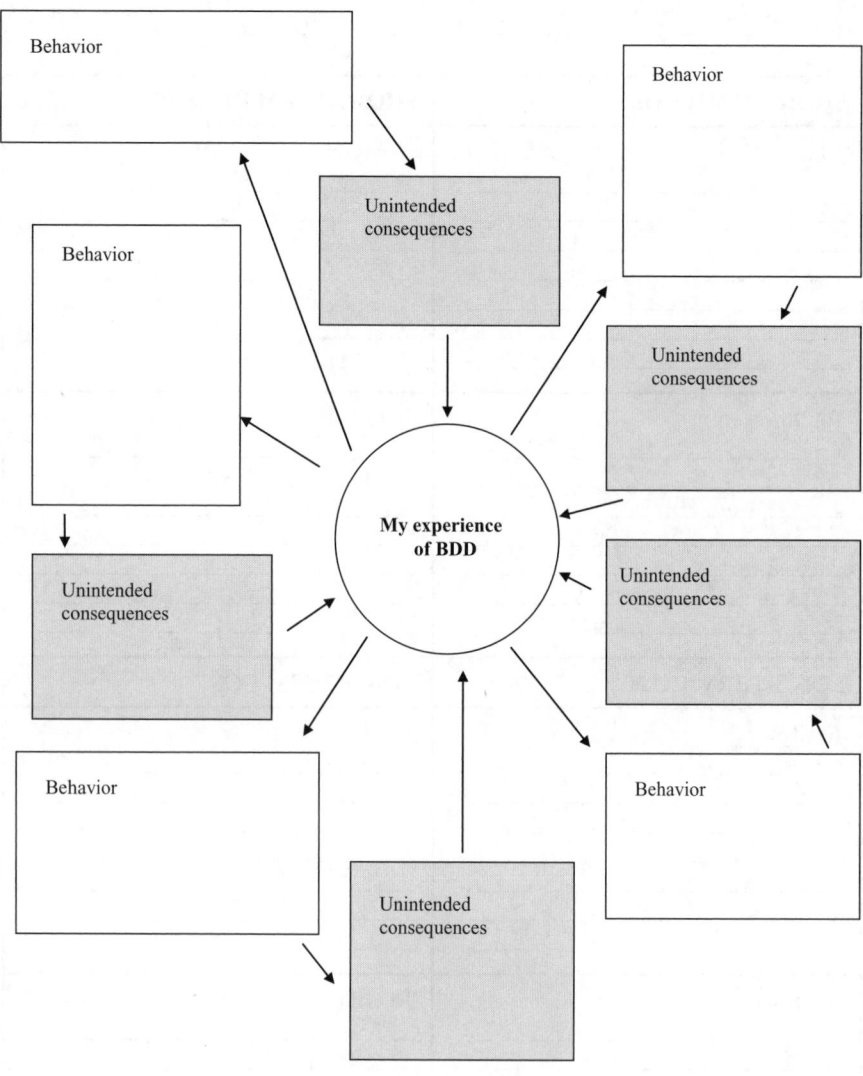

Skin picking monitoring form
Part 1

This form is for monitoring skin picking. The purpose is to help you and your therapist learn more about your behavior, especially the pattern and the contexts in which it occurs. Try to write down the details that occur immediately after the behavior (not later that day or the following days) as that way it will be fresh in your mind.

Date/Time	Duration: How long did you pick for?	Location: Where were you?	Activity: What were you doing before picking?	Strength of urge to pick on a scale of 0 to 10, (where 0 is no urge)	Degree of awareness of picking on a scale of 0 to 10, where 0 is no awareness	Notable feelings before you picked	Notable thoughts or images before you picked	Notable sensations before you picked (e.g. itching or burning)
1								
2								
3								
4								
5								

Skin picking monitoring form
Part 2

Site: Where did you pick?	What effect did picking have on your feelings?	What effect did picking have on your thoughts?	What effect did picking have on your sensations?	How strong was your effort to resist on a scale of 0 to 10 (0 is no effort at all)	What did you do to try to resist picking?
1					
2					
3					
4					
5					

Competing response self-monitoring form

Time/date	Location "Where were you?"	Activity "What were you doing"	Strength of urge to pick (0–10) (where 0 is no urge to pick)	Did I use a competing response with no urge or before, during or after picking?	Result of competing response	Other comments
1						
2						
3						
4						
5						
6						
7						

Appendix 3

Resources for BDD

Further Reading

These are all books suitable for people with BDD and body image problems.

Cash, T. F. (2008). *The Body Image Workbook: An 8-Step Program for Learning to Like Your Looks* (2nd edition.) Oakland, CA: New Harbinger Publications.

Claiborn, J. & Pedrick, C. (2002). *The BDD Workbook*. Oakland, CA: New Harbinger Publications.

Phillips, K. (1996). *The Broken Mirror: Understanding and Treating Body Dysmorphic Disorder*. Oxford: Oxford University Press.

Pope, H., Phillips, K. & Olivardia, R. (2000). *The Adonis Complex – How to Identify, Treat, and Prevent Body Obsession in Men and Boys*. New York: Simon & Schuster.

Veale, D. Willson, R. & Clark, A. (2009). *Overcoming Body Image Problems (Including Body Dysmorphic Disorder)*. London: Robinson.

Wilhelm, S. (2006). *Feeling Good About the Way You Look*. New York: Guilford Publications.

Body Dysmorphic Disorder: A Treatment Manual. David Veale and Fugen Neziroglu
© 2010 John Wiley & Sons, Ltd.

Useful Contacts and Information

Australia

Anxiety Recovery Centre Victoria
Obsessive Compulsive and Anxiety Disorders Foundation of Victoria
42 High Street Road
Ashwood
Victoria 3147
OCD & Anxiety Helpline Tel: 03 9886 9377
Office Tel: 03 9886 9233
Fax: 03 9886 9411
Website: www.arcvic.com.au
Email: arcmail@arcvic.com.au
The Anxiety Recovery Centre Victoria is an organization for people living
with anxiety disorders.

Argentina

Bio-behavioral Institute
Av. del Libertador 930 4 piso 2 cuerpo
Buenos Aires. – Argentina
Tania Borda y Ricardo Perez-Rivera
Tel. 54 (011) 4812-5904
E: info@bio-behavioral.com.ar

Canada

Obsessive Compulsive Information and Support Centre
R. 204–825 Sherbrook Street
Winnipeg MB R3A 1M5
Tel: 204 942 3331
Fax: 204 975 3027
Email: occmanitoba@shaw.ca
Website: www.members.shaw.ca/occmanitoba/
This website provides assistance and education for people affected by OCD
and related disorders such as BDD.

South Africa

OCD Association of South Africa
PO Box 87127
Houghton 2041
South Africa
Tel: +27 (0)11 786 7030
Email: pserebro@iafrica.com
The website provides a place for people with OCD and their families to share
common ground, information and support.

United Kingdom

The BDD Foundation
Website: www.thebddfoundation.org
Email: admin@thebddfoundation.com
The BDD Foundation aims to increase awareness and understanding of body
dysmorphic disorder.

BDD Help
Website: http://www.bddhelp.com/
Email: emma@bddhelp.com
Information about overcoming BDD. The website is maintained by someone
who has recovered from BDD.

British Association of Behavioural and Cognitive Psychotherapies
BABCP
Victoria Buildings
9–13 Silver Street
Bury BL9 0EU
Tel: 0161 797 4484
Fax: 0161 797 2670
Website: www.babcp.com
Register of accredited therapists: www.cbtukregister.com
Email: babcp@babcp.com

OCD Action
Davina House
Suites 506-507
137–149 Goswell Road
London EC1V 7ET
Office Tel: 0870 360 6232
Helpline: 0845 390 6232
Fax: 020 7288 0828
Email: info@ocdaction.org.uk
Website: www.ocdaction.org.uk/
OCD Action is a user-led charity for individuals with OCD and BDD.

Centre for Anxiety Disorders and Trauma
South London and Maudsley Trust
99 Denmark Hill
London SE5 8AZ
http://psychology.iop.kcl.ac.uk/cadat/GPs/BDD.aspx
Tel: 020 3228 2101
Specialist NHS out-patient clinic and residential unit for treating BDD directed
   by Dr David Veale

The Priory Hospital North London
The Bourne
Southgate
London N14 6RA
Tel: 020 8882 8191
Specialist private clinic and in-patient unit for BDD directed by Dr David
   Veale

United States of America

Association for Behavioral and Cognitive Therapies
305 7th Avenue
16th Floor
New York NY 10001
Tel: 212 647 1890
Fax: 212 647 1865
Website: www.aabt.org

BDD Central
Website: www.bddcentral.com
Email: bddcentral@gmail.com
Website and forum for people with BDD. Also lists various specialists in BDD
around the world.

OC Foundation
337 Notch Hill Road
North Branford, CT 06471
Tel: 203 315 2190
Fax: 203 315 2196
Email: info@ocfoundation.org
Website: www.ocfoundation.org/
The OC Foundation is a non-profit organization for people with OCD and
related disorders such as BDD.

Bio-Behavioural Institute
935 Northern Boulevard, Suite 102
Great Neck, New York 11021
Tel: (516) 487-7116
Email: info@biobehavioralinstitute.com
Website: www.biobehavioralinstitute.com
Specialist clinic for BDD directed by Dr Fugen Neziroglu

Body Image Program
Butler Hospital
345 Blackstone Blvd
Providence, RI 02906.
T: 401-455-6466
E: Katharine_Phillips@Brown.edu.
W: www.bodyimageprogram.com.
Specialist research clinic in BDD directed by Dr Katharine Phillips

Los Angeles Body Dysmorphic Disorder and Body Image Clinic
10850 Wilshire Blvd., Suite 240
Los Angeles, CA, 90024
T: 310-741-2000
E: Director@BDDClinic.com
W: www.bddclinic.com
Directed by Arie Winograd

Massachusetts General Hospital
BDD Clinic and Research Unit
Charles River Plaza
Simches Research Building
185 Cambridge St., Suite 2000
Boston, MA 02115
T: 617-726 6766
W: www2.massgeneral.org/bdd/
E: kscales1@partners.org
Research Clinic Directed by Dr Sabine Wilhelm

OCD Center of Los Angeles
10921 Wilshire Blvd., #502
Los Angeles, CA, 90024
T: 310-335-5443
W: www.ocdla.com
Clinic Directed by Tom Corboy

UCLA Semel Institute for Neuroscience and Human Behavior
300 UCLA Medical Plaza, Suite 2200
Los Angeles, CA 90095
W: www.semel.ucla.edu/bdd
BDD Research Program directed by Professor James Feusner

References

Al-Adawi, S., Martin, R., Al-Naamani, A. et al. (2001). Body dysmorphic disorder in Oman: cultural and neurpsychological findings [journal]. *La Revue de santé de la mediterranée orientale*, *7*(3), 562–567.

Albertini, R. S. & Phillips, K. A. (1999). Thirty-three cases of body dysmorphic disorder in children and adolescents. *Journal of the American Academy of Child & Adolescent Psychiatry*, *38*(4), 453–459.

Allan, S. & Gilbert, P. (1995). A social comparison scale: Psychometric properties and relationship to psychopathology. *Personality and Individual Differences*, *19*(3) (September), 293–299.

Allan, S. & Gilbert, P. (1997). Submissive behavior and psychopathology. *British Journal of Clinical Psychology*, *36*(4), 467–488.

American Psychiatric Association (1980). *Diagnostic and Statistical Manual of Mental Disorders*, 3rd edition. Washington, DC: American Psychiatric Assocation.

American Psychiatric Association (1994). *Diagnostic and Statistical Manual of Mental disorders*, 4th edition. Washington, DC: APA.

American Society for Aesthetic Plastic Surgeons (2008). *ASAPS 2008 Statistics on Cosmetic Surgery*. www.surgery.org/press/statistics.php.

Andreasen, N. C., Endicott, J., Spitzer, R. L. & Winokur, G. (1977). The family history method using diagnostic criteria. Reliability and validity. *Archives of General Psychiatry*, *34*(10), 1229–1235.

Andrews, B. (1995). Bodily shame as a mediator between abusive experiences and depression. *Journal of Abnormal Psychology*, *104*(3), 277–285.

Andrews, B. (1997). Bodily shame in relation to abuse in childhood and bulimia: a preliminary investigation. *British Journal of Clinical Psychology*, *36*, 41–49.

Andrews, B., Qian, M. & Valentine, J. D. (2002). Predicting depressive symptoms with a new measure of shame: the experience of shame scale. *British Journal of Clinical Psychology*, *41*(Pt 1), 29–42.

Anson, M. (2008). Social evaluative concerns and processes in body dysmorphic disorder. PhD thesis, Institute of Psychiatry, King's College, London.

Anson, M., Veale, D. & De Silva, P. (2003). Social evaluative concerns and processes in body dysmorphic disorder. In *Proceedings of the Papers Presented at Conference Innovation in Cognitive Behavior Therapy for BDD*, London.

Anson, M., Veale, D., De Silva, P. & Mansell, W. (in submission). Attention to faces in BDD.

Aouizerate, B., Pujol, H., Grabot, D. et al. (2003). Body dysmorphic disorder in a sample of cosmetic surgery applicants. *European Psychiatry*, *18*(7), 365–368.

Archer, R. P. & Cash, T. F. (1985). Physical attractiveness and maladjustment among psychiatric inpatients. *Journal of Social and Clinical Psychology*, *3*(2), 170–180.

Arnold, L. M., Auchenbach, M. B. & McElroy, S. L. (2001). Psychogenic excoriation. Clinical features, proposed diagnostic criteria, epidemiology and approaches to treatment. *CNS Drugs*, *15*(5), 351–359.

Arnold, L. M., McElroy, S. L., Mutasim, D. F. et al. (1998). Characteristics of 34 adults with psychogenic excoriation [see comments]. *Journal of Clinical Psychiatry*, *59*(10), 509–514.

Arnold, L. M., Mutasim, D. F., Dwight, M. M. et al. (1999). An open clinical trial of fluvoxamine treatment of psychogenic excoriation. *Journal of Clinical Psychopharmacology*, *19*(1), 15–18.

Arntz, A. & Weertman, A. (1999). Treatment of childhood memories: theory and practice. *Behavior Research and Therapy*, *37*(8), 715–740.

Atiullah, N. & Phillips, K. A. (2001). Fatal body dysmorphic disorder by proxy. *Journal of Clinical Psychiatry*, *62*(3), 204–205.

Azrin, N. H. & Nunn, R. G. (1973). Habit reversal: a method of eliminating nervous habits and tics. *Behavior Research and Therapy*, *11*, 619–628.

Azrin, N. H., Nunn, R. G. & Frantz, S. E. (1980). Treatment of hair pulling (trichotillomania): a comparative study of habit reversal and negative practice training. *Journal of Behavior Therapy and Experimental Psychiatry*, *11*(1), 13–20.

Bach, M. & Bach, D. (1993). Psychiatric and psychometric issues in acne excoriée. *Psychotherapy and Psychosomatics*, *60*, 207–210.

Baer, L. (1994). Factor analysis of symptom subtypes of obsessive compulsive disorder and their relation to personality and tic disorders. *Journal of Clinical Psychiatry*, *55*, 18–23.

Barr, L. C., Goodman, W. K. & Price, L. H. (1992). Acute exacerbation of body dysmorphic disorder during tryptophan depletion [letter]. *American Journal of Psychiatry*, *149*(10), 1406–1407.

Bartsch, D. (2007) Prevalence of body dysmorphic disorder symptoms and associated clinical features among Australian university students. *Clinical Psychologist*, *11*(1) 16–23.

Bass, C., Bolton, J. & Wilkinson, P. (2002). Referrals to a liaisons psychiatry out-patient clinic in a UK general hospital: a report on 900 cases. *Acta Psychiatrica Scandinavica*, *105*, 117–125.

Beck A T. (1969). *Depression: Clinical, Experimental and Theoretical Aspects*. London: Staples Press.

Beck, A. T. & Beck, A. T. (1976). Meaning and emotions. In *Cognitive Therapy and the Emotional Disorders* (pp. 47–75). London: Penguin.

Beck, A. T., Epstein, N., Brown, G. & Steer, R. A. (1988). An inventory for measuring clinical anxiety: psychometric properties. *Journal of Consulting & Clinical Psychology*, *56*(6), 893–897.

Beck, A. T., Rush, A. J., Shaw, B. F. & Emery, G. (1979). *Cognitive Therapy of Depression*. New York: Guilford Press.

Beck, A. T., Steer, R. A. & Brown, G. K. (1996). *Beck Depression Inventory II*. San Antonio, TX: The Psychological Corporation.

Beck, A. T., Ward, C. H., Mendelson, M. et al. (1961). An inventory for measuring depression. *Archives of General Psychiatry*, *4*, 561–571.

Bellino, S., Zinna, M. & Paradiso, E. (2003). Body dysmorphic disorder and personality disorders: A clinical investigation in patients seeking cosmetic surgery. *Italian Journal of Psychopathology*, *9*, 149–156.

Ben-Tovim, D. I., Tuschen, C. B. & Florin, I. (1998). Body image and the experienced body. In *Recent Research in Eating Disorders* (pp. 1–9). Mannheim: Springer Verlag.

Biby, E. L. (1998). The relationship between body dysmorphic disorder and depression, self-esteem, somatization, and obsessive-compulsive disorder. *Journal of Clinical Psychology*, *54*(4), 489–499.

Bienvenu, O. J., Samuels, J. F., Riddle, M. A. et al. (2000). The relationship of obsessive-compulsive disorder to possible spectrum disorders: results from a family study. *Biological Psychiatry*, *48*, 287–293.

Biondi, M., Arcangeli, T. & Petrucci, R. M. (2000). Paroxetine in a case of psychogenic pruritus and neurotic excoriations. *Psychotherapy & Psychosomatics*, *69*, 165–166.

Blanch, J., Grimalt, F., Massana, G. & Navarro, V. (2004). Efficacy of olanzapine in the treatment of psychogenic excoriation. *British Journal of Dermatology*, *151*(3), 714–716.

Bloch, M. R., Elliott, M., Thompson, H. & Koran, L. M. (2000). Fluoxetine for skin-picking. Paper presented at the Psychosomatics, Boca Raton, FL.

Bloch, S. & Glue, P. (1988). Psychotherapy and dysmorphophobia: a case report. *British Journal of Psychiatry*, *152*, 271–274.

Boesiger, P., Conny, F., Ishai, A. & Schmidt. (2005). Face perception is mediated by a distributed cortical network. *Brain Research Bulletin*, *67*(1–2), 87–93.

Bögels, S. M. (2006) Task concentration training versus applied relaxation, in combination with cognitive therapy, for social phobia patients with fear of blushing, trembling, and sweating. *44*(8), 1199–1210.

Bogels, S. M., Mulkens, S. & de Jong, P. J. (1997). Task concentration training and fear of blushing. *Clinical Psychology and Psychotherapy*, *4*(4), 251–258.

Bohne, A., Keuthen, N. J., Wilhelm, S. et al. (2002). BDD symptom prevalence and its correlates: a cross-cultural comparison. *Psychosomatics*, *43*, 486–490.

Bohne, A., Wilhelm, S., Keuthen, N. J. et al. (2002a). Prevalence of Body Dysmorphic Disorder in a German college student sample. *Psychiatry Research*, *109*, 101–104.

Bohne, A., Wilhelm, S., Keuthen, N. J. et al. (2002b). Skin picking in German students. Prevalence, phenomenology, and associated characteristics. *Behavior Modification*, *26*(3), 320–339.

Bowe, W. P., Leyden, J. J., Crerand, C. E. et al. (2007). Body dysmorphic disorder symptoms among patients with acne vulgaris. *Journal of the American Academy of Dermatology*, *57*(2), 222–230.

Bowes, L. E. & Alster, T. S. (2004). Treatment of facial scarring and ulceration resulting from acne excoriée with 585-nm pulsed dye laser irradiation and cognitive psychotherapy. *Dermatologic Surgery*, *30*(6), 934–938.

Braddock, L. E. (1982). Dysmorphophobia in adolescence: a case report. *British Journal of Psychiatry, 140*, 199–201.

Bramwell, R., Morland, C. & Garden, A. S. (2007). Expectations and experience of labial reduction: a qualitative study. *BJOG: An International Journal of Obstetrics & Gynaecology, 114*(12), 1493–1499.

Brawman-Mintzer, O., Lydiard, R. B., Phillips, K. A. et al. (1995). Body dysmorphic disorder in patients with anxiety disorders and major depression: a comorbidity study. *American Journal of Psychiatry, 152*(11), 1665–1667.

Brod, M. (1995). *Franz Kafka: A Biography*, New York: Da Capo Press.

Brown, K. W., McGoldrick, T. & Buchanan, R. (1997). Body dysmorphic disorder: seven cases treated with eye movement desensitization and reprocessing. *Behavioral and Cognitive Psychotherapy, 25*(203), 202

Brown, T. A. & Barlow, D. H. (1992). Comorbidity among anxiety disorders: implications for treatment and DSM-IV. *Journal of Consulting & Clinical Psychology, 60*, 835–844.

Brunswick, R. M. (1928). A supplement to Freud's "History of an Infantile Neurosis." *International Journal of Psycho-Analysis, 9*, 439–476.

Brunswick, R. M. (1971). Pertaining to the Wolf Man: A supplement to Freud's The History of an Infantile Neurosis. *Revista de Psicoanalisis, 35*, 5–46.

Buhlmann, U., Cook, L. M., Fama, J. M. & Wilhelm, S. (2007) Teasing experiences in Body Dysmorphic Disorder. *Body Image, 4*(4), 381–385.

Buhlmann, U., Etcoff, N. L., McNally, R. J. et al. (2004). Emotion recognition deficits in body dysmorphic disorder. *Journal of Psychiatric Research, 38*, 201–206.

Buhlmann, U., Etcoff, N. L. & Wilhelm, S. (2006). Emotion recognition bias for contempt and anger in body dysmorphic disorder. *Journal of Psychiatric Research, 40*, 105–111.

Bulik, C. M., Devlin, B., Bacanu, S. A. et al. (2003). Significant linkage on chromosome 10p in families with bulimia nervosa. *American Journal of Human Genetics, 72*(1), 200–207.

Bulik, C. M., Sullivan, P. F. & Kendler, K. S. (2003). Genetic and environmental contributions to obesity and binge eating. *International Journal of Eating Disorders, 33*(3), 293–298.

Butters, J. W. & Cash, T. F. (1987). Cognitive behavioral treatment of women's body image dissatisfaction. *Journal of Consulting and Clinical Psychology, 55*(6), 889–897.

Calikusu, C., Yucel, B., Polat, A. & Baykal, C. (2003). The relation of psychogenic excoriation with psychiatric disorders: a comparative study. *Comprehensive Psychiatry, 44*(3), 256–261.

Campisi, T. A. (1995). Exposure and response prevention in the treatment of body dysmorphic disorder. PhD thesis, Hofstra University, Hampstead, NY.

Cansever, A., Uzun, O., Donmez, E. & Ozsahin, A. (2003). The prevalence and clinical features of body dysmorphic disorder in college students: a study in a Turkish sample. *Comprehensive Psychiatry, 44*(1), 60–64.

Carey, P., Seedat, S., Warwick, J. et al. (2004). SPECT imaging of body dysmorphic disorder. *Journal of Neuropsychiatry and Clinical Neurosciences, 16*, 357–359.

Carroll, B. J., Yendrek, R., Degroot, C. & Fanin, H. (1994). Response of major depression with psychosis and body dysmorphic disorder to ECT [letter; comment]. *American Journal of Psychiatry, 151*(2), 288–289.

Carter, L. (2001) Body dysmorphia. Electronic response to: K. A. Phillips & D. J. Castle, body dysmorphic disorder in men. *British Medical Journal, 323,* 1015–1016. http://bmj.com/cgi/letters/323/7320/1015#17324.

Cartwright, R. & Cardozo, L. (2008) Cosmetic Vulvovaginal surgery. *Obstetrics, Gynaecology and Reproductive Medicine, 18,* 285–286.

Cartwright-Hatton, S. & Wells, A. (1997). Beleifs about worry and intrusions: the metacognitions questionnaire and its correlates. *Journal of Anxiety Disorders, 11,* 279–315.

Cash, T. F. (1990). The psychology of physical appearance: aesthetics, attributes, and images. In T. F. Cash & T. Pruzinsky (eds.) *Body Images: Development, Deviance, and Change* (pp. 51–79). New York: Guilford Press.

Cash, T. F. (1991). *Body-Image Therapy: A Program for Self-Directed Change.* New York: Guilford Press.

Cash, T. F. (2000) *The Multidimensional Body–Self Relations Questionnaire and MBSRQ Users' Manual.* www.body-images.com.

Cash, T. F. (2002). Cognitive behavioral perspectives on body image. In T. F. Cash & T. Pruzinsky (eds.), *Body Image: A Handbook of Theory, Research, and Clinical Practice.* New York: Guilford Press.

Cash, T. F. (2008). *The body image workbook: An 8 step programme for learning to like your looks.* Oakland, CA: New Harbinger.

Cash, T. F. & Fleming, E. C. (2002). The impact of body-image experiences: development of the Body Image Quality of Life Inventory. *International Journal of Eating Disorders, 31*(4), 455–460.

Cash, T. F., Phillips, K. A., Santos, M. T. & Hrabosky, J. I. (2004). Measuring "negative body image": validation of the body image disturbance questionnaire in a nonclinical population. *Body Image: An International Journal of Research, 1,* 363–372.

Cash, T. F. & Pruzinsky, T. (2002). *Body Image: A Handbook of Theory, Research, and Clinical Practice.* New York: Guilford Press.

Castelnuovo-Tedesco, P. (1992). Body dysmorphic disorder [letter; comment]. *American Journal of Psychiatry, 149*(5), 718.

Castle, D. J., Honigman, R. J. & Phillips, K. A. (2002). Does cosmetic surgery improve psychosocial wellbeing? *Medical Journal of Australia, 176*(12), 601–604.

Castle, D. J., Molton, M., Hoffman, K. et al. (2004). Correlates of dysmorphic concern in people seeking cosmetic enhancement. *Australian and New Zealand Journal of Psychiatry, 38*(6), 439–444.

Cavanagh, M. & Franklin, J. (2000). Attention training and hypochondriasis: preliminary results of a controlled treatment trial. Paper presented at the World Congress of Cognitive and Behavioral Therapy. Vancouver, Canada.

Chamberlain, S., Fineberg, N. A., Blackwell, A. et al. (2006). Motor inhibition and cognitive flexability. *American Journal of Psychiatry, 163,* 1282–1284.

Chapman, L. J., Chapman, J. P. & Raulin, M. L. (1978). Body-image aberration in schizophrenia. *Journal of Abnormal Psychology, 87*(4), 399–407.

Chen, Y. P., Ehlers, A., Clark, D. M. & Mansell, W. (2002). Patients with generalized social phobia direct their attention away from faces. *Behavior Research and Therapy*, *40*, 677–687.

Cheng, S. T. (1996). A critical review of Chinese Koro. *Culture, Medicine and Psychiatry*, *20*(1), 67–82.

Chowdhury, A. N. (1998). Hundred years of koro: the history of a culture-bound syndrome. *International Journal of Social Psychiatry*, *44*, 181–188.

Clark, D. M. (2001). A cognitive perspective on social phobia. In W. R. Crozier & L. E. Alden (eds.) *International Handbook of Social Anxiety: Concept, Research and Interventions Relating to the Self and Shyness* (pp. 405–430). Chichester: John Wiley & Sons.

Clark, D. M., Ehlers, A., McManus, F. et al. (2003), Cognitive therapy versus fluoxetine in generalized social phobia: a randomized placebo-controlled trial. *Journal of Consulting and Clinical Psychology*, *71*(6), 1058–1067.

Clark, D. M., Salkovskis, P. M., Hackmann, A. et al. (1998). Two psychological treatments for hypochondriasis. A randomised controlled trial. *British Journal of Psychiatry*, *173*, 218–225.

Clark, D. M. & Wells, A. (1995). A cognitive model of social phobia. In R. G. Heimberg, et al. (eds.) *Social Phobia – Diagnosis, Assessment, and Treatment* (pp. 69–93). New York: Guilford Press.

Coles, M. E., Phillips, K. A., Menard, W. et al. (2005). Body Dysmorphic Disorder and social phobia: cross-sectional and prospective data. *Depression and Anxiety*, *23*(1), 26–33

Concar, D. (1995). Sex and the symmetrical body. *New Scientist*, *146*, 40–44.

Connolly, F. H. & Gibson, M. (1978). Dysmorphophobia – a long-term study. *British Journal of Psychiatry*, *132*, 568–570.

Conroy, M., Menard, W, Fleming-Ives, K. et al. (2008) Prevalence and clinical characteristics of body dysmorphic disorder in an adult inpatient setting. *General Hospital Psychiatry*, *30*(1), 67–72.

Cook, S. A., Rosser, R., Meah, S. et al. (2003). Clinical decision guidelines for NHS cosmetic surgery: analysis of current limitations and recommendations for future development. *British Journal of Plastic Surgery*, *56*, 429–436.

Cooper, Z. & Fairburn, C. G. (1987). The eating disorder examination: a semi-structured interview for the assessment of the specific psychopathology of eating disorders. *International Journal of Eating Disorders*, *6*, 1–8.

Cotterill, J. A. (1981). Dermatological non-disease: a common and potentially fatal disturbance of cutaneous body image. *British Journal of Dermatology*, *104*(6), 611–619.

Cotterill, J. A. (1981). Dermatological non-disease: a common and potentially fatal disturbance of cutaneous body image. *British Journal of Dermatology*, *104*(6), 611–619.

Cotterill, J. A. & Cunliffe, W. J. (1997). Suicide in dermatological patients. *British Journal of Dermatology*, *137*(2), 246–250.

Craven, J. L. & Rodin, G. M. (1987). Cyproheptadine dependence associated with an atypical somatoform disorder. *Canadian Journal of Psychiatry*, *32*, 143–145.

Cromarty, P. & Marks, I. (1995). Does rational role-play enhance the outcome of exposure therapy in dysmorphophobia? A case study. *British Journal of Psychiatry*, *167*, 399–402.

Cuijpers, P., van Straten, A. & Warmerdam, L (2007) Behavioral activation treatments of depression: a meta-analysis. *Clinical Psychology Review*, *27*(3), 318–326.

Cunningham, S. J., Bryant, C. J., Manisali, M. et al. (1996). Dysmorphophobia: recent developments of interest to the maxillofacial surgeon. *British Journal of Oral & Maxillofacial Surgery*, *34*(5), 368–374.

de Houwer, J., Thomas, S. & Baeyens, F. (2001). Associative learning of likes and dislikes: a review of 25 years of research on human evaluative conditioning. *Psychological Bulletin*, *127*(6), 853–869.

de Jongh, A. & Adair, P. (2004). Mental disorders in dental practice: a case report of body dysmorphic disorder. *Special Care in Dentistry*, *24*(2), 61–64.

de Jongh, A., Oosterink, F. M. D, van Rood, Y. R. & Aartman, I. H. A. (2008). Preoccupation with one's appearance: a motivating factor for cosmetic dental treatment? *British Dental Journal*, *204*, 691–695.

De Waal, M. W. M., Arnold, I. A., Eekhof, J. A. H. & Van Hemert, A. M. (2004). Prevalence, functional impairment and comorbidity with anxiety and depressive disorders. *British Journal of Psychiatry*, *184*, 479–476.

Deckersbach, T., Wilhelm, S., Buhlmann, U. et al. (2000). Characteristics of memory dysfunction in body dysmorphic disorder. *Journal of the International Neuropsychological Society*, *6*(6), 673–681.

Deckersbach, T., Wilhelm, S., Keuthen, N. J. et al. (2002). Cognitive-behavior therapy for self-injurious skin picking. A case series. *Behavior Modification*, *26*(3), 361–377.

Denys, D., van Megen, H. J. & Westenberg, H. G. (2003). Emerging skin picking behavior after serotonin reuptake inhibitor treatment in patients with obsessive-compulsive disorder: possible mechanism and implications for clinical care. *Psychopharmacology*, *17*(1), 127–129.

Department of Health (2000). *National Minimum Standards and Regulations for Independent Health Care*. London: TSO.

Didie, E. R., Tortolani, C. C., Pope, C. G. et al. (2006). Childhood abuse and neglect in body dysmorphic disorder. *Child Abuse and Neglect*, *30*, 1105–1115.

Didie, E. R., Tortolani, C., Walters, M. et al. (2006). Social functioning in body dysmorphic disorder: assessment considerations. *Psychiatric Quarterly*, *77*(3), 223–229.

Dimidjian, S., Hollon S. D., Dobson, K. S. et al. (2006). Randomized trial of behavioral activation, cognitive therapy, and antidepressant medication in the acute treatment of adults with major depression. *Journal of Consulting and Clinical Psychology*, *74*(4), 658–670.

Dion, K. K. & Berscheid, E. (1974). Physical attractiveness and peer perception among children. *Sociometry*, *37*(1), 1–12.

Dion, K. K., Berscheid, E. & Walster. (1972). What is beautiful is good. *Journal of Personality and Social Psychology*, *24*(3), 285–290.

Dollard, J. & Miller, N. (1950) *Personality and Psychotherapy: An Analysis in Terms of Learning, Thinking and Culture*. New York: McGraw-Hill.

Downing, P. E., Jiang, Y., Shuman, M. & Kanwisher, N. (2001). A cortical area selective for visual processing of the human body. *Science*, *293*(5539), 2410–2473.

Downs, A. C. & Lyons, P. M. (1991). Natural observations of the links between attractiveness and initial legal judgements. *Personality and Social Psychology Bulletin*, *17*, 541–547.

Drieschner, K. H., Lammers, S. M. M. & van der Staak, C. P. F. (2004). Treatment motivation: an attempt for clarification of an ambiguous concept. *Clinical Psychology Review*, *23*, 1115–1137.

Dryden, W. (1998). *Developing Self-acceptance*. Chichester: John Wiley & Sons.

Dryden, W. (1999) *A Positive Thought for Every Day*. London: Sheldon Press.

Dufresne Jr, R. G., Phillips, K. A., Vittorio, C. C. & Wilkel, C. S. (2001). A screening questionnaire for Body Dysmorphic Disorder in a cosmetic dermatologic surgery practice. *Dermatological Surgery*, *27*, 457–462.

Duke, E. E. (1983). Clinical experience with pimozide: emphasis on its use in postherpetic neuralgia. *Journal of American Academy of Dermatology*, *8*, 845–850.

Dyl, J., Kittler, J., Phillips, K. A. & Hunt, J. I. (2006). Body dysmorphic disorder and other clinically significant body image concerns in adolescent psychiatric inpatients: prevalence and clinical characteristics. *Child Psychiatry and Human Development*, *36*(4), 369–382.

Ehlers, A. & Clark, D. M. (2000). A cognitive model of posttraumatic stress disorder. *Behavior Research and Therapy*, *38*(4), 319–345.

Eisen, J. L., Phillips, K. A., Baer, L. et al. (1998). The Brown Assessment of Beliefs Scale: reliability and validity. *American Journal of Psychiatry*, *155*(1), 102–108.

el-Khatib, H. E. & Dickey, T. O., III. (1995). Sertraline for body dysmorphic disorder [letter]. *Journal of the American Academy of Child & Adolescent Psychiatry*, *34*(11), 1404–1405.

Elliot, A. J. & Thrash, T. M. (2002) Approach-avoidance in motivation in personality: approach and avoidance temperaments in and goals. *Journal of Personality and Social Psychology*, *82*, 804–818.

Etcoff, N. (1999). *Survival of the Prettiest: The Science of Beauty*. New York: Doubleday.

Fairburn, C. G., Cooper, Z. & Shafran, R. (2003). Cognitive behaviour therapy for eating disorders: a "transdiagnostic" theory and treatment. *Behaviour Research and Therapy*, *41*, 509–528.

Fairburn, C. G. & Harrison, P. J. (2003). Eating disorders. *Lancet*, *361*(9355), 407–416.

Fairburn, C. G., Welch, S. L., Doll, H. A. & Davies, B. (1997). Risk factors for Bulimia nervosa. *Archives of General Psychiatry*, *54*, 509–517.

Faravelli, C., Salvatori, S., Galassi, F. et al. (1997). Epidemiology of somatoform disorders: a community survey in Florence. *Social Psychiatry & Psychiatric Epidemiology*, *32*(1), 24–29.

Farrell, C., Shafran R., Lee, M. & Fairburn, C. G. (2005). Testing a brief cognitive-behavioral intervention to improve extreme shape concern: a case series. *Behavioral and Cognitive Psychotherapy*, *33*(2), 189–200.

Favazza, A., Simeon, D., Hollander, E. & Stein, D. J. (1995). Self-mutilation. In E. Hollander and D. J. Stein (eds.) *Impulsivity and Aggression* (pp. 185–200). Chichester: John Wiley & Sons.

Fenigstein, A., Scheier, M. F. & Buss, A. H. (1975). Public and private self-consciousness: assessment and theory. *Journal of Consulting and Clinical Psychology*, *43*(4), 522–527, American Psychological Association.

Ferster, C. B. (1973). A functional analysis of depression, *American Psychologist*, *28*(10), 857–870.

Festinger, L. (1954) A theory of social comparison processes. *Human Relations, 7,* 117–140.

Feusner, J. D, Townsend, J, Bystritsky, A. & Bookheimer, S. (2007) Visual information processing of faces in body dysmorphic disorder. *Archives of General Psychiatry, 64*(12), 1417–1426.

Feusner, J. D, Yaryura-Tobias, J. & Saxena, S. (2008) The pathophysiology of body dysmorphic disorder. *Body Image, 5,* 3–12.

First, M. B. (2005). Desire for amputation of a limb: paraphilia, psychosis, or a new type of identity disorder. *Psychological Medicine, 35,* 919–928.

Fisher, E., Dunn, M. & Thompson, J. K. (2002). Social comparison and body image: an investigation of body comparison processes using multidimensional scaling. *Journal of Social and Clinical Psychology, 21,* 566–579.

Fisher, K. & Smith, R. (2000) Letter: more work is needed to explain why patients ask for amputation of healthy limbs. *British Medical Journal, 320,* 1147.

Fitts, S. N., Gibson, P., Redding, C. A. & Deiter, P. J. (1989). Body dysmorphic disorder: implications for its validity as a DSM-III-R clinical syndrome. *Psychological Reports, 64*(2), 655–658.

Frecska, E. & Arato, M. (2002). Opiate sensitivity test in patients with stereotypic movement disorder and trichotillomania. *Progress in Neuropsychopharmacology Biological Psychiatry, 26*(5), 909–912.

Fredrickson, B. L., Roberts, T. A., Noll, S. M. et al. (1998). That swimsuit becomes you: sex differences in self-objectification, restrained eating, and math performance. *Journal of Personality & Social Psychology, 75*(1), 269–284.

Freud, S. (1959). *Three Case Histories: The Wolf Man, the Rat Man, and the Psychotic Doctor,* Albany, NY: Schreber

Frisch, M. B. (1994). *The Quality of Life Inventory.* Minneapolis, MN: National Computer Systems, Inc.

Frost, R. O., Marten, P. A., Lahart, C. & Rosenblate, R. (1990). The dimensions of perfectionism. *Cognitive Therapy and Research, 14,* 449–468.

Furth, G. M., Smith, R, & Kübler-Ross, E. (2000). *Amputee Identity Disorder: Information, Questions, Answers, and Recommendations about Self-Demand Amputation*: Bukingham: 1st Books Library.

Fux, M., Levine, J., Aviv, A. & Belmaker, R. H. (1996). Inositol treatment of obsessive-compulsive disorder. *American Journal of Physiology, 153*(9), 1219–1221.

Gabbay, V., Asnis, G. M., Bello, J. A. et al. (2003). New onset of body dysmorphic disorder following fronto-temporal lesion. *Neurology, 61*(1), 123–125.

Gangestad, S. W., Thornhill, R. & Yeo, R. A. (1994). Facial attractiveness, developmental stability, and fluctuating asymmetry. *Ethology and Sociobiology, 15,* 73–85.

Garcia-Coll, C., Kagan, J. & Reznick, J. S. (1984). Behavioral inhibition in young children. *Child Development, 55,* 1005–1019.

Garnis-Jones, S., Collins, S. & Rosenthal, D. (2000). Treatment of self-mutilation with olanzapine. *Journal of Cutaneous Medical & Surgery, 4*(3), 161–163.

Geremia, G. & Neziroglu, F. (2001). Cognitive therapy in the treatment of body dysmorphic disorder. *Clinical Psychology and Psychotherapy, 8,* 243–251.

Giesen-Bloo, J., Van Dyck, R., Spinhoven, P. et al. (2006). Outpatient psychotherapy for borderline personality disorder: Randomized controlled trial of schema-focused therapy vs transference-focused psychotherapy. *Archives of General Psychiatry, 63,* 649–658.

Gilbert, P. (ed.) (2005). *Compassion: Conceptualisations Research and Use in Psychotherapy.* London: Brunner-Routledge.

Gilbert, P. (2007). *Psychotherapy and Counselling for Depression.* London: Sage.

Gilbert, P. (2009). *The Compassionate Mind.* London: Constable & Robinson.

Gilbert, P. & Bailey, K. G. (2000). *Genes on the Couch. Explorations in Evolutionary Psychotherapy.* Hove: Brunner-Routledge

Gilbert, P. & Miles, J. (2002). A biopsychosocial conceptualisation and overview with treatment implications. In P. Gilbert & J. Miles (eds.), *Body Shame: Conceptualisation, Research and Treatment* (pp. 3–55). London: Brunner-Routledge.

Gluhoski, V. L. (1995). A cognitive approach for treating trichotillomania. *Journal of Psychotherapy Practice and Research, 4,* 277–285.

Gombrich, E. H. (1984). *The Sense of Order. A Study in the Psychology of Decorative Art.* London: Phaidon.

Gomez Perez, J. C., Marks, I. M. & Gutierrez Fisac, J. L. (1994). Dysmorphophobia: clinical features and outcome with behavior therapy. *European Psychiatry, 9,* 229–235.

Goodman, W. K., Price, L. H., Delgado, P. L. & Palumbo, J. (1990). Specificity of serotonin reuptake inhibitors in the treatment of obsessive-compulsive disorder: comparison of fluvoxamine and desipramine. *Archives of General Psychiatry, 47,* 577–585.

Gortner, E. T., Gollan, J. K., Dobson, K. S. & Jacobson, N. S. (1998) Cognitive behavioral treatment for depression: relapse prevention. *Journal of Consulting and Clinical Psychology, 66*(2), 377–384.

Grant, J. E., Kim, S. W. & Crow, S. J. (2001). Prevalence and clinical features of body dysmorphic disorder in adolescent and adult psychiatric inpatients. *Journal of Clinical Psychiatry, 62,* 517–522.

Grant, J. E., Menard, W., Pagano, M. et al. (2005). Substance use disorders in individuals with body dysmorphic disorder. *Journal of Clinical Psychiatry, 66*(3), 309–316.

Grant, J. E., Won Kim, S. & Crow, S. J. (2001). Prevalence and clinical features of body dysmorphic disorder in adolescent and adult psychiatric inpatients. *Journal of Clinical Psychiatry, 62,* 517–522.

Grant, J. E., Won Kim, S. & Eckert, E. D. (2002). Body dysmorphic disorder in patients with anorexia nervosa: prevalence, clinical features, and delusionality of body image. *International Journal of Eating Disorders, 32,* 291–300.

Graybiel, A. M. (1998). The basal ganglia and chunking of action repertoires. *Neurobiology of Learning and Memory, 70,* 119–136.

Greist, J. H., Marks, I. M., Baer, L. et al. (1998). Self-treatment for obsessive compulsive disorder using a manual and a computerised telephone interview: a U.S.–U.K. study. *M.D. Computing, 15*(3), 149–157.

Griesemer, R. D. (1978). Emotionally triggered disease in a dermatologic practice. *Psychiatric Annals, 8,* 407–412.

Grindlinger, H. M. & Ramsay, E. (1991). Compulsive feather picking in birds. *Archives of General Psychiatry, 48,* 857–857.

Groves, P. M. & Lynch, G. S. (1972). Mechanisms of habituation in the brainstem. *Psychology Review*, *79*(3), 237–244.

Gunstad, J. & Phillips, K. A. (2003). Axis I comorbidity in Body Dysmorphic Disorder. *Comprehensive Psychiatry*, *44*(4), 270–278.

Gupta, M. A. & Gupta, A. K. (1993). Fluoxetine is an effective treatment for neurotic excoriations: case report. *Cutaneous Medicine for the Practitioner*, *51*(5), 386–387.

Gupta, M. A. & Gupta, A. K. (2000). Olanzapine is effective in the management of some self-induced dermatoses: three case reports. *Cutaneous Medicine for the Practitioner*, *66*(2), 143–146.

Gupta, M. A., Gupta, A. K. & Haberman, H. F. (1986). Neurotic excoriations: a review and some new perspectives. *Comprehensive Psychiatry*, *27*(4), 381–386.

Hackmann, A. (2005). Compassionate imagery in the treatment of early memories in Axis I anxiety disorders. In P. Gilbert (ed.) *Compassion: Conceptualisations Research and Use in Psychotherapy* (pp. 352–368). London: Brunner-Routledge.

Hackmann, A., Clark, D. M. & McManus, F. (2000). Recurrent images and early memories in social phobia. *Behavior Research and Therapy*, *38*, 601–610.

Hackmann, A. & Hersen, M. (1998). Working with images in clinical psychology. In *Comprehensive Clinical Psychology* (pp. 301–317): Amsterdam: Elsevier.

Hackmann, A., Surawy, C. & Clark, D. M. (1998). Seeing yourself through others' eyes: a study of spontaneously occurring images in social phobia. *Behavioral and Cognitive Psychotherapy*, *26*, 3–12.

Haidt, J., McCauley, C. & Rozin, P. (1994). Individual differences in sensitivity to disgust: a scale sampling seven domains of disgust elicitors. *Personality and Individual Differences 16*(5), 701–713.

Hamilton, M. (1974). *Fish's Clinical Psychopathology*. Bristol: John Wright.

Hanes, K. R. (1995). Body dysmorphic disorder: an underestimated entity? [letter]. *Australasian Journal of Dermatology*, *36*(4), 227–228.

Hanes, K. R. (1996) Serotonin, psilocybin, and body dysmorphic disorder: a case report. *J. Clin. Psychopharmacology*, *16*(2), 188–189.

Hanes, K. R. (1998). Neuropsychological performance in body dysmorphic disorder. *Journal of the International Neuropsychological Society*, *4*(2), 167–171.

Harris, D. L. (1982). Cosmetic surgery – where does it begin? *British Journal of Plastic Surgery*, *35*, 281–286.

Harris, D. L. & Carr, A. T. (2001). Prevalance of concern about physical appearance in the general population. *British Journal of Plastic Surgery*, *54*(3), 223–226.

Hartenberg, P. (1901). *Les timides et la timidité*. Paris: Alcan.

Harvey, A. G., Clark, D .M., Ehlers, A. & Rapee, R.M. (2000) Social anxiety and self-impression: cognitive preparation enhances the beneficial effects of video feedback following a stressful social task. *Behavior Research and Therapy*, *38* (12), 1183–1192.

Harvey, A. G., Watkins, E., Mansell, W. & Shafran, R. (2004). *Cognitive Behavioural Processes across Psychological Disorders*. Oxford: Oxford University Press.

Hawton, K., Salkovskis, P. M, Kirk, J. & Clark, D. M. (eds.) (1992). *Cognitive Behavior Therapy for Psychiatric Problems: A Practical Guide*. Oxford: Medical Publications.

Hay, G. G. & Heather, B. B. (1973). Changes in psychometric test results following cosmetic nasal operations. *British Journal of Psychiatry, 122,* 89–90.

Hayes, S. C., Barnes-Holmes, D. & Roche, B. (eds.) 2001. *Relational Frame Theory: A Post-Skinnerian Account of Human Language and Cognition.* New York: Plenum Press.

Hayes, S. C., Strosahl, K. & Wilson, K. G. (1999). *Acceptance and Commitment Therapy: An Experiential Approach to Behavior Change.* New York: Guilford Press.

Hayward, C., Killen, J. D., Kraemer, H. C. & Taylor, C. B. (1998). Linking self – reported childhood behavioral inhibition to adolescent social phobia. *Journal of American Academy of Child and Adolescent Psychiatry, 37,* 1308–1316.

Heinberg, L. & Thompson, J. (1992). Social comparison: gender target importance ratings and relation to body image disturbance. *Journal of Social Behavior and Personality, 7,* 335–344.

Helman, C. G. (1990). *Culture, Health and Illness* (second edition.). London: Wright.

Hewitt, P. L. & Flett, G. L. (1991). Dimensions of perfectionism in unipolar depression. *Journal of Abnormal Psychology, 100,* 98–101.

Hewitt, P. L. & Flett, G. L. (2002). Perfectionism and stress processes in psychopathology. In G. L. Flett & P. L. Hewitt, (eds.), *Perfectionism: Theory, Research and Treatment* (pp. 255–256). Washington, DC: American Psychological Association.

Higgins, E. T. (1987). Self-discrepancy: a theory relating self and affect. *Psychological Review, 94*(3), 319–340.

Higgins, E. T., Bond, R. N., Klein, R. & Strauman, T. (1986). Self-discrepancies and emotional vulnerability: how magnitude, accessibility and type of discrepancy influence affect. *Journal of Personality and Social Psychology, 51*(1), 5–15.

Hoehn-Saric, R., Ninan, P., Black, D. W. et al. (2000) Multicenter double-blind comparison of sertraline and desipramine for concurrent obsessive-compulsive and major depressive disorders. *Archives of General Psychiatry, 57,* 76–82.

Holland, A. (2006) *DClinPsy thesis.* London: University College.

Hollander, E. (1993). Obsessive-compulsive spectrum disorders: an overview. *Psychiatric Annals, 23,* 355–358.

Hollander, E., Allen, A., Kwon, J. et al. (1999). Clomipramine vs desipramine crossover trial in body dysmorphic disorder: selective efficacy of a serotonin reuptake inhibitor in imagined ugliness. *Archives of General Psychiatry, 56*(11), 1033–1042.

Hollander, E. & Hollander, E. (1993). Introduction. In *Obsessive Compulsive Related Disorders* (pp. 1–16). Washington, DC: American Psychiatric Press.

Hollander, E., Liebowitz, M. R., Winchel, R. et al. (1989). Treatment of body-dysmorphic disorder with serotonin reuptake inhibitors. *American Journal of Psychiatry, 146,* 768–770.

Hollander, E., Neville, D., Frenkel, M. et al. (1992). Body dysmorphic disorder. Diagnostic issues and related disorders [review] [71 refs]. *Psychosomatics, 33*(2), 156–165.

Hollander, E, Stein, D. J. & Decaria, C. M. (1994) Unpublished observations. Cited in Hollander, E. & Wong, C. M. (1995). Body dysmorphic disorder, pathological gambling, and sexual compulsions. *Journal of Clinical Psychiatry, 56* (Suppl 4), 7–12.

Holmes, E. A., Arntz, A. & Smucker, M. R. (2007). Imagery rescripting in cognitive behavior therapy: images, treatment techniques and outcomes. *Journal of Behavior Therapy and Experimental Psychiatry, 38*(4), 297–305.

Holmes, E. A. & Mathews, A. (2005). Mental imagery and emotion: a special relationship. *Emotion*, 5(4), 489–497.

Hopko, D. R., Lejuez, C. W., Lepage, J. P. et al. (2003). A brief behavioral activation treatment for depression; a randomized pilot trial within an inpatient psychiatric hospital. *Behavior Modification*, 27, 458–469.

Horowitz, K., Gorfinkle, K., Lewis, O. & Phillips, K. A. (2002). Body dysmorphic disorder in an adolescent girl. *Journal of American Academy of Child and Adolescent Psychiatry*, 41(12), 1503–1509.

Horowitz, M. J. (1970). *Image Formation and Cognition*. New York: Appleton-Century-Crofts.

Hrabosky, J. I., Cash, T. F, Veale, D, et al. (2009). Multidimensional body image comparisons of eating disorders, body dysmorphic disorder, and clinical controls: a multisite study. *Body Image*, 6(3), 155–163.

Ingram, R. E. (1990). Self-focused attention in clinical disorders: review and a conceptual model. *Psychological Bulletin*, 107(2), 156–176.

Ishigooka, J., Iwao, M., Suzuki, M. et al. (1998). Demographic features of patients seeking cosmetic surgery. *Psychiatry and Clinical Neurosciences*, 52(3), 283–287.

Jacobson, N. S., Dobson, K. S., Truax, P. A. et al. (1996). A component analysis of cognitive-behavioral treatment for depression. *Journal of Consulting and Clinical Psychology*, 64, 295–304.

Jagger, R. G. & Korszun, A. (2004). Phantom bite revisited. *British Dental Journal*, 197(5), 241–243.

Jahrreiss, W. (1930) Das hypochondrische Denken. *Archiv der Psychiatrie und Nervenkrankheiten*, 92, 686–923.

Janet, P. (1903). *Obsessions et la psychasthénie*. Paris: Alcan.

Jansen, A., Nederkoorn, C. & Mulkens, S. (2005) Selective attention for ugly and beautiful body parts in eating disorders. *Behavior Research and Therapy*, 43, 183–196.

Jansen, A., Smeets, T., Martijn, C. & Nederkoorn, C. (2006). I see what you see: the lack of a self-serving body-image bias in eating disorders: *British Journal of Clinical Psychology*, 45(1), 123–135.

Jaspers, K. ([1959]1963). *General Psychopathology*, trans. J. Koenig and M. W. Hamilton, Manchester: Manchester University Press.

Jaycox, L. H., Foa, E. B. & Morral, A. R. (1998). Influence of emotional engagement and habituation of exposure therapy for PTSD. *Journal of Consulting and Clinical Psychology*, 66, 185–192.

Jenike, M. A. (1984). A case report of successful treatment of dysmorphophobia with tranylcypromine. *American Journal of Psychiatry*, 141(11), 1463–1464.

Jerome, L. (1992). Body dysmorphic disorder: a controlled study of patients requesting cosmetic rhinoplasty [letter]. *American Journal of Psychiatry*, 149(4), 577–578.

Jerome, L. (2001). Dysmorphophobia and taphephobia: two hitherto undescribed forms of insanity with fixed ideas. A new translation of Enrico Morselli's original article. Classic Text No. 45. *History of Psychiatry*, 12, 103–114.

Johnston, V. S. & Franklin, M. (1993). Is beauty in the eye of the beholder? *Ethology and Sociobiology*, 13, 183–199.

Josephson, S. C. & Hollander, E. (1997). Body dysmorphic disorder by proxy [letter]. *Journal of Clinical Psychiatry, 58*(2), 86–87.

Judd, L. L., Kessler, R. C., Paulus, M. P. et al. (1998). Comorbidity as a fundamental feature of generalized anxiety disorders: results from the National Comorbidity Study (NCS). *Acta Psychiatrica Scandinavia, 98*, 6–11.

Kaan, H. (1892). *Der neurasthenische Angsteffekt bei Zwangvorstellungen und der primordiale Grubelzwang*. Leipzig: Deutike.

Kaats, G. R. & Davis, K. E. (1970). The dynamics of sexual behavior of college students. *Journal of Marriage and the Family, 32*(3), 390–399.

Kalivas, J. (2003). Dermatitis artefacta vs. dermatitis factitia [letters to the editor]. *Dermatology and Psychosomatics, 4*(168).

Kalivas, J., Kalivas, L., Gilman, D. & Hayden, C. T. (1996). Sertraline in the treatment of neurotic excoriations and related disorders. *Archives of Dermatology, 132*(5), 589–590.

Kalsi, J. S., Arya, M., Paters, J. et al. (2002). Grease gun injury to the penis. *Journal of Royal Society of Medicine, 95*, 254.

Kanter, J. W., Busch, A. M. & Rusch A. C. (2009) *Behavioral Activation: Distinctive Features*. London: Routledge.

Kaplan, R. (2000). What should plastic surgeons do when crazy patients demand work? *The New York Observer, 7* March, 1.

Kells, B. E., Kime, D. L., Kennedy, J. G. & Freeman, R. (1996). Dysmorphophobia: a case successfully treated using a multidisciplinary approach. *Dental Update, 23*(10), 402–404.

Kent, A., & Drummond, L. M. (1989). Acne excoriée – a case report of treatment using habit reversal. *Clinical and Experimental Dermatology, 14*(2), 163–164.

Keuthen, N. J., Deckersbach, T., Wilhelm, S. et al. (2000). Repetitive skin picking in a student population and comparison with a sample of self-injurious skin-pickers. *Psychosomatics, 41*(3), 210–215.

Keuthen, N. J., Deckersbach, T., Wilhelm, S. et al. (2001a). The Skin Picking Impact Scale (SPIS): scale development and psychometric analyses. *Psychosomatics, 42*(5), 397–403.

Keuthen, N. J., Wilhelm, S., Deckersbach, T., et al. (2001b) The Skin Picking Scale: scale construction and psychometric analyses. *Journal of Psychosomatic Research, 50*, 337–341.

Khemlani-Patel, S. (2001). Cognitive and behavioral therapy for body dysmorphic disorder: A comparative investigation. PhD thesis, Hofstra University, Hempstead, NY.

Klassen, A., Jenkinson, C., Fitzpatrick, R., & Goodacre, T. (1996). Patients' health-related quality of life before and after aesthetic surgery. *British Journal of Plastic Surgery, 49*(7), 433–438.

Koblenzer, C. S. (1992). Cutaneous manifestations of psychiatric disease that commonly present to the dermatologist: diagnosis and treatment. *International Journal of Psychiatry in Medicine, 22*, 47–63.

Kohlenberg, R. J., Kanter, J. W. & Bolling, M. (2004). Functional analytic psychotherapy, cognitive therapy, and acceptance. In S. C. Hayes, V. M. Follette & M. M. Linehan (eds.) *Mindfulness and Acceptance: Expanding the Cognitive-behavioral Tradition* (pp. 96–119). New York: Guilford Press.

Koran, L., Abujaoude, E., Large, M. & Serpe, R. (2008). The prevalence of Body Dysmorphic Disorder in the United States adult population. *CNS Spectrums*, *13*(4), 316–322.

Korkina, M. V. & Morozov, P. V. (1979). Dysmorphophobic disorders. *Zh. Neuropath. Psikhiat. Korsakov*, *79*(111).

Kosslyn, S. M., Brunn, J., Cave, K. R. & Wallach, R. W. (1985). Individual differences in mental imagery ability: a computational analysis. *Cognition*, *18*(1–3), 195–243.

Kraepelin, E. (1909). *Psychiatrie: Ein Lehrbuch fur Studierende und Arzte, Klinische Psychiatrie*. Leipzig: Barth.

Krupp, N. E. (1977). Self-caused skin ulcers. *Psychosomatics*, *18*(2), 15–19.

Lacey, J. H. & Birtchnell, S. (1986). Body image and its disturbances. *Journal of Psychosomatic Research*, *90*(6), 623–631.

Ladee, G. A. (1966). *Hypochondriacal Syndromes*. Amsterdam: Elsevier.

Lambrou, C. (2006). *The Role of Aesthetic Sensitivity in Body Dysmorphic Disorder*, London: Institute of Psychiatry, University of London.

Langlois, J. H. & Roggman, L. A. (1987). Attractive faces are only average. *Psychological Science*, *1*, 115–121.

Laniti, M. & Neziroglu, F. (in submission) Neuropsychological performance of individuals with body dysmorphic disorder and obsessive compulsive disorder. Doctorate dissertation.

Lansdown, R., Rumsey, N., Bradbury, E. et al. (1997). *Visibly Different*. Oxford: Butterworth-Heinemann.

Laugharne, R., Upex, T. & Palazidou, E. (1998). Dysmorphophobia by proxy. *Journal of the Royal Society of Medicine*, *9*(5), 266.

Layden, M. A., Newman, C. F., Freeman, A. & Morse, S. B. (1993). *Cognitive Therapy of Borderline Personality Disorder*. Boston, MA: Allyn & Bacon.

Lazarus, A. (1977). Towards an egoless state of being. In A. Ellis & R. Grieger (eds.) *Handbook of Rational Emotive Therapy*, Volume 1 (pp. 113–118). New York: Springer.

Lazarus, A., Ellis, A. & Grieger, R. (1977). Towards an egoless state of being. In *Handbook of Rational Emotive Therapy*, Volume 1 (pp. 113–118). New York: Springer.

Lewinsohn, P. M., Biglan, A. & Zeiss, A. S. (1976) Behavioral treatment of depression. In P. O. Davidson (ed.) *The Behavioral Management of Anxiety, Depression and Pain* (pp. 91–146). New York: Brunner/Mazel.

Li, C., Kayes, O., Kell, P. D., Christopher, N. et al. (2006). Penile suspensory ligament division for penile augmentation: indications and results. *European Urology*, *49*, 729–733

Liao, L. M. & Creighton S. M. (2007) Requests for cosmetic genitoplasty: how should healthcare providers respond? *British Medical Journal*, *334* (26 May), 1090–1092.

Lienemann, J. & Walker, F. D. (1989). Reversal of self-abusive behavior with naltrexone. *Journal of Clinical Psychopharmacology*, *9*(6), 448–449.

Linehan, M. M. (1993). *Skills Training Manual*. New York: Guilford Press.

Lipkens, G., Hayes, S. C. & Hayes, L. J. (1993) Longitudinal study of derived stimulus relations in an infant. *Journal of Experimental Child Psychology*, *56*, 201–239.

Livesley, W. J., Jackson, D. N. & Schroeder, M. L. (1989) A study of the factorial structure of personality pathology. *Journal of Personality Disorders*, *3*, 292–306.

Lloyd, J., Crouch, N. S., Minto, C. L. et al. (2005) Female genital appearance: "normality" unfolds. *BJOG: An International Journal of Obstetrics & Gynaecology, 112,* 643–646.

Lochner, C., Simeon, D., Niehaus, D. J. & Stein, D. J. (2002). Trichotillomania and skin picking: a phenomenological comparison. *Depression and Anxiety, 15*(2), 83–86.

Lochner, C., Vythilingum, B. & Stein, D. J. (2001). Olfactory reference syndrome: diagnostic criteria and differential diagnosis. *Primary Care Psychiatry, 7*(2), 55–59.

Longmore, R. J. & Worrell, M. (2007) Do we need to challenge thoughts in cognitive behavior therapy? *Clinical Psychology Review, 27,* 173–187.

Losee, J. E., Serletti, J. M., Kreipe, R. E. & Caldwell, E. H. (1997). Reduction mammaplasty in patients with bulimia nervosa. *Annals of Plastic Surgery, 39*(5), 443–446.

Lucas, P. (2002). Body dysmorphic disorder and violence: case report and literature review. *Journal of Forensic Psychiatry, 13*(1), 145–156.

Lundgren, J. D., Anderson, D. A. & Thompson, J. K. (2004). Fear of negative appearance evaluation: development and evaluation of a new construct for risk factor work in the field of eating disorders. *Eating Behaviors, 5,* 75–84.

MacGregor, F. (1981). The place of the patient in society. *Aesthetic Plastic Surgery, 5,* 85–93.

MacLeod, A., Matthews, A. & Tata, P. (1986). Attentional bias in emotional disorders. *Journal of Abnormal Psychology, 95,* 15–20.

Maisonneuve, J. & Bruchon-Schweitzer, M. (1981). *Modèles du corps et psychologie esthétique.* Paris: Universitaires de France.

Mancini C., van Ameringen, M. & Farvolden, P. (2002) Does SSRI augmentation with antidepressants that influence noradrenergic function resolve depression in obsessive-compulsive disorder? *Journal Affective Disorders, 68*(1), 59–65.

Mannuzza, S., Fyer, A. J., Liebowitz, M. R. & Klein, D. F. (1990). Delineating the boundaries of social phobia: its relationship to panic disorder and agoraphobia. *Journal of Anxiety Disorders, 4,* 41–59.

Mansell, W., Clark, D., Ehlers, A. & Chen, Y. P. (1999). Social anxiety and attention away from emotional faces. *Cognition and Emotion, 13,* 673–690.

Mansueto, C. S., Golomb, R. G., Thomas, A. M. & Stemberger, R. M. T. (1999). A comprehensive model for behavioral treatment of trichotillomania. *Cognitive and Behavioral Practice, 6,* 23–43.

Marazziti, D., Dell'Osso, L., Presta, S. et al. (1999) Platelet [3H]paroxetine binding in patients with OCD-related disorders. *Psychiatry Research, 89*(3), 223–228.

Marbach, J. J. (1976). Phantom bite. *American Journal of Orthodontics, 70*(2), 190–199.

Marbach, J. J. (1978). Phantom bite syndrome. *American Journal of Psychiatry, 135,* 476–479.

Marks, I. M. (1986). *Behavioural Psychotherapy – Maudsley Pocket Book of Clinical Management.* Bristol: Wright.

Marks, I. & Mishan, J. (1988). Dysmorphophobic avoidance with disturbed bodily perception. A pilot study of exposure therapy. *British Journal of Psychiatry, 152,* 674–678.

Martell, C., Addis, M. E. & Jacobson, N.S. (2001) *Depression in Context: Strategies for Guided Action.* New York: W. W. Norton.

Masters, F. W. & Greaves, D. C. (1987). The Quasimodo complex. *British Journal of Plastic Surgery*, *20*, 10–204.

Mataix-Coles, D. & van den Heuvel, O. A. (2006). Common and distinct neural correlates of obsessive compulsive and related disorders. *Psychiatric Clinics of North America*, *29*, 391–410.

Mathew, A. (2001). Pediatric autoimmune neuropsychiatric disorders variant and body dysmorphic disorder [letter]. *American Journal of Psychiatry*, *158*(963).

Mattick, R. P. & Clarke, J. C. (1998). *Development* and validation of measures of social phobia scrutiny fear and social interaction anxiety. *Behavior Research and Therapy*, *36*, 455–470.

Mayville, S., Katz, R. C., Gipson, M. T. & Cabral, K. (1999). Assessing the prevalence of body dysmorphic disorder in an ethnically diverse group of adolescents. *Journal of Child and Family Studies*, *8*(3), 357–362.

McConnaughy, E. A., Prochaska, J. O. & Velicer, W. F. (1983). Stages of change in psychotherapy: measurement of sample profiles. *Psychotherapy: Theory, Research and Practice*, *20*, 368–375.

McGlynn, S. M. & Schacter, D. L. (1989). Unawareness of deficits in neuropsychological syndromes. *Journal of Clinical and Experimental Neuropsychology*, *11*(2), 143–205.

McIntosh, V. V., Britt, E. & Bulik, C. M. (1994). Cosmetic breast augmentation and eating disorders. *New Zealand Medical Journal*, *27*(107), 151–152.

McKay, D. (1999). Two-year follow-up of behavioral treatment and maintenance for body dysmorphic disorder. *Behavior Modification*, *23*(4), 620–629.

McKay, D. & Neziroglu, F. (in press) The spectrum of obsessive-compulsive disorders: methodological issues with body dysmorphic disorder and hypochondriasis as examples. *Psychiatry Research*.

McKay, D., Neziroglu, F. & Yaryura-Tobias, J. A. (1997). Comparison of clinical characteristics in obsessive-compulsive disorder and body dysmorphic disorder. *Journal of Anxiety Disorders*, *11*(4), 447–454.

McKay, D., Todaro, J., Neziroglu, F. et al. (1997). Body dysmorphic disorder: a preliminary evaluation of treatment and maintenance using exposure with response prevention. *Behavior Research and Therapy*, *35*(1), 67–70.

McKenna, P. J. (1984). Disorders with overvalued ideas. *British Journal of Psychiatry*, *145*, 579–585.

McMahon, C. E. (1973). Images as motives and motivators: a historical perspective. *American Journal of Psychology*, *86*(465), 490.

McVey-Noble, M. E., Khemlani-Patel, S. & Neziroglu, F. (2006), *When Your Child Is Cutting: A Parent's Guide to Helping Children Overcome Self-injury*, Oakland, CA, New Harbinger Publications.

Mick, M. A. & Telch, M. J. (1998). Social anxiety and history of behavioral inhibition in young adults. *Journal of Anxiety Disorders*, *12*, 1–20.

Miller, W. R. & Rollnick, S. (1991). *Motivational Interviewing*. New York: Guilford Press.

Mills, R. S. L., Rubin, K. H., Rubin, K. H. & Asendorpf, J. B. (1993). Socialization factors in the development of social withdrawal. In *Social Withdrawal, Inhibition, and Shyness in Childhood* (pp. 117–148). Hillsdale, NJ: Lawrence Erlbaum.

Mogg, K. & Bradley, B. P. (1998). A cognitive-motivational analysis of anxiety. *Behavior Research and Therapy*, *36*, 809–848.

Moller, A. P. (1993). Female preference for apparently symmetrical male sexual ornaments in the barn swallow, *Hirundo rustica*. *Behavioral Ecology and Sociobiology*, *32*, 371–376.

Moller, A. P., Soler, M. & Thornhill, R. (1995). Breast asymmetry, sexual selection, and human reproductive success. *Ethology and Sociobiology*, *16*, 207–219.

Money, J., Jobaris, R. & Furth, G. (1977). Apotemnophilia. *Journal of Sexual Research*, *13*(115), 125.

Morgan, M. & Jones, J. (1993). Intentional self-infection with HIV by long-term partners of HIV-positive homosexual men: four case reports. *AIDS Patient Care*, *7*(1), 10–15.

Morselli, E. (1891). Sulla dismorfofobia e sulla tafefobia. *Boll Accad Med (Genova)*, *VI*, 110–119.

Mulkens, S. (2007) Task concentration training in Body Dysmorphic Disorder. Presentation at World Congress of Behavior and Cognitive Therapies, Barcelona, Spain.

Mulkens, S., Bögels, S. M. & de Jong, P. J. (1999). Attentional focus and fear of blushing: A case study. *Behavioral and Cognitive Psychotherapy*, *27*, 153–164.

Mulkens, S., Bögels, S. M., de Jong, P. J. & Louwers, J. (2001). Fear of blushing: effects of task concentration training versus exposure *in vivo* on fear and physiology. *Journal of Anxiety Disorders*, *15*, 413–432.

Munjack, D. (1978). Behavioral treatment of dysmorphophobia. *Journal of Behavioral Therapy and Experimental Psychiatry*, *9*, 53–56.

Munro, A. & Stewart, M. (1991). Body dysmorphic disorder and the DSM-IV: the demise of dysmorphophobia [see comments]. *Canadian Journal of Psychiatry. Revue Canadienne de Psychiatrie*, *36*, 91–96.

Naga. A. A., Devinsky, O. & Barr, W. B. (2004) Somatoform disorders after temporal lobectomy. *Cognitive and Behavioral Neurology*, *17*(2), 57–61.

Napoleon, T., Chassin, L. & Young, R. (1980). A replication and extension of "Physical attractiveness and mental illness." *Journal of Abnormal Psychology*, *89*, 250–253.

National Collaborating Centre for Mental Health (2004). *Obsessive Compulsive Disorder: The Management of Obsessive Compulsive Disorder in Children and Adults in Primary and Secondary Care*. London: Gaskell and BPS.

National Collaborating Centre for Mental Health (2006). *Obsessive Compulsive Disorder: Core Interventions in the Treatment of Obsessive Compulsive Disorder and Body Dysmorphic Disorder*. London: Gaskell and BPS.

Newell, R. & Shrubb, S. (1994). Attitude change and behavior therapy in body dysmorphic disorder: two case reports. *Behavioral and Cognitive Psychotherapy*, *22*, 163–169.

Neziroglu, F. (2004) How to apply cognitive and behavior therapy for body dysmorphic disorder. Paper presented at the American Psychiatric Association, 157th Annual Meeting; May 1–6. New York.

Neziroglu, F., Anderson, M. C. & Yaryura-Tobias, J. A. (1999). An in-depth review of obsessive compulsive disorder, body dysmorphic disorder, hypochondriasis, and trichotillomania: therapeutic issues and current research. *Crisis Intervention*, *5*, 59–94.

Neziroglu, F., Hickey, M. et al. (2009, in press). Psychophysiological and self-report components of disgust in body dysmorphic disorder: the effects of repeated exposure. *International Journal of Cognitive Therapy.*

Neziroglu, F. & Khemlani-Patel, S. (2002). A review of cognitive and behavioral treatment for body dysmorphic disorder. *CNS Spectrums, 7,* 464–471.

Neziroglu, F., & Khemlani-Patel, S. (2003) Therapeutic approaches to body dysmorphic disorder. *Brief Treatment and Crisis Intervention, 3,* 301–322

Neziroglu, F., Khemlani-Patel, S. & Jacofsky, M. (2009). Body dysmorphic disorder: symptoms, models and treatment interventions. In Simos Gregoris (ed.), *Cognitive Behavior Therapy: A Guide for the Practising Clinician* (pp. 94–111). London: Routledge.

Neziroglu, F., Khemlani-Patel, S. & Veale, D. (2008). Social learning theory and cognitive behavioral models of body dysmorphic disorder. *Body Image, 5,* 28–38.

Neziroglu, F., Khemlani-Patel, S. & Yaryura-Tobias, J. A. (2006). Rates of abuse in Body Dysmorphic Disorder and Obsessive Compulsive Disorder. *Body Image, 3*(2), 189–193.

Neziroglu, F., McKay, D., Todaro, J. & Yaryura Tobias, J. A. (1996). Effects of cognitive behavior therapy on persons with body dysmorphic disorder and comorbid Axis II diagnoses. *Behavior Therapy, 27,* 67–77.

Neziroglu, F., McKay, D., Yaryura-Tobias, J. A. & Stevens, K. P. (1999). The overvalued ideas scale: development, reliability, and validity in obsessive compulsive disorder. *Behaviour Research and Therapy, 37*(881), 902.

Neziroglu, F., Rabinowitz, D., Breytman, A. & Jacofsky, M. (2008) Skin picking: phenomenology and severity comparison. *The Primary Care Companion. 10*(4), 306–312.

Neziroglu, F., Roberts, M. & Yaryura-Tobias, J. A. (2004) A behavioral model for body dysmorphic disorder. *Psychiatric Annals, 34,* 915–920.

Neziroglu, F., Stevens, K. P., McKay, D. & Yaryura-Tobias, J. A. (2001). Predictive validity of the overvalued ideas scale: outcome in obsessive-compulsive and body dysmorphic disorders. *Behavior Research Therapy, 39,* 745–756.

Neziroglu, F. & Yaryura-Tobias, J. A. (1993a). Body Dysmorphic Disorder: phenomenology and case descriptions. *Behavioural Psychotherapy, 21,* 27–36.

Neziroglu, F. & Yaryura Tobias, J. A. (1993b). Exposure, response prevention, and cognitive therapy in the treatment of body dysmorphic disorder. *Behavior Therapy, 24,* 431–438.

Neziroglu, F. & Yaryura-Tobias, J. A. (1997). A review of cognitive behavioral and pharmacological treatment of body dysmorphic disorder. *Behavior Modification, 21*(3), 324–340.

Nirenberg, A. A., Phillips, K. A., Petersen, T. J. et al. (2002). Body dysmorphic disorder in outpatients with major depression. *Journal of Affective Disorders, 69,* 141–148.

Norris, D. L. (1984). The effects of mirror confrontation on self-estimation in anorexia nervosa, bulimia and two control groups. *Psychological Medicine, 32,* 573–577.

Obholzer, K. (1982). *The Wolf-Man: Sixty Years Later.* London: Routledge & Kegan Paul.

O'Connor, K. (2005) *Cognitive-Behavioral Management of Tic Disorder.* Chichester: John Wiley.

Oosthuizen, P., Lambert, T. & Castle, D. (1998). Dysmorphic concern: prevalence and associations with clinical variables. *Australian and New Zealand Journal of Psychiatry, 32*, 129–132.

Osman, S., Cooper, M., Hackmann, A. & Veale, D. (2004). Spontaneously occurring images and early memories in people with body dysmorphic disorder. *Memory, 12*, 428–436.

O'Sullivan, R. L., Phillips, K. A., Keuthen, N. J. & Wilhelm, S. (1999). Near-fatal skin picking from delusional body dysmorphic disorder responsive to fluvoxamine. *Psychosomatics, 40*(1), 79–81.

Ottenbreit, N. D. & Dobson, K. S. (2004). Avoidance and depression: the construction of the Cognitive-Behavioral Avoidance Scale. *Behavior Research and Therapy, 42*, 292–313.

Ottens, A. J. (1981). Multifaceted treatment of compulsive hair pulling. *Journal Behavior Therapy & Experimental Psychiatry, 12*(1), 77–80.

Otto, M. W., Wilhelm, S., Cohen, L. S. & Harlow, B. (2001). Prevalence of body dysmorphic disorder in a community sample of women. *American Journal of Psychiatry, 158*(12), 2061–2063.

Padesky, C. A. (1997). Developing cognitive therapist competency: teaching and supervision models. In P. M. Salkovskis (ed.) *Frontiers of Cognitive Therapy* (pp. 266–292). New York: Guilford Press.

Pallanti, S. & Koran, L. M. (1996). Intravenous, pulse loaded clomipramine in body dysmorphic disorder: two case reports. *CNS Spectrums, 1*, 54–57.

Papageorgiou, C., & Wells, A. (1998). Effects of attention training on hypochondriasis: a brief case series. *Psychological Medicine, 28*, 193–200.

Papageorgiou, C. & Wells, A. (2000). Treatment of recurrent major depression with attention training. *Cognitive and Behavioral Practice, 7*, 407–413.

Penzel, F. (2003). *The Hair-pulling Problem: A Complete Guide to Trichotillomania.* New York: Oxford University Press

Perez Jimenez, J. P., Gomez Bajo, G. J., Lopez Castillo, J. J. et al. (1994). Psychiatric consultation and post-traumatic stress disorder in burned patients. *Burns, 20*(6), 532–536.

Perovic, S. V., Byun, J.-S., Scheplev, P. et al. (2006). New perspectives of penile enhancement surgery: tissue engineering with biodegradable scaffolds. *European Urology, 49*(1), 139–147.

Perrett, D. I., Lee, K. J., Penton-Voak, I. et al. (1998). Effects of sexual dimorphism in facial attractiveness. *Nature, 394*, 884–887.

Perugi, G., Akiskal, H. S., Giannotti, D. et al. (1997). Gender-related differences in body dysmorphic disorder (dysmorphophobia). *Journal of Nervous & Mental Disease, 185*(9), 578–582.

Perugi, G., Giannotti, D., Di Vaio, S. et al. (1996). Fluvoxamine in the treatment of body dysmorphic disorder (dysmorphophobia). *International Clinical Psychopharmacology, 11*(4), 247–254.

Philippopoulos, G. S. (1979). The analysis of a case of dysmorfobia. *Canadian Journal of Psychiatry – Revue Canadienne de Psychiatrie, 24*, 379–401.

Phillips, K. A. (1991). Body dysmorphic disorder: the distress of imagined ugliness. *American Journal of Psychiatry, 148*(9), 1138–1149.

Phillips, K. A. (1996a). *The Broken Mirror – Understanding and Treating Body Dysmorphic Disorder*. New York: Oxford University Press.

Phillips, K. A. (1996b). Body dysmorphic disorder: diagnosis and treatment of imagined ugliness. *Journal of Clinical Psychiatry*, *57* (Suppl 8), 61–64.

Phillips, K. A. (1996c). An open study of buspirone augmentation of serotonin-reuptake inhibitors in body dysmorphic disorder. *Psychopharmacology Bulletin*, *32*(1), 175–180.

Phillips, K. A. (1996d). Pharmacologic treatment of body dysmorphic disorder. *Psychopharmacology Bulletin*, *32*(4), 597–605.

Phillips, K. A. (1998). Body dysmorphic disorder: clinical aspects and treatment strategies. *Bulletin of the Menninger Clinic*, *62*(4 Suppl A), A33–A48.

Phillips, K. A. (2000). Quality of life for patients with body dysmorphic disorder. *Journal of Nervous and Mental Disease*, *188*, 170–175.

Phillips, K. A. (2001) Body dysmorphic disorder. In K. A. Phillips (ed.) *Somatoform and Factitious Disorders* (pp. 67–94). Washington, DC: American Psychiatric Publishing.

Phillips, K. A. (2002). Pharmacologic treatment of body dysmorphic disorder: review of the evidence and a recommended treatment approach. *CNS Spectrums*, *7*(6), 453–463.

Phillips, K. A. (2005). Placebo-controlled study of pimozide augmentation of fluoxetine in body dysmorphic disorder. *American Journal of Psychiatry*, *162*(2), 377–379.

Phillips, K. A., Albertini, R. S. & Rasmussen, S. A. (2002). A randomized placebo-controlled trial of fluoxetine in body dysmorphic disorder. *Archives of General Psychiatry*, *59*, 381–388.

Phillips, K. A., Albertini, R. S., Siniscalchi, J. M., et al. (2001). Effectiveness of pharmacotherapy for body dysmorphic disorder: a chart-review study. *Journal of Clinical Psychiatry*, *62*, 721–727.

Phillips, K. A., Atala, K. D. & Pope, H. G. (1995). Diagnostic instruments for body dysmorphic disorder [published abstract]. *New Research Programs and Abstracts*, Miami, FL.

Phillips, K. A., Coles, M., Menard, W. et al. (2005). Suicidal ideation and suicide attempts in body dysmorphic disorder. *Journal of Clinical Psychiatry*, *66*(6), 717–725.

Phillips, K. A., Conroy, M., Dufresne, R. G. et al. (2006). Tanning in body dysmorphic disorder. *Psychiatric Quarterly*, *77*(2), 129–138.

Phillips, K. A., Didie, E. R., Menard, W. et al. (2006). Clinical features of Body Dysmorphic Disorder in adolescents and adults. *Psychiatry Research*, *141*(3), 305–314.

Phillips, K. A., Dufresne, R. G., Jr. et al. (2000). Rate of body dysmorphic disorder in dermatology patients. *Journal of the American Academy of Dermatology*, *42*, 436–444.

Phillips, K. A. & Diaz, S. F. (1997). Gender differences in body dysmorphic disorder. *Journal of Nervous & Mental Disease*, *185*(9), 570–577.

Phillips, K. A., Dufresne, R. G., Jr., Wilkel, C. S. et al. (2000). Rate of body dysmorphic disorder in dermatology patients. *Journal of the American Academy of Dermatology*, *42*, 436–444.

Phillips, K. A., Dwight, M. M. & McElroy, S. L. (1998). Efficacy and safety of fluvoxamine in body dysmorphic disorder. *Journal of Clinical Psychiatry*, *59*(4), 165–171.

Phillips, K. A., Grant, J. E., Siniscalchi, J. M. et al. (2005). A retrospective follow-up study of body dysmorphic disorder. *Comprehensive Psychiatry, 46*(5), 315–321.

Phillips, K. A. & Hollander, E. (2008). Treating body dysmorphic disorder with medication: evidence, misconceptions, and a suggested approach. *Body Image, 5*(1), 13–27.

Phillips, K. A., Hollander, E., Rasmussen, S. A. et al. (1997). A severity rating scale for body dysmorphic disorder: development, reliability, and validity of a modified version of the Yale-Brown Obsessive Compulsive Scale. *Psychopharmacology Bulletin, 33*(1), 17–22.

Phillips, K. A. & McElroy, S. L. (1992). Obsessive-compulsive disorder in relation to body dysmorphic disorder: reply. *American Journal of Psychiatry, 149*, 1284.

Phillips, K. A. & McElroy, S. L. (1993). Insight, overvalued ideation, and delusional thinking in body dysmorphic disorder: theoretical and treatment implications. *Journal of Nervous & Mental Disease, 181*(11), 699–702.

Phillips, K. A. & McElroy, S. L. (2000). Personality disorders and traits in patients with body dysmorphic disorder. *Comprehensive Psychiatry, 41*(4), 229–236.

Phillips, K. A., McElroy, S. L., Hudson, J. I., & Pope, H. G. Jr. (1995). Body dysmorphic disorder: an obsessive-compulsive spectrum disorder, a form of affective spectrum disorder, or both? *Journal of Clinical Psychiatry, 56* (Suppl 4), 41–51.

Phillips, K. A., McElroy, S. L., Keck, P. E., Jr. et al. (1993). Body dysmorphic disorder: 30 cases of imagined ugliness. *American Journal of Psychiatry, 150*(2), 302–308.

Phillips, K. A., McElroy, S. L., Keck, P. E., Jr. et al. (1994). A comparison of delusional and non-delusional body dysmorphic disorder in 100 cases. *Psychopharmacology Bulletin, 30*(2), 179–186.

Phillips, K. A. & Menard, W. (2004). Body dysmorphic disorder and art background. *American Journal of Psychiatry, 161*, 927–928.

Phillips, K. A. & Menard, W. (2006). Suicidality in Body Dysmorphic Disorder: a prospective study. *American Journal of Psychiatry, 163*(7), 1280–1282.

Phillips, K. A., Menard, W. & Fay, C. (2006). Gender similarities and differences in 200 individuals with body dysmorphic disorder. *Comprehensive Psychiatry, 47*(2), 77–87.

Phillips, K. A., Menard, W., Pagano, M. E. et al. (2006). Delusional versus nondelusional body dysmorphic disorder: clinical features and course of illness. *Journal of Psychiatric Research. 40*(2), 95–104.

Phillips, K. A. & Najjar, F. (2003). An open-label study of citalopram in body dysmorphic disorder. *Journal of Clinical Psychiatry, 64*(6), 715–720.

Phillips, K. A., Nierenberg, A. A., Brendel, G. & Fava, M. (1996). Prevalence and clinical features of body dysmorphic disorder in atypical major depression. *Journal of Nervous & Mental Disease, 184*(2), 125–129.

Phillips, K. A., Pagano, M. E., Menard, W. & Stout, R. L. (2006). A 12-month follow-up study of the course of body dysmorphic disorder. *American Journal of Psychiatry, 163*(5), 907–912.

Phillips, K. A. Pinto, A. Menard, W. et al. (2007). Obsessive-compulsive disorder versus body dysmorphic disorder: a comparison study of two possibly related disorders. *Depression & Anxiety, 24*(6) 399–409.

Phillips, K. A. & Taub, S. L. (1995). Skin picking as a symptom of body dysmorphic disorder. *Psychopharmacology Bulletin, 31*(2), 279–288.

Pinto, A. & Phillips, K. A. (2005). Social anxiety in Body Dysmorphic Disorder. *Body Image, 2*, 401–405.

Pitman, R. K. (1987). Pierre Janet on obsessive compulsive disorder (1903): review and commentary. *Archives of General Psychiatry, 44*, 226–232.

Pittenger, J. B. & Baskett, L. M. (1984). Facial self-perception: Its relation to objective appearance and self-concept. *Bulletin of the Psychonomic Society, 22*(3) (May), 167–170.

Pittenger, C., Bloch, M., Wegner, R. & Teitelbaum, C. (2006) Glutamergic dysfunction in obsessive compulsive disorder and the potential clinical utility of Glutamate-modulating agents, *Primary Psychiating, 13*(10) 65–77.

Plath, S. (2000). Journal 28 August 1957–14 October 1958: Northampton, Massachusetts. In K. V. Kukil (ed.), *The Journals of Sylvia Plath 1950–1962*, London: Faber and Faber.

Pope, C. G., Pope, H. G., Menard, W. et al. (2005). Clinical features of muscle dysmorphia among males with BDD, *Body Image 2*(4), 395–400.

Priebe, S. & Rohricht, F. (2001). Specific body image pathology in acute schizophrenia. *Psychiatry Research, 101*(3), 289–301.

Prior, M. (1992). Childhood temperament. *Journal of Child Psychology and Psychiatry and Allied Disciplines, 33*, 249–279.

Pruzinsky, T. & Borkovec, T. D. (1990). Cognitive and personality characteristics of worriers. *Behavior Research and Therapy, 28*(6), 507–512.

Pryse-Phillips, W. (1971). An olfactory reference syndrome. *Acta Psychiatrica Scandinavica, 47*(4), 484–509.

Rabinowitz, D., Neziroglu, F. & Roberts, M. (2007). Clinical application of a behavioral model for the treatment of body dysmorphic disorder. *Cognitive and Behavioral Practice*, 231–237.

Radika, L. M., Hayslip, B., Cash, T. F. & Pruzinsky, T. (2002). Projective techniques to assess body image. *Body Image: A Handbook of Theory, Research, and Clinical Practice*. (pp. 156–157). New York: Guilford Press.

Rapee, R. M. & Hayman, K. (1996). The effects of video feedback on the self-evaluation of performance in socially anxious subjects. *Behavior Research and Therapy, 34*, 315–322.

Rapoport, J. L., Ryland, D. H. & Kriete, M. (1992). Drug treatment of canine acral lick: an animal model of obsessive-compulsive disorder. *Archives of General Psychiatry, 49*, 517–521.

Rauch, S. L., Phillips, K. A., Segal, E. et al. (2003). A preliminary morphometric magnetic resonance imaging study of regional brain volumes in body dysmorphic disorder. *Psychiatry Research, 122*(1), 13–19.

Rauch, S. L., Shin, L. M. & Wright, C.I. (2003). Neuroimaging studies of amygdala function in anxiety disorders. *Annals of the New York Academy of Sciences, 985*, 389–410.

Rhodes, G., Hickford, C. & Jeffery, L. (2000). Sex-typicality and attractiveness: are supermale and superfemale faces superattractive? *British Journal of Psychology, 91*, 125–140.

Rhodes, G., Sumich, A. & Byatt, G. (1999). Are average facial configurations only attractive because of their symmetry and averageness. *Journal of Comparative Psychology*, *108*, 233–242.

Rich, N., Rosen, J. C., Orosan, P. G. & Reiter, J. T. (1992). *Prevalence of Body Dysmorphic Disorder in Non-clinical Populations*. Presentation at Association for Advancement of Behavior Therapy, Boston, MA.

Richards, C. H. & Salkovskis P. M. (1995). The cognitive phenomenology of OCD repeated rituals. Poster presented at World Congress of Behavioral and Cognitive Therapies, Copenhagen, Denmark.

Richter, M. A., Tharmalingham, S., Burroughs, E. et al. (2004). A preliminary genetics investigation of BDD and OCD. *Neuropsychopharmacology*, *29* (suppl 1), S200.

Riding, J. & Munro, A. (1975). Pimozide in the treatment of monosymptomatic hypochondriacal psychosis. *Acta Psychiatrica Scandinavica*, *53*, 23–30.

Rief, W., Buhlmann, U., Wilhelm, S. et al. (2006). The prevalence of body dysmorphic disorder: a population-based survey. *Psychological Medicine*, *36*(6), 877–885.

Roberts, L. F., Brett, M.A., Johnson, T. W. & Wassersug, R. J. (2007), Passion for castration: characterizing men who are fascinated with castration, but have not been castrated. *Journal of Sexual Medicine*, *5*(7) 1669–1680.

Robinson, E. (1997). Psychological research on visible differences in adults. In R. Lansdown et al. (eds.) *Visibly Different. Coping with Disfigurement* (pp. 102–111). Oxford: Butterworth-Heinemann.

Rosen, J. C. & Reiter, J. (1995). *Development* of the body dysmorphic disorder examination. *Behavior Research and Therapy*, *34*(9), 755–766.

Rosen, J. C. & Reiter, J. (1996). *Development* of the body dysmorphic disorder examination. *Behavior Research and Therapy*, *34*(9), 755–766.

Rosen, J. C., Reiter, J. & Orosan, P. (1995a). Cognitive-behavioral body image therapy for body dysmorphic disorder. *Journal of Consulting and Clinical Psychology*, *63*, 263–269.

Rosen, J. C., Reiter, J. & Orosan, P. (1995b). Assessment of body image in eating disorders with the body dysmorphic disorder examination. *Behaviour Research and Therapy*, *33*(1), 77–84.

Rosenbaum, M. S. & Ayllon, T. (1981). The behavioral treatment of neurodermatitis through habit reversal. *Behavior Research and Therapy*, *19*(4), 313–318.

Rothbaum, B. O. (1992). The behavioral treatment of trichotillomania, *20/1* (85–90), 85–90.

Rozin, P. & Fallon, A. (1987). A perspective on disgust. *Psychological Review*, *94*, 23–41.

Rubin, K. H., Nelson, L. J., Hastings, P. & Asendorpf, J. (1999). Transaction between parents' perceptions of their children's shyness and their parenting styles. *International Journal of Behavioral Development*, *23*, 937–957.

Ruffolo, J., Phillips, KA, Menard, W. et al. (2006). Comorbidity of body dysmorphic disorder and eating disorders: severity of psychopathology and body image disturbance. *International Journal of Eating Disorders*, *39*(1), 11–19.

Salib, E. A. (1988). Subacute sclerosing panencephalitis (SSPE) presenting at the age of 21 as a schizophrenia-like state with bizarre dysmorphophobic features. *British Journal of Psychiatry*, *152*, 709–710.

Salkovskis, P. M. (1985). Obsessive-compulsive problems: a cognitive behavioral analysis. *Behavior Research and Therapy, 23*, 571–583.

Salkovskis, P. M. (1991). The importance of behavior in the maintenance of anxiety and panic. *Behavioral Psychotherapy, 19*, 6–19.

Salkovskis, P. M. (1999). Understanding and treating obsessive compulsive disorder. *Behavior Research and Therapy, 37* (suppl. 1), S29–S52.

Salkovskis, P. M., Clark, D. M. & Gelder, M. G. (1996). Cognition–behavior links in the persistence of panic. *Behavior Research and Therapy, 34*(5–6), 453–458.

Salkovskis, P. M. & Kirk, J (2009). Obsessional disorders. In K. Hawton, (ed.) *Cognitive Behavior Therapy for Psychiatric Problems: A Practical Guide.* Oxford: Oxford University Press.

Salkovskis, P. M., Richards, C. & Forrester, E. (2000). Psychological treatment of refractory obsessive-compulsive disorder and related problems. In W. K. Goodman, J. D. Maser & M. V. Rudorfer (eds.) *Obsessive-Compulsive Disorder: Contemporary Issues in Treatment* (pp. 201–221). Mahwah, NJ: Lawrence Erlbaum.

Sarwer, D. B. (2002) Awareness and Identification of body dysmorphic by aesthetic surgeons: Results of a survey of American society for aesthetic surgery members. *Aesthic Surgery Journal, 22*(6) 531–535.

Sarwer, D. B., Pertschuk, M. J., Wadden, T. A. & Whitaker, L. A. (1998). Psychological investigations in cosmetic surgery: a look back and a look ahead. *Plastic & Reconstructive Surgery, 101*, 1136–1142.

Sarwer, D. B., Wadden, T. A., Pertschuk, M. J. & Whitaker, L. A. (1998). Body image dissatisfaction and body dysmorphic disorder in 100 cosmetic surgery patients. *Plastic & Reconstructive Surgery, 101*(6), 1644–1649.

Saxena, S. & Feusner, J. D. (2006) Toward a neurobiology of Body Dysmorphic Disorder, *Primary Psychiatry, 13*, 41–50.

Schmidt, N. B. & Harrington, P. (1995). Cognitive-behavioral treatment of body dysmorphic disorder: a case report. *Journal of Behavior Therapy & Experimental Psychiatry, 26*(2), 161–167.

Schneier, F., Johnson, J., Hornig, C. D. et al. (1992). Social phobia: comorbidity and morbidity in an epidemiological sample. *Archives of General Psychiatry, 49*, 282–288.

Schwalberg, M. D., Barlow, D. H., Alger, S. A. & Howard, L. J. (1992). Comparison of bulimics, obese binge eaters, social phobics, and individuals with panic disorder on comorbidity across DSM-III-R anxiety disorders. *Journal of Abnormal Psychology, 101*, 675–681.

Schwartz, C. E., Snidman, N. & Kagan, J. (1999). Adolescent social anxiety as an outcome of inhibited temperament in childhood. *Journal of American Academy of Child and Adolescent Psychiatry, 38*, 1008–1015.

Semiz, U., Basoglu, C, Ceti, M. et al. (2008) Body dysmorphic disorder in patients with borderline personality disorder: prevalence, clinical characteristics, and role of childhood trauma. *Acta Neuropsychiatrica, 20*(1), 33–40.

Shafran, R., Cooper, Z. & Fairburn, C. G. (2002). Clinical perfectionism: a cognitive-behavioral analysis. *Behavior Research and Therapy, 40*, 773–791.

Sherry, S. B. & Vriend, J. L. (2009) Perfectionism dimensions, appearance schemas, and symptoms of body image disturbance in community members and university students. *Body Image.*

Siegle, G. J., Ghinassi, F. & Thase, M. E. (2007). Neurobehavioral therapies in the 21st century: summary of an emerging field and an extended example of Cognitive Control Training for depression. *Cognitive Therapy and Research 31*(2), 235–262.

Simeon, D., Favazza, A., Simeon, D. & Hollander, E. (2001). Self-injurious behaviors: phenomenology and assessment. In *Self-injurious Behaviors: Assessment & Treatment*. Washington, DC: American Psychiatric Press, pp. 1–28.

Simeon, D., Hollander, E., Stein, D. J. et al. (1995). Body dysmorphic disorder in the DSM-IV field trial for obsessive-compulsive disorder. *American Journal of Psychiatry, 152*(8), 1207–1209.

Simeon, D., Stein, D. J., Gross, S. et al. (1997). A double-blind trial of fluoxetine in pathologic skin picking. *Journal of Clinical Psychiatry, 58*(8), 341–347.

Smith, R. & Fisher, K. (2003). Healthy limb amputation: ethical and legal aspects. *Clinical Medicine, 3*(2), 188.

Smucker, M. R. & Dancu, C. V. (1999). *Cognitive Behavioral Treatment for Adult Survivors of Childhood Trauma: Rescripting and Reprocessing*. Northvale, NJ: Jason Aronson.

Smucker, M. R., Dancu, C., Foa, E. B. & Niederee, J. L. (1995). Imagery rescripting: a new treatment for survivors of childhood sexual abuse suffering from posttraumatic stress. *Journal of Cognitive Psychotherapy, 9*(1), 3–17.

Smucker, M. R. & Niederee, J. (1995). Treating incest-related PTSD and pathogenic schemas through imaginal exposure and rescripting. *Cognitive and Behavioral Practice 2*(1), 63–92.

Sobanski, E. & Schmidt, M. H. (2000). "Everybody looks at my pubic bone" – a case report of an adolescent patient with body dysmorphic disorder. *Acta Psychiatrica Scandinavica, 101*(1), 80–82.

Solyom, L., DiNicola, V. F., Phil, M. et al. (1985). Is there an obsessive psychosis? Aetiological and prognostic factors of an atypical form of obsessive-compulsive neurosis. *Canadian Journal of Psychiatry, 30*, 372–379.

Sondheimer, A. (1988). Clomipramine treatment of Delusional Disorder-Somatic type. *Journal of the American Academy of Child and Adolescent Psychiatry, 27*, 188–192.

Spyropoulos, E., Christoforidis, C., Borousas, D. et al. (2005). Augmentation phalloplasty surgery for penile dysmorphophobia in young adults: considerations regarding patient selection, outcome evaluation and techniques applied. *European Urology, 48*(1), 121–128.

Stein, D. J. & Hollander, E. (1992). Dermatology and conditions related to obsessive-compulsive disorder [see comments]. [Review] [55 refs]. *Journal of the American Academy of Dermatology, 26*(2 Pt 1), 237–242.

Stein, D. J., Hutt, C. S., Spitz, J. L. & Hollander, E. (1993). Compulsive picking and obsessive-compulsive disorder. *Psychosomatics, 34*(2), 177–181.

Stein, D. J. & Simeon, D. (1999). The nosology of compulsive skin picking. *Journal of Clinical Psychiatry, 60*(9), 618–619.

Stice, E. (2002) Risk and maintenance factors for eating pathology: a meta-analytical review. *Psychological Bulletin, 1218*, 825–848.

Stopa, L. & Spurr, J. M. (2003). The observer perspective: Effects on social anxiety and performance. *Behavior Research and Therapy, 41*(9) (September), 1009–1028.

Stormer, S. & Thompson, J. (1996). Explanations of body image disturbance: a test of maturational status, negative verbal commentary, social comparison, and sociocultural hypotheses. *International Journal of Eating Disorders, 19*, 193–202.

Stout, R. J. (1990). Fluoxetine for the treatment of compulsive facial picking. *American Journal of Psychiatry, 147*, 370–370.

Stutte, H. (1962). Thersites-komplex. *A Crianca Portuguesa, 21*, 451–456.

Suzuki, K., Takei, N., Iwata, Y. et al. (2004). Do olfactory reference syndrome and jiko-shu-kyofu (a subtype of *taijin-kyofu*) share a common entity? *Acta Psychiatrica Scandinavica, 109*(2), 150–155.

Sverd, J., Kerbeshian, J., Montero, G. et al. (1997). Co-occurrence of body dysmorphic disorder and Tourette's disorder. Three patient examples. *Psychosomatics, 38*(6), 578–581.

Symons, D. (1987). *The Evolution of Human Sexuality*: Oxford: Oxford University Press.

Tamam, L. & Ozpoyraz, N. (2002). Comorbidity of anxiety disorder among patients with bipolar I disorder in remission. *Psychopathology, 35*, 203–209.

Tanzi, E. (1909). *A Textbook of Mental Diseases*, trans. W. F. Robertson and T. C. MacKenzie, London: Rebman.

Taqui, A..M., Shaikh, M., Gowani, S. A. et al. (2008) Body Dysmorphic Disorder: gender differences and prevalence in a Pakistani medical student population. *BMC Psychiatry*, 8:20 (doi:10.1186/1471-244X-8-20).

Teng, E. J., Woods, D. W., Twohig, M. P. & Marcks, B. A. (2002). Body-focused repetitive behavior problems. Prevalence in a nonreferred population and differences in perceived somatic activity. *Behavior Modification, 26*(3), 340–360.

Teri, L., Logsdon, R. G., Uomoto, J. & McCurry, S. M. (1997). Behavioral treatment of depression in dementia patients: a controlled clinical trial. *Journal of Gerontology*. Series B, Psychological Sciences Social Sciences, *52*, P159–P166.

Thomas, C. M., Keery, H., Williams, R. & Thompson, J. K. (1998). The fear of negative appearance evaluation scale: Development and preliminary validation. Paper presented at the Annual Meeting of the Association for the Advancement of Behavior Therapy, Boston, MA.

Thomas, C. S. (1984). Dysmorphophobia: a question of definition. *British Journal of Psychiatry, 144*, 513–516.

Thomas, C. S. (1990). Stress and facial appearance. *Stress Medicine, 6*, 299–304.

Thomas, C. S. & Goldberg, D. P. (1995). Appearance, body image and distress in facial dysmorphophobia. *Acta Psychiatrica Scandinavica, 92*, 231–236.

Thomas, N. & Edward, N. Z. (2001). Mental imagery. In *The Stanford Encyclopedia of Philosophy*, Winter edition.

Thompson, J. K., Heinberg, L. J., Altabe, M. & Tantleff-Dunn, S. (1999). *Exacting Beauty: Theory, Assessment, and Treatment of Body Image Disturbance*. Washington, DC: American Psychological Association.

Thompson, J. K., Reed, D. L., Brannick, M. T. & Sacco, W. P. (1991). Development and validation of the Physical Appearance State and Trait Anxiety Scale (PASTAS), *Journal of Anxiety Disorders, 5*(4), 323–332.

Thompson, J. M., Baxter, L. R. & Schwartz, J. M. (1992). Freud, obsessive-compulsive disorder and neurobiology. *Psychoanalysis and Contemporary Thought, 15*, 483–505.

Thornhill, R. & Gangestad, S. W. (1993). Human facial beauty averageness, symmetry, and parasite resistance. *Human Nature, 4*(3), 237–269.

Thornhill, R. & Gangestad, S. W. (1994). Human fluctuating asymmetry and sexual behavior. *Psychological Science, 5*(5), 297–302.

Thornhill, R. & Gangestad, S. W. (2000). Facial attractiveness. *Trends in Cognitive Sciences, 3*, 452–460.

Thornhill, R. & Grammer, K. (1994). Human (Homo sapiens) facial attractiveness and sexual selection: the role of symmetry and averageness. *Journal of Comparative Psychology, 108*(3), 233–242.

Thornhill, R. & Moller, A. P. (1997). Developmental stability, disease and medicine. *Biological Reviews, 72*, 497–548.

Tignol, J., Biraben-Gotzamanis, L., Martin-Guehl, C. et al. (2007) Body dysmorphic disorder and cosmetic surgery: evolution of 24 subjects with a minimal defect in appearance 5 years after their request for cosmetic surgery. *European Psychiatry, 22*(8), 520–524.

Traub, A. C., Olson, R., Orbach, J. & Cardone, S. S. (1967). Psychophysical studies of body-image. 3. Initial studies of disturbances in a chronic schizophrenic group. *Archives of General Psychiatry, 17*(6), 664–670.

Treasure, J. L. & Ward, A. (1997). A practical guide to the use of motivational interviewing. *European Eating Disorders Review, 5*, 102–114.

Trimble, M. R. (1988). Body image and the temporal lobes. *British Journal of Psychiatry*, Supplement, 12–14.

Twohig, M. P. & Woods, D. W. (2001). Habit reversal as a treatment for chronic skin picking in typical developing adult male siblings. *Journal of Applied Behavior Analysis, 34*(2), 217–220.

Uzun, O., Basoglu, C., Akar, A. et al. (2003). Body dysmorphic disorder in patients with acne. *Comprehensive Psychiatry, 44*(5), 415–419.

van Rood, Y. R., den Hollander-Gisman, M. A., de Jongh, A. & de Beurs, E. (unpublished). Development and validation of the screening instrument for Body Dysmorphic Disorder: the SI-BDD (described in de Jongh et al., 2008).

Veale, D. (2000). Outcome of cosmetic surgery and "D.I.Y" surgery in patients with body dysmorphic disorder. *Psychiatric Bulletin, 24*, 218–221.

Veale, D. (2002). Overvalued ideas: a conceptual analysis. *Behavior Research and Therapy, 40*(4), 383–400.

Veale, D. (2004). Advances in a cognitive behavioral model of body dysmorphic disorder. *Body Image, 1*, 113–125.

Veale, D. (2006). A compelling desire for deafness. *The Journal of Deaf Studies and Deaf Education, 11*(3), 369–372.

Veale, D., Boocock, A., Gournay, K. et al. (1996). Body dysmorphic disorder. A survey of fifty cases. *British Journal of Psychiatry, 169*(2), 196–201.

Veale, D. & Chapman, H. (2005). Classification approach [letter]. *British Dental Journal, 198*(1), 2–3.

Veale, D., De Haro, L. & Lambrou, C. (2003). Cosmetic rhinoplasty in body dysmorphic disorder. *British Journal of Plastic Surgery, 56*(6), 546–551.

Veale, D., Ennis, M. & Lambrou, C. (2002). Possible association of body dysmorphic disorder with an occupation or education in art and design. *American Journal of Psychiatry, 159*(10), 1788–1790.

Veale, D., Gournay, K., Dryden, W. et al. (1996). Body dysmorphic disorder: a cognitive behavioral model and pilot randomized controlled trial. *Behavior Research and Therapy, 34*(9), 717–729.

Veale, D., Kinderman, P., Riley, S. & Lambrou, C. (2003). Self-discrepancy in body dysmorphic disorder. *British Journal of Clinical Psychology, 42*, 157–169.

Veale, D. M. & Lambrou, C. (2002). The importance of aesthetics in body dysmorphic disorder. *CNS Spectrums, 7*(6), 429–431.

Veale, D., Menzies, J. & De Silva, P. (2003). Obsessive compulsive spectrum disorders. In *Obsessive Compulsive Disorder* (pp. 221–236). Chichester: John Wiley.

Veale, D. & Riley, S. (2001). Mirror, mirror on the wall, who is the ugliest of them all? The psychopathology of mirror gazing in body dysmorphic disorder. *Behavior Research and Therapy, 39*, 1381–1393.

Veale, D. & Willson, R. (2007) *Manage Your Mood*. London: Constable & Robinson.

Veale, D., Willson, R. & Clark, A. (2009) Overcoming Body Image Problems. London: Robinson.

Villano, M. (1998). *Stages of Change Assessment in Obsessive-Compulsive Disorder*. New York: Hofstra University.

Vindigni, V., Pavan, C., Semenzin, S. et al. (2002). The importance of recognizing body dysmorphic disorder in cosmetic surgery patients: do our patients need a preoperative psychistric evaluation? *European Journal of Plastic Surgery, 25*, 305–308.

Vitiello, B. & de Leon, J. (1990). Dysmorphophobia misdiagnosed as obsessive-compulsive disorder. *Psychosomatics, 31*, 220–222.

Vittorio, C. C. & Phillips, K. A. (1997). Treatment of habit-tic deformity with fluoxetine. *Archives of Dermatology, 133*(10), 1203–1204.

Vrana, S. R., Cuthbert, B. N. & Lang, P. J. (1986). Fear imagery and text processing. *Psychophysiology, 23*(3), 247–253.

Vulink, N. C., Sigurdsson, V., Kon, M. et al. (2006). Body dysmorphic disorder in 3–8% of patients in outpatient dermatology and plastic surgery clinics [English abstract]. *Nederlands Tijdschrift voor Geneeskunde, 150*(2), 97–100.

Walster, E. A., Aronson, V., Abrahams, D. & Rottman, L. (1966). Importance of physical attractiveness in dating behavior. *Journal of Personality and Social Psychology, 4*, 508–516.

Warhol, A. (1975). *The Philosophy of Andy Warhol: From A to B and Back Again*, San Diego, CA: Harcourt.

Warwick, H. & Salkovskis, P. M. (1990). Hypochondriasis. *Behavior Research and Therapy, 28*(2), 105–117.

Watkins, E., Scott, J., Wingrove, J. et al. (2007). Rumination-focused cognitive behavior therapy for residual depression: a case series. *Behavior Research and Therapy, 45*(9), 2144–2154.

Watson, D. & Friend, R. (1969). Measurement of social evaluative anxiety. *Journal of Consulting and Clinical Psychology, 33*(4), 448–457.

Watts, F. N. (1990). Aversion to personal body hair: a case study in the integration of behavioral and interpretative methods. *British Journal of Medical Psychology, 63*, 335–340.

Webster, M. & Driskell, J. E. (1983). Beauty as status. *Am. J. Sociol., 89*, 140–165.

Wells, A. (1990). Panic disorder in association with relaxation induced anxiety: an attentional training approach to treatment. *Behavior Therapy, 21*, 273–280.

Wells, A. (2000). *Emotional Disorders and Metacognition: Innovative Cognitive Therapy.* Chichester: Wiley.

Wells, A. (2005). Detached mindfulness in cognitive therapy: a metacognitive analysis and ten techniques. *Journal of Rational-Emotive & Cognitive-Behavior Therapy, 23,* 337–355.

Wells, A. (2009). *Meta-cognitive Therapy for Anxiety and Depression.* New York: Guilford Press.

Wells, A. & Davies, M. I. (1994). The thought control questionnaire: a measure of individual differences in the control of unwanted thoughts. *Behaviour Research and Therapy, 32,* 871–878.

Wells, A. & Hackmann, A. (1993). Imagery and core beliefs in health anxiety: contents and origins. *Behavioral and Cognitive Psychotherapy, 21*(3), 265–273.

Wells, A. & Papageorgiou, C. (1998) Social phobia – effects of external attention on anxiety, negative beliefs, and perspective taking. *Behavior Therapy, 29,* 357–370.

Wells, A., White, J. & Carter, K. E. (1997). Attention training: effects on anxiety and beliefs in panic and social phobia. *Clinical Psychology and Psychotherapy, 4,* 226–232.

Wernicke, C. (1900). *Grundriss der Psychiatrie.* Leipzig: Verlag von Georg Thieme.

Wessells, H., Lue, T. F. & McAninch, J. W. (1996). Penile length in the flaccid and erect states: guidelines for penile augmentation. *The Journal of Urology, 156*(3), 995–997.

Whiteside, S. P., Port, J. D. & Abramowitz, J. S. (2004). A meta-analysis of functional neuroimaging in obsessive compulsive disorder. *Psychiatry Research, 132,* 69–79.

Wild, J., Hackmann, A. & Clark, D. M. (2008). Rescripting early memories linked to negative images in social phobia: a pilot study. *Behavior Therapy, 39*(1), 47–56.

Wilhelm, S. (2006). *Feeling Good about the Way You Look: A Program for Overcoming Body Image Problems.* New York: Guilford Press.

Wilhelm, S., Buhlmann, U., Etcoff, N. et al. (2001). Ratings of facial attractiveness in Body Dysmorphic Disorder. Paper presented at the World Congress of Behavioral and Cognitive Therapies, Vancouver, Canada.

Wilhelm, S., Buhlmann, U., Tolin, D. F. et al. (2008). Augmentation of behavior therapy with D-cycloserine for obsessive compulsive disorder. *American Journal of Psychiatry, 165*(3), 335–341.

Wilhelm, S., Keuthen, N. J., Deckersbach, T. et al. (1999). Self-injurious skin picking: clinical characteristics and comorbidity. *Journal of Clinical Psychiatry, 60*(7), 454–459.

Wilhelm, S. & Neziroglu, F. (2002). Cognitive theory of body dysmorphic disorder. In R. Frost & G. Steketee (eds.), *Cognitive Approaches to Obsessions and Compulsions: Theory, Assessment, and Treatment.* (203–214). Amsterdam: Pergamon/Elsevier Science.

Wilhelm, S., Otto, M. W., Lohr, B. & Deckersbach, T. (1999). Cognitive behavior group therapy for body dysmorphic disorder: a case series. *Behavior Research and Therapy, 37*(1), 71–75.

Wilhelm, S., Otto, M. W., Zucker, B. G. & Pollack, M. H. (1997). Prevalence of body dysmorphic disorder in patients with anxiety disorders. *Journal of Anxiety Disorders*, *11*(5), 499–502.

Williams, J., Hadjistavropoulos, T. & Sharpe, D. (2006). A meta-analysis of psychological and pharmacological treatments for Body Dysmorphic Disorder. *Behavior Research and Therapy*, *44*, 99–111.

Woodruff-Borden, J., Brothers, A. J. & Lister, S. (2001). Self-focused attention: Commonalities across psychopathologies and predictors. *Behavioral and Cognitive Psychology*, *29*(169), 178.

Woody, S. R., Steketee, G., Chambless, D. L. et al. (1995). Reliability and validity of the Yale-Brown Obsessive-Compulsive Scale. [Research Support, US Gov't, P.H.S.]. *Behavior Research & Therapy*, *33*(5), 597–605.

World Health Organization (1992) *The ICD-10. Classification of Mental and Behavioural Disorders*, Geneva: World Health Organization.

Yaryura-Tobias, J. A. & Neziroglu, F. (1997a). *Obsessive-Compulsive Disorder Spectrum: Pathogenesis, Diagnosis and Treatment*. Washington, DC: American Psychiatric Press.

Yaryura-Tobias, J. A. & Neziroglu, F. (1997b). *Bio-behavioral Treatments of Obsessive Compulsive Disorders*. Boston, MA: Norton.

Yaryura-Tobias, J. A., Neziroglu, F., Chang, R. et al. (2002). Computerized perceptual analysis of patients with body dysmorphic disorder. *CNS Spectrums*, *7*(6), 444–452.

Yaryura-Tobias, J. A., Neziroglu, F. & Torres-Gallegos, M. (2002). Neuroanatomical correlates and somatosensorial disturbances in body dysmorphic disorder. *CNS Spectrums*, *7*, 432–434.

Yaryura-Tobias, J. A., Pinto, A. & Neziroglu, F. (2001). The integration of primary anorexia nervosa and obsessive-compulsive disorder. *Eating & Weight Disorders*, *6*(4), 174–180.

Yates, A., Shisslak, C. M., Allender, J. R. & Wolman, W. (1988). Plastic surgery and the bulimic patient. *International Journal of Eating Disorders*, *7*(4), 557–560.

Yates, F. A. (1966). *The Art of Memory*. London: Routledge & Kegan Paul.

Zaidens, S. H. (1950). Dermatologic hypochondriasis: a form of schizophrenia. *Psychosomatic Medicine*, *12*(4), 250–253.

Zaidens, S. H. (1951a). Self-inflicted dermatoses and their psychodynamics. *Journal of Nervous and Mental Disease*, *113*, 395–404.

Zaidens, S. H. (1951b). The skin: psychodynamic and psychopathologic concepts. *Journal of Nervous and Mental Disease*, *113*, 388–394.

Zebrowitz, L. A., Voinescu, L. & Collins, M. A. (1996). "Wide-eyed" and "crooked-faced": determinants of perceived and real honesty across the life span. *Personality and Social Psychology Bulletin*, *22*(12) (December), 1258–1269.

Zigmond, A. & Snaith, R. P. (1983). The hospital depression and anxiety scale. *Acta Psychiatrica Scandinavica*, *67*, 361–370.

Zimmerman, M. & Mattia, J. I. (1998). Body dysmorphic disorder in psychiatric outpatients: recognition, prevalence, comorbidity, demographic, and clinical correlates. *Comprehensive Psychiatry*, *39*(5), 265–270.

Zimmerman, M. & Mattia, J. I. (1999). Is post-traumatic stress disorder underdiagnosed in routine clinical settings? *Journal of Nervous and Mental Disease*, *187*, 420–428.

Index

Body Dysmorphic Disorder: A Treatment Manual. David Veale and Fugen Neziroglu
© 2010 John Wiley & Sons, Ltd.